WHERE TO WATCH BIRDS IN SOUTHEAST ENGLAND
ESSEX, LONDON AND KENT

DAVID CALLAHAN

H E L M

LONDON • OXFORD • NEW YORK • NEW DELHI • SYDNEY

HELM
Bloomsbury Publishing Plc
50 Bedford Square, London, WC1B 3DP, UK
29 Earlsfort Terrace, Dublin 2, Ireland

BLOOMSBURY, HELM and the Helm logo are
trademarks of Bloomsbury Publishing Plc

First published in the United Kingdom 2024

A catalogue record for this book is available from the British Library.
Library of Congress Cataloguing-in-Publication data has been applied for.

ISBN: PB: 978–1-3994–0360–3; ePub: 978–1-3994–0361–0;
ePDF: 978–1-3994–0362–7

2 4 6 8 10 9 7 5 3 1

Typeset in the UK by Mark Heslington

Maps by Brian Southern

Printed and bound in Great Britain by CPI Group (UK) Ltd, Croydon CR0 4YY

To find out more about our authors and books visit
www.bloomsbury.com and sign up for our newsletters.

Cover photographs. Front: Nightingale (t), Roger Wilmshurst; Avocet and
Shelduck (b), Mike Powles. Back: Smew (l), Ian Fox; Red Kite (c), Giedriius;
Hawfinch (r), Erni. Spine: Black Redstart, Dusty Gedge

CONTENTS

Contents

ACKNOWLEDGEMENTS

Though it's as up-to-date as possible, this is far from being the first book to cover birding in the counties and region concerned, and I'm very much standing on the shoulders of giants in using the most important of these works as starting points for my own. That said, birds, sites and humans all change, and I've strived to make the book as useful, comprehensive and informative as possible for anyone thinking of venturing outdoors to see birds in London, Essex or Kent going forward in the twenty-first century.

However, it wouldn't be anywhere near as accurate or up-to-date as it is without the considerable help of John Cantelo, Howard Vaughan, Andrew Self, Matt Turner and Paul Hawkins. These major figures in local birding read through the sections with which they are most familiar and highlighted the changes and criticisms necessary to make this book much better. Suffice it to say, I'm extremely grateful for their help. I should also add that any remaining mistakes, quirks or inaccuracies in the text or maps are solely my responsibility. Josh Jones, Jamie Partridge and David Bradshaw also commented invaluably on certain aspects during the writing of the book. Steve Swaby and John Sutherby also provided useful information and contacts.

More pragmatic and material support came from the Society of Authors, whose help is essential to the completion of so many books; it would have been almost impossible to finish this project without it.

INTRODUCTION

It's often a given that the best places to go birdwatching are considered to be remote coastal marshes or offshore islands. However, most birders live in more urban areas and need to visit less wild places to get their regular fix of the pastime.

The fact is that everyone is close to some kind of birding hotspot – even if you live in London, and certainly if you're based in the most bird-rich of the city's satellite counties: Kent and Essex. South-East England is blessed with the best public transport system in the country and cycling is well catered for. It also has many internationally and nationally important reserves and surrounds one of Europe's biggest river estuaries. While the shoreline of much of the Thames Estuary is built-up and has been drained, the Essex and Kent coasts still feel wild and support huge numbers of wildfowl and waders.

The two counties mentioned, therefore, are easy to get to from London and this urbanised triumvirate is a logical combination for a 'Where to Watch' guide. At the forefront of my mind while writing the book was to include those places most likely to provide an exciting day's birding for both the beginner and the more experienced wielder of binoculars. There are several well-known large reserves in the region where you are likely to see a lot of birds, both in number and kind. There are a lot of well-watched local patches, with plenty of information available, and I also wanted to include some under-watched or lesser-known spots, to encourage you to visit or even regularly if you're nearby – perhaps such a site could become your local patch.

Getting the most out of your region or local area is of paramount importance as national and international travelling is increasingly highlighted as being damaging to our environment. What better time to familiarise yourself with birds closer to home if you're a seasoned world birder? And what better time to acquaint or reacquaint yourself with the potential of even our most built-up regions to produce an intimate knowledge of commoner birds and throw in the curveballs of less-expected species? London, with its brownfield sites and green belt, Essex, with its huge reservoirs and wild coast, and Kent with its deep forests and expansive marshes are all primed to satisfy your birding desires, no matter how ambitious.

HOW TO USE THIS BOOK

The sites are organised by county (with London defined as one by proxy), and each entry adheres as closely as possible to a site's geographical situation and proximity to others. The entries all follow the same format (simplified for less-productive sites), which is as follows:

Site name in bold: the official name of the site concerned with its management organisation or owner. Older or more colloquial site names are usually mentioned in the 'Your visit' section of the text below.

The most useful street address for visitors, with the nearest postcode to aid sat-nav users; this is usually the site entrance or the address of the main or most useful parking area for a birding visit.

Website: usually a site's official web page where one exists, but otherwise the most directly helpful pages on the internet.

Ordnance Survey (OS) map reference: this is taken to the nearest six-digit reference, rendered in the format of two letters and six digits; i.e. 'XX000000'. Many birders still use OS grid references and squares for surveys and watching their patches, and some continue to use the more traditional paper map for navigation. I have omitted to mention the differently scaled commercially available OS-branded maps, but these can be bought or found easily online if needed. Hopefully, the maps included in this book will be all you need to find your way around each main site.

What3Words app location: this increasingly popular app can locate any part of a landscape down to the nearest 3 square metres using fixed words from the dictionary. The app is available free for all mobile phones and each location is rendered 'word.word.word'. It's also fun seeing which combinations of words the app comes up with, which are sometimes strangely appropriate (or amusingly inappropriate).

Phone: this should be the most useful number available at the time of writing, and where possible will connect you directly with the person or department most responsible for the site and its birds.

Email: this should be the most useful email address available, and where possible will connect you directly to the person or department most responsible for the site and its birds.

Open: the days and times at which the site is officially accessible for birding visits, at the time of writing. Please note that some sites can be at least partially open outside the stated times and dates. Also, note that the times can change according to management whim, public holidays or maintenance, so make sure you ring or check the site's website where possible. Under this section you'll also find details of the facilities available on-site or nearby, the condition of the paths and whether the site is open to wheelchairs, bicycles, prams or dogs.

Conservation status: the official status of the site or part of it with regard to governmental and scientific status. All sites listed are in some way important for nature at various scales, but it's sometimes useful to know whether a site is protected and to which level. For instance, an SSSI has less protection under the law than, say, a Ramsar site.

Area of site: given in hectares and acres, in parentheses, where known.

A one-sentence introductory summary of the headline attributes of the site: this is meant to whet your appetite and highlight the key importance of each site with regard to its birds.

Species: this section is a blunt tool and includes only those species of birding interest to the visitor. This does not mean you are guaranteed to see all the species mentioned or that they are confined completely to the season listed. For example, both summer and winter visitors are seen during migration. The commonest species of the region are dealt with in the introduction below – they are so universal to sites that it avoids repetition to include them in the front sections rather than under every site heading. Rarities, whether local or national, are always unlikely and aren't generally included in any of the sections, though some are mentioned in the text to give you a flavour of what might occur (with a great deal of luck).

The generalised seasons are:

All year: resident species or those with at least a few individuals present at the site in all months. For example, it is possible to see one or two non-breeding Yellow-legged Gulls in every month of the year at a few sites on the Thames, but it's generally a migrant.

Summer: breeding visitors only.

Winter: generally northern migrants that linger throughout the colder months, which can sometimes be present from late summer through to late spring.

Migration: those species that are usually just passing through in spring and autumn on their way to points further north or south. For some species in this particular context, 'spring' movements can begin in February (e.g. Black Redstart) and last into June (some Arctic-breeding waders), whereas for others autumn can start in late June (some Arctic-breeding waders) and finish in November or even early December (some seabirds or wildfowl).

Access: this section highlights the best way to get to the site using major modes of transport. It's taken as read that once you get there you'll usually be getting around on foot.

The four sections are:

Bike: cycling is to be encouraged whenever possible in these days of exacerbated climate change, but many of the sites don't include this section because almost all roads around the vast majority of sites are cyclable (except motorways). Wherever you are, you'll often need to secure your bike at your own risk, whether on an official bike rack or to a handy fence (paying due consideration to its owner and the surroundings). That said, I have highlighted official national bike routes on or close to the site, as well as any tracks or paths that can be used by cyclists and whether there are bike racks present. Bikes can be taken on most trains, but there may be time limits so check with the train company before you depart.

Bus: the bus routes that pass closest to the site are listed here, generally along with the company that runs them and sometimes which stop might be used. Please check times and availability online using the bus company website.

Train: the nearest station is included in this section, along with the company that runs the trains and the termini. If you need more detail, you're advised to search for the timetables online on the train companies' websites.

Car: driving routes can be convoluted, so I have generally only included the nearest streets in this section, along with the nearest main A or M road. I've endeavoured to include all the parking spaces for a site with postcodes, grid references and what3words codes. Most phones now have sat-nav apps for you to input the postcode or street address and find the most direct route. I've omitted parking information for some Inner London sites, as these are best reached by public transport and parking can be oversubscribed and expensive.

YOUR VISIT

This section should include all the information you need to maximise the birding success of your visit, including how much time you should allow. Where relevant and possible, I've tried to give an example or examples of productive routes or circuits around each site, with details of where a site's best locations might be, depending on the season. I've generally only mentioned the more unusual or interesting species, though rarities are sometimes mentioned for reasons of context.

The maps: it's impossible to give finer detail of the landscape for many sites, but I've tried to highlight the best areas and all parts of any site mentioned in the text so you know where you are at any point. It's hoped that you will take this book out with you into the field, and the maps have been created to help with your route around the site as well as getting there from nearby. I have aimed to make this book a fixture in your glove compartment or backpack side pocket.

GENERAL REMARKS ON THE TEXT

As is traditional in bird books, the English names of all species mentioned (whether animal or vegetable) are capitalised, while those of large groups of species are not (e.g. Common Cuckoo, the species, and cuckoos, the family of birds). Subspecies with English names are placed in inverted commas, e.g. 'Pied' Wagtail (the British subspecies of White Wagtail). Scientific generic and specific names, where used, are given in italics with capitalised generic qualifiers and lower-case species names, as is the usual protocol. Levels of classification above species level are given in roman type.

THE SITES

There are many different kinds of sites to visit in the area covered by this book, ranging from urban parks to commons, to huge wetland reserves. All are open to the public within the hours given, and most are at least partially open all day, every day. Some great birding sites are private or prohibit people from visiting – fortunately, there aren't too many, and I hope I have made it clear which these are and how it might be possible to scan or visit them in certain circumstances.

All RSPB reserves are free to members, but a charge is payable by non-members, often at the visitor centre (VC) and less often using an honesty box. Wildlife Trust reserves are generally free to enter, though the parking places are often pay-and-display. I've tried to let you know when you might have to pay a fee, but please look around in case any changes have occurred post-publication.

With the pandemic and lockdown somewhat fresh in the memory, many city and town dwellers have become more interested in, and acquainted with, the natural world, particularly the one they experienced while taking their government-approved walks. The hobby of birdwatching (or 'birding' as most active participants end up calling it) benefited from this newfound awareness of wildlife. This guide hopes not only to appeal to experienced birders looking to expand their knowledge of the region's sites and more interesting species but also to those recently awakened to the joys of the pastime. It's hoped that such nascent enthusiasts might want to discover more places and birds all the better to sustain their interest.

I've included helpful websites in the appendices (page 318) that should help make your birding journey as informed and pleasant as it is exciting. London, Essex and Kent can provide some of Britain's finest birding experiences if you know where to look, and this guide intends to point you definitively in the right direction.

The proximity of many of the capital's green spaces to residential areas and excellent public transport make many of the sites covered in this guide ideal for Londoners and their compatriots in the Home Counties for watching as a local patch. This maintains engagement and personal involvement with nature and creates a low carbon footprint. Patch-watchers are key contributors to our increasingly detailed knowledge of the South-East's ever-changing birdlife.

The best sites are often watched almost continually by committed and heavily invested groups of birders using Facebook, WhatsApp, Yahoo!, Wiki and Twitter groups to inform each other of sightings and discuss changes in their patches. I recommend joining one or more of these groups to enhance your enjoyment and knowledge, and to help contribute yourself. As often as not, chatting with fellow birders in the field can result in an invitation to join a group, and taking part will be a boon to your birding. Most are friendly, helpful and all too willing to offer gen and good company to young and old alike.

As well as this, the South-East has an impressive infrastructure enabling even the most obscure reaches of Essex and Kent to be reached by public transport, motorways and A-roads. The bigger roads are not so great for cycling, but a huge network of cycle routes and paths covers the area in this guide. The region as a whole is heavily built-up and industrialised, but despite that concentration of human activity, it also has some of the most bird-rich regions in the country. This is helped by its complex coastlines with many unique and internationally valuable habitats, and the fact that the Continental coastline and the edges of Britain are part of a major migratory route: the East Atlantic Flyway. The rivers Thames and Lea and their valleys and floodplains (or what's left of them) are also important for the navigation of birds on the move.

The region covered by the book includes most of the area enclosed by the London Bird Club's recording area (see page 27). All the Outer London Boroughs encroach on the countryside and there are several important nature reserves even within the M25 orbital road. I have also included a few of the more bird-rich parks of the Inner London Boroughs – partly because visitors to the capital might stay centrally, but also to illustrate that some good birds can penetrate even one of the world's biggest and longest-standing cities. And, if it's your first time in Britain, they're good places to familiarise yourself with our staple species.

The region covered also includes the globally important, ecologically rich Greater Thames Estuary – the areas of low-lying mudflats, beaches and saltmarsh that form the coastlines of north Kent and east Essex, which sometimes flood during spring tides, depositing the fecund silts and muds that enrich their substrates and provide huge areas of bird habitat that support an impressive biomass. This massive, internationally important estuary is fed by the tributaries of other significant rivers such as the Blackwater, Colne, Crouch and Medway and annexes coastal islands such as Canvey, Osea and Sheppey. Most of the islands have great birding opportunities and many can be visited by road or rail. I won't ignore the potential for the inshore English Channel and the North Sea to produce good seabirds, either.

To summarise, this book incorporates the largest county in South-east England (Kent), the closest East Anglian county to London (Essex) and the London Natural History Society's (LNHS) Greater London Urban Area – and all are under the influence of one of the world's great rivers. Despite its large human population and the presence and demands of heavy industry, retail parks, recreational areas and housing, it's not the most polluted region of Britain. Much progress has been made in bringing nature back to a historically badly degraded estuarine environment that prehistorically rivalled many of those across Eurasia.

Nature reserves have proliferated in the late twentieth and early twenty-first centuries, and many European wetland birds are staging a comeback – though this is unfortunately partly due to climate change. However, the same cannot yet be said of many radically declining farmland and woodland species. Even so, a birdwatcher based in London has an exciting choice of species to see within easy driving or public-transport distance. An obvious choice of destination might be Suffolk, Norfolk or Cambridgeshire (see my own *Where to Watch Birds in East Anglia*), but there are almost no species found in that region that cannot be seen by a diligent observer within an hour or two of London.

The marshes and mudflats of the Thames Estuary attract hordes of migrating waders, including internationally important numbers of Dunlin, Knot, Avocet, Bar-tailed and Black-tailed Godwits, Lapwing, Curlew and Oystercatcher. The adjacent wetlands and fields support dramatic numbers of Wigeon and Brent Geese, along with Shelduck, Pintail, Shoveler and Teal, while the more brackish and freshwater marshlands and wetlands provide habitat for burgeoning populations of Marsh Harrier and Bearded Tit, which means both now have toeholds within the M25.

Regional woodlands have lost Willow Tit but gained Firecrest, while the likes of Lesser Spotted Woodpecker, Turtle Dove, Tree Pipit and Spotted Flycatcher just about cling on as breeding species. However, the classic woodland passerines – Pied Flycatcher, Redstart and Wood Warbler – are all overwhelmingly seen now as scarce but annual passage migrants.

The parks and farmlands are rapidly losing Grey Partridge – the species has gone completely from Greater London, despite the influx of captive-bred birds every year – but it hangs on in more rural areas, as do Grasshopper Warbler, Corn Bunting and Yellowhammer. Cuckoo still remains relatively widespread each summer despite its clearly shrinking numbers.

Geo-ecological worries aside, even the most built-up parts of Central London can provide ornithological interest from what might at first seem like meagre pickings. Black Redstart is nationally scarce but breeds in its greatest numbers in the West End, City and East End of London, though you'll often have to strain to hear it singing above the traffic. Grey Wagtail has made urban inroads via the canals and parks and breeds in many seemingly barren urban areas. The city's Feral Pigeons are kept anxious by the drama of stooping or soaring Peregrines, while any urban gathering of gulls outside the breeding season can potentially contain a Mediterranean, Yellow-legged or Caspian Gull.

The region as a whole, therefore, has a good deal of ornithological interest, although this is constantly in conflict with the interests of humans. Birders are, by and large, used to getting up early to catch the worm, and this helps avoid our jogging, cycling and dog-walking conspecifics. Few sites included in this book manage to entirely avoid such disturbance, so take it in good humour and just get out early.

You can take it for granted that barbecues and fires are not permitted at any of the sites discussed for very good reasons, and picnics and other small gatherings, if allowed, should only occur in designated areas. Dog-walkers should refer to the individual site entry to find out if their four-legged companions are welcome (they generally aren't but there are exceptions). Please also bear in mind that a tranche of recent research has overwhelmingly shown that dogs contribute to the destruction of habitat and disturbance of breeding birds, so please at least keep 'Tyson' on lead.

Most of the site addresses I've given relate to the main entrance and include the nearest postcode. I've omitted grid references from the vast majority of Inner London sites as they are most likely to be visited via a street address, but I've included them for all other sites. App-friendly readers will find a 'What3Words' designation for sites and key locations within them; this three-word code pinpoints any area (or sighting, if you're passing the news on to others) to a three-metre square defined by a unique set of three words.

I've also included the main website addresses for every site where available so that visitors are able to refer to the most up-to-date information regarding visiting – this is particularly important in these times of pandemics, floods and constant habitat change.

TYPICAL HABITATS AND THEIR SPECIES

Most of the major habitats in London and the Thames Estuary counties have their typical, often ubiquitous, species. To avoid repetition, I have summarised the most common in each habitat here, so that the more unusual and desirable species can be focused on without being lost among a list of more predictable species. This isn't to dismiss those familiar birds, but almost no one will need this book to find and see them. If you're just starting out as a birder, you should familiarise yourself with all the plumages, sounds and habits of the following species; they're fascinating in their own right, and such knowledge will also help you pick out more unusual or scarcer species.

Habitats that border each other will, of course, share species; for example, farmland will provide foraging for Jackdaws and Rooks, which may then roost or nest in wooded areas or around buildings, while built-up areas will share their Woodpigeons, Collared Doves and Feral Pigeons with neighbouring fields and trees, where they will mingle with Stock Doves. Certain species such as Blackbird, Blue and Great Tits, Dunnock, Wren, Carrion Crow and Magpie are omnipresent in almost all habitats.

WOODLAND

Woodland will invariably produce those species typical of parks and gardens in the rest of the region: songbirds will include Dunnock, Robin, Wren, Blackbird, and Blue, Great and Long-tailed Tits, while non-passerines will come in the form of Woodpigeon and Stock Dove. Predators will include Sparrowhawk and, less often, Buzzard and Red Kite – these last two often revealing their presence by circling on thermal air currents high overhead.

More specialist species such as Jay will be present. However, the likes of Marsh Tit, Hawfinch and Lesser Spotted Woodpecker are declining fast and are only found in a few woodlands these days. I have highlighted these sites where appropriate. Other species such as Willow Tit have sadly now been extirpated from the entire region.

Woodland edges and scrub will hold significant numbers of migratory warblers in summer, with Blackcap and Whitethroat the most common, while Chiffchaff will be present all year, but with much smaller numbers in winter. Sparser in distribution are Lesser Whitethroat and Willow Warbler, while Garden Warbler is often just passing through, though there are regional breeding hotspots for this plainest of species. I generally mention if a site hosts these last three species in the relevant entry.

Song Thrush is still fairly common despite a decline, while larger, more wooded parkland will usually produce Mistle Thrush or Stock Dove. Great Spotted Woodpecker will be fairly obvious in most stands of trees, even in urban environments, while Green Woodpecker will likely be 'yaffling' from patches of tree-lined grass in the bigger green spaces. Goldcrest is frequent around the region's stands of conifers, even ornamental ones, but is more wide-ranging in winter; Coal Tit may also be found in similar habitats but is scarcer. Chaffinch is ubiquitous in wooded and scrubby areas, though can be elusive.

GRASSLAND, FARMLAND AND LANDFILL SITES

Areas with relatively short, unmown grass (commons, extensive parkland, playing field and landfill edges, fallow farmland) still produce the odd Meadow Pipit or Skylark, though the activities of dog-walkers and sportspeople can put paid to their chances of breeding, the closer one gets to the cities and towns. As grass and weeds grow higher and longer, and scrub begins to take over, Greenfinch, Goldfinch and, slightly less often, Linnet become more likely.

The region's landfill sites are now gradually being closed down, as welcome recycling sees organic food waste turned into compost, but the few remaining open dumps still attract thousands of gulls. All five of the commoner gull species (Black-headed, Common, Lesser Black-backed, Herring and, less often, Great Black-backed) are attracted to them to rest and feed (with Common Gull mostly outside the breeding season). They can also be seen on the short turf of sports grounds, parks, playing fields and pitches, though they are often subject to recreational disturbance. Pied Wagtails also frequent shorter grass (along with car parks and reservoir banks).

Nearby buildings will still support gradually recovering numbers of House Sparrows and far greater numbers of Starlings.

WETLANDS AND RESERVOIRS

Every patch of reeds in the region is likely to have its own pair of Reed Warblers by the end of April, while the more extensive sites will produce Sedge Warblers and Reed Buntings.

Any extensive area of open water will feature Mallard and probably Tufted Ducks, with a few Pochard. Coot and Moorhen are very likely. Great Crested and Little Grebes will dive and surface all year round, while pterosaurian Cormorants will fish out on the water and pass overhead.

ESTUARY AND COASTAL MARSHES

The region's coasts overlook the relatively shallow waters of the Thames Estuary and the North Sea, allowing birders to observe most of our commoner seabirds at the right time of year. The absence of coastal cliffs and hilltops means that auks, skuas, Kittiwakes and Gannets are unlikely during the breeding season, but they certainly turn up – sometimes even on inland waters after bad weather. The same is true of seaduck, some of which migrate overland, and divers and the scarcer grebes.

The extensive mudflats of the Thames and other rivers that empty into the North Sea, as well as the coast itself, also gift birds copious feeding opportunities, with large flocks of waders present outside of summer, along with Shelduck. Redshank, Oystercatcher and Lapwing stay to breed, often inland on the marshes, but most are just passing through. The changeover is sometimes almost imperceptible, so waders heading north will be heading south just a couple of weeks later in the summer. Internationally important numbers of Avocet use the Greater Thames estuary (more than 3,000 in winter), with hundreds remaining to breed.

Saltmarshes are largely relict on the Thames but become more prevalent the further out of London one gets. Those areas and the coastal grasslands heavily feature flocks of geese in winter, especially on the Essex side. These will overwhelmingly comprise Canada and Greylag Geese, but Brent Geese (of the Dark-bellied form) are profuse in winter on the northern side of the Thames and around tributary estuaries. Among them, Barnacle (often from feral populations) and White-fronted Geese can turn up in small numbers.

Wild swans are scarce (though they are regularly found in winter as far south as Romney Marsh in Kent), but Mute Swan is part of the furniture. Other winter wild-fowl will include Wigeon in similar habitats, while any sizeable areas of water should hold Teal, Shoveler and sometimes Pintail, as well as the ubiquitous Mallard, Tufted Duck and Pochard.

Many of the birds that feature in wetlands will also appear in more maritime habitats.

OFFSHORE

While Essex has an extensive coastline, its mudflats and saltmarshes, as well as its more industrialised flanks, create a complex border from which seabirds can be observed. Kent has some great seawatching owing to the presence of several promontories jutting into the English Channel and North Sea.

All the regular gull species (including Yellow-legged and Caspian) are possible on any of these coasts, along with Kittiwake and Mediterranean Gull, both of which have notable dispersal movements in late winter and late summer. Gannet, Guillemot, Razorbill and Red-throated Diver all have sizeable pelagic populations in the North Sea outside the breeding season and can be seen from many points on the coast, particularly with onshore winds. Please refer to the relevant sites for details on the best weather and wind conditions under which to visit.

URBAN AREAS

While often thought of as an ecological desert, inner-city London is far from bird-free. In fact, there is a small number of species that can be as easily seen in town than out, and one – Black Redstart – which is mostly present as a breeding species in built-up areas. While exact nest locations are kept secret, there are healthy populations of this mostly continental chat in the West End and City of London, as well as in East London from Stratford down to the Isle of Dogs. It can even be heard singing in late winter and spring over the shoppers and traffic at Westfield Stratford City and around Oxford Street and Soho.

Other largely urban species include London's wide-ranging Peregrine population (with much of the city parcelled into their adjoining territories) and the huge numbers of Feral Pigeons on which Peregrines feed. The scarcer two of the large white-headed gull species can also be found with their much commoner congeners, with places like Billingsgate fish market in Poplar regularly – though unpredictably – producing Yellow-legged and Caspian Gulls, particularly in late summer (see page 306). The green oases of Kensington Gardens and Hyde Park hold the most central breeding Treecreepers, Nuthatches and Goldcrests in small numbers, along with Tawny Owls, which can be very showy in late spring when their chicks are leaving the nest.

Another key urban species is the ever-growing population of introduced Ring-necked Parakeets, which have now spread from their former south-of-the-Thames strongholds to encompass all of Greater London and many of the medium-to-large towns in Essex and Kent. Their roosts can occasionally number in their thousands and create quite the spectacle in inner-city parks and around suburban playing fields.

Areas of water in the city also provide habitat and attract species such as feral Mandarin Duck and Red-crested Pochard to the inner city, along with the more regular species. Gadwall is still officially a scarce breeding species, and the Thames area is the epicentre of its British population, with counts of more than a thousand over the whole region; it sometimes seems to be the commonest species at some sites in winter. The introduced Egyptian Goose is now making inroads into most urban reservoirs, lakes and ponds. Grey Herons nest colonially even near the centre of towns, while Little Egret is now widespread and often joins them.

As you can see, there are huge areas of bird-productive wetlands, woodlands, farmland and open country in the region covered, despite overwhelming human interference. Combine this with an extensive coastline, some of which faces south (favourable in spring) and some north and east (beneficial in autumn), and you have a region in pole position to receive migrants and boost its summering and wintering species.

Whether you're just taking up the beautiful pastime of birding, a hardened patch watcher and county lister, or even a seasoned ornithologist and bird surveyor, I hope that you'll find inspiration and suggestions in this book to help broaden your experience and provide memorable sightings in the years to come.

GLOSSARY OF SPECIES NAMES

Throughout this book, I've used the names that British birders most commonly use when referring to particular species. These overwhelmingly tend to be short-hand for the commonest species that are found in Britain.

For example, while seven species of Wheatear *Oenanthe* are accepted as having occurred in Britain, birdwatchers themselves refer to Northern Wheatear simply as 'Wheatear' while the others are given their full names (Desert Wheatear, Eastern Black-eared Wheatear and so forth). Almost every UK birder knows that 'Wheatear' refers to Northern Wheatear, and the same is true for all the species listed below.

However, for the benefit of users of this book from overseas I have here included the IOC's international standardised English names to avoid confusion if you're unfamiliar with those used in the field. I've also included a few colloquial terms commonly used by birders to refer to familiar species.

Avocet Pied Avocet *Recurvirostra avosetta*
Bittern Eurasian Bittern *Botaurus stellaris*
Blackbird European Blackbird *Turdus merula*
Black-necked Grebe Eared Grebe *Podiceps nigricollis*
Buzzard Common Buzzard *Buteo buteo*
Cattle Egret Western Cattle Egret *Bubulcus ibis*
Coot Eurasian Coot *Fulica atra*
Cormorant Great Cormorant *Phalacrocorax carbo*
Crossbill Common Crossbill *Loxia curvirostra*
Cuckoo Common Cuckoo *Cuculus canorus*
Curlew Eurasian Curlew *Numenius arquata*
Fulmar Northern Fulmar *Fulmarus glacialis*
Goldeneye Common Goldeneye *Bucephala clangula*
Golden Plover European Golden Plover *Pluvialis dominica*
Goldfinch European Goldfinch *Carduelis carduelis*
Goshawk Northern Goshawk *Accipiter gentilis*
Guillemot Common Guillemot *Uria aalge*
Herring Gull European Herring Gull *Larus argentatus*
Hobby Eurasian Hobby *Falco subbuteo*
Honey-buzzard European Honey-buzzard *Pernis apivorus*
Jay Eurasian Jay *Garrulus glandarius*
Kestrel Common Kestrel *Falco tinnunculus*
Kingfisher Common Kingfisher *Alcedo atthis*
Kittiwake Black-legged Kittiwake *Rissa tridactyla*
Knot Red Knot *Calidris canutus*
'Large white-headed gull' Member of the Herring Gull species complex, including European Herring, Yellow-legged and Caspian Gulls
Lapwing Northern Lapwing *Vanellus vanellus*
Linnet Common Linnet *Linaria cannabina*
'LRP' Little Ringed Plover *Charadrius dubius*
Marsh Harrier Western Marsh Harrier *Circus aeruginosus*

Mealy Redpoll Common Redpoll *Acanthis flammea flammea*, as distinct from the British subspecies, which is Lesser Redpoll *Acanthis flammea cabaret*

Moorhen Common Moorhen *Gallinula chloropus*

Night Heron Black-crowned Night-heron *Nycticorax nycticorax*

Nightingale Common Nightingale *Luscinia luscinia*

Nightjar European Nightjar *Caprimulgus europaeus*

Oystercatcher Eurasian Oystercatcher *Haematopus ostralegus*

Peregrine Peregrine Falcon *Falco peregrinus*

Pied Wagtail *Motacilla alba yarrellii* British form of White Wagtail *Motacilla alba alba*

'Pink-foot' Pink-footed Goose *Anser brachyrhynchus*

Pochard Common Pochard *Aythya ferina*

Quail Common Quail *Coturnix coturnix*

Raven Northern Raven *Corvus corax*

Redshank Common Redshank *Tringa totanus*

Redpoll Lesser Redpoll *Acanthis flammea cabaret*

Redstart Common Redstart *Phoenicurus phoenicurus*

Reed Bunting Western Reed Bunting *Emberiza schoeniclus*

Scaup Greater Scaup *Aythya marila*

Shag European Shag *Phalacrocorax aristotelis*

Shelduck Eurasian Shelduck *Tadorna tadorna*

Shoveler Northern Shoveler *Anas clypeata*

Siskin Eurasian Siskin *Spinus spinus*

Skylark Eurasian Skylark *Alauda arvensis*

Slavonian Grebe Eared Grebe *Podiceps auritus*

Sparrowhawk Eurasian Sparrowhawk *Accipiter nisus*

Spoonbill Eurasian Spoonbill *Platalea leucorodia*

Starling Common or European Starling *Sturnus vulgaris*

Stonechat European Stonechat *Saxicola rubicola*

Teal Eurasian or Common Teal *Anas crecca*

Turtle Dove European Turtle Dove *Streptopelia turtur*

Wheatear Northern Wheatear *Oenanthe oenanthe*

'White-front' White-fronted Goose *Anser albifrons*

Whitethroat Common Whitethroat *Silvia communis*

White Wagtail *Motacilla alba alba* (the continental form of Pied Wagtail *Motacilla alba yarrellii*)

'White-winger' or **'white-winged gull'** Iceland Gull *Larus glaucoides* or Glaucous Gull *Larus hyperboreus*

Wigeon Eurasian Wigeon *Mareca penelope*

GLOSSARY OF TERMS AND ACRONYMS

Ancient woodland Areas of woodland in England that have persisted since 1600 and have remained relatively unchanged by human interference. They contain mature communities and ecosystems of plants, fungi and animals, and are able to support the complete avifauna that relies on that habitat.

AONB Area of Outstanding Natural Beauty. Land protected by the Countryside and Rights of Way Act 2000 (CROW Act).

BBRC British Birds Rarities Committee. This committee is a panel of experts assessing reports of all rare birds in Britain.

Bins Birders' colloquial term for binoculars.

Borrow dyke A trench created by the excavation of soil while making a seawall or dyke. This often fills with water to form a ditch or small waterbody that supports small ecosystems.

BTO The British Trust for Ornithology. A UK conservation charity formed to increase the knowledge of birds through empirical scientific research.

CP Country park. A green area created and designated for members of the public to use for recreation or enjoyment, usually close to a built-up area. Country parks provide a rural atmosphere for their users but are not necessarily part of the actual countryside.

CPB Coastal Protection Belt. A protected area of coastal land designated to protect the rural coastline from development that might adversely affect its character or wildlife.

Common land Land over which people who are not the owners are able to exercise certain legal rights, such as gazing their livestock, collecting firewood, cutting turf or walking at will.

Darvic ring A numbered plastic ring used to help track individual birds' movements.

DEFRA Department for Environment, Food and Rural Affairs. The government ministerial department responsible for protecting and improving the environment.

Desire line Any unplanned path worn into a grassy or muddy surface by the passage of feet.

Diurnal The condition of being active during the daylight hours.

Drift migrant A migrating bird blown off course by wind during flight. For example, this may happen to birds migrating south from northern Europe, which are regularly 'drifted' across the North Sea.

EA Environment Agency. A non-departmental public body responsible for protecting and improving the environment in England, funded by DEFRA (see above); conservation, flood management and the control of land and water pollution all come under its remit.

ESA Environmentally Sensitive Area. An agricultural area designated for special protection by Natural England due to its ecological value.

EWT Essex Wildlife Trust.

'Fall' The grounding of large numbers of migrating birds en route by severe or unusual weather conditions. Birds will often stay put for a while to recuperate from exhaustion when this happens.

FC Forestry Commission. A non-ministerial government department responsible for the management, regulation and improvement of publicly owned forests in England.

Forestry England That part of the Forestry Commission that acts as a business agency.

FSC Field Studies Council. An outdoors educational charity providing residential and day courses and visits to reserves and centres, including London parks.

GIGL Greenspace Information for Greater London. A collating organisation and website for observational data donated by amateur and professional naturalists. *www.gigl.org.uk*.

GP Gravel pit. A quarry from which gravel has been or continues to be extracted.

Green Flag status Recognition and reward of a good standard of outdoor recreational space management under The Green Flag Award Scheme.

Heligoland trap A large, building-sized netting or wire mesh structure comprising a funnel with a box trap at the end, designed for trapping birds for ringing or measuring biometric data. Named after the site of the first trap in Germany. The funnels are so layered and constructed that birds can't leave once they're inside.

Hirundine A member of the swallows and martins family Hirundinidae. The term is sometimes used inaccurately by birders to include the unrelated swifts Apidae, owing to their similar lifestyle and appearance.

HMWT Hertfordshire and Middlesex Wildlife Trust.

In-off Description of a migrant bird seen arriving from the sea and heading inland.

Irruption The sudden influx of a bird species into a usually extralimital area due to an expansion in population size within its usual range.

KGV King George V Reservoir (see page 44).

KOS Kent Ornithological Society.

KWT Kent Wildlife Trust.

Lammas Lands farmed privately but which are subject to the rights of common ownership outside the growing season. Traditionally, such lands became commons on 12 August, at the end of the growing season.

Larid A member of the gull family, Laridae.

Larophile The colloquial birding term for those who favour gull-watching over other forms of the pastime.

LNR Local Nature Reserve. A governmentally designated nature reserve of local importance for its wildlife. There are now more than 1,280 LNRs in England.

LWS Local Wildlife Site. A site selected for protection and management by the government for its 'substantive nature conservation value' within a region.

LVRP Lee Valley Regional Park.

LVRPA The Lee Valley Regional Park Authority, which manages the entire LVRP (see above).

LWT London Wildlife Trust.

MCZ Marine Conservation Zone. The 91 MCZs were created to protect nationally important or threatened habitats on the coast of England in a designated 'blue belt'.

MOD Ministry of Defence.

Natura 2000 A protected EU-wide network of protected core breeding and stop-over sites on land and sea for threatened species.

NDC Nature Discovery Centre.

NNR National Nature Reserve. Significant locations designated and managed by NT in partnership with NGOs as key sites for wildlife and nature in England. There are currently 229 NNRs covering 363 square miles (939km^2).

NR Nature reserve.

NT National Trust. A charity founded in 1895 founded for the conservation of heritage sites in England. Many of its managed properties are historical buildings and stately homes, but much of the land is important for nature and managed as such. The NT is one of the biggest landowners in the UK.

'Obs' Bird observatory. A place or building where research on birds, including ringing and monitoring, occurs.

OS Ordnance Survey. The government's national mapping agency for Great Britain.

Patch/Local patch/Patch birder A birder's patch is usually the local site or nature reserve where they spend most of their time indulging in their pastime. Most birders are obsessive about their patch and visit it as often as possible. Many of the observations from those visits are contributed to national databases such as BirdTrack and eBird, and help track the fortunes of the country's avifauna.

Permissive footpath A footpath that the owner of the land allows the public to use, though not actually a public right of way.

'Phyllosc' Birder's shorthand for leaf warblers of the genus *Phylloscopus*.

RADAR key A blue and silver key that opens most of the disabled toilets available in the UK. It can be purchased for £5 by anyone with a permanent disability from Tourist Information Centres and from *www.radarkey.org*.

Ramsar site A major wetland designated as internationally important and protected under the Ramsar Convention, the environmental treaty signed by 173 countries in 1971 in the Iranian city of Ramsar.

RSPB The Royal Society for the Protection of Birds.

SAC Special Areas of Conservation. Part of the government-designated network of protected 'important high-quality conservation sites' in the UK, originally established under the EU Habitats Directive.

Salting An area of coastal land regularly covered by the tide.

Sawbill A species of duck (Anatidae) belonging to the tribe Merginae which has serrated bill edges and includes the mergansers and Smew.

SBBO Sandwich Bay Bird Observatory.

SBBOT Sandwich Bay Bird Observatory Trust. The organisation that runs the SBBO.

'Scope' Birders' colloquial term for telescope.

Scrape A shallow depression, often dug on purpose, filled with water and mud or sand for wading and other birds to feed on invertebrates.

Seaduck Maritime duck species, including scoters, Long-tailed Duck, Scaup and Red-breasted Merganser.

Secondary woodland Woodland that has developed through natural processes on land previously cleared of trees. It is usually species-poor when compared with ancient woodland.

SINC Site of Importance for Nature Conservation. A location designated by local authorities in England to ensure protection of important sites for wildlife, under the aegis of DEFRA, to help deliver the UK's Biodiversity Action Plans.

SLINC Site of Local Importance for Nature Conservation (see SINC above).

SMINC Site of Metropolitan Importance for Nature Conservation (see SINC above).

SPA Special Protected Area. Locations specifically protected for birds under the Conservation of Habitats and Species Regulations 2017 in England and Wales.

SSSI Site of Special Scientific Interest. A site designated as being of particular interest to science owing to its flora or fauna.

SWT Sussex Wildlife Trust.

Thermalling The soaring of birds using columns of warm air to assist their progress in flight – particularly common behaviour among raptors and large waterbirds.

VC Visitor centre.

Vis-mig Visible migration. Birders' shorthand for the observation or logging of migrating birds that can be seen and counted; often referred to as 'vis-migging'.

WeBS Wetland Bird Survey. The BTO's (see page 22) nationwide monthly continuous bird count of waterbird species on wetlands. The counts are the basis on which wetland nature reserves are chosen and designated.

WHCG Welsh Harp Conservation Group. The group of birders involved with the protection and promotion of Brent Reservoir (page 108).

WT Woodland Trust. The UK's biggest woodland conservation charity, which protects, replants and helps restore ancient woodland.

KEY TO THE MAPS

�	Sea/inland water
▢	Area of interest, eg. reserve
Ⓟ	Car parking
Ⓗ	Birdwatching hide
★	Viewpoint/screen
⊕	Church
■	Building
⚇	Sewage farm
Ⓥ	Visitor centre
ⓌⒸ	Toilet
▞▞▞	Railway
╱	Main roads
╱	Minor roads
- - - -	Footpath
🌳	Woodland
▰	Towns

GREATER LONDON

London is a huge conurbation in South-East England with a history stretching back for more than 2,000 years. It formed on the banks of the River Thames and has since spread to cover much of the great river's floodplain, its natural marshland being extensively drained and built on as a consequence.

London has been measured or delimited in many ways for many purposes, whether it be as Greater London, the Greater London Built-up Area, or the area within the M25 or North Circular. However, the divisions considered by the LNHS are the most relevant to this book.

This august body formed from two local natural history societies in 1913 and set the limit to its studies as a 20-mile (32.19-km) radius around St Paul's Cathedral – and, so, this somewhat arbitrary limit has remained to this day. However, the LNHS Recording Area incorporates (sometimes large) areas of seven of the eight home counties because of this definition – not just Essex and Kent, but Buckinghamshire, Hertfordshire, Surrey, Berkshire and Middlesex (though this last county is essentially incorporated into Greater London and completely encircles Inner London). Though sightings in those counties are included in London's bird records, some of the more outlying sites are less likely to be visited by someone based in the city or Essex and

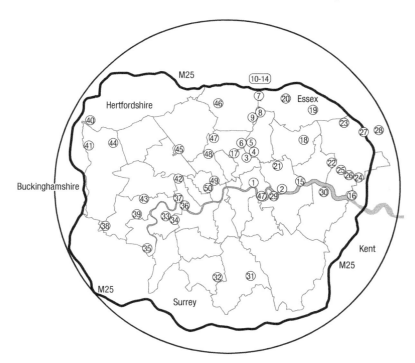

The Greater London Urban Area as used in this book, defined by the LNHS. Numbers correspond to the sites in the Greater London section.

Kent, unless they're a hardcore London lister. I've included location details of the best of these sites at the end of the book (see page 301), should you be interested.

The LNHS also maps London by means of its Watsonian vice-counties, a system based on the ancient borders of counties and generally only used for biological recording these days out of tradition. Despite their usefulness in context, they're a somewhat obscure method of delineating regional borders and create a division through the centre of Inner London.

Putting those definitions aside, we're left with the Greater London Urban Area, as illustrated on the map on page 27 and defined by the LNHS. This outlines a comprehensive area of the city and suburbs that most people would intuitively consider part of Greater London and omits much of the Home Counties other than Essex and Kent. This definition of London when combined with the two latter counties provides an excellent and highly accessible region of South-East England to go birding in – you'll get some of the best birding in Britain, for visitors and residents alike, combined with its best transport infrastructure and facilities.

Perhaps, on the face it, you might not expect London to have much in the way of birdlife. However, the LNHS Recording Area has logged an impressive 371 wild bird species at the time of writing (though some are outside the remit of the book within the above-mentioned definition).

For more in-depth information on the capital's birds and their history, see *The Birds of London* by Andrew Self (2014).

EAST LONDON

THE LEA VALLEY

While the floodplain of the River Lea (confusingly spelled 'Lee' by the Lee Valley Regional Park Authority) extends north through Hertfordshire to its source in the Bedfordshire Chilterns, many of the most productive sites fall within the LNHS recording area and can be reached easily by public transport or car. There are plenty of walking and cycling paths throughout the whole area, which is extensive and provides some of the best birding habitats in London.

The valley forms a minor flyway, enabling many regular migrants to be seen (though its winding shape means that routes aren't always obvious), and several scarcer breeding and wintering species make the valley their home, including Gadwall, Bittern, Little Ringed Plover, Oystercatcher, Nightingale and Garden Warbler.

Many of the sites are sizeable, especially the further north you get, so allow plenty of time to explore – it's bound to pay off sooner or later.

1 BOW CREEK ECOLOGY PARK AND EAST INDIA DOCK BASIN NR

Bow Creek: Bidder Street, London E16 4ST; TQ391813; coffee.milky.sling
East India Dock: Orchard Place, London E14 9QS; TQ389809; guilty.fairly.silent
Website: www.visitleevalley.org.uk/bow-creek-and-east-india-dock-basin
Phone: 03000 030 610
Email: Bow Creek info@leevalleypark.org.uk; East India Dock lvprojects@leevalleypark.org.uk
Open: 8am–dusk
(Bow Creek 2.5 hectares; 6.18 acres; East India Dock 6.61 hectares; 16.33 acres)

Two small urban reserves that can be combined in one visit, and featuring spring Little Ringed Plovers with the odd surprise during migration.

SPECIES

All year: Peregrine Falcon, Cetti's Warbler, Black Redstart (now scarce).

Summer: Common Tern, Little Ringed Plover, Sand Martin, Reed Bunting, Reed and Sedge Warblers.

Winter: commoner winter ducks, Water Rail (scarce), Oystercatcher, Redshank, Yellow-legged and Caspian Gulls, Kingfisher, finches, Chiffchaff.

Migration: Common Sandpiper, other waders, terns, House Martin, Swallow, warblers, Stonechat, Wheatear.

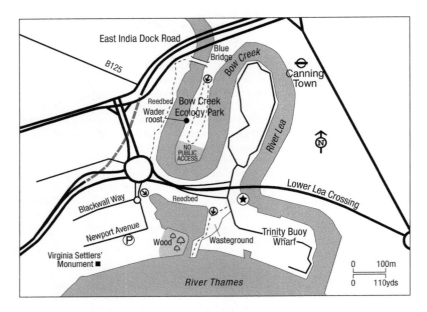

ACCESS

Bike: there are bike racks at each reserve, and the footpaths are all surfaced and level.

Bus: TfL route D3 stops at East India DLR, two minutes from the reserve; many other buses stop on East India Dock Road.

Train: Canning Town DLR (for Bow Creek) and East India (for East India Dock NR) are both a short walk from the sites.

Car: there are few parking places close to the sites, but NCP car parks and paid residential places can be found.

YOUR VISIT

Though they are in two different boroughs, these sites neighbour each other and can be combined and explored easily in no more than a couple of hours. They're best visited early in the morning to avoid courting couples, smokers, joggers, tai chi exponents and dog-walkers. The dock is sometimes left unlocked, but it's often better to start at **Bow Creek** (BCEP) for the chance to view the River Lea as you walk down the wide footpath from Canning Town DLR station.

If possible, consult tide times, as in winter there can be a high-tide Redshank roost on the River Lea's bank alongside BCEP. Common Sandpiper, Oystercatcher, Shelduck and Teal are all likely at low tide. A spring visit can produce Lesser Whitethroat along with other commoner migrants, but adverse weather will bring the inner-city scarcities that keep the regular birders coming.

Complete your Bow Creek circuit and exit over the Blue Bridge. Turn left toward **East India Dock** (EIDB). Keep an eye on the Lea as you pass the tall, litter-strewn reeds that fringe its banks, where Reed Warbler nests in summer. At low tide, the mud at the southernmost bend attracts lots of gulls, Grey Herons and other common waterbirds.

The dock, now mostly filled with mud, remains tidal and is a regular site for Little Ringed Plover (LRP) in spring and summer. LRPs visit to forage and display, and probably breed on nearby wasteground. There are two small wooden rafts that hold a few Common Tern nests most summers, but make sure you scan offshore and downriver from the Thames side of the reserve during migration for Arctic and even Black Tern. There is sometimes a wintering Water Rail in the reeds, which hold Reed Bunting and Reed and Sedge Warblers in summer.

EIDB used to be the most reliable site in London for Black Redstart, with up to five birds present in winter and two or three pairs breeding, but now, sadly, it's far from regular. EIDB has a reputation for producing random London rarities, and astonishingly the site has produced two Barred Warblers in the last 20 years, along with two Roseate Terns that stayed for an afternoon. The likes of Scaup, Jack Snipe, Nightingale and Whinchat have also occurred. As both sites are at the mouth of the River Lea flyway, many species unusual for Inner London have been logged.

Scan the mud in front of the O2 Arena (formerly the Millennium Dome) on the opposite side of the Thames (a scope is good) for gulls and wildfowl on the mud at low tide. A Common Seal frequented nearby Limehouse Basin for several years and was sometimes seen attempting to supplement its diet with Teal in front of the O2 Arena. Caspian and Yellow-legged Gulls are sometimes present, while Peregrine regularly perches on the yellow support towers above the O2 Arena (three territories intersect directly over EIDB). The occasional Buzzard or Red Kite has been noted overhead.

There is a small supermarket by East India Dock DLR for snacks and drinks, but the area is subject to continuous development and may have more shops (and people!) in the near future.

2 THE THAMES BARRIER AREA: LYLE AND THAMES BARRIER PARKS

Lyle Park: Royal Docks, London E16 2BG; TQ406800; plant.baked.deep
Thames Barrier Park: North Woolwich Rd, London E16 2HP; TQ411800; doors.gold.wanted
Phone: 020 7476 3741
Email: royaldocks@london.gov.uk
Open: Lyle Park 7am–10pm; Thames Barrier Park dawn until dusk, though opening times in spring and summer are from 7am only; the cafe and toilets open at 9am.
(7 hectares; 17.3 acres)

Two small urban parks on the Thames that can provide excellent gull-watching and the odd surprise.

SPECIES
All year: Peregrine, Black Redstart (scarce).

Summer: common species.

Winter: Shelduck, Teal, Mediterranean, Yellow-legged and Caspian Gulls.

Migration: terns, gulls, waders, songbirds.

ACCESS

Bike: bikes can be taken onto DLR trains, except between 7.30–9.30am and 4–7pm on weekdays; there are cyclable paths around the sites.

Bus: TfL routes 330 and 474 run along the A1020 North Woolwich Road to both sites.

Train: use Pontoon Dock DLR for Thames Barrier Park and West Silvertown DLR for Lyle Park.

Car: limited paid parking is available in neighbouring streets.

YOUR VISIT

These two small patches of urban greenspace are close to each other and have become known among larophiles owing to the hard work of several patch birders.

Huge flocks of gulls gather on the Thames mud at low tide from late summer through to spring and can be surveyed at close quarters, preferably with a scope. Mediterranean, Yellow-legged and Caspian Gulls are regular, while scarcer species such as Iceland Gull have occurred. The many hundreds of gulls that assemble during annual test drills involving the Thames Barrier are well worth investigating, but there's always a huge mass of them away from high tide.

Black Redstart and Peregrine are also possible, along with the commonest finches and garden birds. Both small parks can be covered with ease on foot and are close to transport. Bear in mind that scanning the gull flocks can take a considerable amount of time.

It can also be worth scanning the Millennium Mills wasteground on the other side of the A1020 for passerines, while the surrounding waters of the disused dockyard can provide shelter for the odd storm-driven waterbird. The area can also be partially scanned with a little difficulty from Mill Road.

3 HACKNEY MARSHES, MIDDLESEX FILTER BEDS NR AND WATERWORKS CENTRE NR

HACKNEY MARSHES

Homerton Rd, London E9 5PF
Website: https://hackney.gov.uk/hackney-marshes
TQ369856; admire.noted.composers
Phone: 020 8986 8615
Email: parks@hackney.gov.uk
Open: all day, every day
(136.01 hectares; 336.1 acres)

MIDDLESEX FILTER BEDS NR

Lea Bridge Road, London E5 9RB
Websites: https://londonbirders.fandom.com/wiki/Middlesex_Filter_Beds;

https://www.leevalleypark.org.uk/middlesex-filter-beds
TQ359864, places.bets.leaps
Email: lvprojects@leevalleypark.org.uk
(4.05 hectares; 10 acres)

WATERWORKS CENTRE NR

Lammas Road (off Lea Bridge Road), Leyton, London E10 7QB
Website: www.visitleevalley.org.uk/waterworks-nature-reserve
TQ362869; tags.forgot.heats
Phone: 03000 030 610
Email: info@leevalleypark.org.uk
Open: 8am–4pm (winter); 8am–6.30pm (summer); closes early on public
holidays and is fully closed on Christmas Day
(5.68 hectares; 14.05 acres)

Two adjacent local reserves with some interesting species that can be covered in one morning or with Walthamstow's more extensive sites just to the north.

A website that covers all these sites is at: https://www.visitleevalley.org.uk/plan-your-visit/plan-your-visit-to-waterworks-centre-nature-reserve-and-field-%26-middlesex-filter-beds

SPECIES

All year: Little Owl, Kingfisher.

Summer: Common Tern, Hobby (scarce), Swift, Sand Martin, Lesser Whitethroat, Garden, Sedge and Reed Warblers.

Winter: Little Grebe, gull flocks, Gadwall, Teal, Shoveler, Snipe, Firecrest (scarce).

Migration: Buzzard, Red Kite, Common Sandpiper, hirundines, Redstart and chats (scarce).

ACCESS

Bike: there are cycle paths all over the site.

Bus: TfL routes 48, 55 and 56 all stop nearby on Lea Bridge Road.

Train: Clapton station (London Liverpool Street–Chingford) is a 10-minute walk away, while Lea Bridge (London Liverpool Street–Bishops Stortford) is just 5 minutes away.

Car: free parking is available at the Lee Valley Ice Centre on Lea Bridge Road or next to the WaterWorks NR, when open. Cross the road from the ice centre and turn right for Middlesex Filter Beds or left for WaterWorks.

YOUR VISIT

Hackney Marshes is a large area of playing fields bordered by tall trees and the River Lea on its eastern edge and the Lea Navigation to its west. At its northern end are two former sewage works: Middlesex Filter Beds and the WaterWorks

Nature Reserve (formerly known as Essex Filter Beds). There are also several small wooded areas and some scrub and rough grassland around the site, which nowadays is a marsh in name only.

All the habitats can be productive for birds, particularly early in the morning during migration. The site is heavily used by human beings and their commensal pets, and many birds don't hang around for long.

The tall trees near the Friends Bridge have recently become home to a pair of London's most reliable Little Owls, but they can be elusive. The bridge is a good place from which to scan for Kingfisher, Grey Wagtail and the occasional Common Sandpiper when the water is low (the river is still tidal at this point).

At the crack of dawn, large flocks of gulls assemble before the people and these can include Yellow-legged Gull, but the flocks disperse quickly, often with dogs hot on their heels.

Spring brings the expected warblers, most just passing through. Lesser Whitethroat and Garden Warbler breed in WaterWorks NR. The surrounding trees throughout support Great Spotted Woodpecker, while the grass allows their Green cousins to forage for ants.

WaterWorks NR is a pleasant place to stroll and is sometimes accessible outside its official times, and it's much less disturbed than the surrounding locale. The area of fenced-off grassland within can produce Whinchat in spring, when Redstart is fairly regular in the bordering hawthorns. A roaming Firecrest or two is usually found in winter (though they can wander as far as Walthamstow Wetlands), while the area of denser hawthorns by the children's play area on the way in has breeding Garden Warbler.

The large circular viewpoint in the reserve's centre is well designed, and allows observation of the open water, long grass and reedbeds covering six former filter beds. In winter, these are home to Teal, Shoveler, Gadwall and Little Grebe, while Kingfisher is resident and sometimes overflies the footpaths between pools. Snipe is also present in winter, but other waders are infrequent, with Green Sandpiper perhaps the most likely. Jack Snipe could well be annual, but only rarely reveals itself in freeze-ups.

Summer brings Reed and Sedge Warblers, Reed Buntings and Sand Martins to the reeds and pools, but the most deafening sound can be the Marsh Frogs.

Have a quick look at the flood relief channel adjacent to the WaterWorks from the road bridge for views of several species of bat as they forage on warmer summer evenings. Little Egret and Grey Heron fish there, often photogenically close.

Middlesex Filter Beds are situated between the River Lea to the north, the canalised Lea Navigation to the south and Hackney Marshes to the east. The site holds another six former filter beds and has two entrances: one to the west from the canal towpath opposite Millfields Park and another to the east from Hackney Marshes. Similar species to the WaterWorks can be seen, though in smaller numbers and variety, though Pied Flycatcher and even Nightjar have occurred.

The adjacent weir on the River Lea is good for Kingfisher and Grey Wagtail. The Princess of Wales pub right on the river at Lea Bridge Road is an ideal refreshment spot (though book well in advance for Sunday lunch), while there are plenty of cafes on nearby Chatsworth Road. Walthamstow Marshes is directly opposite on the other side of the Lea Bridge Road, and directly connected to Walthamstow Wetlands when it's open.

The disused industrial area between the Old River Lea/Middlesex Filter Beds NR and the WaterWorks Centre NR has recently been proposed for development as 'East London Waterworks Park'. In addition to recreation, this should see a bit more habitat appearing on the WaterWorks' western edge, potentially making it better for wildlife.

4 WALTHAMSTOW MARSHES

Lea Bridge Road, London E10 7QL
Website: www.visitleevalley.org.uk/nature-reserves-and-open-spaces/ walthamstow-marshes
TQ350875; punch.vanish.fired
Phone: 020 8988 7565
Email: LVRPA Ranger Services Manager (Ges Hoddinott) at *ghoddinott@ leevalleypark.org.uk*
Open: all day, every day
SSSI
(36.7 hectares; 91 acres)

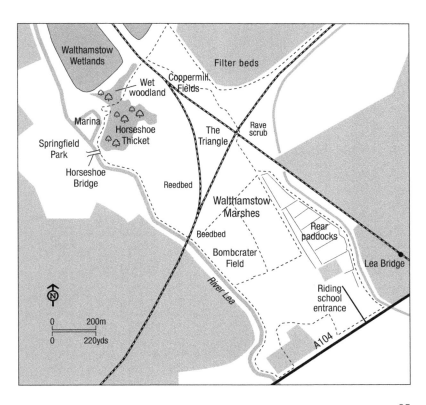

A remnant patch of river-valley grassland, Walthamstow Marshes supports a wide variety of migrants and breeding songbirds.

SPECIES

All year: Little Egret, Peregrine Falcon, Meadow Pipit, Cetti's Warbler, Linnet, Reed Bunting.

Summer: Lesser Whitethroat, Reed and Sedge Warblers.

Winter: Snipe and Jack Snipe, Fieldfare, Redwing, Goldcrest, Firecrest, Brambling.

Migration: common raptors, Yellow Wagtail, pipits, warblers, Wheatear, Redstart, Black Redstart, Stonechat, Whinchat, flycatchers.

ACCESS

Bike: there are broad gravel paths on both sides of the marsh suitable for cycling.

Bus: TfL routes 48, 55 and 56 stop outside the ice rink on Lea Bridge Road.

Train: the newly opened Lea Bridge station is on the Greater Anglia line between Stratford and Tottenham Hale.

Car: use the large car park at Lee Valley Ice Centre; there's another car park on Coppermill Lane (TQ350880; noting.video.eating) near the official public entrance.

YOUR VISIT

Walthamstow Marshes can be approached from any direction via neighbouring streets, but the best start point is probably at Lea Bridge Road. This enables you to walk through the entrance gate to the riding school and check the paddocks and surrounding trees in winter for Redwing, Fieldfare and finch flocks, as well as Green Woodpecker. The occasional Spotted or Pied Flycatcher has been noted in the trees during migration, while Mistle Thrush is possible all year.

Bear right onto the grassy footpath past the stables, then turn left until you see the three fenced-off paddocks to your left. Pay careful attention to these during migration as Yellow Wagtail and Wheatear are regular, while Redstart and Black Redstart are annual. There will also be flocks of Goldfinches, Greenfinches, Linnets and Chaffinches, and these occasionally hold scarcer species such as Brambling and Yellowhammer. Stock Dove breeds in the dead elms, though the formerly reliable Little Owls have now deserted the site.

Bear left at the north of the paddocks onto a wide gravel path overlooking Leyton Marsh. This is heavily used by dog-walkers and joggers, but there is a fenced-off wet meadow and reedy area with a boardwalk straight ahead, between the main path and River Lea. Migration periods produce reliable Whinchats in the taller vegetation, with multiple and long-staying individuals at times. Meadow Pipit and Reed Bunting breed.

This area can flood in winter, when it can attract quite large numbers of gulls, which have included Mediterranean. Ring Ouzel has occurred and Rook (a scarce bird in London Transport Zones 1–4) can fly through.

Follow the mature elms towards the canalised River Lea, keeping your eyes open for Sand Martin, which breeds in summer. Swallow and House Martin pass through on migration. Turn right along the gravel path past a boggy area known as the Bombcrater Field; this grazed area can hold Snipe in winter, but Jack Snipe and Green Sandpiper are much less regular.

Continue under the working viaduct and turn right onto 'true' Walthamstow Marshes. During freeze-ups, the ditch by the path can produce intimate views of Water Rail, though these are more likely to be heard and not seen in the larger reedbed most years.

Follow the worn desire line across the marsh. Reed and Sedge Warblers and Reed Buntings breed in the extensive area of reeds to your right, and the latter can linger into winter. The area is often flooded and has attracted Little and (rarely) Great Egrets, Teal and Shoveler. Much of the site can be muddy in winter so wellies are advised.

At the northern end of the marsh is Horseshoe Copse, a productive area for singing warblers (including, once, one of the subalpine species) and Greenfinch in spring. Firecrest and even Dusky Warbler have wintered and it's worth checking the scrubby edges for Redstart and Cuckoo in spring.

Opposite this copse is Horseshoe Bridge, crossing the River Lea to Springfield Park. While the park is not usually very productive, the nearest trees have held migrant Spotted and Pied Flycatchers and good numbers of warblers, while Mistle Thrush breeds. Red-crested Pochards of dubious origin are also seen on Springfield Park Pond, but it's best to turn back to the marsh after checking for passerines.

Walk past the marina to your left and turn right to walk alongside Walthamstow Wetlands, checking the patches of wet woodland to your left, where Firecrest has wintered. Cetti's Warbler is resident and Chiffchaff is very likely, while Siskin and Redpoll have been seen in winter, though neither is anywhere near as frequent as they were. This is another good spot for Water Rail, and the local population of Water Voles may be seen along the horsetail-ridden ditch.

Continue east under the low railway crossing bridge. Walk straight ahead if you have decided to visit the Wetlands (the entrance is a short distance on your left and opens at 9.30am) or turn right and explore the bushes and trees of Coppermill Fields. Peregrine often overflies and more warblers may be seen.

The path south will take you past the filter beds, through some scrub and under a tunnel graffitied with wildlife themes. This will enable scanning of the filter beds from the top of a slope, where plentiful gulls may be present in winter. There's a summer House Martin colony and Grey Wagtail breeds.

A detour left down a muddy slope along the edge of the railway leads to an area known as the 'Rave Scrub', owing to its summertime abuse by revellers. Nightingale has been heard, while migration periods can produce a profusion of warblers and possibly Redstart.

Regular watching of Walthamstow Marshes over the last couple of decades has produced a tasty array of scarce species, including Bar-tailed Godwit, Water Pipit, Dusky and Yellow-browed Warblers and Common Rosefinch.

5 WALTHAMSTOW WETLANDS

2 Forest Road, London N17 9NH
Websites: *www.wildlondon.org.uk/walthamstow-wetlands-nature-reserve;*
www.thameswater.co.uk/about-us/responsibility/days-out/walthamstow-
wetlands; http://walthamstowbirders.blogspot.com
TQ349891; combining.share.food
Phone: 0203 989 7448
Email: walthamstow@wildlondon.org.uk
Open: 9.30–5pm to the general public (with limited access to paths); 7am
(summer) or 8am (winter) until dusk for permit holders (see website for
changeover dates)
SSSI, Ramsar, SPA, Site of Metropolitan Importance for Nature Conservation
(211 hectares; 520 acres)

*A huge urban wetland which supports most of the common waterbirds – and
always the potential for unexpected sightings.*

SPECIES
All year: Little Egret, Water Rail, Stock Dove, Kingfisher, Peregrine, Cetti's
Warbler, Linnet, Grey Wagtail, Reed Bunting.

Summer: Shelduck, heronry, Cormorant colony, Great Black-backed Gull,
Common Tern, Hobby, Swift, House and Sand Martins, Lesser Whitethroat, Reed
and Sedge Warblers.

Winter: Wigeon, Teal, Shoveler, Goosander, Goldeneye, Lapwing, Green
Sandpiper, Snipe, Common Gull, Fieldfare, Redwing, Goldcrest.

Migration: Garganey, Red-crested Pochard, Common Scoter, Buzzard, Red Kite,
Black-necked Grebe, Great Egret, Ringed and Little Ringed Plovers, Greenshank,
Dunlin, Kittiwake, Arctic, Sandwich, Little and Black Terns, Cuckoo, Swallow,
Yellow Wagtail, Meadow and Rock Pipits, Garden and Willow Warblers, Wheatear,
Redstart, Black Redstart, Stonechat, Whinchat, Spotted Flycatcher, Firecrest,
Brambling, Siskin, Redpoll.

ACCESS
Bike: cycling is permitted on some of the footpaths and there are bike stands by
the VC. Please don't cycle on the top of the reservoir embankments. There is a
comfortable café and shop in the Engine House.

Bus: more than 20 bus routes coalesce at Tottenham Hale, 10 minutes from the
entrance; TfL routes 123 (Lordship Lane–Hainault) and 230 (Wood Green–Upper
Walthamstow) stop directly outside.

Train: Blackhorse Road and Tottenham Hale tube stations (Victoria Line) are both
a 10-minute walk away. The Greater Anglia Liverpool Street–Cambridge line
stops at Tottenham Hale.

Car: there is pay-and-display parking at the Forest Road entrance (permit holders
park for free by the site office). More spaces are available next to the Coppermill
Lane entrance and 100m further on at the Coppermill Fields Car Park on
Walthamstow Marshes.

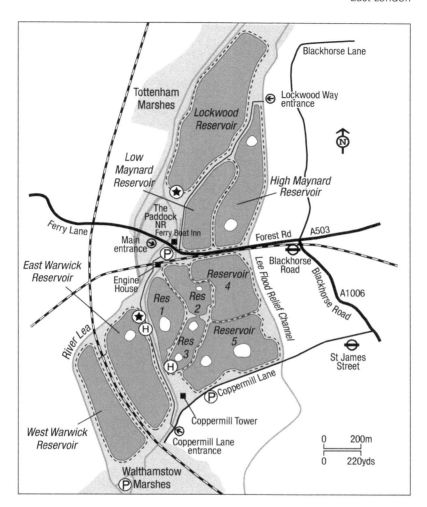

NB: Birdwatching permits allowing full access to the entire site and outside official visiting hours can no longer be obtained at the gatehouse and must be applied for via the Engine House shop. A limited number are available each year and there's always a long list of applicants.

YOUR VISIT

This complex of 10 reservoirs – 11 if you count Banbury Reservoir just to the north, which has no public access – is managed by Thames Water and very popular with anglers and local birders, and – since it officially opened to the public – cyclists, walkers, toddlers and joggers.

The site was always open to the public before it officially became a nature reserve for the nominal sum of £1 and was perhaps London birding's best-kept secret. However, the publicity that accompanied the management takeover by the LWT has radically increased the site's usage by casual visitors. This, in turn, has created crowd-management and conservation problems, and the LWT and Thames Water don't always sing from the same hymn sheet. Despite this, the Walthamstow Wetlands area remains attractive to species that are often scarce in other parts of London, and it's watched regularly and enthusiastically by a healthy number of regulars. There are also two WhatsApp groups to join to keep informed about sightings.

Formerly known as Walthamstow Reservoirs, Walthamstow Wetlands remains a working Thames Water site, supplying water to 3.5 million households and workplaces. It hosts a publicly accessible nature reserve managed by the LWT. The three large waterbodies on the northern side of Ferry Lane and the seven to the south comprise one of the largest urban wetland reserves in Europe.

Bordered by Walthamstow Marshes to the south-east and Tottenham Marshes to the north-west, about a third of the Wetlands is accessible to non-permit holders. This can be frustrating, as more interesting birds are often in inaccessible areas. That said, the site is worth visiting at any time and some of the best birds have appeared during the day and in the most accessible places.

The larger waterbodies have concrete banks, sometimes attractive to migrating waders despite their austere appearance. Green and Common Sandpipers and Snipe are most likely, but Lapwing, Little Ringed and Ringed Plovers, Dunlin, Greenshank, Redshank and even Avocet are annual, while most scarcer waders have occurred. Lockwood Reservoir is often the most productive for waterbirds, especially in the early morning or during spells of rain. The open water pulls in a Black-necked Grebe most years, but other scarce grebes and divers are less likely and Little and Great Crested Grebes are the stalwarts.

Spring sees the chance of migrant warblers, flycatchers, pipits and wagtails, which can occur anywhere. Summer sees common breeding species settling in to raise their young, but there's still interest: one of southern England's largest Cormorant colonies is present on islands at Reservoir No5. Both *sinensis* and *carbo* subspecies can be present, though only the former breeds, with 134 occupied nests in 2020. No5 also has small numbers of Great Black-backed Gulls nesting among the Lesser Black-backed and Herring, and Kingfisher breeds in the island's sandy bank (and elsewhere on site). The breeding Barnacle Geese are feral, however.

There is an impressive heronry on the islands of Reservoirs 1, 2 and 3, which currently hosts about 45 pairs as well as more than 30 pairs of Little Egret, while a few Stock Doves nest in holes in the dead trees. Common Terns are obvious over the whole site in summer, though numbers vary according to the condition of the tern rafts, which are often neglected.

Nationally important numbers of Tufted Duck assemble in late summer, peaking at around 2,000 – though half that figure is usual most years. These monochrome rafts bear scrutiny as they can conceal Scaup. Other cold-season wildfowl include Teal and Shoveler, while a few Goosanders linger every year but can be very flighty. Garganey and Red-crested Pochard are annual – usually in spring, though the former has wintered – while the odd Wigeon or Pintail turns up towards the end of the year. Shelduck breeds but usually abandons the site in autumn.

Gulls are omnipresent in autumn and winter, but their numbers change seasonally. Scan the adjacent filter beds or examine any larid gathering in March for Mediterranean Gull and late summer for Yellow-legged Gull; Iceland, Glaucous and Caspian Gulls have also been noted rarely. A recent development has been a near-annual arrival of Little Gull flocks on West Warwick and Lockwood in late April and early May, though lone individuals are more likely; check movements around the rest of the country to increase your odds of connecting. Arctic, Sandwich and Little Terns are annual on passage, and Black Tern is almost annual, but none are reliable and they can occur anywhere.

The open water pulls in hundreds of Swifts in late summer; it's a real thrill to have these birds whizzing past you at eye level, often close enough to feel the air from their wings. Large numbers of Swallows and House and Sand Martins can also occur during migration, especially in overcast or drizzly conditions. There is a colony of about 30 pairs of House Martins on the filter beds.

The most frequent scarcer passerine migrants are Yellow Wagtail, Wheatear and Whinchat, while Stonechat often winters between East and West Warwick. Rock Pipit is annual but Meadow is much more likely. The commoner finch species are ever-present – with Linnet the scarcest of them. Reed Bunting is generally on site somewhere, though often elusive.

Most commoner migrant warbler species breed, and Willow and Garden Warblers pass through every spring and autumn; the resident Cetti's Warblers have been obvious since they colonised the site at the turn of the century. Early autumn will bring a Spotted Flycatcher or two, and Redstart and Black Redstart are annual. Please note that, despite a preponderance of eBird records, Coal Tit is an extreme rarity at this site.

Regular watching has paid off with a long list of scarce and rare visitors over the years. These have included Black Kite, Gannet, Purple and Night Herons, Cattle Egret, Kittiwake, Wood Sandpiper, Little Stint, Hoopoe, Yellow-browed Warbler, Bearded Tit, Bluethroat, Serin and Little Bunting.

Note that there is a small wooded nature reserve called The Paddock NR (TQ349893; dine.ahead.played) on the west side of the Ferry Boat Inn near the Wetlands entrance. This has always looked good for songbird migrants like Firecrest, warblers and flycatchers, though little has been found and there can be some 'interesting' human activity to make an early visit uncomfortable.

6 NEARBY: TOTTENHAM MARSHES

Main entrances: Watermead Way, London N17 0XD (TQ350905; edgy. sentences.foal) or Ferry Lane N17 9NE (TQ347894; darker.value.during)
Website: Friends of Tottenham Marshes: *www.tottenhammarshes.org*
Phone: 020 8808 1341
Email: contact@tottenhammarshes.org
Open: all day, every day
(40.47 hectares; 100 acres)

Scrub and grassland that hosts common parkland and scrub species, with the possibility of interesting migrants.

YOUR VISIT
This extensive green space on the River Lea floodplain's ancient lammas meadows is heavily used by dog-walkers, joggers and cyclists – however, 'good' birds can still be found.

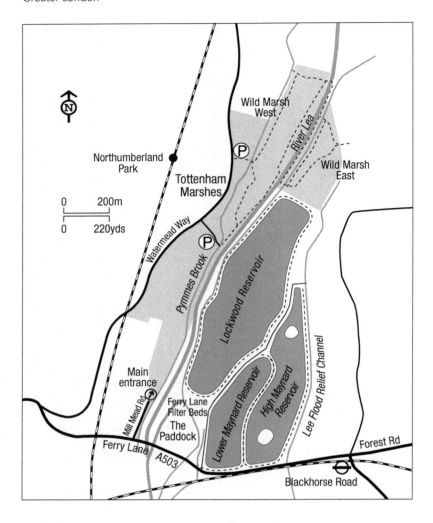

Tottenham Marshes expansive area of flat, scrubby grass broken up by allotments and a few tall trees stretches north to south from Ferry Lane (near Tottenham Hale station) to Northumberland Park station. It's bordered to the west and east by Watermead Way (A1055) and Walthamstow Wetlands respectively. Its habitat is defined on each side by the River Lea and its flood channels, and an industrial estate.

The expected common scrub and garden birds are present, and most common migrants pass through – especially warblers. This is a reliable site for Whinchat and Stonechat on passage, though usually bettered by Walthamstow Marshes, and can be incorporated into a longer visit to Walthamstow Wetlands. Keep an eye on the drainage channels for Goosander and Little Egret in winter, while a fly-through Kingfisher is always possible.

Regular observation has resulted in several scarcities being located, including

Short-eared and Barn Owls, Great Egret, Yellow-browed Warbler and Common Rosefinch.

There are several entrances, the main one being at the car park on Watermead Way, where you'll find a cafe and toilets. A further entrance with limited parking can be found on Leeside Road, from which a small bridge crosses Pymmes Brook to the Wild Marsh.

7 RAMMEY MARSH

Smeaton Road, Enfield Lock, EN3 6HR (car park)
Website: www.visitleevalley.org.uk/gunpowder-park
TQ372993; wage.sung.sleepy
Phone: 03000 030 610
Email: info@leevalleypark.org.uk
Open: all day, every day. There are plenty of grassy footpaths; a few are suitable for wheelchairs.
(42 hectares; 100 acres)

This accessible area of marshy grassland and scrub is one of the more reliable sites in London for Grasshopper Warbler in spring and Jack Snipe in winter.

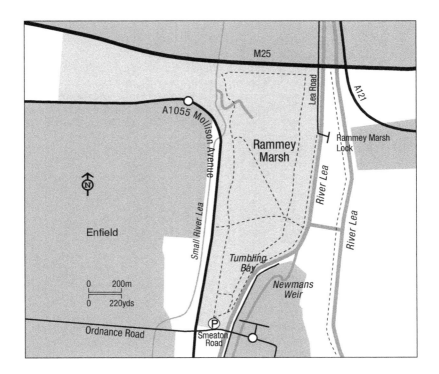

SPECIES

All year: Red-legged Partridge (scarce), Buzzard, Sparrowhawk, Kestrel, Chiffchaff.

Summer: Cuckoo, Grasshopper Warbler and common breeding migrants.

Winter: Snipe, Jack Snipe, Short-eared Owl (scarce).

Migration: Red Kite, Hobby, Ring Ouzel, chats, warblers.

ACCESS

Bike: National Cycle Route 1 (River Lea footpath) crosses the site.

Bus: route 121 (Enfield Island–Turnpike Lane) stops right by the site; route 491 (Waltham Cross–North Middlesex Hospital) goes to Enfield Lock.

Train: the nearest station is Enfield Lock on the Greater Anglia London Liverpool Street–Hertford East/Bishop's Stortford line. Exit and walk east along Ordnance Road, crossing Mollison Avenue to Smeaton Road.

Car: there is a small free car park just off Smeaton Road at the southern entrance and a larger car park on South Ordnance Road by the Swan and Pike Pool.

YOUR VISIT

Just north-west of Gunpowder Park, this discrete area of scrub, trees and grassland has enough boggy areas to provide a few waterbirds as well as commoner species. It's a reliable site for Grasshopper Warbler in spring and Jack Snipe in winter but holds interest for most of the year.

The open grassland attracts Wheatear, Whinchat and Stonechat in spring, with Redstart and Ring Ouzel also possible. Grasshopper Warbler should be buzzing away from mid-April, particularly where bushes are surrounded by long grass.

The northern boggy area holds Snipe in winter, but the scarcer Jack Snipe will be your prize. Short-eared Owl is also possible. Overhead, Buzzard is likely, Red Kite appears on passage and Hobby is infrequent in summer, when there is still a chance of Cuckoo. This is also one of London's few regular sites for Red-legged Partridge, but this is becoming much scarcer.

Rammey Marsh can be covered thoroughly in a couple of hours, with respite at the Greyhound pub almost opposite, on South Ordnance Road.

8 WILLIAM GIRLING AND KING GEORGE V RESERVOIRS

King George V Reservoir: Lea Valley Road, Chingford, London E4 7PX
TQ373950; enable.camera.calls
(170 hectares; 420 acres)
Mansfield Park (for William Girling Reservoir): Old Church Road (A112), London E4 7ST
TQ373942; credit.movie.basic

(Reservoir: 135 hectares; 334 acres)
Open: all day, every day for Walthamstow Wetlands permit holders only
(a key or code number is issued with your birdwatching permit). William
Girling is closed to the public but can be partially scoped from nearby
Mansfield Park. A separate permit can now be purchased solely for KGV
from the Wetland Centre.

*Two huge expanses of open water attracting scarce waterbirds aplenty, especially
during passage or in winter.*

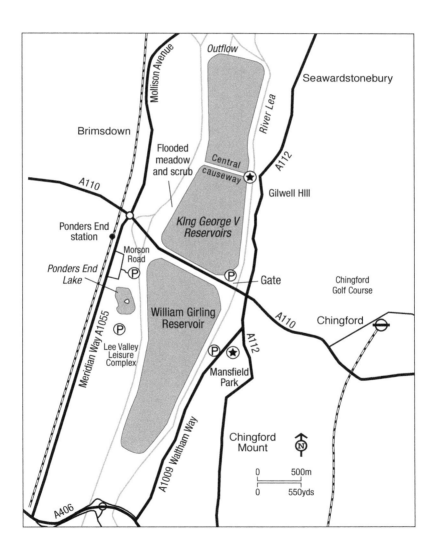

SPECIES

All year: Little Egret, Buzzard, Red Kite, Kingfisher, Peregrine, Cetti's Warbler, Black Redstart, Grey Wagtail, Raven, Linnet, Reed Bunting.

Summer: Common Tern, Hobby, Swift, House and Sand Martins, Swallow, warblers.

Winter: divers, scarce grebes, Wigeon, Teal, Shoveler, Goosander, Goldeneye, Fieldfare, Redwing.

Migration: Garganey, Red-crested Pochard, Common Scoter, Black-necked Grebe, lost seabirds, Ringed and Little Ringed Plovers, Greenshank, Dunlin, Kittiwake, Little Gull, Arctic, Sandwich, Little and Black Terns, Yellow Wagtail, Meadow and Rock Pipits, Wheatear, Stonechat, scarcities.

ACCESS

Bike: permit holders can lock bikes in the car park, or dismount and walk them along the top of the reservoir bank.

Bus: route 313 (Chingford–Potters Bar) stops outside the gate at King George Sailing Club, while the 121 (Enfield Island–Turnpike Lane) and 491 (Waltham Cross–North Middlesex Hospital) both stop at Mollison Avenue, Ponders End, at the western end of Lea Valley Road.

Train: the nearest station is Ponders End on the Greater Anglia service from London Liverpool Street–Hertford East. Exit and walk down Wharf Road onto Lea Valley Road and head east for 10 minutes to the entrance, perhaps via Ponders End Lake (page 47).

Car: permit holders can turn into the short driveway at the gate, unlock it with their key or code and use the gravel parking area. Lock the gate behind you.

YOUR VISIT

The usual strategy to cover this huge area of water is to walk the eastern side of the south basin from the car park past the sailing club, stopping and scanning regularly. To cover the whole of **King George V Reservoir**, follow the bank all the way around to where you started. A scope is essential owing to the size of the two basins and will reduce the temptation to walk on the central causeway, which is frowned upon by regulars (you'll probably flush unseen waders).

This is a large site, needing a minimum of three hours to cover fully. It's most productive during passage and winter, so dress appropriately – KGV can be bracingly bleak. Regulars spend much of their time at the east end of the causeway, scoping the edges and water of both basins.

Passage sees waders dropping into the banks below the causeway between the two basins – these are usually single birds that rarely stay for long but have included the likes of Little Stint and Pectoral Sandpiper. Pipits and wagtails are also worth checking.

A few raptor species breed locally, and Buzzard, Red Kite, Hobby and Peregrine may all be seen. The commoner warblers and finches will be present, though often distant, in the scrub trees and on adjacent farmland. The wasteground and industrial estate at Brimsdown on the western side gives you a chance at Black Redstart; keep scanning the fence line, where the birds often perch.

Autumn passage will see wildfowl arriving. Seaduck such as Scaup (annual), Red-breasted Merganser and Velvet Scoter are possible, though Common Scoter is more likely than the latter. Goosander winters; check the drainage channels to the north and east of the site, if none are on the reservoirs. Scarce grebes are also possible, with Black-necked the most likely (more are usually on William Girling Reservoir). Most winters feature a diver, with Great Northern the most regular.

The northern outflow churns up the water enough for hordes of duck and gulls to hang around, among which scarcities have been located. In fact, everything from Long-tailed Skua to Citrine Wagtail and Snow Bunting has pitched up. It's worth braving all weathers during migration to discover such species in an exciting London context.

William Girling Reservoir, with its deeper, wider water and less disturbance, has also proved very attractive to unusual birds. There's a large gull roost from autumn to spring (with overspill onto KGV), and Black-necked Grebe numbers in double figures sometimes. The lack of access has not prevented good London birds such as Velvet Scoter and Leach's Storm-petrel from being discovered when scoped from Mansfield Park.

9 NEARBY: PONDERS END LAKE

Entrances: Morson Road lay-by (TQ361950; wing.game.alien);
Lea Valley Leisure Centre car park (TQ360945; reason.winks.work)
Lake location: TQ362947; down.jobs.broken
Open: all day, every day

This area of open water fringed by trees and reeds, and set in the middle of a golf course, punches above its weight for scarcities.

YOUR VISIT

Despite being in the middle of a golf course, birders are free to visit this small lake any time, but it's best during passage when it comes into its own.

Most common migrants turn up, but regular watching has produced scarcities and even the odd rarity, including a singing Iberian Chiffchaff in May 2020 – only the second for London. Otherwise, a small mud island in the lake draws in Lapwings and Redshanks, along with the odd migrant tern and gull, while Common Tern nests. The open water attracts hirundine and swift flocks in late summer, and Garganey can drop in on passage. A recently refurbished bird hide overlooks the lake and one hopes this remains intact, despite its urban location.

Ponders End Lake is perhaps most worth a look when visiting King George V Reservoir (where a permit is required). Ponders End station on the London Liverpool Street line is just a short walk to the north. From the station, turn down Meridian Way, then onto Morson Road. Bus W8 from Chase Farm Hospital, Enfield, terminates at Picketts Lock/Lea Valley Leisure Centre, right next to the golf course.

For drivers, there is a small lay-by with parking spaces and fly-tipped rubbish on Morson Road – it's possible to access the golf course from there, and you'll see the lake ahead to your left. More reliable is the larger free car park at the leisure centre, slightly south of the lake.

RIVER LEE COUNTRY PARK

Website: www.visitleevalley.org.uk/river-lee-country-park
Phone: 03000 030610
Email: info@leevalleypark.org.uk

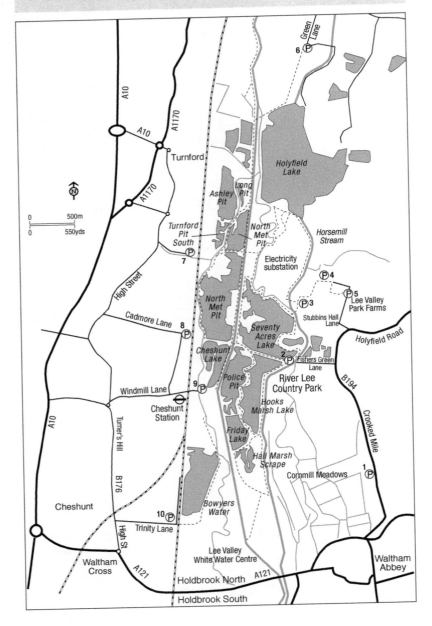

This huge river valley is home to a profusion of waterbirds and songbirds. It's one of the few reliable sites for Smew and Bittern in London in winter, and the city's best area for Nightingale in spring, despite being a popular recreational destination.

This large area is where the River Lea's floodplain opens out upriver, and there is much less urban intrusion than in the sites above. There's still plenty of disturbance, and the river is tidal and water levels everywhere can vary seasonally.

The mid-Lea Valley provides substantial amounts of riverine, lacustrine, reedbed, marshland, woodland and grassland habitats. Consequently, there are largely healthy populations of most of the species you would expect in those environments in South-east England. It is managed for wildlife by the LVRPA and there are well-maintained bird hides in key locations.

Despite being such an extensive park, it's possible to explore most of it in one day with the judicious use of a car. There are plenty of spacious car parks very close to the most bird-rich areas and plenty of obscure nooks to search.

This is the largest self-contained part of the LVRP and comprises several large lakes formed from former gravel pits, some of which are used for boating or fishing. There are also smaller pools, drainage ditches, marshes, scrub, grassland and regenerative and secondary wooded areas. The greater area of habitat measures about 5 miles (8km) in length by 1.5 miles (2.4km) in width and is bordered by farmland to the east and suburbia to the west.

Strategies for birding such a large area are many. It's best broken up into two or three main areas that can be walked around with relative ease. On foot, you could devote an entire day to getting the best out of the area. However, there are several car parks around the park's perimeter which can be used as bases.

ACCESS

Bike: the footpaths connecting and surrounding the park's lakes are mostly cyclable.

Bus: TfL route 251 (Hammond Street–Upshire) stops at Lea Road, Waltham Cross, and McDonald's, Waltham Abbey, at the very southern end of the park, just a short walk to Bowyers Water and Hall Marsh Scrape.

Train: use Cheshunt station on the West Anglia Main Line from London Liverpool Street for the southern two-thirds of the park. The next station to the north is Broxbourne, from which the northern part can be explored.

Car: there are 10 mostly pay-and-display car parks serving this extensive site. From south to north, they are:

1. Cornmill Meadows (TL383015; rate.cool.voter) – less than a mile out of Waltham Abbey on the western side of Crooked Mile (B194);

2. Hooks Marsh (TL377027; upper.exists.each) – turn left onto Fishers Green Lane from Crooked Mile, drive down the rough track and pass over the small bridge to park right by the water;

3. Fishers Green (TL377032; shops.fence.expert) – turn left at the T-junction at the end of Crooked Mile onto Stubbins Hall Lane and park in the wooded area by the public toilets;

4. Fishers Green overspill (TL378037; keen.force.react) – park by the electricity substation;

5. Lee Valley Park Farms (TL382034; fled.bright.aims) – a large, free car park with many spaces, ideal for walking to the goose fields;

6. Green Lane (TL377057; drums.hardly.likely) – free, but isolated on a dirt track; allows the quickest access to Holyfield Lake through scrub and grassland;

7. Turnford Brook (TL366037; likely.than.monks) – behind a housing estate, allowing a long walk over a railway bridge and through secondary woodland to view Holyfield Lake. This is a good option for Ashley Pit and the North Metropolitan pit, but there is a 2-m height restriction;

8. North Metropolitan Pit (TL366028; racing.plan.scores) – an anglers' car park (check there are no new restrictions signposted) that allows quicker access to Cheshunt Lake and the North Metropolitan Pits;

9. Cheshunt Country Walk (TL367024; rises.storms.bleak) – a long walk alongside the River Lea to Bowyers Water;

10. Trinity Lane (TL365011; spin.curiosity.update) – roadside parking for a quick visit to Bowyers Water.

10 CORNMILL MEADOWS

Crooked Mile/B194, Waltham Abbey, Essex EN9 2ES
Website: www.visitleevalley.org.uk/waltham-abbey-gardens
TL383015; rate.cool.voter
Open: all day, every day
SSSI
(24.6 hectares; 61 acres)

This compact site at the southern end of the park is one of the few surviving examples of floodplain grassland in the valley. There are some choice pockets of woodland and marshland to explore. A roughly rectangular circuit leads right or left from the car park on often waterlogged grass. I favour the right-hand option, taking you through the wooded areas first, then skirting the edges of the productive marshland. A small hide at the southern end overlooks open water.

Spring sees singing warblers among the woodland, hedgerows and scrub, including Garden Warbler – and even the occasional Grasshopper Warbler. The park's wintering Redpolls and Siskins pop in to feed on the alders, but Bullfinch can be seen in the hawthorns year-round. Lesser Spotted Woodpecker hung on into the early twenty-first century but hasn't been seen for years.

The Wake Hide to the south is good for commoner reedbed species but is sometimes vandalised. It provides a limited panorama over the reeds and lake, where scarcities such as Garganey, Great Egret and Wood Sandpiper are annual, and even Spotted Crake has occurred. Water Rail and Cetti's Warbler are ever-present, and Lapwing, Golden Plover, Redshank, Greenshank, Ruff, Black-tailed Godwit and Common and Green Sandpipers pass through every year. The likes of Snipe and Green Sandpiper winter, and cold-season wildfowl will include Wigeon, Shoveler, Teal and the occasional Pintail.

Winter may see Barn Owl hunting over the area, while summertime Hobbies are likely among the commoner raptors.

11 BOWYERS WATER, FRIDAY LAKE AND CHESHUNT

Parking/entrances: Windmill Lane (north) or Trinity Lane (south), Cheshunt, Herts
Website: www.visitleevalley.org.uk/places-to-fish/bowyers-water
TL367014; icon.mental.leap
Phone: 03000 030 622
Email: fisheries@leevalleypark.org.uk
Open: all day, every day
(Bowyers Water: 14.16 hectares; 35 acres)

Bowyers Water is one of the best locations in the LVRP for Smew and Goldeneye in winter. **Friday Lake** is a short walk over the River Lea to the east and also affords a chance to possibly see these attractive species. Its wide expanse of open water and depth attracts diving ducks and gulls, among which the occasional scarcity has been found.

The surrounding reeds, scrub and trees support the expected woodland, scrub and garden birds. Warblers sing in spring and summer, among them Garden and Willow Warblers and Lesser Whitethroat. The scrub is a chance at Grasshopper Warbler in this part of the Lea Valley in spring, when denser areas of tall bushes should hold Nightingale. Away from the breeding season, roving flocks of Redpoll and Siskin pass through, while the scrub holds a few elusive Bullfinches and shelters Redwing and Fieldfare in winter.

If you're walking, the longer route from **Cheshunt** railway station can be productive. From the station, turn right down Windmill Lane and turn left before the River Lea to head towards Bowyers Water. You can also cross the Lea and turn left for a long walk towards Fishers Green. In summer, Hobby hunts over the whole area, while in winter most of the site's specialities can be picked up along this latter route.

12 FISHERS GREEN AND HALL MARSH SCRAPE

Fishers Green Lane, Waltham Abbey, Essex, EN8 9AN
Website: www.visitleevalley.org.uk/walking-running-and-cycling-routes/fishers-green-foray
TL376026; whips.device.lifts
Phone: 03000 030 610
Email: info@leevalleypark.org.uk
Open: all day, every day

YOUR VISIT

This large expanse of open water, reedbeds, woodland and scrub is usually the most productive in the park. It's the best place to see Bittern, particularly from the Bittern Watchpoint next to the bridge that leads from Fishers Green car park (TL377032; glitz.silly.dots). Views can be intimate – hence the hide's popularity with photographers – but also unpredictable. However, close-up Water Rails and Reeves's Muntjac can offer compensation while waiting.

May mornings can be thrilling at **Fishers Green**, as the songs of Cetti's and Garden Warblers and Nightingales merge with a background of Reed and Sedge Warblers, Whitethroats and Lesser Whitethroats, Blackcaps and Reed Buntings, with the klaxon of a Cuckoo in pursuit. Hobby strafes the spring reedbeds for dragonflies, even before first light.

The Hooks Marsh car park (TL376026; larger.gravy.baking) is another good place to start from, parking by Seventy Acres Lake. The expected wintering wildfowl can be checked, when there's a chance of Pintail – and even a rarity (Ring-necked Duck and Green-winged Teal have occurred recently).

There are two main routes from there:

- The footbridge (TL374026; buzz.liver.volunteered) over the short channel between Seventy Acres and Hooks Marsh Lakes (a circular walk);
- The left-hand path south alongside Horsemill Stream (Waltons Walk – TL375026; looks.bricks.super) towards Hall Marsh Scrape.

If taking the first option, look out for Water Rail among the low reeds and trees to your left before the bridge. Garden Warblers regularly nest in the brambles there, and there will be others en route. Singing Willow Warbler, Lesser Whitethroat and other warblers should all be obvious, and Nightingales will be letting rip by the end of April (though they quickly quieten down from mid-May).

As you walk the edge of the lake, keep a watchful eye on the reedy channels for Water Rail and Bittern. Smew can linger into spring, when Garganey is regular. The warmer months supply breeding Common Terns among the thriving Black-headed Gull colony on the rafts.

Reaching the last third of your walk, the Bittern Watchpoint will be well signposted and a patient vigil there could pay off, as up to four birds can be present in the tiny reedbed. There is a 'recent sightings' board in the hide, giving an indication of where to concentrate your efforts around the valley.

Turn right out of the hide to return to the Hooks Marsh car park. Now take the left-hand path, leading you down a wide tarmac path favoured by joggers, walkers and cyclists. Despite this, the alders and hawthorns lining the path are frequented by small flocks of Siskin and Redpoll in winter. There will be commoner finches, Chiffchaff in the tit flocks and even Lesser Spotted Woodpecker has turned up.

You'll soon come to an expanse of flooded grass and marsh surrounded by hawthorns: **Hall Marsh Scrape**. The right turn will bring you to two screens (TL371017; wants.hunt.plus) where point-blank encounters with Water Rail, Lapwing, Snipe and Cetti's Warbler are possible early on a winter's morning.

There will also be a profusion of duck, including Wigeon, Teal, Gadwall and Shoveler. Cattle Egret occasionally occurs and can stick around, while Wood Sandpiper and even Glossy Ibis have popped in during passage. Little Ringed Plover has bred, but water levels are often too high. Passage Green and Common Sandpipers are likely, as is Kingfisher.

Continue with the scrape to your left and you will come to a fork in the path

(TL372018; picked.clocks.relay). The route straight ahead leads to Bowyers Water (page 51) via Friday Lake (TL370018; jacket.last.places), but turning left will afford more chances to scrutinise Hall Marsh Scrape (TL371016; salads.flash.twin), although the hide that was formerly there has now been demolished. Tit flocks work the tall trees in winter, with Treecreeper, Goldcrest and even Firecrest sometimes accompanying them. Fieldfare and Redwing should be apparent on the fields emerging to your right, where there is a small Little Egret roost, and good numbers of gulls often forage on the flooded areas in winter.

A short gravel path leads to the Snipe Hide (TL372015; sport.units.film), allowing further views of the scrape, but be alert for the occasional 'self-absorbed' smoker or courting couple as you approach. There are a few feral Green Pheasants among their commoner relations, and this is a good place to see Reeves's Muntjac. A Red Kite may circle overhead, while the pylons provide perches for Peregrine and sometimes Raven. Circle back and return to the car park, looking out for Siskin and Redpoll.

13 HOLYFIELD VIEWPOINT AND THE GOOSE FIELDS

Parking: Lea Valley Park Farms, Stubbins Hall Lane, Fishers Green, Waltham Abbey, Essex EN9 2EH
TL385036; maple.comical.custom
Open: all day, every day

A 10-minute walk from the Fishers Green car park, this expanse of farmland can be incorporated into a longer visit, though the Lea Valley Park Farms car park (TL380033; into.saving.stole) is closer and it takes just two minutes to change parking location (though a further fee applies).

On foot, the extensive scrub and trees between the two locations can produce winter thrushes, finch and tit flocks, woodpeckers and Nightingale in the appropriate seasons. Lesser Whitethroat, Garden Warbler, Bullfinch, Chiffchaff and Willow Warbler are also possible, and Buzzard, Red Kite, Peregrine and Hobby can all appear overhead.

From the Lea Valley Park Farms car park, turn north onto Stubbins Park Lane past the large field (TL382034; chin.soon.frock), which can produce Skylark, Meadow Pipit and Pied Wagtail before the corn sprouts, while its edges support wintering Stonechat, and Wheatear and Whinchat have been noted. Little Owl is sometimes in the taller hedgerows.

To your left, behind the hedge, is some rough grazing (TL381036; jams.zoom. eaten), which is good for winter thrushes, Green Woodpecker, Linnet and other scrub birds. The resident flock of feral wildfowl includes Egyptian Geese and sometimes Shelduck. Temporary pools form on the fields after rain, and occasionally attract Green or Common Sandpiper.

Turn right along the edge of the ploughed field before you enter the private Holyfield Hall Farm. A few Yellowhammer breed on the farm, while Chaffinch flocks have concealed Brambling in winter. More geese assemble in the fields (colloquially known as the 'goosefields') up the hill (TL387039; wants.city.basket), which are famous for luring in 'proper' wild geese in winter, including White-fronted, feral Barnacle and, more rarely, Pink-footed.

14 HOLYFIELD LAKE

Parking (15 minutes walk from the lake): Slipe Lane, London EN10 6HB
TL368051; parent.image.buns
Open: all day, every day
(73 hectares; 180 acres)

Formerly known as Langridge Lake, this large waterbody is less accessible than its southerly cousins and you'll need to park for free some distance away on residential Slipe Lane. Cross the railway via the footbridge, turn right and walk through the secondary woodland. Another option is to take the long walk along the River Lea from Fishers Green, following one of three footpaths north. Bring a scope to save walking all the way around the very large lake.

Despite the presence of a sailing club, Holyfield Lake is attractive to wildfowl in winter, and Goldeneye and Goosander are usually present. Kingfisher and Grey Wagtail are expected, and the surrounding dense trees and bushes are good for warblers and Nightingales in spring. In summer, Hobby hunts overhead while Common Terns fish. The lake has drawn in scarcities and rarities, including Ring-necked and Ferruginous Ducks.

During migration, contemplate checking the pools around Valley Grown Nurseries on Paynes Lane, immediately to the north-east of the lake (TL381049; curry.print.brush), as well as those a little further north along Paynes Lane (TL382055; guard.lied.blows). Parking can be precarious, but the more northerly pools can hide wildfowl, and the more southerly ones have held Greenshank, Spotted Redshank and Bar-tailed Godwit among commoner species when water levels have been low. In front of the weir (TL376052; shins.stress.chip) is a good place for Common and sometimes Green Sandpipers on passage.

Ashley Pit (TL370042; feels.much.every) is also worth visiting in winter, as it's the most regular site for Goosander and other scarce wildfowl occasionally occur. It's just over the railway bridge and to the north of Turnford Brook car park (see page 50), and close to Holyfield Lake and the North Metropolitan Pit, but can also be accessed by walking south from Slipe Lane via some smaller fishing pits.

THE URBAN NORTH THAMES

15 GALLIONS REACH

Atlantis Avenue, London, E16 2BF
TQ444808; cats.grabs.stared
Open: all day, every day

A very urban riverside site that has a good reputation for seabirds under the right conditions.

ACCESS

Bike: the Capital Ring Footpath is cyclable and runs east from North Woolwich along the Thames to Atlantis Avenue.

Bus: bus routes 101, 262, 366, 474 and N551 run to Gallions Reach DLR station. The 24-hour 474 route runs along Albert Road and takes you almost to King George V DLR station.

Train: Gallions Reach DLR is nearest to the Beckton end; alight, turn left and walk east along Atlantis Avenue past the Co-Op, turning right at the river. King George V DLR is closest to the North Woolwich end; turn right onto Pier Road all the way to the Thames, then turn left onto the Capital Ring Footpath.

Car: there are no close parking facilities.

YOUR VISIT

This is a good place to observe the northern bank of the Inner Thames. Gallions Reach also has areas of rough ground to attract migrants and most of it can be scanned from the handy path by the Thames.

This is about as far as seabirds ever penetrate into central London, apart from in truly exceptional circumstances. Some waders also find the mud of the Thames foreshore and its tributaries there to their liking. Gulls can be usefully sifted at this point, along with the nearby mouth of the River Roding. At the time of writing, the wasteground inland of the path is still undeveloped and hosts a pair of Kestrels and passerine migrants.

A serviceable route around the site starts at Gallions Reach DLR and follows Atlantis Avenue to the river. Walk upstream towards the Albert Dock lock for waders on ascending or descending tides, or seabirds and ducks at high tide; birds on the mud can be very distant at low tide. Check the Albert and King George Docks thoroughly during rough or cold weather. The footpath crosses the docks and you may have to turn inland a little if the riverside path gate is locked. This route takes you to Woolwich Ferry, a short distance to King George V DLR.

Regular watching of this site has produced wandering seabirds fairly often, including Red-breasted Merganser, Fulmar, Guillemot, Razorbill, Puffin, Sabine's Gull and Great and Arctic Skuas, though none are usually likely. Passage waders can be a bit more numerous, and both godwits, Dunlin and Whimbrel occasionally penetrate this far upriver. Terns have included Black and Roseate, while gulls have included Caspian, Glaucous, Iceland and even Bonaparte's.

This isn't a songbird hotspot, but Wheatear and Rock Pipit sometimes occur, and Siberian Chiffchaff, Firecrest and both redstarts have been seen around the gasworks at its eastern end. This is a site that rewards dedication but can be worth visiting spontaneously in promising conditions.

16 RSPB RAINHAM MARSHES

New Tank Hill Rd, Purfleet, Essex, RM19 1SZ
Website: www.rspb.org.uk/reserves-and-events/reserves-a-z/rainham-marshes
VC: TQ547787; light.strain.reef
Phone: 01708 899840
Email: rainham.marshes@rspb.org.uk
Open: all day, every day. The reserve *sensu stricto* is open 9.30am–5pm (March–October) or 9.30am–4pm (November–March); check the website for public holiday hours.
SSSI
(411 hectares; 1,015.6 acres)

The jewel in the crown of London's nature reserves, this extensive site is arguably the most reliable location in the country for Caspian Gull and holds breeding Marsh Harrier, Bearded Tit and Corn Bunting – all within the M25!

SPECIES

All year: Gadwall, Shoveler, Shelduck, Marsh Harrier, Peregrine, Little, Great and Cattle Egrets, Spoonbill, Barn Owl, Water Rail, Lapwing, Redshank, Avocet, Oystercatcher, Ringed Plover, Yellow-legged and Caspian Gulls, Kingfisher, Stonechat, Black Redstart (scarce, but breeds sometimes), Cetti's Warbler, Bearded Tit, Reed and Corn Buntings.

Summer: Hobby, Common Tern, Swift, hirundines, Lesser Whitethroat, Grasshopper Warbler, Marsh Warbler (scarce).

Winter: Wigeon, Teal, Golden Plover, Curlew, Black-tailed Godwit, Snipe, Jack Snipe, Short-eared Owl, Dartford Warbler, Firecrest.

Migration: Garganey, Common Scoter, Grey Plover, Greenshank, Ruff, Common, Green and Wood Sandpipers, Dunlin, Whimbrel, Bar-tailed Godwit, Little and Mediterranean Gulls, Arctic and Black Terns, Wheatear, Whinchat, warblers, finches.

ACCESS

Bike: the Thames Path is flat and cyclable and provides many places to stop to scan the water and shoreline. The path across the West Marsh is cycle-friendly, but you'll need to lock your bike at the RSPB VC to walk the enclosed reserve. The whole area is wheelchair accessible.

Bus: Ensignbus route 44 (Lakeside Thurrock–Grays) stops on New Tank Hill Road, close to the entrance road. Numbers 103, 173, 287 and 372 stop at Rainham station. Alight, go through the level crossing and walk over the footbridge to the West Marsh.

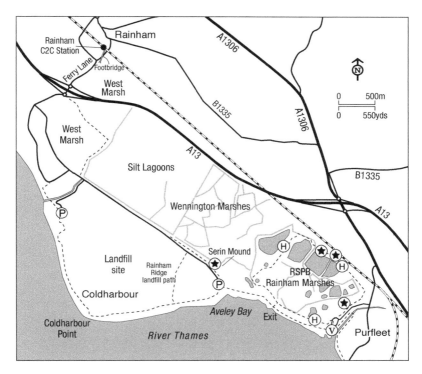

Train: for the West Marsh, take the c2c train to Rainham station on the Fenchurch Street–Grays line and use the level crossing. Stay on until the next stop, Purfleet, if you wish to go to the RSPB VC directly. Turn right out of Purfleet station onto London Road and walk west over the level crossing; the reserve and footpaths are well signposted and you can check the river as you walk through Purfleet Heritage Park (I've had Black Redstart and Sandwich Tern from there).

Car: by car, there are five main parking locations, all free:

Riverside car park (aka the **Concrete Barges**, at TQ516800; trials.able.clear);

Aveley Bay car park (aka 'dump car park', at TQ534792; sank.waddle.stove);

RSPB car park (TQ547788; pile.cost.meant), park here to visit the enclosed reserve;

West Marsh (TQ518804; owners.loaf.cover);

Salamons Way (TQ514814; react.makes.think), on-road parking by some industrial premises, which can be used to explore the West Marsh from the western end; best at weekends, otherwise the road is very busy and dirty.

YOUR VISIT

This huge site can be tackled in several ways. The site is treated here as if walked from west to east, though this route can be reversed or cherry-picked.

THE WEST MARSH

As you walk onto the ramp from the footbridge over the railway (TQ520819; career.minute.remit), you will be greeted with a widescreen view of the northern part of the West Marsh (as well as the ever-busy A13). Descending the ramp, choose whether to go down the steps to the right onto the road and explore the large area of rough ground, reeds and pools immediately below (which can also be scanned from the footbridge) or continue towards the A13 flyover along the tarmac footpath.

This first area is underwatched and produces Water Rail regularly. It holds the common scrub and garden birds – and sometimes singing Grasshopper Warbler in spring. If you have time, enter via the wide black metal gate (TQ521819; matter. posed.return) and follow the path straight ahead for a full circular walk or turn right to explore the small reedbeds and shallow pools close to the path.

Continue along the tarmac path under the A13, heading south along Ferry Lane. Cross the roundabout and enter the second section of the West Marsh using the small bridge and boardwalk (TQ516814; crest.broom.total). If parked on Salamons Way, turn left and walk north for 100m on Ferry Lane to use the same entrance.

Follow the tarmac path through the reedbeds, turning right at the bend (TQ521809; glue.broke.pounds), parallel to the huge raised area of the Silt Lagoons. These overgrown areas, formerly used to dump dredgings from the Thames, have been closed off for years, but are gradually being prepared for reopening. This is an exciting prospect because the old lagoons produced many rarities among the hordes of waders that roosted there. Currently, the area is closed and is mostly scrub and long grass. Even so, it's produced Woodcock, Short-eared Owl and Grasshopper Warbler in recent years, and even a singing Golden Oriole one spring day.

Walking the West Marsh, listen for Cetti's Warbler, as well as Reed and Sedge Warblers and Reed Bunting in the breeding season. Spring will see Garden Warbler (occasionally) and Lesser Whitethroat there, while Marsh Warbler has bred. Marsh Harrier and Barn and Short-eared Owls sometimes overfly, particularly in winter. This is also not a bad place for visible migration, as a broad expanse of sky can be seen. It's often the best place to see Cuckoo in spring and summer, and Turtle Dove has flown through. The channels and ditches hold breeding Gadwall and Little Grebe.

THE CONCRETE BARGES

When you come to a wooded area around the path (TQ518805; hired.river. winner), either retrace your steps back to your car and drive to other areas, or cross the road and head down the single-lane road to the Riverside car park. By the entrance, there's a small car park (TQ518804; owners.loaf.cover) with four spaces that you can use to explore the West Marsh from the southern end, but otherwise walk or drive slowly until you turn left into the Riverside car park. It's worth checking the reedbed and stream by the side of the road for Water Rail, Kingfisher and Reed and Sedge Warblers, and the dense blackthorn and hawthorn hedge to the left hides winter thrushes and finches.

The feeder in the car park (TQ516800; scarf.guards.paying) attracts rats and birds in equal measure, but your main purpose at this point is to scan the river, barges and outflow pipe. Gulls taking a break from feeding on the dump perch on the pipe, and these can include scarcer species. Away from summer, there is sometimes a large roost of Black-tailed Godwits and other waders on the barges, while the small patch of saltmarsh in front provides your first chance of Water Pipit in winter – up to six are regularly counted over the site as a whole, almost matching the number of Scandinavian Rock Pipit that turn up at the same time.

The hedgerows along the edge of the dump give migrants and overwintering songbirds shelter, and everything from Stonechat to Ring Ouzel and Yellowhammer has been seen. This is also a good place to scan the Thames (try watching from TQ516797; crest.hill.void), and a rising tide will bring the best chance of random seabirds such as Kittiwake or Sandwich Tern.

Return to your car and drive to the Aveley Bay car park, or continue walking along the Thames Path to Coldharbour Point (TQ519788; funds.gift.bikes) and the Purfleet riverfront. The latter involves a mile-long hike past some industrial zones and the edge of the dump, but is recommended for a thorough check of the foreshore area. The pigeons on the warehouse (TQ518791; voted.start.envy) at Coldharbour Point attract Peregrine, the rough grassland on the dump is good for chats and Skylark, and the helipad has plenty of wagtails and pipits outside the breeding season. Ducks, waders and pipits use the shoreline in winter.

Depending on the landfill's working schedule, the path provides some of the best views of the masses of gulls as they loaf on the water and foreshore, or fly overhead. Yellow-legged Gulls can number more than 50 in late summer, while several Caspian Gulls may be present in winter and the odd Mediterranean Gull may mingle with the hordes. The dump can be scanned from one or two places, but views are generally not so good and entering the dump is strictly forbidden. Gull numbers are best when the dump is working on a weekday or Saturday morning, away from high tide, and there will be constant toing and froing from the dump to the foreshore, river and Wennington Marsh (see below).

The foreshore provides good views of waders such as Dunlin, Black-tailed Godwit, Oystercatcher, Avocet and Redshank, while both Scandinavian Rock and Water Pipits can be seen in winter. You will eventually come to Aveley Bay car park (TQ534792; curving.sleep.manliness), or you can walk over the grassy hill at the edge of the dump using the gate and footpath (TQ531790; stages.curvy.slimy) – both will eventually bring you to the mound overlooking Wennington Marsh (TQ533794; rising.dime.cape). The south side of the hill is by far your best chance at Corn Bunting, while Skylark, Meadow Pipit and Reed Bunting all breed, and Wheatear and Whinchat are regular on migration.

WENNINGTON MARSH

From the Aveley Bay car park, you can explore the foreshore as above or leave the car park along the path to the north to scan Wennington Marsh. Follow the tarmac path curving round to the left and you'll see a grassy promontory covered with Buddleia, from which the whole vista of the marshes can be scoped (TQ533794; wisdom.singer.foam). This is known as the 'Serin Mound' owing to a family party of that species that once spent the winter there. There will almost certainly be one or two Marsh Harriers in the air, while Buzzard and Red Kite are regular. Peregrine rests out on the grass at times, Merlin is possible in winter and Hobby can appear in numbers in late spring. This is the best place to see Ravens if they are visiting from the Kent side of the Thames, while the feral geese can sometimes attract wild species.

You can see the wetter areas in the distance, where Spoonbill and Great and Cattle Egrets are regular, if unpredictable. Sightings of White Stork are increasing. Gulls rest on the marsh, and Caspian and Yellow-legged are often picked out in scope views. Don't ignore the scrub and brambles around the mound, as these have produced the likes of Marsh Warbler, Serin and Lapland Bunting in the past. The small pool at the foot of the mound attracts Green Sandpiper when water levels are low and has held Spotted Crake and even Slavonian Grebe.

It's sometimes worth walking towards the 'silts' to scope the marsh from a lower level and view the open channel (TQ529797; boat.insist.codes) at the west end of Wennington Marsh. Now, walk east towards the reserve along the seawall or return to your car and drive for 15 minutes to the RSPB car park via the A13.

THE RSPB RESERVE

While almost all of the site I've discussed is leased by the RSPB, only the enclosed area of the reserve – accessible via the VC (TQ547787; pace.improving.awake) – is currently managed for visitors. You'll find a well-stocked shop, a cafe featuring home-made cakes, a sightings board and helpful staff. A circular, 2.5-mile system of boardwalks guides you around the site; there are four hides and several viewpoints.

The VC has a broad view over the reserve and is good for scanning Purfleet Scrape for wildfowl and waders. Wigeon (2,000 were counted recently), Teal and Shoveler winter, Avocet and Oystercatcher breed, Garganey pops in on migration (occasionally summering) and there are winter high-tide roosts of Black-tailed Godwits and Curlew – all visible from the comfort of an armchair with a coffee in your hand. Marsh Harriers and Hobbies sometimes swing close. The decking at the front of the VC, overlooking the Thames, can serve as a proxy seawatching view-point, particularly when there is bad weather and winds are blowing into the Thames.

Leaving the VC, walk down the slope and turn left or right – either is fine. You'll find wooden boardwalks or tarmac paths on a circular route. At the bottom of the slope down, there is a bench with great views over the scrape.

Turning right, follow the path into the 'woodland', which often attracts migrants; Redstart is regular in early autumn, while a wandering Firecrest or two can overwin-ter. Explore the Cordite Store (TQ549790; bill.daring.sound) for migrant and nesting warblers, plus the occasional flycatcher on passage. Don't ignore the play-ground, which also holds migrants in its bushes. The woodland can be explored on its own circular mini-route before you continue or return to the VC.

The path ahead meanders through reeds and willow scrub, and as it emerges into the open, you'll see a wooden fence overlooking the east end of the reserve. There is a Barn Owl box low down in the row of tall trees to your left, and the occu-pants can be visible at times.

You'll now come to the Ken Barrett Hide (TQ548794; brand.feel.prep). This green, converted container overlooks muddy pools that are most productive with low water levels (as is most of the reserve). Snipe, Teal, Pochard and Gadwall are often obvious, but there is a chance of Jack Snipe in winter, other waders on passage, and Kingfisher pops in regularly.

Continuing along the Northern Boardwalk, you'll find two observation platforms overlooking Aveley Pools (TQ547796 and TQ546796; tent.prone.fishery and delay. taken.clever) where there's a good chance of a scarce passage wader, the wildfowl are worth sifting and Mediterranean, Yellow-legged or Caspian Gulls sometimes drop in. Great and Cattle Egrets can be hidden there, while rarities have included White-tailed and Sociable Lapwing and Marsh Sandpiper.

Continue through some open habitat until the boardwalk takes an abrupt left turn. The water just before the turn is known as the Tringa Pool (TQ544797; songs. eagle.robe) and is good for waders if levels are low, while it's worth scanning the pylons ahead for Peregrine.

Turning south (left) you'll see the (Shooting) Butts Hide (TQ542796; cheat.drums. edit), which overlooks the Butts Scrape to the east and Target Pools to the west. There are plenty of stools to sit on and the wide windows operate on pulley systems. The Butts Scrape can hold Water Pipit in winter and Little Ringed Plover in summer, and often pulls in scarcities during passage.

The species on the Target Pools depend on water levels – if high, wildfowl and gulls benefit, while the wet grass and mud around the edges will produce waders, which can include Ruff in winter and Wood Sandpiper on passage. As levels descend, more waders will appear, though the pools can be almost birdless when dry. The reeds at the back have recently hosted nesting Marsh Harriers (up to four pairs nest in the area), while Hobby is often most apparent from this hide.

Continuing south, there's a small observation deck to your right (TQ540795; poems.clots.slowly) which allows different views of the Target Pools. Bearded Tit favours the reeds in this area, but can be elusive, particularly in stronger winds, though up to three pairs manage to breed. There is a gritting tray placed on the edge of the reeds in the Dragonfly Pool (TQ539794; rating.jeeps.filed) for this species, which is often easy to photograph here.

Head towards the seawall and turn left at the numbered targets. You have a good chance of hearing or seeing Bearded Tit all the way around to the next hide (TQ541790; broke.shows.finely), overlooking the Marshland Discovery Zone (MDZ). The hide sometimes allows good (photogenic) views of Kingfishers, down to a few metres. Forge ahead towards the VC to visit the Purfleet Hide (TQ546788; jump. forks.teeth) and view the more hidden corners of Purfleet Scrape.

There's always something worth seeing at Rainham. Birds can be distant and the sun is often in your eyes watching the river, particularly during mid-morning. Early or late visits are best, but it's easy to spend a whole day on site. It's London's best birding site, the mix of habitats rivalling some more rural reserves. In late spring, it's not unheard of for people to log more than 100 species in a day.

17 WOODBERRY WETLANDS LWT

West entrance via New River Path, Lordship Road, London N16 5HQ
Websites: www.wildlondon.org.uk/woodberry-wetlands-nature-reserve;
https://sites.google.com/site/stokenewingtonreservoirs/home
TQ325874; desks.asset.birds
Phone: 020 7261 0447
Email: enquiries@wildlondon.org.uk
Open: 9am–4pm every day
(4.5 hectares; 11 acres)

The commoner wetland and garden birds are numerous at this urban oasis, and the odd scarcity is possible.

YOUR VISIT

Formerly known as Stoke Newington Reservoirs, the 12 hectares (30 acres) of Woodberry Wetlands can reasonably be described as a 'wildlife oasis' in the built-up borough of Hackney.

Consisting of twin waterbodies (the East and West Reservoirs), Woodberry Wetlands is sandwiched between Stoke Newington and Finsbury Park. There are entrances on the New River Path from Lordship Road (TQ325874; shady.almost.driver) and on Newnton Close (TQ328877; engage.fast.fully). The name Woodberry Wetlands more strictly refers to the East Reservoir, but it's possible to scan the West Reservoir through the fence.

This site has long been known to birders, who gained access occasionally via London Wildlife Trust staff, but otherwise had to peer through the fence. The site opened to the public in 2016 and has become popular with locals. This has coincided with a slight decline in birding value, although migrants still turn up.

The reserve is owned by Thames Water and managed by the LWT, and the East Reservoir has the public-facing conservation focus. It supports common waterbirds and produces winter wildfowl including Gadwall, Shoveler and Teal. Water Rail, Green Sandpiper, Fieldfare, Redwing and Siskin are also possible then.

In summer, Little and Great Crested Grebes, Cetti's, Reed and Sedge Warblers and Reed Bunting breed, along with Blackcap and Chiffchaff, and there's a small colony of Lesser Black-backed Gulls. Sizeable agglomerations of Swifts appear in summer.

Surprises are possible, and these have included Scaup, Bittern and Golden Oriole, while the few trees on the eastern side pull in Spotted and Pied Flycatchers and Redstart every autumn. Six species of bat are possible in the evening.

Buses from Finsbury Park and Manor House tube stations (Piccadilly Line) and Stamford Hill railway station (from Liverpool Street) are frequent. Take the 253, 254, 259 or 279 along Seven Sisters Road and alight at Woodberry Grove. Driving is not advised, though parking can be found on nearby residential streets. There's a cafe, picnic area and toilets, and room to walk around part of the reserve, though running and jogging are not permitted.

18 FAIRLOP WATERS

Forest Rd, Ilford IG6 3HN
Website: www.redbridge.gov.uk/leisure-sport-and-the-arts/parks/fairlop-waters-country-park
Car park: TQ453905; rating.varieties.lows
Phone: 020 8500 9911
Email: parks.enquiries@visionrcl.org.uk; fairlopwaters@vision-rcl.org.uk
Open: the VC is open from 7am–11pm (Monday–Thursday), 7am–midnight (Friday–Saturday) and 7am–10.30pm (Sunday); the whole site is open all day, every day
SINC
(593 hectares; 1,465.33 acres)

An extensive area of parkland with a full suite of common species and the chance of a surprise on passage.

SPECIES

All year: Red-legged Partridge, Little Owl, Kestrel, Sparrowhawk, Green and Great Spotted Woodpeckers, Stock Dove, Skylark, Meadow Pipit, Reed Bunting.

Summer: warblers, hirundines, Swift.

Winter: Teal, Gadwall, Shoveler, Water Rail, gull roost, Lapwing, Golden Plover, Green Sandpiper, Snipe, Woodcock, Short-eared Owl (some years), Kingfisher, Stonechat, Redwing, Fieldfare, Siskin, Redpoll.

Migration: Common and Arctic Terns, waders, Hobby, Lesser Whitethroat, Spotted Flycatcher, Wheatear, Whinchat, Yellow Wagtail.

ACCESS

Bike: there are many cyclable paths throughout, plus bike racks and bikes for hire.

Bus: Fairlop Waters is one stop from Fairlop station.

Train: the park is a short walk from Fairlop and Barkingside stations (Central Line). Barkingside is closest to the gravel works. Exit the station, turn right down Station Approach, then double back to walk uphill along Station Road. Just past the peak of this low hill, after you've crossed the railway track on a bridge, you'll see a gap in the hedgerow north of the station, where a grassy track heads east, taking you

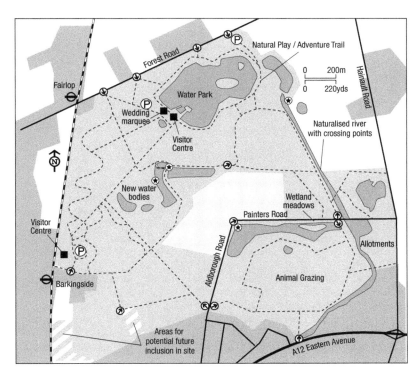

along the south side of the rewilded former golf course. Continue along Station Road and turn right (south) after you reach the barrier. Turn left again at the end, just after Aldborough Hatch Farm, into fields skirting some houses. Turn left (north) again onto Aldborough Road North. This bends right and becomes Painters Road.

Car: the site is signposted and easily accessible from the A12 (via Forest Road).

YOUR VISIT

Fairlop Waters is a large area of well-used parkland on the eastern side of the London Borough of Redbridge, not far from Hainault Forest. It has five water-bodies and Seven Kings Water, a tributary of the River Roding, plus areas of farmland, woodland and heathland, with a quarry and a small landfill site adjacent. The habitat in the park is largely open and extensive. Because of its recreational popularity, an early start is recommended if you want to see anything other than the commonest species.

Fairlop's birding reputation comes from the rarities and scarcities that have appeared over the years (including Radde's and Hume's Warblers) and the formerly sizeable winter flocks of Golden Plover and Lapwing. Golden Plover numbers, which once reached more than 2,000, now don't attain three figures, but it's still worth checking adjacent farmland for the small modern wintering flock. Up to 120 species are recorded annually.

Concentrate on the lakes during passage and after hard weather, as divers, grebes and seaduck have dropped in. While the open areas can lure in wagtails, pipits and chats, it's the areas of scrub, trees and shrubs you should explore in spring and autumn, when warblers, flycatchers and finches can be anticipated.

Fairlop Gravel Works are off limits to the public as gravel extraction is still taking place. Most of the habitat is to the north of Painters Road and west of Hainault Road but this is currently fenced off. The grassland is flat and grazed by cattle, with viewing made difficult by hedges and fences.

The grass and scrub attract Ring Ouzel some years, and Stonechat lingers over the winter period. Other migrating songbirds include Wheatear, Whinchat and Yellow Wagtail into double figures every year. 'White' Wagtail is often found among the large numbers of Pied Wagtails. The commoner warblers breed, including Reed and Sedge, and there is a chance of Grasshopper Warbler in spring.

Waterlogged areas can hold more than 20 Snipe and several Green Sandpipers each winter, and Jack Snipe has occurred. Shelduck is often present among the commoner ducks. Breeding waders include a few pairs of Lapwing and Little Ringed Plover. Woodcock and Water Rail are fairly reliable in winter, while even Spotted Crake was once recorded on passage. Expected passage waders include Whimbrel, Black-tailed Godwit, Greenshank, Oystercatcher and Dunlin.

The gravel works area is surprisingly productive for raptors, with Little Owl all year and Hobby in summer, as well as a chance of Merlin, Marsh Harrier and Barn Owl.

Progress in preserving this productive suburban site for nature has been made, and its future status as an official nature reserve seems assured. Its current name appears to be Aldborough Hall NR (though older signs indicate its name as Fairlop Quarry NR). There are plans for onsite facilities, said to include a car park and hides, and an idea for incorporating the workings into a circular route including the country park has been mooted. The gravel pits may yet be filled in, but local birders and conservationists are fighting to keep them as a wetland.

19 HAINAULT FOREST CP

Manor Road, Chigwell Row, Essex RM4 1NH (TQ478943; lands.vibe.state)
or Hainault Forest CP car park (TQ476926; stable.encounter.oldest), Fox
Burrow Road, Essex IG7 4QN (further south of the wooded area)
Websites: www.woodlandtrust.org.uk/visiting-woods/woods/hainault-forest;
www.woodlandtrust.org.uk/visiting-woods/woods/hainault-forest-country-
park; https://hainaultforest.net
Phone: 0330 333 3300 (office hours)
Email: enquiries@woodlandtrust.org.uk; england@woodlandtrust.org.uk
Open: all day, every day
(113 hectares; 280 acres)

*A large area of ancient forest in north-east London where a good range of wood-
land species can be seen.*

SPECIES

All year: Tawny and Little Owls, Lesser Spotted Woodpecker, Coal Tit, Nuthatch,
Treecreeper, Bullfinch.

Summer: Hobby, Cuckoo, Swallow, Skylark, Garden Warbler.

Winter: Wigeon, Gadwall, Teal, Shoveler, Golden Plover, Woodcock, Snipe,
Redwing, Fieldfare, Firecrest, Brambling, Siskin, Redpoll.

Migration: Common Sandpiper, Swift, hirundines, Tree Pipit, Yellow Wagtail,
Redstart, Whinchat, Wheatear, Ring Ouzel, warblers.

ACCESS

Bike: there are tarmac-surfaced cycle routes throughout the park.

Bus: the nearest stop is Fowler Road on routes 247 (Romford–Barkingside) and
362 (Chadwell Heath–Barkingside), directly opposite Fox Burrow Road which
leads to the main car park.

Train: the nearest tube station is Grange Hill (Central Line), 0.6 miles (1km) from
the park's north-west corner, though a better ploy is to alight at Hainault and take
bus 247 to Fowler Road.

Car: the site is 3.5 miles from Junction 5 of the M11. One car park is on Lambourne
Road opposite Chigwell Row Primary School, and there are also two pay-and-
display car parks on Fox Burrow Road by the main entrance and two free WT car
parks on Manor Road, on the northern edge of the site. All these car parks are
open during daylight hours.

YOUR VISIT

Hainault Forest is north-west of Romford, Essex, and north-east of Fairlop Waters
(see page 62). It comprises a large area of ancient and secondary woodland and
pasture owned by Redbridge Council. Also considered part of the park is the 54
hectares (134 acres) of arable land that makes up Havering Park Farm. Both are
managed by the Woodland Trust.

Hainault Forest CP is a large urban oasis surrounded by residential areas to the

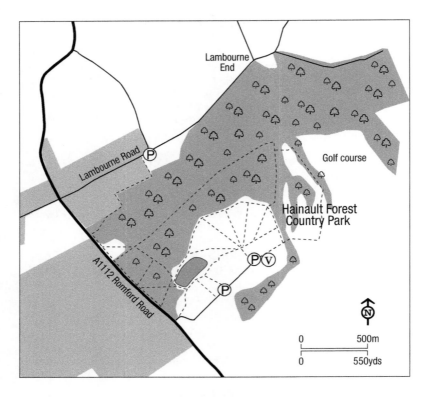

west, a golf course to the east and south and mostly agricultural land to the north. Historically, the site was part of the huge royal hunting forest that incorporated Epping Forest too and provided sport and meat for the chosen few.

There are 14 entrances: 10 for pedestrians, accessed through kissing gates and gaps in the fence, and four permissive bridleways. There are plenty of footpaths throughout, some of which are flat and surfaced, and can allow disabled access to most of the main areas. Many can become muddy, though.

Hainault holds similar species to Epping Forest but is more workable despite also being large. Its human popularity doesn't stop it from maintaining a decent understorey among its oaks, hornbeams and beech trees. The central lake near Romford Road provides some variety, as do the small patches of conifers, scrub and grassland.

For a chance of Lesser Spotted Woodpecker, concentrate on the older woodland at the northern end, but otherwise, a long, circular route can take in most of the habitats, as you see fit. Starting at dawn is best.

20 EPPING FOREST

Website: www.cityoflondon.gov.uk/things-to-do/green-spaces/epping-forest
(2,400 hectares; 5,900 acres)

*Common woodland birds can be seen in good numbers in London's largest
forest, while a few scarce species still hang on.*

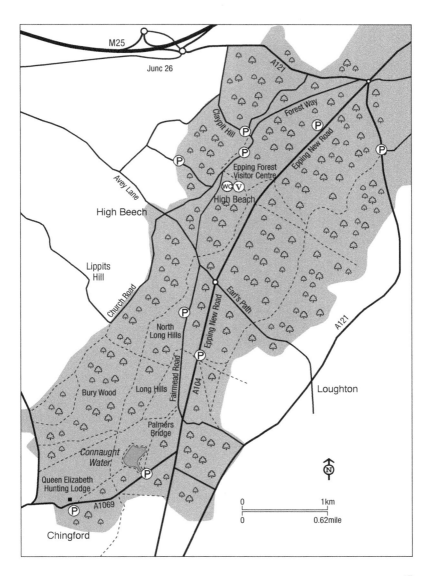

SPECIES

All year: Mandarin Duck, raptors, Lesser Spotted Woodpecker, Woodcock, Tawny and Little Owls, Bullfinch.

Summer: Common Tern, Hobby, Cuckoo, Nuthatch, Treecreeper, Willow Warbler and other warblers and songbirds.

Winter: Gadwall, Shoveler, Goosander, Kingfisher, Fieldfare, Redwing, Brambling, Siskin, Redpoll, Crossbill, Hawfinch.

Migration: warblers, chats, thrushes.

YOUR VISIT

Extending from the M25 in the north-east to Upper Walthamstow in the south-west, and enclosing Theydon Bois, Loughton and Chingford, Epping Forest is the biggest area of forest in London. Despite this, its popularity with visitors and the large amount of residential properties all work against it supporting a richer avifauna. That said, there are still good birds in some of its hidden pockets – you just have to find them!

Epping is partly a remnant of the medieval hunting forest that once extended far out into Essex. The dominant woodland conceals smaller areas of grassland, scrub and several ponds. You are advised to concentrate your efforts at the hotspots listed below. Start early to avoid the worst of the disturbance.

There are footpaths and cycling routes throughout the forest (though mountain bikes have been responsible for some serious degradation of habitat).

CONNAUGHT WATER

Ranger's Road, Buckhurst Hill, Essex IG10 4RP
Website: www.cityoflondon.gov.uk/things-to-do/green-spaces/epping-forest/where-to-go-in-epping-forest/connaught-water
TQ404950; like.older.served
Phone: 020 8532 1010
Email: epping.forest@cityoflondon.gov.uk
Open: all day, every day
(3.2 hectares; 8 acres)

In combination with the adjacent Chingford Plain (see page 69), this lake offers the best selection of habitats and species. Infamous for its constant changeover of exotic wildfowl escapees, with everything from Black-bellied Whistling Duck to Cinnamon Teal popping in, it's also probably the easiest place in the region covered by this book to see Mandarin Duck. Up to 20 pairs breed in the forest with the largest numbers at Connaught Water, where a total of 50 post-breeding birds has been counted in September. This naturalised Asian oak woodland specialist could almost be considered an accidental reintroduction, as fossil bones assigned to the genus *Aix* have been identified from fossil beds in West Runton, Norfolk, dated at about 350,000 years in age.

The lake also attracts commoner winter wildfowl such as Shoveler and Teal, while up to five Goosanders are seen along with occasional Goldeneye. Kingfisher winters, while Common Terns fish and mate in summer, but nest elsewhere.

Venturing into the surrounding woodland should produce commoner woodland species such as Great Spotted Woodpecker, Nuthatch and Treecreeper, but Lesser

Spotted Woodpecker is only occasional these days. Hawfinch did breed but is now generally seen only as a rare fly-over. Crossbill may linger in an irruption year but is otherwise very unlikely.

There are bike racks in the car park, and bus routes 97, 179, 212, 313, 379, 385, 397, 444 and N26 stop at Chingford London Overground station (from London Liverpool Street), 0.9 miles (1.5km) away. Chingford Plain can also be reached by this route.

CHINGFORD PLAIN

Bury Road, Chingford, London E4 7QJ
TQ394949; choice.sparks.monkey

This was once the most reliable site for Tree Pipit in London, but the species has declined radically and is only likely to be seen as an occasional migrant. Commoner scrub species such as Linnet, Whitethroat and Lesser Whitethroat breed, and Chingford Plain is still a reasonable bet for migrants such as Ring Ouzel, Whinchat, Wheatear and Redstart.

The open sky allows for good raptor watching, and Buzzard, Red Kite, Sparrowhawk and Peregrine are likely overhead, along with Hobby in summer. A few Garden and Willow Warblers hang on in summer but are most likely on passage, along with the occasional Grasshopper Warbler. It's also possible that one or two of the passing Spotted Flycatchers still linger to breed. Try the plentiful birches, willows and alders in the area for the unpredictable winter appearances of Siskin and Redpoll; I've very occasionally seen wandering Lesser Spotted Woodpeckers in those same trees.

HIGH BEACH

Parking: Epping Forest Visitor Centre, Nursery Road, High Beech, Loughton, Essex IG10 4AF
Out-of-hours parking: Pillow Mounds Car Park, Wake Road, Loughton, Essex IG10 4AE
Website: www.cityoflondon.gov.uk/things-to-do/green-spaces/epping-forest/where-to-go-in-epping-forest/high-beach-and-pauls-nursery
TQ412981; shirts.motel.chip
(225 hectares; 556 acres)

Named for its exposed sands and gravels, there are also plentiful beech trees nearby and the fallen mast can attract large flocks of Chaffinches in autumn and winter, feeding on the forest floor. Among them are often a few Brambling and even Hawfinch has very occasionally been noted. Explore the area to the south and behind the FSC building. One or two pairs of Lesser Spotted Woodpeckers still nest in the stretch between High Beach and Staples Hill (TQ418972; index. oldest.soaks), Loughton, but are likely to be very elusive.

The nearest tube station is Loughton (Central Line), 45 minutes' walk away to the south-east, served by bus routes 20 (Walthamstow–Debden), 167 (Ilford–Loughton), 397 (Walthamstow–Loughton) and 677 (Ilford–Loughton).

COPPED HALL

Crown Hill, Epping, Essex CM16 5HS
Website: www.coppedhalltrust.org.uk/index.php/wildlife
TL430012; hung.hears.snows
Phone: 07799 473108
Email: info@coppedhalltrust.org.uk
Open: all day, every day
Conservation Area, LWS
(350.9 hectares; 142 acres)

The farmland surrounding this eighteenth-century Georgian country house has Red-legged Partridge (scarce in London) and Yellowhammer, with Grey Partridge still putting in occasional appearances. Barn and Little Owls are present all year, and winter is the best time to see them. The trees around the gardens and Epping Forest, across the M25 footbridge, host resident Tawny Owl, Nuthatch, Treecreeper and Green and Great Spotted Woodpeckers – all in healthy numbers. Winter finch flocks sometimes contain Brambling, while Hawfinch is occasionally noted flying over the nearby forest. The lucky rambler around the denser wooded areas may spook a roosting Woodcock. Spring migrants will include Garden Warbler, while the odd Cuckoo, Skylark and Meadow Pipit can be heard in spring.

Copped Hall has a good reputation for raptors. Stand halfway down the entrance track at the far end of Lodge Road, which overlooks a sizeable part of Epping Forest, and scan the forest on the opposite side of the M25. With patience, you may see a complete suite of the commoner birds of prey: Red Kite (especially in spring), Buzzard, Sparrowhawk, Kestrel and Peregrine, with Hobby in spring. Goshawk has been noted relatively often.

The site is at least 1.5 miles from any public transport stops and routes; a long walk from Waltham Abbey (from London Liverpool Street), Theydon Bois or Epping (both Central Line) stations is the best choice, if not driving.

ONGAR PARK WOOD

Epping Road, Stapleford Tawney, Woodhatch, Epping Forest, Essex CM16 7PX
TL499022; grades.wage.movies

This sizeable but isolated patch of deciduous woodland to the north-east of Epping is notable in that at least two pairs of Firecrest breed (though one or two pairs also use the northern end of the main part of the forest on occasion). Up to eight Hawfinches were present in 2022, favouring the Hornbeams near the Colliers Hatch car park (TL500022). Tawny Owl, Nuthatch, Treecreeper and other woodland specialists are also in residence.

21 WANSTEAD PARK AND FLATS

For addresses and coordinates, see Access.
Websites: www.wansteadwildlife.org.uk/index.php/en;
http://wansteadbirding.blogspot.com
SSSI
(*Wanstead Flats*: 187 hectares; 462 acres;
Wanstead Park: 74 hectares; 182.86 acres)

An extensive urban park and almost-adjacent expanse of grassland that are good for migrants, and host most of the city's commoner species.

SPECIES

All year: Little Owl, Kingfisher, Skylark, Grey Wagtail.

Summer: Hobby, Swift, hirundines.

Winter: Woodcock, gulls, Redwing, Fieldfare, Firecrest, Redpoll, Siskin.

Migration: Wryneck, Yellow Wagtail, Ring Ouzel, Pied and Spotted Flycatchers, Wheatear, Whinchat, Stonechat, Redstart, warblers.

ACCESS

Bike: there are cyclable paths and roads throughout.

Bus: routes 58 (Walthamstow–East Ham) and 308 (Homerton–Clapton) stop at Jubilee Pond on Dames Road, while Wanstead Park is served by routes 101 (Wanstead–Beckton), 308 (Homerton–Clapton) and W19 (Walthamstow–Ilford), stopping at Blake Hall Crescent.

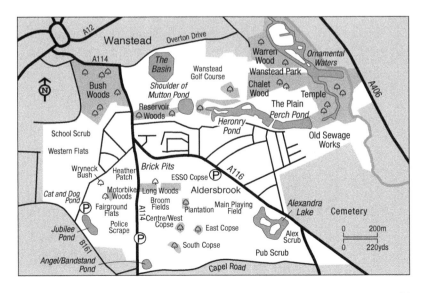

Train: Wanstead and Redbridge tube stations (Central Line) are just beyond the northern edge of Wanstead Park, while Forest Gate (Liverpool Street–Shenfield/Southend) and Wanstead Park (Barking–Gospel Oak) overground stations serve the southern end of the park.

Car: there are five entrances to Wanstead Park, of which the Warren Road car park (TQ413876; metro.shop.super) is the closest to the wooded areas. There are several parking places around the perimeter of Wanstead Flats; the most convenient for birding are those at Alexandra Lake (TQ414864; point.pepper.lies) and Central Road (TQ405861; broken.noting.until).

YOUR VISIT

This open expanse of grassland, scrub, trees and lakes is at the southernmost extreme of Epping Forest and extends from Leytonstone and Wanstead to Forest Gate.

There are plenty of nooks to explore, and local birders are enthusiastic and committed, and have made many choice discoveries over the years. That said, the site generally features common birds, though more than 190 species have been seen.

Unusually for a site within the M25 orbital motorway, there is a small population of Skylarks and Meadow Pipits breeding in the less-disturbed areas of grass, which are now fenced off for their protection. The shortest turf on the playing fields attracts hundreds of loafing gulls during daylight hours, with the odd interesting form on occasion. The groups of old oaks in the open areas are the home of Little Owl, which can be hard to see. Winter Redpoll flocks are sporadic and favour the SSSI area (TQ403867; rental.belong.exchanges), but more than 50 are sometimes counted.

The whole site comes into its own during migration. Wanstead Flats is the best area for migrants, having a more complex mosaic of grass, scrub and woodland. Spring produces Yellow Wagtail, Ring Ouzel and Wheatear. Autumn gears up with the same species and Redstart, Stonechat, Whinchat and Spotted and Pied Flycatchers likely, while scarcer species such as Wryneck, Red-backed Shrike, Yellow-browed Warbler and even Rustic Bunting have turned up. The scrub has occasionally held Dartford Warbler in recent years. However, the holly and ivy in Wanstead Park are your best bet for the Firecrests that winter most years.

The small ponds and lakes tend to host the commoner wildfowl species and can attract the odd Snipe or Common Sandpiper early in the morning.

22 THE CHASE LNR

The Millennium Centre, The Chase, Dagenham Road, Rush Green, Romford, Essex RM7 0SS.
Websites: www.thameschase.org.uk/visitor-centres/dagenham-and-romford/the-chase-local-nature-reserve
TQ509860; tides.guilty.seated
Phone: 0208 595 4155; 01708 642970
Email: enquiries@thameschase.org.uk; parksandcountryside@lbbd.gov.uk

Open: all day, every day; the Millennium Centre and cafe is open from 10am–5pm (summer) or 10am–4pm (winter) but check the website for changeover dates
LNR, SSSI
(48.5 hectares; 119.85 acres)

SPECIES

All year: Gadwall, Little Owl, Kingfisher, Cetti's Warbler, Bullfinch.

Summer: Common Tern, Swift, hirundines, warblers.

Winter: Water Rail, Lapwing, Green Sandpiper, Snipe, Jack Snipe, Firecrest.

Migration: Garganey, freshwater waders including Common Sandpiper, Ring Ouzel, Redstart, Whinchat, Stonechat, Spotted Flycatcher, Siskin, Redpoll.

ACCESS

Bike: most of the footpaths are appropriate for bikes and wheelchair accessible, though the areas around The Slack are less so.

Bus: route 174 (Dagenham Heathway–Romford) stops directly outside the reserve.

Train: Dagenham East (District Line) is the nearest tube, and is within walking distance. Turn left out of the station onto Rainham Road South (A112) for about 100m, then cross over and walk down the obscure footpath called Foxlands Lane (TQ502852; unique.prove.chops), which leads to the south end of The Chase. Alternatively, continue north along Rainham Road South for about 0.5 miles, turn right at the crossroads down Dagenham Road and continue until the road bends to the north. Turn down The Chase, between the reserve and Eastbrookend CP.

Car: leave the A12 for Dagenham East, then follow the instructions above. Park at the Millennium Centre car park on the no-through road.

YOUR VISIT

Popularly known among birders as 'Dagenham Chase', this very urban nature reserve managed by the London Borough of Barking and Dagenham is a classic local patch with a good reputation for attracting scarcities during migration.

Thorough coverage of this large site can take a few hours. Its habitats include scrub, woodland and grazed grassland, along with smaller areas of marsh and a few ponds and lakes. Larger areas of water can be found at Eastbrookend CP.

Focus your birding on the small, shallow wetland known as 'The Slack', which attracts ducks, gulls and waders during passage and in winter. The area is popular with joggers, cyclists and dog-walkers, meaning that birds may not linger. There are roosting Little Egrets in the fringing bushes and Great Egret now overflies annually. Garganey is regular in spring, while Little Ringed Plover, Lapwing and Kingfisher all breed.

Passerine migrants can appear almost anywhere, but the open grassland, hawthorn scrub and the stand of Black Poplars by the River Rom are all productive. Skylark hangs on as a breeder on the grasslands. The willows and reeds fringing the Tom Thumb and BARDAG fishing lakes can be productive for Willow and Cetti's

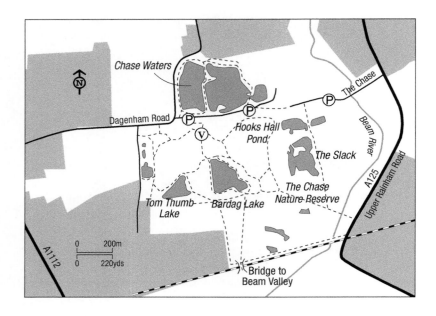

Warblers, Chiffchaff and Lesser Whitethroat, as can most of the trees and scrub; Marsh Warbler has bred in the past. The rough ground surrounding The Slack is good for Ring Ouzel and Wheatear in spring and autumn. Another area that is good for passerine migrants is the dense scrub just to the south of, and in between, the main BARDAG lake and The Slack, known as Crowfoot by locals.

Eastbrookend Pond (TQ509862; will.tribes.below) and **Chase Waters/White Hart Lakes** (TQ512861; retain.lazy.sober) just to the north are former gravel pits, popular with anglers. They produce species that need deeper waters than The Slack. A few Common Terns hunt over them in summer, but Black-necked, Red-necked and Slavonian Grebes have occurred in recent years, including a pair of 'Slavs' that lingered for weeks in spring. **Eastbrookend CP**, which surrounds Eastbrookend Pond, and the wasteground to the west (TQ506863; sock.rice.horns) have grassland, scrub and trees that are worth exploring on quieter days.

Scan adjacent **Eastbrook School playing fields** (TQ504858; when.spoke.added) for gulls, Lapwing and (occasionally) Golden Plover. Eastbrookend Cemetery (TQ514862; stocks.loud.divide) to the east of Chase Waters looks promising for woodland and scrub species, but locals omit it out of respect.

At the south-western end, you can cross the railway line via the footbridge and explore **Beam Valley CP** (TQ518848; wounds.wrong.lodge), which has a small heronry, good areas of scrub, a lake and some marshy areas, as well as regular Kingfisher along the Beam River.

There is always the chance of a surprise at The Chase, and famous rarities have included Pine Bunting and Great Snipe, along with scarcities such as Temminck's Stint, Spotted Crake and Lapland Bunting.

23 THE MANOR LNR AND DAGNAM PARK

Settle Road, Harold Hill, Romford RM3 9YA
*Websites: www.havering.gov.uk/directory_record/104/the_manor_nature_
reserve;*
Website: www.havering.gov.uk/info/20037/parks/700/dagnam_park
Car park: TQ550928; wing.motel.rises
Phone: 01708 434743
Open: 8am–half an hour after dusk
*LNR, Site of Metropolitan Importance for Nature Conservation, Site of
Borough Importance for Nature Conservation (Duck Wood), Ancient Forest*
(28 hectares; 69 acres)

SPECIES

All year: Mandarin Duck, Red-legged Partridge, Little Owl, Lesser Spotted Woodpecker, Yellowhammer.

Summer: Cuckoo, Swift, hirundines, warblers.

Winter: Firecrest, Hawfinch.

Migration: Tree Pipit, Yellow Wagtail, Ring Ouzel, Redstart, Whinchat, Spotted and Pied Flycatchers, warblers.

ACCESS

Bike: there is an extensive network of cycle paths.

Bus: routes 174 (Rainham–Dagnam Park), 496 (Romford–Harold Wood) and 674 (Romford–Dagnam Park) stop on Dagnam Park Drive.

Train: the nearest station is Harold Wood (London Liverpool Street–Southend), from where buses can be taken.

Car: the site is close to the M25 and A12, with free parking on Settle Road.

This community green resource near the large housing estates of Harold Hill has ancient forest, grassland and meadows. The Manor incorporates Dagnam Park and some decent tracts of woodland in the form of Hatters Wood, Duck Wood and Fir Wood.

Mandarin Duck can be found close to the small ponds in the woods. Lesser Spotted Woodpecker and Hawfinch are occasionally seen; the latter no longer breeds but can sometimes be found in winter.

Hobby and farmland songbirds such as Yellowhammer breed. Cuckoo can still be found in summer, but Turtle Dove has gone. Most of the expected migrants turn up and have included Pied Flycatcher and Wood Warbler. The scrub hides the odd Redstart in spring or autumn, while Whinchat, Stonechat and Wheatear pass through the open areas and grassland. It's an extensive site that pays off with regular watching and can be combined with visits to nearby Tylers Common and Warley Place.

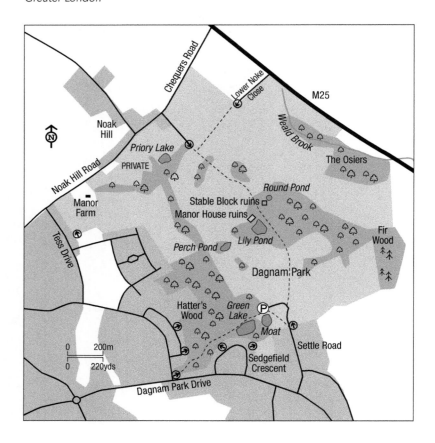

24 BELHUS WOODS CP AND CELY WOODS

Belhus Woods: Romford Road, Aveley, South Ockendon RM15 4XJ; TQ565825; take.feared.town
Cely Woods: Warwick Lane, RM13 9EW; TQ560833; cats.shape.rush
Websites: www.thameschase.org.uk/visitor-centres/ockendon/belhus-country-park; www.explore-essex.com/places-to-go/find-whats-near-me/belhus-woods-country-park
Phone: 01708 865628
Email: belhuswcpr@essex.gov.uk
Open: Cely Woods is all day, every day, though the official hours are 8am–dusk. Belhus Woods VC is open from 10am–4pm, and has a cafe, toilets, baby-changing, and picnic and barbecue areas.
(*Belhus Woods:* 121 hectares; 300 acres; *Cely Woods:* 57 hectares; 140 acres)

One of the very few reliable locations for Lesser Spotted Woodpecker in Greater London.

SPECIES

All year: Lesser Spotted Woodpecker, Nuthatch, Treecreeper, Bullfinch.

Summer: Little Ringed Plover, Shelduck, Lapwing and Redshank, Willow Warbler.

Winter: winter thrushes, Brambling, Siskin, Redpoll.

Migration: commoner warblers.

ACCESS

Bike: footpaths throughout the site are cyclable. Cely and Belhus Woods have good wheelchair access on fairly flat paths.

Bus: route 372 (Hornchurch–Lakeside Thurrock) serves the sites and can be caught from Rainham station.

Train: Rainham is the nearest train station and is on the c2c Fenchurch Street–Southend line.

Car: leave the A13 at the turn-off for 'Wennington, West Thurrock, Purfleet and Aveley', and take the first turning off the roundabout ('Rainham/Wennington/Aveley'). Turn right at the next roundabout onto Sandy Lane, and then take the first left (Romford Road) at the following roundabout. The parking is pay-and-display (£2 at the time of writing).

YOUR VISIT

Belhus Woods CP is a mosaic of ancient woodland, newly planted trees, coppices, scrub, hedgerows, grassland streams and lakes. It's part of the Thames Chase Community Forest project (see page 78), part-owned by the Woodland Trust and Forestry Commission, and was once part of an estate landscaped by Capability Brown during the mid-eighteenth century.

Lesser Spotted Woodpecker often frequents the area around the VC. The birds are most vocal in late winter and early spring. If you have no luck at Belhus Woods, then try **Cely Woods**, a much more compact area with some older trees that attract a pair most years. They can be found in Warwick Wood or White Post Wood to the south of the car park, from where they can be heard at times.

Other species present – mostly at Belhus Woods – include Bullfinch and Marsh Tit (both rapidly declining) and commoner wintering and summering passerines. Belhus Woods is one of the few places in Essex where one or two pairs of Willow Warbler stay long enough to breed. Siskin and Redpoll (63 in November 2020) are possible in the colder months when Snipe and Lapwing are ensconced around the fishing lakes. Interesting wildfowl can pop in. Common Tern nests and Water Rail winters. Migration can also turn up good birds, with the usual warblers, chats, pipits, wagtails and finches passing through.

In winter, **Damyns Hall Aerodrome** – across the road to Cely Woods – hosts large numbers of Greylag and Canada Geese which pull in stray Pink-feet and White-fronts. Scan from just opposite the car park entrance (TQ559833; roofs.races.gain).

To the north of the Damyns Hall area is **Bonnetts Wood** (RM14 2XR; TQ552843; skip.other.spent), which holds a decent selection of common woodland birds and is now linked to Berwick Glades and Berwick Woods (page 81).

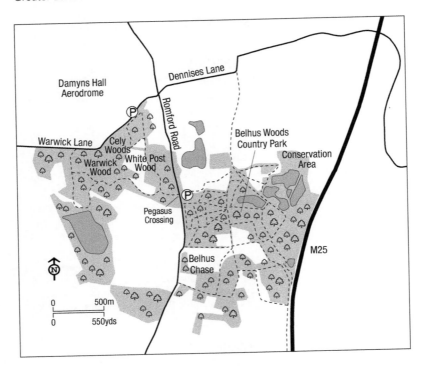

THAMES CHASE COMMUNITY FOREST

Website: www.thameschase.org.uk/visitor-centres/upminster-and-harold-wood/tylers-common
A landscape-scale community nature scheme that supports interesting species, including reliable Grasshopper Warblers.

YOUR VISIT

Thames Chase is an ambitious plan to recreate an extensive forest across a broad swathe of East London and south-west Essex for recreation and to combat climate change.

First established in 1990, the scheme aims to restore and maintain extensive native woodland by creating a huge wildlife corridor and increasing local biodiversity. The tree planting has gradually spread over much of the London Borough of Havering.

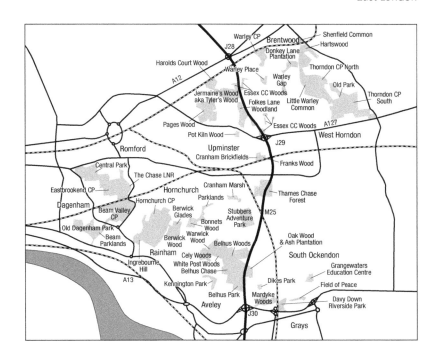

25 INGREBOURNE MARSHES AND HORNCHURCH CP

Ingrebourne Valley LNR car park: Squadrons Approach, Hornchurch, Essex RM12 6DF (sat nav: RM12 6TS)
Website: www.essexwt.org.uk/nature-reserves/ingrebourne
TQ536849; swaps.juror.cycles
Phone: 01708 520364
Email: ingrebourne@essexwt.org.uk
Open: all day, every day, but the official hours are 10am–4pm
(1 November–31 March); 10am–5pm (1 April–31 October)
(261 hectares; 645 acres)
SSSI, LNR, Site of Metropolitan Importance for Nature Conservation
Hornchurch CP: South End Road, South Hornchurch, Essex RM12 5LS
Website: www.thameschase.org.uk/visitor-centres/rainham-hornchurch/
hornchurch-country-park
TQ528839; loaded.pump.cross
Phone: 01708 434743
Email: parks@havering.gov.uk
Open: 9am–4pm (1 November–31 March); 9am–5pm (1 April–31 October).
(105.5 hectares; 258 acres)

Extensive suburban wetlands, scrub and woodland punching above their weight during passage.

SPECIES

All year: Gadwall, Teal, Red-legged Partridge, heronry, Water Rail, Buzzard, Red Kite, Marsh Harrier, Lapwing, Redshank, Little, Barn and Tawny Owls, Kingfisher, Skylark, Cetti's Warbler, Bullfinch, Reed Bunting, Yellowhammer.

Summer: Little Ringed Plover, Common Tern, Hobby, Cuckoo, Nightingale, and Reed, Sedge, Garden, Willow and Grasshopper Warblers.

Winter: Shoveler and other ducks, Snipe, Jack Snipe, Green Sandpiper, Bearded Tit.

Migration: Garganey, waders, hirundines, warblers, Ring Ouzel, chats, flycatchers, Yellow Wagtail, Tree Pipit.

ACCESS

Bike: the Greenway and some other footpaths are suitable for bikes and wheelchairs.

Bus: cross the road from Hornchurch tube station to bus stop M for the 252. Alight at the Hornchurch CP stop (A), where you will see the park on your left. Bus 256 terminates one stop before this.

Train: Hornchurch (District Line) is the nearest tube station, one mile from the VC.

Car: for the northern end of Hornchurch CP, Squadron Approach is at the bend in the road where Airfield Way become Suttons Lane; the car park is clearly signposted. For the southern car park, take the signposted but unnamed tarmac track off South End Road.

YOUR VISIT

Incorporating Ingrebourne Valley LNR, the Ingrebourne Nature Discovery Centre and Ingrebourne Marshes EWT, the Ingrebourne Valley and its floodplain comprises river, open water, marsh, grassland, reedbed, ancient and secondary woodland, scrub and hedgerows. It includes the sizeable Hornchurch CP, a former airfield, and other smaller nature reserves. Within its borders is the largest uninterrupted reedbed in London. The Nature Discovery Centre opened in 2015 and has a shop, café, toilets and playground.

Hornchurch CP hit world headlines in 2015, when a Weasel was photographed jumping onto a Green Woodpecker's back. The birding is usually less dramatic than the 'Weaselpecker' incident, but some 61 bird species breed, including Marsh Harrier, Little Ringed Plover, Cuckoo, Nightingale and occasional Grasshopper and Garden Warblers.

While there is plenty to explore, most of **Ingrebourne Marshes** is closed to the public. However, it can be viewed from the platform (TQ536844; third.list.files) just south of the VC. The southern part of the marshes can also be scanned from the bridge (TQ537842; traps.sunset.select) crossing the river that also joins up with Berwick Ponds (page 81). Otherwise, there are plenty of footpaths leading around the site, including the central Ingrebourne Valley Greenway.

Make sure you explore the reserve as far as its southernmost point, as the pool by St Albyn's Farm (St Albyn's Pit) can produce good birds, and even the picnic area has revealed Firecrest in the past.

Several scarcities have appeared in recent years, including Spotted Crake, Pectoral Sandpiper and Waxwing.

26 NEARBY: BERWICK PONDS

Berwick Pond Road, Romford, Essex RM14 2XS
Websites: www.thameschase.org.uk/visitor-centres/rainham-hornchurch/
berwick-woods; www.thameschase.org.uk/visitor-centres/rainham-hornchurch/
berwick-glades;www.woodlandtrust.org.uk/visiting-woods/woods/berwick-glades
TQ542838; award.deeply.banana
Phone: 0800 1 218 218
Email: enquiries@tarmac.com
Open: all day, every day
(25.2 hectares; 72.03 acres)

These popular fishing ponds are set in farmland on the very edge of London. The site is mainly composed of two long fishing ponds bordered by trees and reeds, and patches of marshland and grassland. It forms a continuous patch of habitat with Hornchurch CP, which lies to the west.

At **Berwick Ponds**, commoner waterbirds include resident Shoveler, wintering Teal, Water Rail all year (a few pairs breed) and Common Tern in summer. Bearded Tit sometimes appears in the reedbeds. Good numbers of Lapwing in winter can be supplemented by Golden Plover on the surrounding land, while Snipe, and sometimes Jack Snipe, use the muddy edges of the reedbeds. Redshank has occasionally bred. Passage sees scarcer waders appearing, and can include Ringed Plover, Greenshank and Wood, Common and Green Sandpipers.

Little Owl can be seen in the surrounding hedges and trees, but Short-eared, Long-eared and Barn Owl sightings are less frequent and usually in winter. Good numbers of hirundines pass through, as do other migrant songbirds, including Yellow Wagtail, Grasshopper and Garden Warblers, Spotted Flycatcher, Redstart, Whinchat, Stonechat, Wheatear and Ring Ouzel. The passerines that stay will be harassed by the odd Cuckoo. Both Rock and Water Pipits have popped up at the water's edge. Yellowhammer may still be present, but Grey Partridge, Turtle Dove and Corn Bunting now seem to have disappeared.

Berwick Woods (25.2 hectares; 72.03 acres) is an area of former gravel extraction bordering Berwick Ponds that has been recently planted with trees, and has a decent area of wet woodland and scrub. It's just a little further to the north of the ponds on Berwick Pond Road but is congruent with that site.

Berwick Glades is a former area of farmland enclosing Bennett's Wood and some scrub, and has a shallow lake bordered by London's largest area of willow carr. It is the northernmost part of the 'Berwick' complex. There's always a chance of migrants here.

For all three sites, catch the c2c service from Fenchurch Street–Grays and alight at Rainham, from where you can catch buses 165 (Romford–Rainham) or 287

(Barking–Rainham) to Abbey Wood Lane. You can then walk into Abbey Wood and cross the wooden bridge to the combined site.

27 NEARBY: TYLERS COMMON, TYLERS WOOD AND HAROLD WOOD PARK

Nag's Head Lane, Harold Wood, Essex RM14 1TS
TQ563906; rash.face.raves
Open: all day, every day
(32 hectares; 79.2 acres)

Also known as Upminster Common, **Tylers Common** is one of the largest areas of common land in Greater London. It mostly consists of rough grazing and scrub, and is probably the most reliable site in London for Grasshopper Warbler, as well as supporting a reasonable number of passage migrants and Woodcock in winter.

Up to four singing Grasshopper Warblers have been found in spring in the more open scrub at the southern side, where there is also a pond that can host Snipe in winter. The trees lining the road there can produce roosting Woodcock, while Little Owl can be elusive along the hedges at the eastern end.

Formerly known as Jermaines Wood, **Tylers Wood** is a little bit further on the public footpath and also supports wintering Woodcock, along with Tawny Owl. Follow the Thames Chase path to the south to **Harold Wood Park** for Yellowhammer in spring and Bullfinch. Scarcities have included Dartford Warbler, Ring Ouzel, Black Redstart, Red-backed Shrike and Waxwing.

28 NEARBY: WARLEY PLACE NR EWT

Thatcher's Arms, Warley Road, Great Warley, Brentwood, Essex CM13 3HU
Website: www.essexwt.org.uk/nature-reserves/warley-place
TQ583907; drops.simply.spaces
Open: all day, every day
LWS
(10.52 hectares; 26 acres)

This compact patch of woodland hosts reliable Firecrests and commoner woodland species in winter.

YOUR VISIT

More strictly in Essex than the Greater London Urban Area, this is a cute bluebell wood on the site of a former Edwardian house and gardens, managed by the EWT. It's pleasant at any time of the year but is most notable for birds in winter. More than one Firecrest is often present and should be easy to locate among the ivy-clad trunks of leafless trees in this small area.

Other species present include Nuthatch, Treecreeper and Coal Tit, while Spotted and Pied Flycatchers can occur on passage, and winter offers the possibility of seeing Redpoll and Bullfinch. Scarcities such as Yellow-browed Warbler, 'Northern' Bullfinch and 'Mealy' Redpoll have occurred.

Brentwood railway station, on the Liverpool Street–Southend Victoria or Elizabeth lines (Forest Gate–Shenfield), is the closest, about a mile to the north-east. First Essex bus route 351 stops halfway there from Brentwood at The Drive, 10 minutes away on foot.

If driving, leave the M25 at the intersection with the A12 and take the A1023 for about 0.5 miles, turning right onto Mascalls Lane. Follow this to the right onto Dark Lane, turn left and then left immediately again into the Thatcher's Arms car park.

SOUTH LONDON

29 GREENWICH ECOLOGY PARK

Greenwich Park, John Harrison Way, London, SE10 0QZ
Websites: http://thelandtrust.org.uk/space/greenwich-ecology-park;
https://londonbirders.fandom.com/wiki/Greenwich_Peninsula;
www.facebook.com/GreenwichEcologyPark
TQ400792; wounds.rock.ozone
Phone: (Joanne Smith) 0208 293 1904
Email: gpep@tcv.org.uk
Open: Outer Lake – all day, every day; Inner Lake – Wednesday–Sunday, 10am–5pm (or dusk, if earlier)
SLINC
(11 hectares; 27 acres)

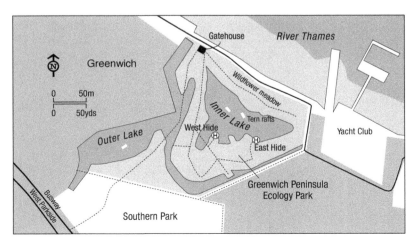

A very urban oasis, this compact municipal site was built to recreate or restore some of the original marshland that existed before urban development.

It holds common species, but has turned up the odd surprise during migration, such as Jack Snipe, Caspian Gull, *heinei* Common Gull, Arctic Tern, Whinchat, Firecrest and Red-backed Shrike.

Separated by the busy Thames Path from the river, the freshwater Inner and Outer Lakes provide shelter to wanderers at times, among the common wildfowl usually present. Boardwalks run around the park: the outer one is a permissive footpath and open all the time. The inner boardwalk, however, has limited opening hours and can only be accessed via the Gatehouse.

The lakes are surrounded by a small marsh, Alder Carr woodland and a wild-flower meadow, and two bird hides overlook the Inner Lake. In winter, you might see Snipe and Water Rail, while Reed Warbler breeds in summer as Swifts whirl overhead, and a few pairs of Common Tern occupy the single rafts on each lake. Little Grebe breeds, while Cetti's Warbler has now colonised and Black Redstart is present in the area.

The park is easily reached by several buses, North Greenwich tube station (Jubilee Line) and riverboat, but driving is inadvisable.

30 CROSSNESS NR AND THAMESMEAD

Norman Road, Belvedere, Kent DA17 6JY
Websites: www.bexleywildlife.org/crossness-nature-reserve;
londonbirders.fandom.com/wiki/Thamesmead_Area
TQ494803; brand.begun.fund
Phone: Karen Sutton on 020 8507 4889
Email: Friends of Crossness NR life membership is £10 and available from
karen.sutton@thameswater.co.uk
Open: all day, every day
SMINC, LNR
(20 hectares; 49 acres)

This large, reclaimed brownfield site has now logged more than 130 species of birds, including rarities and scarcities, and significant numbers of waders and wildfowl.

SPECIES

All year: Teal, Water Rail, Little Egret, Lapwing, Barn Owl, Skylark, Linnet, Reed Bunting.

Summer: Little Ringed Plover, Caspian and Yellow-legged Gulls possible, Cuckoo, commoner warblers including Willow Warbler and Lesser Whitethroat.

Winter: Pintail, Teal, Wigeon, Gadwall, Shoveler, Lapwing, Avocet, Dunlin, Green Sandpiper, Redshank, Snipe, Jack Snipe, Black-tailed Godwit, Short-eared Owl.

Migration: Garganey, Common Scoter, Common Sandpiper, Greenshank and other commoner waders, terns, gulls, Hobby, Black Redstart, Whinchat, Stonechat, Wheatear, Ring Ouzel, warblers and other songbirds.

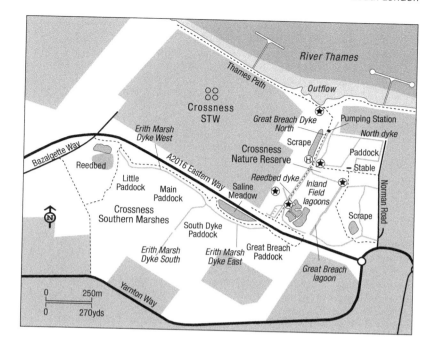

ACCESS

Bike: most of the paths within the reserve are unsuitable for cycling and sometimes wet, particularly those leading north to the river.

Bus: from Abbey Wood station, take the 229 to Crossway and walk to the reserve along the Thames Path. From Belvedere station, take the 401 to just west of the Norman Road/Eastern Way junction (the 180 from Lewisham to Belvedere also stops there), and then take the public footpath across the reserve.

Train: Belvedere, the nearest train stop, is on the Thameslink and North Kent Line out of Charing Cross, while Abbey Wood is an eastern terminus on the Elizabeth Line out of Stratford.

Car: turn north off the Eastern Way/A2016, just to the east of Crossness Sewage Treatment Works. Though there is no official parking for the reserve, there is limited street parking on Norman Road (TQ496802; loss.twice.weds), from where you can walk straight onto the reserve. If intending to look at the Thames foreshore first, park by the disused Thamesview Golf Course centre at the eastern end of Fairway Drive, Thamesmead, SE28 8PP (TQ481812; fact.settle.rushed), just to the west of the sewage works. From there, the reserve can be entered via the Thames Path, 0.8 miles (1.3km) to the east of the reserve along the river.

YOUR VISIT

Formerly known as Erith and Belvedere Marshes, this relatively new nature reserve (it opened in 2006) has had its profile raised as a London hotspot by the committed patch-watching of a few regulars. It's a wildlife-rich, urban brownfield site that's still evolving into a valuable community nature reserve, and currently holds a patchwork of grazing marsh, reedbeds, open water, ditches, scrub, secondary woodland and rough grassland. The reserve now stretches onto both sides of the Eastern Way, with the northern part known as Crossness NR (aka the 'North Marsh') and the southern part, across a busy road, helpfully termed the Southern Marsh. Most of the site is owned by Thames Water.

If coming from the golf centre, check the sewage outlet on the river side of the Thames Path (TQ490808; panels.blitz.tooth), which attracts many gulls, terns and ducks at high tide, and the fence along the path is often used as a perch, so be careful how you approach. The entrance to the reserve will appear to your right just after you've passed the sewage works.

A couple of public footpaths also lead off Norman Road and allow the visitor to view all the habitats, which include the grazing fields, wet meadows, ponds and a fairly large area of open water fringed by reeds, called the Great Breach Lagoon. The easiest path to take is from the corner of Norman Road and the A2016 (just as you turn into Norman Road). You can park anywhere on Norman Road, but much of the reserve is security-fenced, there's a lot of fly-tipping and the road can get busy with lorries and vans. If you're paying a short visit, you can probably park at the Asda distribution centre (TQ497803; intervals.attend.pillow), which is opposite that side of the reserve. The access gates are only open to vehicles belonging to the Friends of Crossness Nature Reserve (FoCNR) or Thames Water.

Most of the site is openly accessible; the most sensitive wildlife area is the fenced-off 'Protected Area' (TQ492805; wonderfully.vast.chest) to the west of the Great Breach Lagoon, which is restricted to FoCNR members and the occasional walk guided by the warden; you can apply for a permit using the email address above. This area contains toilets, a two-storey, concrete hide overlooking the wader scrape, and a Sand Martin wall made from reclaimed concrete pilings sourced locally.

There is little disabled access, but Thames Water has plans to improve this situation, and a map of disabled access points and suitable areas can be obtained from the contacts above.

To get to the reedy ponds, ditches, grassland and scrub of the Southern Marsh, either use the path between the fields to the east of Southmere Lake or the one running off Waldron Way on the west side of the dyke. There is also an Eastern Way gate immediately to the west of the Hailey Way Industrial Estate. If covering the whole site on foot, there's a footpath running directly to Horse Head Dyke from the southern side opposite the Eastern Way Gate (TQ492799; finds.camp.wiser), but you'll have to cross the road to access this via a metal kissing gate.

Walking to the reserve from Belvedere and Abbey Wood stations can also take you through some marsh. Of the specific locations at the site, try the Great Breach Lagoon for wintering wildfowl, while there is a regular high-tide wader roost on the wet meadow. Little Ringed Plover has bred on the shingle island, while the scrape regularly attracts migrant Common Sandpiper, Greenshank, Snipe and scarcer species.

Crossness is one of only two sites in Greater London with regular breeding Barn Owls (the other being Rainham Marshes). The reedbed has breeding Water Rail, Sedge and Reed Warblers and Reed Bunting. On an incoming or outgoing tide, try to time your visit to scan the Thameside mud, where large numbers of waders, gulls and duck feed, particularly when viewing Halfway Reach Bay from the seawall.

Rarities and scarcities have included Quail, Great Egret, Purple and Squacco

Herons, Temminck's Stint, Penduline Tit and Great Reed Warbler – astonishing for such a post-industrial site.

The lakes nearby are good for gulls and the commoner wildfowl species, though occasional unusual birds have been seen, such as a Ferruginous Duck on the West Lake in January 2012.

31 SOUTH NORWOOD CP

Albert Road, London SE25 4QL
Website: https://croydon-birders.fandom.com/wiki/South_Norwood_Coun try_Park
Parking: TQ350680; occurs.sheet.smiles
Phone: 020 8726 6900
Email: parks@croydon.gov.uk
Open: all day, every day
(50 hectares; 123.5 acres)

SPECIES

All year: Tawny Owl, Reed Bunting.

Summer: Swift, House Martin, warblers.

Winter: Water Rail, Snipe, Jack Snipe, Kingfisher, Firecrest, Redwing, Fieldfare, Stonechat, Siskin, Redpoll.

Migration: Common Sandpiper, Cuckoo, pipits, wagtails, Whinchat, Wheatear, flycatchers, Ring Ouzel, warblers.

ACCESS

Bike: 24-hour access from several points.

Bus: routes 197, 312, 356 and 289 all stop close to the park. Croydon's Tramlink route bisects the park, stopping at Harrington Road in the west and Arena in the south.

Train: Elmers End, a short distance to the east, is the nearest station, with regular services from London Charing Cross and London Cannon Street.

Car: there are several car parks open from 8am–dusk (weekdays), and from 9am on weekends and public holidays.

YOUR VISIT

This former sewage farm has gradually developed a respectable range of habitats since it first opened as a country park in 1989, including a landscaped lake and some wet meadows. There are also small areas of grassland, woodland and scrub.

Most common species are present, along with a notable Shoveler flock in winter, sometimes joined by Shelduck, Goosander and Pintail. Both common grebes and

Kingfisher breed. Reed Bunting is resident, while Water Rail winters, but can be elusive. The wet meadow attracts Snipe most years, among which Jack Snipe has been found.

Trees are plentiful enough to attract winter finch flocks, and Fieldfare and Redwing pop in, with the occasional addition of a Firecrest. Regular watching has added several species to Croydon's modest list, including both Great Grey and Red-backed Shrikes, Bearded Tit and Twite.

32 BEDDINGTON FARMLANDS

Mile Rd, Croydon, Wallington SM6 7NN
Websites:bfnr.org.uk;wandlevalleypark.co.uk/interests/wildlife-and-natural-environment; mitchamcommon.org
Entrance: TQ287661; broken.eaten.rally
Email: (Peter Alfrey) littleoakgroup@btinternet.com
Open: all day, every day
Site of Metropolitan Importance for Nature Conservation
(161 hectares; 400 acres)

SPECIES

All year: Shelduck, Gadwall, Peregrine, Lapwing, Redshank, Barn and Little Owls, Kingfisher, Skylark, Cetti's Warbler, Reed Bunting.

Summer: Hobby, Little Ringed Plover, Common Tern, Cuckoo, Swift, hirundines, Sedge, Reed and Garden Warblers, Yellow Wagtail.

Winter: Wigeon, Shoveler, Teal, Pintail, Water Rail, Golden Plover, Green Sandpiper, Ruff, Snipe, Jack Snipe, Woodcock, Curlew, Caspian Gull, Short-eared Owl, Coal Tit, Firecrest, Water Pipit, Brambling, Siskin, Redpoll.

Migration: Brent Goose, Garganey, Goosander, Great Egret, Osprey, waders including Wood and Common Sandpipers, Little, Mediterranean and Yellow-legged Gulls, terns, Turtle Dove, Raven, Ring Ouzel, Spotted and Pied Flycatchers, Wheatear, Whinchat, Stonechat.

ACCESS

Bus: routes 151 (Worcester Park–Wallington) and 127 (Purley–Tooting Broadway) stop at Hackbridge station. From there, walk right down Mile Road over Mile Road Bridge to enter between the North and South Lakes.

Train: the nearest station is Hackbridge (5 minutes' walk) on the Thameslink or Southern services from London Victoria or London Waterloo.

Car: arrive via the A237 on the reserve's western edge and park in the surrounding streets close to Mile Road. You may have to pay for a temporary permit by phone. Perhaps better, though, is the free parking at Beddington Car Park West in Beddington Park, close to the Farmlands' southern entrance.

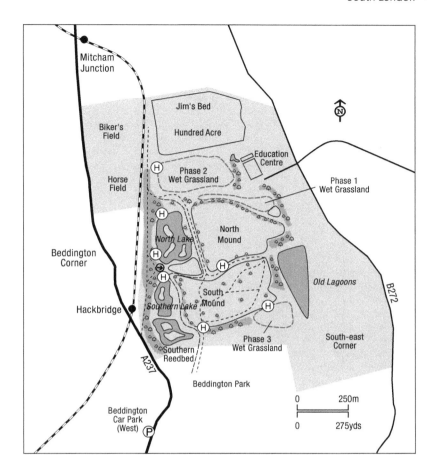

YOUR VISIT

Though an ongoing LNR development project, part of Beddington Farmlands is now open to the public, along with a footpath and three new hides on its western side. With Mitcham Common and Beddington Park, it forms part of the greater Wandle Valley Regional Park, intended to be the conservation and recreational equivalent of the LVRP in north-east London (page 48), with contiguous habitat running from Wandsworth to Wallington.

The new entrance is midway along a permissive footpath that runs south from Mitcham Common along its western edge from Beddington Farmlands to Beddington Park. Three hides made from reconditioned shipping containers now overlook the North (TQ287665; tries.amuse.fire) and South (TQ286659; plot.handy. arts) Lakes – two of the site's most bird-rich areas – and the wet grassland (TQ287666; wells.swear.boxing). Please note that much of the site is still only accessible to members of the Beddington Farm Group, although more areas are expected to open soon; check the website before you visit. At the time of writing, the site – which was expected to be fully open to the public by the end of 2023 – is still under public consultation with Valencia Waste Management, the new owners, who are seeking to make unspecified changes to the site's restoration plan.

One of London's greatest birding sites (along with Rainham Marshes and the London Wetland Centre), which has logged many rarities over the years, access to the site has long been partial and difficult. A commitment to creating a nature reserve from the former landfill site and sewage works was one of the conditions placed on Valencia Waste Management for building a new waste incinerator. Time will see if the company fulfils its obligations, which previous waste companies appear to have failed to do. The site was well known for hosting London's last breeding population of Tree Sparrows, but its decline has been depressingly rapid and the species no longer breeds here, or anywhere in the city, while gull numbers have decreased since the landfill site became inactive. It's also the case that numbers of several of the regular species have declined, although there were still a few Water Pipits in winter 2023.

The site is currently very simple to visit, as you can only officially visit the three hides on the western edge, but it's hoped that this will change in future. Early mornings are best.

Some 262 bird species have been recorded at Beddington, and exciting rarities and scarcities over the years have included Pacific Golden Plover, Killdeer, Glaucous-winged and Sabine's Gulls and Citrine Wagtail.

During migration, it's sometimes worth wandering north to the adjacent **Mitcham Common**, which has scrub, open grassland and trees that attract the more frequent migrants and support Little Owl (which has also been seen recently on **Wandsworth Common**, further north).

Beddington Park (SM6 7BT; TQ288654; polite.sticks.rents) is a short distance left out of Hackbridge station, forms a contiguous green space, includes the River Wandle and a lake, and is worth passing through on your way on a loop to the Farmlands, particularly for migrants and parkland birds.

33 RICHMOND PARK

Pen Ponds Car Park, Broomfield Hill, London SW15 3PF
Websites: www.royalparks.org.uk/parks/richmond-park; www.frp.org.uk
TQ204726; moods.navy.drove
Phone: 0300 061 2200
Email: www.royalparks.org.uk/about-us/contact-us
Open: 7am–dusk (summer), 7.30am–dusk (winter), except on deer-culling days (see the website)
NNR, SSSI, SAC
(950 hectares; 2,347.5 acres)

SPECIES

All year: Mandarin Duck, Water Rail, Lesser Spotted Woodpecker, Tawny and Little Owls, Skylark, Stonechat, Nuthatch, Treecreeper, Reed Bunting.

Summer: Common Tern, Hobby, Swift, warblers including Reed.

Winter: Gadwall, Redwing, Fieldfare, Dartford Warbler, Siskin, Redpoll.

Migration: Common Sandpiper, Hobby, hirundines, chats, Spotted Flycatcher.

ACCESS

Bike: most paths are cyclable.

Bus: numerous routes service all sides of this huge park (see website).

Train: the nearest station is Richmond, which is serviced by the District Line and National Rail.

Car: there are eight car parks, including four with disabled bays for blue badge holders (see: *www.royalparks.org.uk/parks/richmond-park/visitor-information/ parking-in-richmond-park*).

YOUR VISIT

Probably the most productive, bird-wise, of the Royal Parks, Richmond Park is also the biggest. With ancient oak woodland, bracken understorey, acid grassland, a stream and some small reed-edged ponds, there's a lot of varied habitat.

Lesser Spotted Woodpecker still breeds in very small numbers and is extremely elusive, but the woods also have Buzzard, Tawny Owl, Coal Tit, Nuthatch and Treecreeper in residence. More open areas sustain a few Little Owls in hawthorns

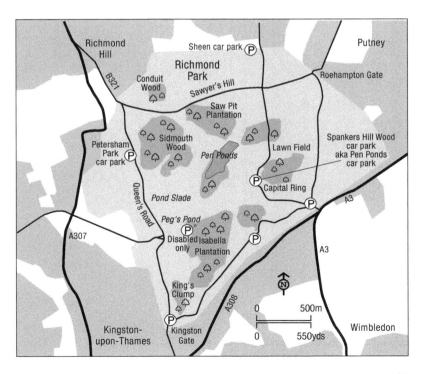

and older isolated trees. Hobby appears every spring and possibly breeds, while Peregrine certainly nests nearby.

The open grass is perhaps over-used by humans, dogs and the park's famous Red and Fallow Deer, but there are still a few Skylarks and Stonechats. The commoner migrant warblers visit in summer and a few Swallows breed.

Vegetation around the ponds sustains Reed Bunting, but Common Tern now seems to have gone. There are good numbers of Mandarin Duck, particularly around Pen Ponds (TQ199728; edge.tones.salads) and Peg's Pond, which has held more than 30 birds in recent winters, while winter brings Gadwall, Teal and Shoveler. Water Rail is elusive but resident, and Snipe and Common Sandpiper appear outside the breeding season. Woodcock winters, generally incognito. The Upper Pen Pond has a Sand Martin breeding wall and Grey Wagtail and Kingfisher are present along the stream.

This is a large park with varied habitats that attract plenty of migrants, and you can safely predict Cuckoo, Yellow Wagtail, Spotted Flycatcher, Ring Ouzel, Redstart, Wheatear and Whinchat each year. The best areas during migration are probably Hawthorn Valley (the northern side of Conduit Wood at TQ190739; rising.brains. garage), Holly Lodge Paddocks (TQ196740; logic.racing.washed), Lawn Field (TQ202730; takes.bill.sadly) and Pond Slade (TQ194723; circle.adjust.choice). Winter sees Redwing and Fieldfare, plus infrequent flocks of Redpoll and Siskin by the Pen Ponds, and in recent years Dartford Warbler has been found annually.

Scarce and rare visitors have included Rough-legged Buzzard, Little Bittern, Hoopoe, Wryneck, Woodchat, Red-backed and Great Grey Shrikes and Golden Oriole.

34 NEARBY: WIMBLEDON AND PUTNEY COMMONS AND PUTNEY HEATH

Windmill Rd, Wimbledon Common, London SW19 5NR
Website: www.wpcc.org.uk/nature/birds
TQ229725; feast.loose.flies (Putney Heath)
Phone: 020 8788 7655
Email: rangersoffice@wpcc.org.uk
SSSI, SAC
(461.34 hectares; 1,140 acres)

Huge areas of community green space that produce good migrants every spring and autumn.

SPECIES
Similar species to Richmond Park (see page 90).

ACCESS
Bike: there are many cyclable paths throughout.

Bus: route 93 (Putney–Wimbledon) runs along the site's eastern edge, while routes 14, 85 and 93 run past Putney Heath.

Train: East Putney (District Line) is the closest underground station, a 10-minute walk from the heath; Wimbledon and Southfields stations are also nearby.

Car: Wimbledon Common and Putney Heath are bordered on the east by Wimbledon Parkside (A219), just south of Roehampton and separated from the south-east side of Richmond Park by the A3. There are four car parks: Windmill Cafe, Windmill Road, SW19 5NQ (7am–9pm); Springwell, SW19 4UW, off Sunset Road (dawn–dusk); Richardson Evans Memorial Playing Field, SW15 3PQ (8am–6pm, but closed at weekends); and Telegraph, SW15 3TU (dawn–dusk). Nearby streets, particularly Wildcroft Road, allow free parking for Putney Heath.

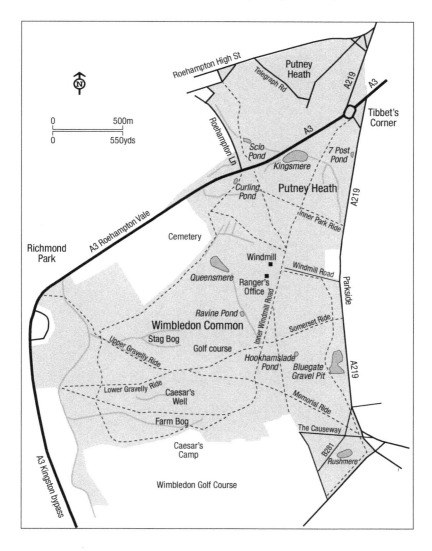

YOUR VISIT

The majority of the combined area of this extensive suburban area eight miles from Central London is taken up by the 364 hectares (900 acres) that comprise Wimbledon and Putney Commons (which also enclose Putney Heath).

Habitats include heathland, open grassland, lakes and secondary and ancient woodland. The whole site is well used by the public, with up to 10,000 people every day letting their dogs run freely – bad news for ground-nesters such as Skylark, now extirpated from the common. This accessibility – it's completely unfenced – means that early mornings generally produce the best birds.

Despite these problems, the site provides a comprehensive cross-section of common species and the chance of the occasional surprise. Residents include Mandarin Duck scattered around the Kingsmere, Fishponds Wood and Bluegate ponds, Tawny Owl and Grey Wagtail, while Reed Bunting may just about hang on. Bullfinch, a former breeder, is now only a scarce winter visitor. Little Owl retains a toehold in the golf course area to the south-west. Some wildfowl are inexplicably scarce, such as Gadwall. Beverley Brook, which connects to Richmond Park, has the occasional Kingfisher.

The commoner finches, warblers and thrushes breed, while raptors such as Hobby and Buzzard appear to be on the verge of establishing a summer presence.

In winter, The Plain has boggy areas that attract Snipe, Woodcock and occasionally Jack Snipe. Firecrests are usually present, and there were an outrageous 43 on site during winter 2022–23, while Dartford Warbler is now regular. A few wintering Fieldfare, more Redwing, plus some Siskins and Redpolls are a given. The playing fields attract hordes of gulls, among which the odd scarcity has been located.

Migration produces a wide range of less usual species such as Cuckoo, Garden and Willow Warblers, Ring Ouzel, Spotted Flycatcher, Wheatear, Whinchat and Stonechat. The heather on the heath has occasionally coaxed in a lost Dartford Warbler.

It is likely that this large area is relatively under-watched and an increase in observers may reveal more surprises in future.

35 BUSHY PARK

Main entrance and office: The Stockyard, Hampton Ct Rd, Hampton TW12 2EJ
Website: www.royalparks.org.uk/parks/bushy-park
TQ157696; intent.reveal.city
Phone: 0300 061 2250
Email: www.royalparks.org.uk/about-us/contact-us
Open: all day, every day
(445 hectares; 1,099 acres)

The second-largest Royal Park boasts all three woodpeckers and Mandarin Duck among a wide array of commoner species.

SPECIES

Similar species to Richmond Park (see page 90).

ACCESS

Bike: cycling is permitted on most paths except when the park is closed for deer-culling in September and November (when opening times revert to 8am–dusk on weekdays). There's a bike rack (TQ152705; neck.heat.stones) and a Companion Riding Scheme for disabled visitors.

Bus: seven bus routes stop at the Hampton Court Gate: 111, 216, 285, 411, 481, X26 and R68.

Train: trains from London Waterloo stop at Teddington, Hampton Wick and Hampton Court, all less than 10 minutes from the park.

Car: there are four free car parks, of which two are close to the wooded areas, ponds and lakes: Cobbler's Walk (TQ153701, shall.scope.exile, accessed via Teddington Gate) and the Diana (TQ160693, supper.panel.minus, via Hampton Court Gate).

YOUR VISIT

Just west of Kingston-upon-Thames, this huge area of grassland, woodland and freshwater holds good populations of most common birds and a couple of specialities. The best place to look for Lesser Spotted Woodpecker, if still present, is the Canal Plantations or Woodland Gardens, where Treecreeper and Nuthatch may also be seen.

Try the Heron Pond for Mandarin Duck; Gadwall are present, while Goosander can appear in winter. Kingfisher, Stonechat, Reed Bunting and Little and Tawny Owls are resident, and Bushy Park is large enough to sustain ground nesters such as Skylark and Meadow Pipit. These days, Dartford Warbler is often present in winter.

Passage produces the expected migrants, particularly in spring. The site is not known for rarities, but a Common Nighthawk photographed flying over the Diana Fountain on 19 October 2019 shows that anything can happen anywhere.

36 LONDON WETLAND CENTRE WWT

Queen Elizabeth Walk, Barnes, London, SW13 9WT
Website: www.wwt.org.uk/wetland-centres/london
TQ226766; cards.misty.cried
Phone: 020 8409 4400
Email: info.london@wwt.org.uk
Open: opening hours are 9.30am–4.30pm (winter) or 9.30am–5.30pm (summer), with the last admissions an hour before closing. The reserve is closed on Christmas Day only. WWT members get in free but it's expensive for non-members, at £15.50 for adults and £9.50 for kids, though there are discounts for families, pensioners, full-time students and the unemployed

There is a large café, a shop, toilets and a heated hide. The paths are wheelchair accessible
(42.5 hectares; 105 acres)

Breeding Little Ringed Plovers and wintering Bitterns are the crown jewels of a site that hosts plenty of waterbirds, and regularly produces scarcities and the odd rarity.

SPECIES

All year: Gadwall, Water Rail, Peregrine, Cetti's Warbler, Goldcrest, Coal Tit.

Summer: Lapwing, Oystercatcher, Little Ringed Plover, Redshank, Common Tern, Sand Martin, Garden Warbler (not annual), warblers.

Winter: Shelduck, Shoveler, Wigeon, Teal, Pintail, Goldeneye, Bittern, Snipe, Jack Snipe, Stonechat, Water Pipit, Siskin, Redpoll, Brambling.

Migration: chance of Brent Goose, Garganey, Red Kite, Marsh Harrier, Osprey, Ringed Plover, Wood, Green and Common Sandpipers, Black-tailed Godwit, Greenshank, Dunlin, Caspian and Yellow-legged Gulls, terns, Ring Ouzel, Wheatear, Whinchat, Redstart, Spotted Flycatcher, Firecrest, Willow Warbler, Yellow and White Wagtails, Rock Pipit.

ACCESS

Bike: the Wetland Centre is on Sustrans Cycle Network Route 4 and the Thames towpath, and there are bike racks and 50 bike cages (which hold up to four bikes) by the VC.

Bus: route 283 runs to the centre from Hammersmith tube station.

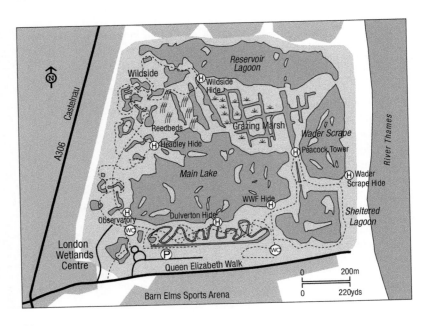

Train: Hammersmith tube station (Piccadilly, District and Hammersmith & City) is nearest. Catch bus number 283 directly to the reserve or, alternatively, walk across Hammersmith Bridge and catch any bus and alight at the Barnes Red Lion stop immediately at the end of Queen Elizabeth Walk.

Car: the tarmac car park is spacious and has disabled spaces.

YOUR VISIT

This site was legendary when it was known as Barn Elms, and some of its former birding potential still remains now that the site is a more managed and publicly accessible 44-ha nature reserve.

The reserve is right next to the River Thames near Hammersmith Bridge. Its grounds hold four decommissioned reservoirs, now converted into lakes and wader scrapes, surrounded by reedbeds, mud, grassland, grazing marsh, scrub and woodland. The disturbance that its heavy public recreational use could cause has been mostly mitigated by building screens along all the paths and allowing views largely from the hides. There are seven of these modern shelters, including the impressive Peacock Tower, which overlooks most of the water and shoreline, and has lifts and comfortable seats on its three floors.

Migration periods are often the best, if you're after surprises, and waders often rest on the scrape on their way north, changing direction from north to south in June. Larger birds of prey are expected and will include the odd Osprey and Marsh Harrier. The scarcer waders (for London) often show up during spring rain on east-erlies. Any of the regular tern species could pass through, while there is a substantial high-tide gull roost, among which Yellow-legged is likely and Caspian possible. Expect the standard chats, with the occasional Greenland form of Wheatear in late April into May. Whinchat can be perched up on the long grass on the fringes, while Ring Ouzel forages on the grassy banks. Scan the islands on the scrape too, as Water and Scandinavian Rock Pipits pass through, and the Pied Wagtail flocks may conceal the odd White Wagtail.

Garganey are more often seen in autumn than spring, and post-breeding waders take on a subtly different character, with Wood Sandpiper, Greenshank and Ruff scarce but more likely. Lapwing flocks build in autumn too. As the weather gets colder and the days shorter, larks, pipits and finches provide some vis mig interest.

The breeding season is busy, and perhaps 10 pairs of Common Tern liven up the rafts as Little Ringed Plovers, Lapwing and Redshank stalk the scrape islands. Avocet breeding attempts have failed so far but success is expected soon. The Sand Martin nest bank can be viewed intimately from the Wader Scrape Hide, and usually hosts about 40 pairs. Marsh Warbler has also bred. Overhead, expect both Hobby and Peregrine, as these breed in the area too.

The site is popular for a winter visit, as both Bittern and Jack Snipe are more regular at this site than most others in the capital. The Nationally Important numbers of Gadwall and Shoveler make for a wildfowl spectacle, and you should be able to see Water Rail from one of the hides as well as hear them squeal.

The Wetland Centre hasn't lost its reputation for good birds and has featured many scarce and rare species in recent years. These have included Black Kite, Crane, Corncrake, Night Heron, Leach's Storm-petrel, Pacific Golden Plover, Pomarine Skua, White-winged Black Tern, Alpine Swift, Bluethroat and Woodchat Shrike.

37 NEARBY: LONSDALE ROAD RESERVOIR

Lonsdale Rd, London SW13 9QN
Website: www.richmond.gov.uk/services/parks_and_open_spaces/
find_a_park/leg_o_mutton
TQ217773; solar.await.budget
(8.19 hectares; 20.2 acres)
LNR

Also known as Leg O'Mutton, this Thames-adjacent waterbody is a short distance from the Wetland Centre and gets some of the commoner waterfowl in winter, including Gadwall, Shoveler and Teal. Common Tern, Reed Warbler and hirundines are seen in summer. Occasional Mandarin Ducks and Red-crested Pochard are noted, but Water Rail isn't annual. Tawny Owl has bred among the commoner woodland species. There is a footpath around most of the perimeter from which the lake can be scanned, but arrive early as there can be disturbance. Notable sightings have included Garganey, Scaup and subalpine warbler.

38 BEDFONT LAKES CP

Clockhouse Lane, Feltham, Middlesex TW14 8QA
Website: www.bedfontlakes.co.uk
TQ076724; kinks.mime.action
There is an entrance by the smaller open area to the east of the main park, next to Bedfont Lake (Bedfont Road, Hounslow, London TW14 8EE; TQ086729; stores.party.sage)
Phone: 01784 259161 or 0845 456 2796; 07525 197 866 (duty ranger)
Email: info@bedfontlakes.co.uk
Open: all day, every day. There is also an area with trees and a reedbed called North Side Private Nature Reserve, which is open to members of the Friends of Bedfont Lakes CP with a £5 membership fee. Non-members can visit the reserve by paying an annual fee of £15 (see website). There's an information centre by the main entrance, plus public toilets (including a disabled WC). There are two designated areas where dog owners can let their charges off the lead, but otherwise please keep dogs leashed.
(75 hectares; 180 acres)

SPECIES

All year: Red Kite, Skylark, Kingfisher, Reed Bunting, Chiffchaff.

Summer: Hobby, Common Tern, Swift, Skylark, hirundines, Meadow Pipit, Garden Warbler, Lesser Whitethroat.

Winter: Gadwall, Teal, Shoveler, Smew (scarce), Goosander, Bittern (scarce), Water Rail, Fieldfare, Redwing, Cetti's Warbler, Firecrest.

Migration: Little Ringed Plover, Lapwing, Common and Green Sandpipers, Yellow Wagtail, Willow Warbler, Wheatear, Whinchat, Stonechat, Redstart, Spotted Flycatcher, Ring Ouzel.

ACCESS

Bus: route 116 runs (Hounslow Bus Station–Ashford Hospital) to Bedfont Green, from where the park is a short walk.

Train: alight at Feltham train station (from London Waterloo–Windsor/Weybridge/ Reading) or Hatton Cross tube (Piccadilly Line) and take the H26 bus (Feltham– Hatton Cross) from either.

Car: there are free car parks at the Clockhouse Lane and Bedfont Road entrances.

YOUR VISIT

Currently somewhat under-watched, this public country park is based on an old landfill and has significant areas of grass meadow, woodland, scrub, reedbed and open water all close to Heathrow Airport. The site is split in half by a railway line but both areas of the park are open to the public, except for the private nature reserve (see page 98). The private reserve encloses a good area of reeds and willow carr. A visit is perhaps best before or after a session at the larger Surrey (formerly Middlesex) reservoirs to the west (not included in this guide, but see the additional site summaries on page 303).

Like most suburban sites, the real birding excitement happens away from the breeding season. Migration will bring the expected scarce warblers and chats, and

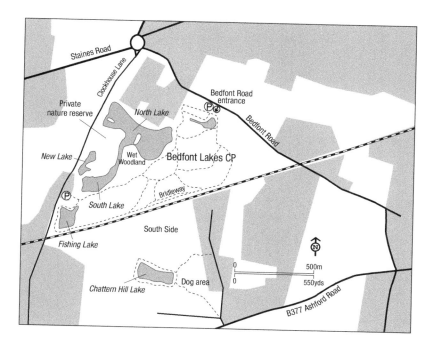

these have been supplemented in recent years by Wryneck, Nightingale and Grasshopper Warbler. Winter sees the chance of Goosander, Smew and Red-breasted Merganser in descending order of likelihood, while Water Rail will haunt the reeds. Don't ignore summer, however – Hobby often hunts overhead and the breeding warblers are very active.

Scarcer species have included Ruddy Shelduck, Hen Harrier, Glossy Ibis and Short-eared Owl. At the time of writing, 163 species have been recorded at the park, though perhaps 100 can be seen every year.

39 NEARBY: HOUNSLOW HEATH

Staines Road, Hounslow, Middlesex TW4 5LJ
TQ119747; bulb.tested.grain
Open: all day, every day
LNR
(80 hectares; 197.68 acres)

This large area of open lowland heath, acid grassland, woodland, scrub, ponds and meadows a couple of miles south-east of Heathrow Airport supports a good selection of commoner scrub and woodland birds, including Skylark, Linnet and Reed Bunting, and it incorporates an LNR. The site is best during migration when the more expected passerines drop into the scrub and small woodland areas – the site has a good reputation for Ring Ouzel in spring. A few Siskins or Redpolls can pop in during winter, while common waterbirds are possible and Woodcock sometimes winters.

WEST LONDON

THE COLNE VALLEY
40 STOCKER'S LAKE

Rickmansworth Aquadrome, Frogmore Lane, Rickmansworth, Hertfordshire WD3 1NF
Website: https://www.hertswildlifetrust.org.uk/nature-reserves/stockers-lake
TQ055937; soap.sleep.wells
Open: all day, every day
LNR
(40 hectares; 98.84 acres)

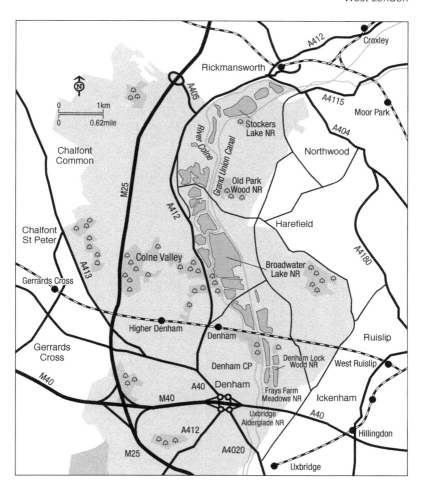

SPECIES

All year: Gadwall, Red-crested Pochard, Red Kite, Tawny and Little Owls, Lesser Spotted Woodpecker, Kingfisher, Cetti's Warbler, Treecreeper.

Summer: Common Tern, Hobby, warblers.

Winter: Wigeon, Gadwall, Shoveler, Teal, Goldeneye, Goosander, Smew, Water Rail, Lapwing, Green Sandpiper, Snipe, Jack Snipe, gull roost, Kingfisher, Fieldfare, Redwing, Chiffchaff (perhaps including Siberian), Firecrest, Siskin, Redpoll.

Migration: Osprey, commoner waders, Peregrine, hirundines, Redstart, Spotted Flycatcher, warblers, wagtails.

ACCESS

Bus: Red Eagle routes R1 and R2 stop at the Tesco superstore stop, from where you can walk half a mile to the Aquadrome.

Train: the Chiltern Railways service (London Marylebone–Aylesbury) stops at Rickmansworth (also on the Metropolitan Line), about 1 mile to the north.

Car: from Harefield Road, turn left onto Frogmore Lane at the edge of Rickmansworth and park in the Aquadrome car park. Turn left out of the car park and the lake is about 200m further on your right, after Bury Lake. You can also enter on foot via Uxbridge Road and Springwell Lane. The paths are good enough for wheelchairs and a RADAR key will get you through the gates that interrupt the roughly circular path. There is a cafe and toilets by Bury Lake.

YOUR VISIT

Probably the most productive of the Colne Valley's waterbodies, Stocker's Lake has Nationally Important numbers of wildfowl, like some of the other lakes nearby. However, it's probably the most reliable for Smew in winter – though there's no guarantee – and has hosted at least 80 breeding species, not all of which are present every year. It supports one of the largest heronries in the UK, which now has Little Egrets nesting among the Grey Herons.

The area of the lake is encircled by the River Colne and the Grand Union Canal, and includes Springwell, Bury and Batchworth Lakes, as well as some smaller pools, all of which can be walked around and explored. There are three hides on the circuit around the lake from the Aquadrome car park, along with a viewpoint over-looking the heronry of more than 60 nests. As well as the lakes, the site has plentiful wet alder woodland, well-vegetated islands and scrub.

Several hundred ducks of the expected species winter on site, and these can include Wigeon, Goosander and – most interestingly – Smew. Red-crested Pochard is now resident.

Hobby can be seen in summer, as it breeds nearby, and Red Kite is seen regularly. The inscrutable Water Rail frequents the wet woodland. There isn't much wader habitat, but Lapwings gather on nearby Stocker's Farm and Snipe can be secreted away anywhere there is mud and cover; any other species is exceptional.

Plenty of gulls use the site after breeding, and scarcer wader feature on occasion. Common Tern breeds on the specially provided rafts but other terns are rare. Turtle Dove has now deserted the site but Cuckoo occasionally still shows up in spring.

With such plentiful woodland, Tawny Owl's presence is unsurprising and Little Owl is sometimes reported from Stocker's Farm. Kingfisher forages on most of the waterbodies in the area. Yellow Wagtail has declined but still passes through on occasion. Chats and flycatchers appear during passage only, but there are plenty of the commoner warblers in summer.

Winter sees Redpolls and, especially, Siskin visiting the alders; more than 50 of the latter have been counted at times.

41 BROADWATER LAKE NR HMWT

Moorhall Road, Harefield, Hillingdon, London UB9 6PB
Website: www.hertswildlifetrust.org.uk/nature-reserves/broadwater-lake
TQ045883; blitz.chefs.small

Open: all day, every day. Enter on foot through the gate with an HMWT sign just east of the River Colne. Follow the footpath along the west bank of the main lake, which has two hides, or walk the rougher second path along the causeway between Broadwater and Harefield Lake.
SSSI
(19.4 hectares; 48 acres)

A large, deep former gravel pit that is one of the more reliable sites for Smew in winter.

SPECIES
Similar species to Stocker's Lake (see page 100).

ACCESS
Bus: route 331 bus runs along Moorhall Road. Alight at the Broadwater Lock Grand Union Canal stop and walk back west to the entrance.

Train: the Chiltern Main Line service (London Paddington–Birmingham Moor Street) stops at Denham, half a mile south-west of the entrance.

Car: park on Link Way, Denham Green (TQ042881; models.freed.paths), a third of a mile from the entrance. Walk along Moorhall Road, which runs between Harefield and Denham Green, to the entrance.

YOUR VISIT
This large former gravel pit in the Colne Valley is now a nature reserve managed by the HMWT. There are three main waterbodies – Broadwater, Harefield and Korda Lakes – surrounded by woodland and bordered by the River Colne. At the time of writing, long-term HS2 development work is taking place, but there is still public foot access. This can't be guaranteed for the seven-year period over which the work is taking place, so visit the website to keep abreast of changes.

Broadwater Lake NR holds Nationally Significant numbers of wildfowl, and winter sees Gadwall, Shoveler, Teal and a few Wigeon present. A few Goosander use the open water and adjacent river, but the site's speciality is Smew – try Korda Lake first, where there are usually one or two present, though the species is declining overall in the UK; Stocker's Lake (see page 100) is more reliable.

The sizeable winter gull roost has produced regular Yellow-legged Gulls, along with the odd Caspian and Iceland. Little Egret also roosts on the islands, but Water Rail is more likely on the river. Passage waders dropping into the gravel at Harefield Lake should include Green and Common Sandpipers, and the odd Lapwing or Oystercatcher. Snipe is nailed on in winter, and Jack Snipe is seen occasionally, though is probably present every year. The tern rafts host plentiful Black-headed gulls, among which Common Terns manage to raise their young too. Black and Arctic Terns and Little Gull are unusual but have occurred in numbers when they do.

The river is well known for hosting double figures of wintering Chiffchaffs in its willows and alders, and 'Siberian' individuals have been found among them, along with the odd Firecrest. Look for Siskins and Redpolls there too.

Late summer sees good numbers of flocking Swifts and hirundines catching flies over the water. They will attract Hobby on occasion, joining the regular raptors, which include Buzzard and Red Kite.

Interesting past drop-ins have included Velvet Scoter, White-headed Duck (not officially accepted), Red-crested Pochard, Black-necked Grebe, Glaucous Gull, Lesser Spotted Woodpecker and Wood Warbler.

42 WORMWOOD SCRUBS

Parking: Linford Christie Stadium, Scrubs Lane, London W12 0DF.
Website: www.friendsofthescrubs.uk
TQ223815; switch.unit.freed.
Open: all day, every day. There are plenty of facilities off site.
LNR.
(75 hectares; 180 acres)

SPECIES

All year: Ring-necked Parrot roost, Meadow Pipit.

Summer: Lesser Whitethroat, Willow Warbler.

Winter: Common species in general.

Migration: Wheatear, Whinchat, Stonechat, Redstart.

ACCESS

Bus: route 220 stops on Scrubs Lane, while numbers 7, 70, 72, 272 and 283 stop on Du Cane Road outside the stadium.

Train: The nearest tube stations are East Acton to the south-west and White City to the south-east (both Central Line), and Latimer Road (Circle and Hammersmith & City); all are 5–10 minutes away on foot.

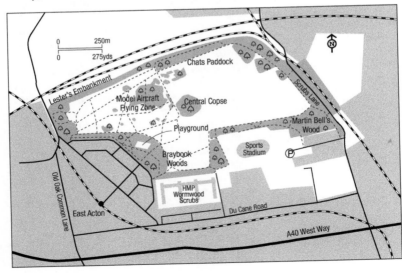

Car: pay-and-display parking is available in the car park off Scrubs Lane. Turn right after entering the signposted track and drive west in front of Linford Christie Stadium to reach the spacious car park.

YOUR VISIT

Wormwood Scrubs ('The Scrubs') is a substantial urban green space of mown playing fields surrounded by trees and scrub, with a copse in the centre. In 2002, English Nature designated seven of its areas of woodland and grassland as an LNR.

The best birds are generally found in the seven more 'natural' areas in the new LNR. These include Central Copse, several small woodlands and two large areas of scrub. There is also a 'mini-Scrubs' – Little Wormwood Scrubs (TQ229819; moral. manual.crush) – on the east side of Scrubs Lane, which is also worth a peek during migration, though work on HS2 has destroyed the northern embankment where many migrants have been seen.

The whole site hosts the usual common scrub and garden birds in good numbers. The rougher areas on the western side sometimes produce Whinchat, Stonechat and Wheatear on passage, with Redstart also possible (one wintered one year). Summer sees breeding warblers, including Lesser Whitethroat and occasionally Willow Warbler. The closest nesting Meadow Pipits to Central London can also be found in this area. There's also the notable daily spectacle of about 5,000 Rose-ringed Parakeet roosting from autumn through to spring.

Over the years, regulars have logged notable species such as Honey-buzzard, Quail, Wryneck, Great Grey and Red-backed Shrikes, Richard's Pipit and Ortolan and Little Buntings.

43 OSTERLEY PARK NT

Nine Acre Trail, Osterley, London TW7 4RB.
TQ148779; blog.paying.swung.
(107.36 hectares; 265.29 acres)

SPECIES

All year: Mandarin Duck, Red Kite, Buzzard, Little and Tawny Owls, Kingfisher, Nuthatch.

Summer: Hobby, warblers.

Winter: Shoveler.

Migration: Common Sandpiper, Snipe, Peregrine, songbirds.

ACCESS

Bike: cycling is allowed throughout via the paths and tracks.

Bus: route H28 stops on St Mary's Crescent, a short walk down Thornbury Road from the main entrance; routes H91, H37, 267, 237 and 117 all stop around the perimeter too.

Train: Osterley tube (Piccadilly line) is five minutes from the entrance. South Western Railway services from London Waterloo–Weybridge stop at Isleworth station, about 0.75 miles away.

Car: there is a spacious car park about 400m from the main gate.

YOUR VISIT

The varied habitats of this large area of parkland, surrounding an NT house in the London Borough of Hounslow, attract more birds than might initially be apparent.

This is a productive site for Mandarin Duck, particularly around the Middle Lake, where Kingfisher is possible, and the small areas of mud in autumn, winter and spring can attract the odd Common Sandpiper or Snipe. Gadwall and Shoveler winter, rarely joined by Wigeon, Goosander and Water Rail. Hobby hunts overhead in summer.

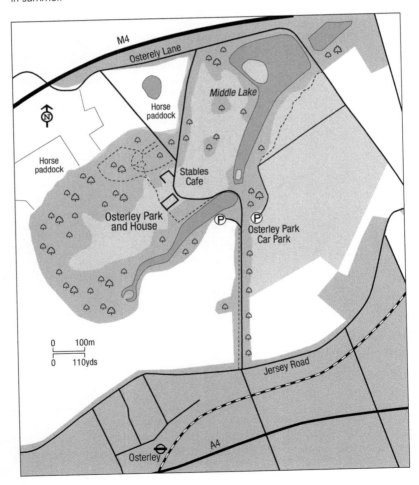

Try the trees lining Nine-Acre Path (the main track) for Little Owl and keep an eye out for Fieldfare and Redwing in the horse paddocks around the road behind Middle Lake; these are also attractive to Whinchat, Wheatear, wagtails and pipits during migration.

Scarcer migrants are possible, and there are records of Hoopoe and Roller.

44 RUISLIP LIDO AND RUISLIP WOODS NNR

Reservoir Road, Ruislip, London HA4 7TY.
TQ085892; trying.nails.behind.
SSSI
(*Ruislip Lido*: 25 hectares; 60 acres;
Ruislip Woods: 11.98 hectares; 29.6 acres)

The first-ever urban NNR, Ruislip Woods – along with Ruislip Lido – has an abundance of acid grassland, heathland and wetland, as well as large areas of woodland. To the east of the Colne Valley, the lido is used for beach, railway and walking excursions, but there are enough undisturbed areas to make the site worth exploring for birds.

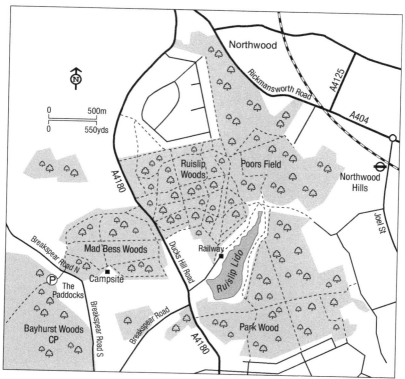

Ruislip Lido provides most of the birding focus, with wintering Goldeneye, Teal, Shoveler, Gadwall and a few Wigeon in winter. Water Rail haunts the North Marsh from autumn when the alders around the lake support small Siskin flocks that may conceal a Redpoll or two. An extensive area of wooded common – Ruislip Woods – surrounds the lido. There is a chance of commoner waders when water levels are low, but otherwise the concrete banks are fairly deserted.

Ruislip Woods NNR is part of four main areas of ancient trees, with notable numbers of Hornbeam, that hold the commoner woodland species. Woodcock is infrequently reported but is probably always present in winter. Lesser Spotted Woodpecker may still breed near the lido or in Copse Wood (TQ083898; raft.tins. poppy), but there are no recent reports. Garden Warbler nests on the more open Poor's Field (TQ088897; phones.single.aura) in summer; check there for chats in spring and autumn too. Mad Bess Wood (TQ079896; quite.memory.loans), just across the A4180 Duck's Hill Road, has very occasional Hawfinches in winter (15 were present in 2017). Scarcer migrants such as Grasshopper Warbler, Black Redstart and Pied Flycatcher occasionally drop in to compliment the bread-and-butter warblers and chats.

The sites can be reached via Ruislip High Street (A4180), which becomes Duck's Hill Road to the north. The lido, Poor's Field, Park Wood (TQ093888; record.pitch. battle) and Copse Wood can be visited from the Reservoir Road car park. Mad Bess and Copse Woods are accessible from the Duck's Hill Road car park, and Bayhurst Wood CP (TQ070890; herb.view.sofa), at the far west end of the site across Breakspear Road, is well signposted and worth exploring on a longer visit. The nearest tubes are Ruislip (Metropolitan and Piccadilly lines) and Northwood Hills (Metropolitan), about 1 mile away. Routes H13 (Pinner–Ruislip Lido, Breakspear Road stop) and 331 (Ruislip–Uxbridge, Reservoir Road stop) pass close to the lido and woods.

NORTH LONDON

45 BRENT RESERVOIR

For parking places, see Access.
Website: brentres.wordpress.com/visiting-brent-reservoir
Email: brentres.wordpress.com/contact
Open: all day, every day, except for the hides. There are several access points. The Main and Heron Hides require a key (via WHCG), but anyone can use the hides if a keyholder is present (most likely on Saturday and Sunday mornings). The Main Hide is usually open during the monthly guided walks, spring and autumn bird counts, and on New Year's Day. The sometimes muddy footpath to the hides leads from the eastern side of the Cool Oak Lane bridge, while another footpath to the west of the bridge leads to the public hide. The viewing platform there is wheelchair accessible, as is the Main Hide if the footpath has been maintained recently.
SSSI, Site of Metropolitan Importance for Nature Conservation, LNR
(79 hectares; 197 acres)

SPECIES

All year: Gadwall, Buzzard, Peregrine, Stock Dove, Tawny Owl, Kingfisher, Cetti's Warbler, Coal Tit.

Summer: Hobby, Common Tern, Swift, Sand and House Martins, Garden Warbler, Reed Bunting.

Winter: Wigeon, Teal, Pintail, Shoveler, Scaup, Goldeneye, Goosander, Little Egret, Water Rail, Snipe, Jack Snipe, Mediterranean Gull, Fieldfare, Redwing, Siskin, Redpoll.

Migration: Shelduck, Garganey, Black-necked Grebe, Red Kite, Little Ringed Plover, Common and Green Sandpipers, Yellow-legged Gull, terns, Skylark, Swallow, pipits, wagtails, Redstart, Whinchat, Stonechat, Wheatear, Spotted Flycatcher.

ACCESS

Bike: cycling is possible but not encouraged on the footpaths.

Bus: routes 32 (Edgware–Kilburn Park), 83 (Golders Green–Ealing Hospital, 142 (Brent Cross–Watford Junction) and 183 (Golders Green–Pinner) all stop at West Hendon Broadway, which is a short walk to the north of Cool Oak Lane. Other routes serve Blackbird Hill and the A406 (North Circular), south-west of the reservoir.

Train: the nearest station is Hendon, a 10-minute walk away on the Thameslink line from several London stations. Alight, walk out of the station, turn right and head down Station Road to West Hendon Broadway. Turn left, cross at the traffic lights and walk down Cool Oak Lane to the paths on either end of the bridge. At the time of writing, there were plans for a new Thameslink station at Brent Cross Shopping Centre, which should be a little closer. Hendon Central tube (Northern Line) is also fairly close; catch bus 83 to West Hendon Broadway, after exiting.

Car: from the A406 North Circular Road, turn onto the A5 (signposted 'Harrow/West Hendon') at the roundabout. Leave the A5 at West Hendon Broadway, turning onto Cool Oak Lane at the traffic lights. Use the free car park further along Cool Oak Lane, on the left, or the ones on Goldsmith Avenue (north of the site), Birchen Grove (to the west) or Aboyne Road (to the south). You can also park on Woolmead Avenue just before the bridge over the reservoir, but you'll get a ticket if you're there between 10am–11am.

YOUR VISIT

One of London's most famous birding destinations due to the work of its committed regulars, Brent Reservoir is a productive patchwork of habitats overseen by the site's very active Welsh Harp Conservation Group (after the site's local name).

Unusually for a capital wetland, Brent has natural water edges rather than concrete banks and this affects the birds using it. Other habitats on site include open water, marshland, rough grassland, woodland, hedgerow, and surrounding gardens, allotments and playing fields. The site is used by a sailing club, though this still leaves much of the water undisturbed.

Like most London sites, Brent Reservoir is best during migration, particularly if the water level is low on the Eastern Marsh, which is helpfully overlooked by two of

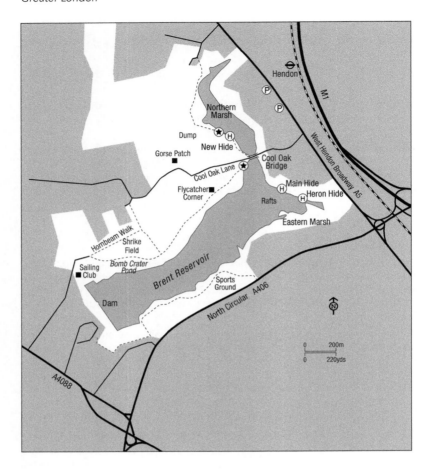

the hides. This has wintering Water Rail and Snipe, and sometimes Jack Snipe. At the same time, the open water will feature Gadwall, Teal and Shoveler, and perhaps a more unusual waterbird keeping them company; Garganey is possible in spring and autumn.

Summer will see a Hobby or two overhead, though the less common raptors are unlikely as Brent isn't on a fly-way. The most likely waders during migration are Common Sandpiper and Little Ringed Plover, while Yellow-legged Gull is annual. Common Tern breeds, but other terns are infrequent. Passage songbirds will feature some of the expected warblers, chats and flycatchers, though the unexpected happens and once included Britain's first Iberian Chiffchaff, on 3 June 1972.

The 121-hectare (299 acres) **Fryent CP** (Fryent Way, Preston, London Borough of Brent, London HA9 9JH; TQ195876; bats.values.shelf) is nearby, just over 0.5 miles to the north-west. It has good numbers of breeding warblers in summer and the commoner woodland birds year-round, including Nuthatch and Treecreeper. The site is somewhat under-watched, so may hold a few surprises during passage when visible migration can be good from the higher points in the park.

46 TRENT CP

Car parks: Cockfosters Road, Enfield, London EN4 0JZ; TQ280969; lasted.
driver.skips;
Hadley Road, Enfield, London EN2 8LA; TQ291981; tame.played.jobs
Websites: trentcountrypark.com; *friendsoftrentcountrypark.org.uk*
Open: all day, every day. There's a VC and cafe next to the main car park.
(167 hectares; 413 acres)

SPECIES

All year: Mandarin Duck, Red-legged Partridge, Kingfisher, Lesser Spotted Woodpecker (scarce), Tawny Owl, Coal Tit, Nuthatch, Treecreeper, Bullfinch, Yellowhammer.

Summer: Hobby, Cuckoo, Swift, Swallow, House Martin, Garden and Willow Warblers.

Winter: Shoveler, Fieldfare, Redwing, Firecrest, Raven, Siskin, Redpoll.

Migration: pipits, warblers, Ring Ouzel, Whinchat, Stonechat, Wheatear, Redstart, Spotted and Pied Flycatchers.

ACCESS

Bike: most of the park's paths are cyclable.

Bus: TfL routes 121, 307 and 377 stop at Oakwood Station and serve the western edge of the park, while 313 runs along the western edge.

Train: Oakwood and Cockfosters Piccadilly Line stations are right on the edge of the park, while Enfield Chase overground (Moorgate–Stevenage/Hertford North) is less than a mile away. From Oakwood, walk uphill on Snakes Lane for no more than 10 minutes to enter the park.

Car: leave the M25 via Junction 24. The CP is just north of the A110 and surrounded by good roads, and it has two sizeable car parks (see above).

YOUR VISIT

The huge Green Belt expanse of Trent CP incorporates meadow grassland, forest, streams and lakes in a mosaic of habitat that proves very attractive to migrants and some interesting resident species. This includes ancient woodland formed from what's left of the Enfield Chase royal hunting ground.

There are many strategies to bird the park, but this suggestion starts at Oakwood tube. Walk up Snake Lane to the main car park, then follow the London Loop right at its northern end into the wood (known as Picnic Wood, but really called Church and Oak Woods) and picnic area. Treecreeper and Goldcrest can be present in the conifers.

Turn left towards the farmland to the north-west, which can produce both species of partridge (though Grey may no longer be resident). Alternatively, you can head north-east from Picnic Wood and walk past the two lakes that are included

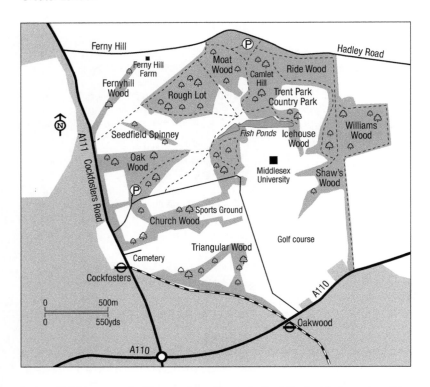

in the official nature walk. These support Mandarin Duck (in double figures) and the odd Goosander in winter among the commoner species.

More extensive, less disturbed woodland spreads from the larger of the lakes' northern shore (Ride and Moat Woods) and will produce better numbers of common woodland species, including Buzzard, though Marsh Tit seems to have gone the way of Willow Tit now. The main path is known as the Horse Trail and will take you onto Vicarage Farm (good for Redstart in autumn), which you can explore using a network of footpaths on the north side of Ferny Hill. The common birds of open farmland will be apparent, including Skylark and perhaps Lapwing or Red-legged Partridge.

On your way back, skirt the eastern side through Williams Wood using the long straight footpath to further woodland in the south-east corner next to the golf course (Shaw's Wood). Check the Trent Park Equestrian Centre paddocks, as Swallow breeds.

While most of the species you'll see will be common and available in most Greater London parks, Trent CP has a good reputation for attracting migrating songbirds and the occasional vagrant, and it is best visited in spring or autumn. Make sure you wander onto the farmland to increase your day list.

47 ALEXANDRA PARK

Parking: Alexandra Palace Way, London, N22 7AY; TQ297901; post.credit. scale
Entrance: Bedford Road, Haringey, London N22 7AX; TQ302903; ideas. gather.fork
Website: apogbirds.blogspot.com
Open: all day, every day
(72 hectares; 180 acres)

SPECIES
All year: Peregrine, Stock Dove, Nuthatch.

Summer: Hobby, Swift, common warblers, House Martin.

Winter: Shoveler, Snipe, Redpoll (scarce), Siskin (scarce).

Migration: Buzzard, Red Kite, Common Sandpiper, chance of Wryneck, hirundines, Treecreeper, Garden Warbler, Whinchat, Stonechat, Wheatear, Redstart, Black Redstart, Spotted and Pied Flycatchers.

ACCESS
Bus: TfL route W3 (Northumberland Park–Finsbury Park) runs through Wood Green and up to Alexandra Palace.

Train: The nearest tube is Wood Green (Piccadilly Line), but Alexandra Palace overground is closer and served by Great Northern services to and from Moorgate.

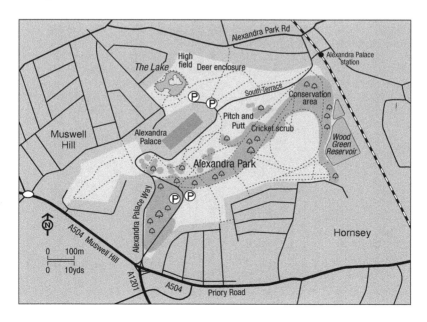

Car: park at The Grove (TQ292898; glare.coats.drip), on the east side of the Palace (TQ297901; proven.taps.work), or on South Terrace (TQ301903; socket. notion.audit).

YOUR VISIT

This extensive urban park on the grounds of Alexandra Palace also includes a small area of water – Wood Green Reservoir (TQ303899; blend.little.muddy) – a boating lake and plenty of woodland, scrub, hedgerows and mown and rough grassland. Lying on a hill between Wood Green (east), Crouch (south) and Muswell Hill (north), the views over London can be impressive and its elevated aspect means it can be good for raptor watching and light visible migration. It's a key landmark for both migrating birds and humans.

A small area of sports pitches is enclosed by a circular perimeter hedge and ditch, remnants of a former racecourse. Next to the pavilion is an area of trees and shrubs known locally as 'the cricket scrub', and during migration times this is the best area to search for warblers (including Garden Warbler and Lesser Whitethroat), chats (Whinchat and Northern Wheatear are regular) and other migrants. Several Wrynecks and Pied Flycatchers have occurred there, and the latter also passes through The Grove to the north-west (TQ291897; quest.drive.tips); Redstart and Spotted Flycatcher are annual. Autumn warbler passage can also be strong on the far edge of the field above the deer enclosure (TQ295903; bars.tennis.again).

Wood Green Reservoir and the adjacent filter beds to the south-east are fed by the New River. These small parcels of water attract wildfowl and gulls in winter, wagtails year-round and even the occasional passage Common Sandpiper. Scarcities dropping in have included Bewick's Swan (in fog), Red-throated Diver (randomly), Slavonian Grebe (in spring) and Black-tailed Godwit (in heavy rain).

Just north of the reservoir, a strip of woodland with an artificial pond has been designated as the Conservation Area. This stretch of waterlogged woodland has attracted everything from Green Sandpiper and Jack Snipe to Yellow-browed and Wood Warblers and Firecrest. Siskin and Redpoll are not as regular as they were but can be looked for in this area too. Water Rail is likely in most winters when a few Woodcock can also be secreted away, and are sometimes watched by torchlight as they feed on the cricket pitch.

At the time of writing, the total number of bird species recorded in the park had topped 180. It's a great urban local patch that pays off with regular watching.

48 HAMPSTEAD HEATH

Main parking: East Heath Road, London NW3 1AL; TQ271859; help.dose. nasal. Kenwood House: Hampstead Lane, London NW3 7JP; TQ267874; path.smooth.fires.
Open: all day, every day. Kenwood is closed at dusk
LNR, Site of Metropolitan Importance, SSSI
(320 hectares; 790 acres)

SPECIES

All year: Mandarin Duck, Gadwall, Buzzard, Green and Great Spotted Woodpeckers, Tawny Owl, Kingfisher, Peregrine, Cetti's Warbler, Goldcrest, Nuthatch, Treecreeper.

Summer: Common Tern, Hobby, Swift, warblers.

Winter: Teal, Shoveler, Water Rail, Woodcock, Fieldfare, Redwing.

Migration: Red Kite, Skylark, hirundines, flycatchers, chats, pipits, wagtails, Siskin, Redpoll, Reed Bunting.

ACCESS

Bike: there is cycling throughout the heath.

Bus: South End Green is served by bus routes 88, 46, 168, 210, 214, 268, C11 and N5, which all stop on the heath's perimeter.

Train: Highgate, Hampstead and Golders Green Northern Line stations are all about 10 minutes from the heath. Hampstead Heath overground station is on the heath's south-west corner, while Gospel Oak is on the south side.

Car: in addition to the main area given above, paid parking is possible on many of the surrounding streets.

YOUR VISIT

London's most famous open green space is best visited at dawn for birding, as it becomes very popular during the day at all times of the year. That said, raptors are often possible from mid-morning, so don't write it off entirely after 9am. The sheer size of the site means that it can take half a day to cover with the tenacity needed to find the best birds.

Its position on an elevated ridge means that the view can be grand on a clear day, especially from Parliament Hill. It's not really a heath, the major habitats being acid grassland, ancient and secondary deciduous woodland and scrub, a few ponds (traditionally for swimming), plus plenty of mown grass. It's mostly within the borough of Camden, managed by the City of London Corporation, and encompasses Kenwood House stately home and its grounds.

Despite its overuse in place, there are quiet corners and regular patch watchers have seen some interesting species over the years. There appear to be a few regulars now, with an annual breeding bird survey and LNHS field meetings, and formerly under-watched areas such as the West Heath are getting coverage along with the more traditionally birded Parliament Hill scrub and cricket pitch area.

The site can be divided into two sections for birding purposes:

West – most accessible from Golders Green tube, this huge area includes the West Heath, Hampstead Heath Extension, Golders Hill Park and Sandy Heath. Much of it holds deciduous woodland, and there are plenty of birch trees fringing some boggy areas. The ponds in the extension are quite productive, as are the lines of trees adjacent.

East – closest to Highgate tube. Contains the bulk of the more well-known areas, including the less-disturbed grounds of Kenwood House, Parliament Hill and the two chains of bathing ponds. This is where most passerine passage occurs. The

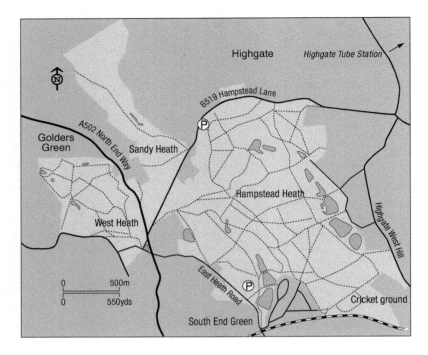

enclosed cricket pitch and some of the thicker scrub around Parliament Hill can be relatively fruitful, even when people are milling around.

The heath's most productive time is during passage periods, and visible migration in autumn can be good just after dawn, particularly at the top of Parliament Hill. Wheatear and Whinchat are often more common than Stonechat in spring and especially in autumn, when Ring Ouzel is possible, Swallows and martins pass through in numbers and warblers can be plentiful in the hedges. Redstart and Spotted Flycatcher are also found most years.

Summer raptor watching can produce fly-over Buzzard, Red Kite, Peregrine and Hobby, especially on warmer days. Winter produces Water Rail, and Woodcock is often present but rarely visible in the grounds of Kenwood House or at West Heath. Alders around the Sanctuary Pond are your best bet for winter finches.

Real surprises have happened over the years, with Gannet, Little Bittern, Bittern, Crane, Montagu's Harrier, Pomarine Skua, Lesser Kestrel and Alpine Swift all being logged.

INNER LONDON

49 REGENT'S PARK

Outer Circle, Marylebone, Westminster, London NW1 4RB
Website: regentsparkbirds.blogspot.com
Open: all day, every day
(197 hectares; 486.8 acres)

This large Central London park produces regular scarce migrants among its comprehensive array of commoner species.

SPECIES

All year: Gadwall, Peregrine, Tawny and Little Owls, common garden and park birds.

Summer: heronry, Hobby, commoner warblers.

Winter: Wigeon, Shoveler, Teal, Pintail, Water Rail, gulls, Redwing, Fieldfare, Goldcrest, Firecrest.

Migration: scarce wildfowl, raptors, hirundines, flycatchers, warblers, chats, finches.

ACCESS

Bus: numerous buses stop very close to the park.

Train: Baker Street, Regent's Park and Great Portland Street tube stations are all very close to the southern end of the park.

Car: NCP and metered parking options are available nearby but are expensive.

YOUR VISIT

Get there as early as possible – preferably during migration – as this park is a popular tourist attraction and recreational resource for residents and workers alike. The sun will also then be behind you when viewing most of the habitat. Perhaps the best place to start is at Clarence Gate, just to the north of Baker Street.

The lake is your first stop. It holds many feral ducks and geese among genuinely wild individuals. Some fully winged Mandarin Ducks and Red-crested Pochards may be present among the captive birds, so make sure you see a wild one! Please don't feed the Grey Herons.

Turning right over the bridge, and then left, you'll swing away from the lake, but stop at the bandstand to scan for Grey Wagtail; Common Sandpiper is regular during passage. There's a sizeable heronry visible in the trees, with up to 26 pairs of Grey Heron (it's the most urban in Europe), and any patch of reeds might hold a Reed Warbler or two in summer, as up to 16 pairs now breed.

Keep scanning the large expanse of sky, as vis mig can be very good (in an urban context), and you can expect Hobby, Peregrine (which nests nearby), hirundines

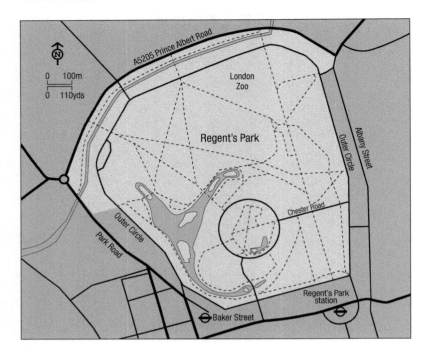

and various other songbirds. The second lake, on your right, has more ducks, including Gadwall and Teal, and a large Cormorant roost.

Continue uphill along the path and cross the Inner Circle road into Queen Mary's Gardens (by the Rose Garden Cafe). Pay particular attention to the more hidden areas, which regularly produce migrant warblers (and Spotted Flycatcher in autumn) – try the shrubbery to the west of the rose wheel.

The more mature trees support breeding Kestrel, Tawny Owl, Stock Dove and Green and Great Spotted Woodpeckers, while Mistle Thrush and other common songbirds forage on the lawns, occasionally joined by a passage Wheatear. Gulls are also attracted to the grass at times and have included Yellow-legged and Mediterranean.

Turn left on Inner Circle, and go through a second park entrance, turning right into the Cricket Pen, a small, enclosed area with trees that have feeders, where Brambling has occurred. This end of the adjacent lake isn't open to the public, but has attracted scarcer waterbirds such as Water Rail, Green Sandpiper and Jack Snipe.

Continue along the path at the northern end of the lake and scan the gorse and rough grassy areas, which are your best bet for Whinchat and Stonechat; there's an outside chance of migrants such as Ring Ouzel. Continue to the Hub Cafe – the sports grounds beyond attracts pipits, wagtails and Wheatear.

Further north-west, another enclosure is good for migrant songbirds, and has held both flycatchers, Firecrest and Wood Warbler. Now turn south-west towards the area known as the Blue Bridges (or Hanover Bridges), where a large reedbed has a channel cut through it, enabling a better chance to see Water Rail. Cetti's Warbler is now found in this area too.

Little Owl breeds, and can generally be found early in the day, just east of the Ready Money Drinking Fountain and the boardwalk that leads to London Zoo. Raptors are often spotted overhead, and regularly include Red Kite.

Regular watching by a few committed observers has revealed that the more sheltered bushes and trees attract Redstart and Pied Flycatcher annually; scarcities have included Lesser Scaup, Osprey, Honey-buzzard, Hoopoe, Wryneck, Red-footed Falcon, Melodious Warbler and Iberian Chiffchaff – and there was a fly-over Cory's Shearwater in September 2016! More than 210 species have been seen over the years, emphasising the park's importance as an urban migratory staging post.

50 HYDE PARK AND KENSINGTON GARDENS

Many entrances and gates surround the entire site
Website: kensingtongardensandhydeparkbirds.blogspot.com
Open: 6am–dusk. Parking is metered and expensive, as are the nearby NCP car parks.
(253 hectares; 625 acres)

A large green space in Inner London, holding most of the commoner woodland and garden species.

SPECIES

All year: Mandarin Duck, Gadwall, Shoveler, Peregrine, Tawny Owl, Cetti's Warbler, Nuthatch, Treecreeper, Goldcrest, Coal Tit, common garden and park birds.

Summer: House Martin, commoner warblers.

Winter: Shoveler, Teal, gulls, Redwing, Fieldfare.

Migration: wildfowl, Common Sandpiper, Common Tern, wagtails, pipits, hirundines, flycatchers, warblers, chats, finches.

ACCESS

Bus: numerous bus routes stop all around the park.

Train: several tube stations are found right on the edge of the park: Marble Arch, Lancaster Gate and Queensway (Central Line), and Hyde Park Corner (Piccadilly Line).

YOUR VISIT

Hyde Park and **Kensington Gardens** are the most productive of the Royal Parks. There is a good selection of habitats that hold most of the common garden and woodland species. It's a good site for first-time visitors to London and the UK to familiarise themselves with these birds before venturing further afield. While the two sites are separate, the combined area is divided by a single road (West Carriage Drive); they share a lake and main road and are considered as one site here.

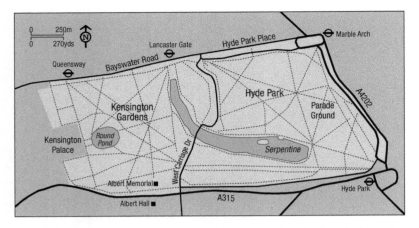

Despite heavy human usage, there are still good birds to be found. The earlier the better is the rule of thumb, and there are footpaths all over the site. Among the mown grass and manicured shrubs and trees, there are patches of rough grassland and wooded areas, and the lake – called the Serpentine in Hyde Park and the Longwater in Kensington Gardens – and Round Pond add to its avian attractions. Almost 200 species have been logged over the years.

There is no waterfowl collection here (thankfully). Concentrate most of your efforts on the areas of trees and bushes. Spring is the best time to locate Tawny Owl and other woodland species such as Nuthatch, Treecreeper and Goldcrest.

Unusual species that have appeared over the years include a long-staying White-winged Black Tern in September 2010 and a pair of Bearded Tits in the very limited Serpentine reeds in January 2013.

Nearby **St James's and Green Parks** form a continuous green area with this site, but they are generally less 'birdy'.

Also nearby, **Holland Park** (W8 6DN; TQ251793; entire.influencing.belong) is a slightly better bet and can be found just off Kensington High Street. Tawny Owl, Coal Tit (probably), Mistle Thrush and Jay provide interest.

51 MUDCHUTE PARK AND MUDCHUTE CITY FARM

Pier Street, Isle of Dogs, London E14 3HP
TQ383788; scan.spits.tins
Phone: 020 7515 5901
Email: info@mudchute.org
Open: there is general access to all the areas all day, every day, but the farm is only open from 10am–4pm.
(13 hectares; 32 acres)

A local park in East London that attracts scarcer migrants and has a small resident population of 'untickable' Monk Parakeets.

SPECIES

Almost all common species.

ACCESS

Bus: routes 277 and N277 (Dalston Junction–Limehouse) stop at Mudchute DLR.

Train: Mudchute station is on the DLR, and trains are every few minutes. It's also possible to alight at Island Gardens and enter through Millwall Park.

Car: there is minimal parking on the surrounding streets for which you may need to pay for a temporary permit. For shorter visits, it's possible to use the Asda car park adjacent.

YOUR VISIT

This park, at the south end of the Isle of Dogs, is worth a visit in spring, winter or autumn for common and scarce migrants or to check the gulls on the river, perhaps while taking in its small population of Monk Parakeets (though they are not yet countable). Visit it in tandem with the adjacent Millwall Park to maximise its limited potential.

The park and farm comprise mostly open grazing, tall trees and scrub. Migration is the best time to visit: commoner warblers sing in spring, flycatchers and chats pop up in the trees, and there's a chance of Ring Ouzel on the paddocks, with the pipits and wagtails. House Sparrow is resident (about the closest it gets to Central London these days). Redwing, Fieldfare and finches visit in winter, Firecrest is present most years.

The site is easily combined with a low-tide visit to the Thames foreshore at Saunders Ness for gulls by crossing the road at the southern end. Yellow-legged Gull is regular, and rarer sightings have included a long-staying Ring-billed Gull, plus Mediterranean, Iceland, Caspian and Little. Leave the Mudchute Equestrian Centre via Pier Street, cross the A1206 and turn right, then turn left onto Newcastle Draw Dock, and left again onto the Thames Path to view the mud.

The parakeets can usually be found in the Undine Road and Falcon Way areas by Mudchute station if they're not on site, and you should see their large stick nests in the London Planes there.

ESSEX

Despite not being the first county that comes to mind when productive birding is mentioned, Essex punches well above its weight, with 389 species having been noted within its recording area at the time of writing – that's three more species than Hampshire and 62 per cent of the BBRC's British List.

Its countryside is often dominated by crop monoculture but there are many ecologically sound locations peppered around the county – especially on the coast. Essex's share of the Thames Estuary, along with the substantial size of the Blackwater estuary and its tributaries, ensures that its coast is of international importance for wildfowl and waders, and there are many sites and reserves that will help you see breathtaking numbers of these species on migration and during winter. There are broad expanses of marshes with typical East Anglian species sometimes present in numbers; Bittern is still scarce but you can expect Marsh Harrier and Bearded Tit. There are sizeable woodlands, meaning that Nightingale and Firecrest are likely and Lesser Spotted Woodpecker, Marsh Tit and a few Hawfinches hang on. Essex manages to sustain perhaps one fifth of the UK's remnant Turtle Dove population.

Most sites detailed here are within an hour's drive of London and well worthy of a day trip or longer visit.

For fascinating and detailed information on Essex and its birds, turn to *The Birds of Essex* by Simon Wood (2007) to discover the county in depth.

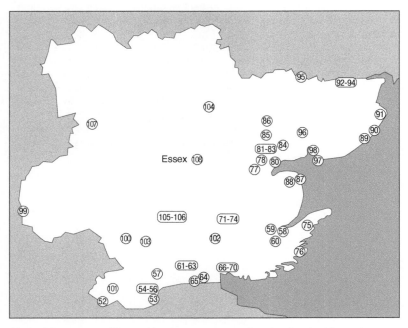

Map of the county of Essex. Numbers correspond to the sites in this section.

COASTAL ESSEX

52 WEST THURROCK MARSHES

Parking: St Clements Church, St Clement's Rd, Grays RM20 4AL
TQ592772; areas.pines.flops
SSSI
(40 hectares; 98.84 acres)

A riverside site with a good selection of waders during winter and migration.

This disused industrial site is past its prime now the outflow has stopped, and the formerly boggy ash lagoons are dry, but it can still be good for viewing Thames-side waders and gulls on a rising or ebbing tide, and Jack Snipe remains possible in winter.

There are remnants of saltmarsh by the river and extensive mudflats at low tide, which can produce a good range of coastal waders, including Grey Plover. Inland there is a substantial area of birches and hawthorns, and some reedbeds and ditches. Overall, the site produces good migrants and the odd surprise.

West Thurrock Lagoon and Marshes were designated an SSSI for the importance of its flooded ash lagoons for wildfowl and waders. Nowadays, the lagoons have gone, leaving black, muddy paths and scrub, though the location is still an insect-rich brownfield site. Currently, it's classified by NE as being in 'an unfavourable condition', and one can only hope that remedial management by the EWT will improve West Thurrock's status as a wetland once more.

This site is still worth visiting when the extensive mudflats are revealed at low tide – probably the greatest expanse in the LNHS recording area. A typical late winter or early spring visit can turn up great numbers of waders such as Avocet, Curlew, Redshank, Lapwing, Snipe, Dunlin and Black-tailed Godwit. Luck or regular visits can supply the likes of Whimbrel, Jack Snipe, Bar-tailed Godwit, Sanderling, Spotted Redshank and Little Stint. Bring a scope!

Currently, there is no public access to the marshes themselves, although people do enter, particularly dirt-bike riders. The habitat is in a parlous state as far as birds are concerned but winter thrushes and finches, Peregrine and Hobby are all possible.

Park by St Clements Church (as featured in the movie *Four Weddings and a Funeral*) and take the footpath opposite through the scrub towards the Thames, then head west along the seawall. Ensign bus 44 (Purfleet–Grays) stops at The Ship, West Thurrock, from where you can walk to the Thames. By train, alight at Grays or Purfleet on the London Fenchurch Street line, then walk along the Thames west from Grays or east from Purfleet.

THE EAST TILBURY AREA

Classic riverine and farmland site, with good migration watching and new nature reserves supporting scarcer breeders.

East Tilbury and Coalhouse Fort have long been known as productive birding sites, with a long history of famous rarities and plenty of scarcities.

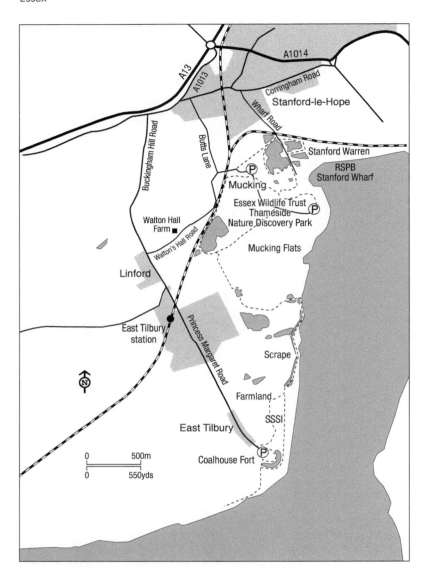

The area used to involve taking a long walk along the seawall, scanning inland and across the Thames, perhaps before or after popping into Mucking to check out Stanford Warren. This is still the case, but the habitats are much more 'joined up' now, with much of the former landfill site scheduled to become a nature reserve or country park. Long, partly circular walks are now possible.

Most of the habitats are accessible to the public, and there are a few joggers and dog-walkers, but the area is big and wild enough to support several choice species in good numbers and provide moments of quiet contemplation. It's on the Thames Path route and the whole area can be walked over a day, though it's a bit of a maze.

SPECIES

All year: Oystercatcher, Avocet, Barn Owl, Skylark, Meadow Pipit, Stonechat, Cetti's Warbler, Yellowhammer, Reed and Corn Buntings.

Summer: Little Ringed Plover, Cuckoo, Nightingale, Lesser Whitethroat, Grasshopper Warbler.

Winter: Lapwing, Ringed and Grey Plovers, Curlew, Redshank, Green Sandpiper, Dunlin, Black-tailed Godwit, Short-eared Owl, Water and Rock Pipits.

Migration: waders, seabirds, Common, Arctic, Sandwich, Little and Black Terns, Caspian, Yellow-legged, Mediterranean and Little Gulls, Whimbrel, Bar-tailed Godwit, Curlew, Wood and Common Sandpipers, Little Stint, Greenshank, Wheatear, Whinchat, Garden Warbler.

53 EAST TILBURY AND COALHOUSE FORT

Parking: Princess Margaret Road, East Tilbury, Essex RM18 8QD
Website: www.thurrock.gov.uk/coalhouse-fort-park/overview
Open: all day, every day
SSSI
(37.4 hectares; 92.42 acres)

After parking by Coalhouse Fort, there are a number of locations to visit and if you've arrived during migration, it's best to check everywhere.

Starting in the car park itself, it's worth scanning the arable field just beyond, as well as sifting through the songbird flocks in the hedges and trees, as warblers, flycatchers and finches are a feature of spring and autumn there.

You can now walk either side of the fort. The right-hand side takes you to a large, abandoned water tower, where a final short path enables you to walk out onto the mud and check east and west along the river foreshore. In spring and autumn, there will be hordes of wading birds away from high tide, and a rising tide will bring them very close to you. You're out in the open, so use the tower's struts to conceal yourself (and shelter from the wind). Everything from Whimbrel to Little Stint – even Semipalmated Sandpiper – has been seen from this vantage point.

The left-hand choice takes you around the north end of the moat, which holds dozens of Little Grebes in winter and provides rocks for Common and Green Sandpipers. You can either follow the edge of the moat to the Thames and walk the seawall east or take the path on the northern side of the SSSI scrub area. The southern option allows you to watch the saltmarsh, where Marsh Harrier and occasionally Short-eared Owl hunt. The northern option adds a few farmland birds to your day list, and the chance of Little, and once or twice Cattle Egret feeding among the sheep. You can also walk straight across the SSSI, checking for larks, pipits, warblers and finches. Grasshopper Warbler breeds (five pairs in recent years) and Dartford Warbler occasionally overwinters.

All three paths converge on the seawall again just before it reaches the fairly new scrape, which is tucked just inland and easily viewable without leaving the path. The habitat there is still developing but includes areas of shallow water, shingle, sand, low vegetation, reeds and trees. Much of your time is best spent checking this area, as winter ducks are plentiful and include Wigeon and Pintail, while waders pop in, particularly at high tide. Among the common species, Little Stint and Curlew Sandpiper are regular and come relatively close, though there will be more distant waders on the mudflats next to the Thames, viewed better at the far eastern end of the scrape. Unusual visitors to the scrape have included three long-staying Stone Curlews (in 2022) and a few Pectoral Sandpipers.

The Thames mud can hold stupendous numbers of Dunlin, Avocet, Lapwing, Black-tailed Godwits and Grey Plovers in autumn (fewer in spring), and scarcer species join them, including Spotted Redshank, Little Stint and Curlew Sandpiper. In late summer, more than 80 Yellow-legged Gulls can assemble.

Spring sees the best numbers of Whimbrel and Bar-tailed Godwits, though some also pass through later in the year. The Thames is also quite good for seabirds, especially during rough weather and easterly blows – expect gulls and terns, with the chance of skuas and others.

Taking up a perch by the scrape also increases your chances of passerine action, and late summer and autumn can see hirundines in their hundreds whizzing over the seawall, while finches, wagtails, pipits and buntings all fly through. The seawall provides brief respite for Stonechat and Wheatear, while Whinchat can be perched on inland vegetation. Dartford Warbler is becoming more regular.

At this point, many turn back to the car park satisfied, but you can continue further east along the seawall to join Thurrock Thameside Nature Park EWT (page 127), a route that should provide you with Nightingale and Grasshopper Warbler in spring.

Parking is currently free by the fort (though there are unpopular moves afoot to start charging), where there are also a cafe and toilets.

54 STANFORD WARREN EWT

Parking: St John the Baptist church, Mucking Wharf Road, Stanford-le-Hope SS17 0RN (there are about four spaces on the verge), or nearby Thurrock Thameside Nature Park (see page 127)
Website: www.essexwt.org.uk/nature-reserves/stanford-warren
TQ685811; foam.fuel.runs
Open: all day, every day
SSSI
(15.38 hectares; 38 acres)

Inland to the north-east of Coalhouse Fort is one of the largest reedbeds in Essex: Stanford Warren, a former gravel pit and a hidden gem of a reserve.

The Warren and adjacent fisheries hold good numbers of Nightingale and Cuckoo in summer, and Cetti's Warbler and a few (very elusive) Bearded Tit are resident, the latter in very small numbers.

A spring and early summer dawn arrival is energising as summer visitors such as Nightingale and various warblers will be plentiful and deafening as they defend their territories. There will be a few Lesser Whitethroats, too, though the breeding Turtle Doves have disappeared. Water Rail is resident and Little Egret is now almost certain to be seen.

A visit to Stanford Warren can easily be combined with Thurrock Thameside and even East Tilbury for the hardier walker.

55 THURROCK THAMESIDE NATURE PARK EWT

Mucking Wharf Road, Mucking, Stanford-Le-Hope, Essex SS17 0RN (80 spaces)
Website: www.essexwt.org.uk/nature-reserves/thurrock-thameside
TQ696806; boost.latter.claps
Phone: 01375 643342
Email: ttnp@essexwt.org.uk
Open: 8.30am–4.30pm (reserve); 10am–5pm (VC)
Ramsar, SSSI, SPA
(97.12 hectares; 240 acres)

What can be rather a bleak, open area also provides a good spot for watching migration and observing waders closely.

After leaving the main car park, follow the footpath to the hide (TQ698805; those.wicked.mutual), which overlooks Mucking Flats (aka RSPB Stanford Wharf, below). For the best wader watching, arrive in the period a couple of hours either side of high tide; otherwise, the birds will be very distant or roosting elsewhere.

Other footpaths around the site lead from Crown Green Cottage (TQ687810; market.horses.best) close to Mucking church, or Mucking Creek Sluice Gate to the north (TQ691808; hurry.twigs.plant), which is accessible via Stanford Warren (see page 126).

The nature reserve was created from the dredgings and refuse of the old Mucking Tip. Opened by David Attenborough in 2013, it has a VC that also allows great views over Mucking Flats and the Thames, with a café, shop, picnic tables and a playground. The car park is a good place to watch Stonechats. The completed park will comprise 342 hectares (845 acres) of habitat, mostly open grassland and scrub away from the river, with a few small clumps of trees.

The grassland has healthy populations of Meadow Pipit, Skylark and Stonechat, which attract Cuckoo in spring. Passage periods feature Wheatear and Whinchat.

Most of the reserve's birding reputation relies on those dramatic views of the Thames, viewable best from the VC's rooftop decking with its 360° viewing area. The view is stunning, but you'll need to go to the hide instead if you arrive before opening hours.

Expect Internationally Important numbers of Avocet and Ringed Plover, and Nationally Important flocks of Black-tailed Godwit, Grey Plover, Dunlin and Redshank – similar foreshore species to the rest of the area, in fact.

56 RSPB STANFORD WHARF

Wharf Rd, Stanford-le-Hope, Essex SS17 0EE
TQ693811; limes.page.camps.
Website: www.rspb.org.uk/reserves-and-events/reserves-a-z/stanford-wharf/
Phone: 01268 498620
Email: southessex@rspb.org.uk
Open: all day, every day
SSSI, SPA.
(35 hectares; 86.49 acres)

For a slightly closer look at the wading birds on Mucking Flats, this tiny RSPB reserve – formerly known as Shell Haven – was designated as compensatory habitat for intertidal marshes lost during the London Gateway Port Development. It's accessible from Stanford Warren (see page 126) via the boardwalk that leads off to the right (TQ688814; dress.island.acute) from the main path as you walk from St John the Baptist Church, or more directly at the end of Wharf Road (TQ692812; badly.delay.loose). If you choose this option, you can use the parking by the fishery (the other car parks are private).

The mudflats can be scoped from the start of the narrow promontory (TQ696808; mixer.memory.weeks) at the end of Wharf Road. The reserve is an intertidal mudflat directly opposite RSPB Cliffe Pools (see page 198). Note that Mucking Creek, the narrow river that borders the promontory, can only be crossed in Stanford Warren via the rickety bridge over the sluice (TQ691808; hurry.twigs.plant).

57 FOBBING MARSH NATURE RESERVE EWT

Marsh Lane, Fobbing, Essex
Parking: High Road, Fobbing
TQ716844; funny.crab.smiles
Website: www.essexwt.org.uk/nature-reserves/fobbing-marsh
LWS, SSSI
(75.67 hectares; 187 acres)

To the south of Wat Tyler CP (see page 134) and north-east of RSPB Stanford Wharf, next to Holehaven Creek, is this area of remnant grazing marsh, a haven for migrants on the western edge of Vange Creek. To reach this very isolated site you have to walk for more than 1 mile (1.6km) along the undrivable Marsh Lane track from High Road, Fobbing.

The walk is picturesque, and Yellow Wagtail, Wheatear and Whinchat can pop up almost anywhere en route during migration, while Corn Bunting and Yellowhammer still breed. It's worth visiting in winter too, as wintering harriers, falcons and owls can all be present, and grazing Wigeon and Teal are present in numbers.

58 RSPB WALLASEA ISLAND

Creeksea Ferry Rd, Rochford, Essex SS4 2HD
Website: www.rspb.org.uk/reserves-and-events/reserves-a-z/wallasea-island
TQ955945; cleans.dinner.hillsides
Phone: 01268 498620
Email: wallasea@rspb.org.uk
Open: all day, every day. There are no facilities on-site, but nearby villages have basic amenities
SPA
(740 hectares; 1,828.6 acres)

An expansive scarcity magnet that hosts impressive numbers of waders and wildfowl in winter, along with raptors and Short-eared Owls.

SPECIES

All year: Shelduck, Great Egret, Spoonbill, Marsh Harrier, Avocet, Oystercatcher, Ringed Plover, Redshank, Mediterranean Gull, Peregrine, Skylark, Corn and Reed Buntings.

Summer: Little Ringed Plover, Hobby, Swallow, Yellow Wagtail.

Winter: Dark-bellied Brent Goose, Shoveler, Teal, Wigeon, Red-throated Diver, Hen Harrier, Greenshank, Grey and Golden Plovers, Knot, Dunlin, Curlew, Bar-tailed and Black-tailed Godwits, Short-eared Owl, Merlin, Rock and Water Pipits.

Migration: Green, Common, Curlew and Wood Sandpipers, Whimbrel, terns, Wheatear, Whinchat.

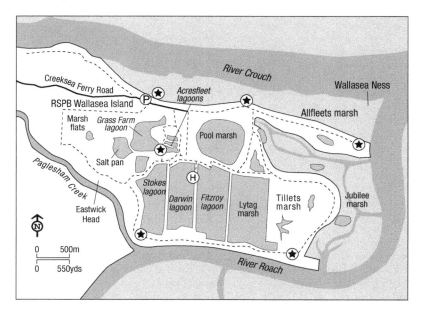

ACCESS

Bike: cycling is not allowed on site but there is a bike rack at the entrance.

Bus: Stephenson's route 60 (Paglesham–Southend-on-Sea) stops at Loftman's Corner, Canewdon, about 1 mile (1.6 km) from the entrance. Walk or cycle east from Canewdon to Creeksea Ferry Road for the entrance.

Train: the nearest station is Rochford, about 6.5 miles (10.5 km) from the entrance.

Car: once on Creeksea Ferry Road, continue past the off-road centre and holiday camp until you get to the reserve car park. The road is narrow but there are passing bays along most of its length. Keep an eye on the fields for geese and raptors.

YOUR VISIT

Nestled between Burnham-on-Crouch, Foulness and Potton Islands and one of a small group of islands between the Crouch and Roach estuaries, this RSPB-managed reserve covers a mosaic of mudflats, open sea, tidal river, saltmarsh, saline lagoons, ditches, wetland, grassland and grazing marsh, abutted by arable farmland.

Large and rich enough to attract almost all the interesting species possible on the Essex coast, Wallasea allows views over excellent estuarine and coastal habitat on three sides. Allow several hours to cover the area effectively – the seawall is about 5.6 miles (9 km) long. Any visit to Wallasea Island will provide a long day list, and wintering wildfowl and wader numbers have topped 30,000 recently, with Brent Geese alone making up almost 8,000 birds in the area. The numbers of Wigeon can also be rather impressive, with 4,149 logged in December 2020.

The reserve was created from 3 million tonnes of earth taken from London's Crossrail/Elizabeth Line tunnel excavations, which allowed the RSPB to raise it above sea level. A system of sluices controls water levels in the saline lagoons, while cattle graze the wet grassland, maintaining it for breeding and roosting waders, and hunting harriers and owls.

You have a choice of three mostly unsurfaced walking routes from the car park (where there is also a festival-style portable toilet): the Jubilee Marsh, Allfleets Marsh and Marsh Flat trails, but the RSPB says it will create more. These can be combined in a longer, site-wide walk if you wish.

Jubilee Marsh Trail – 1.5 miles (2.4 km) long, leading eastwards between the River Crouch and the lagoons. It leads south between Jubilee Marsh and the wet grassland and ends up at a shelter overlooking the River Roach.

Allfleets Marsh Trail – 2 miles (3.2 km) long, taking in a peninsula along the Crouch, between Allfleets Marsh and Jubilee Marsh, passing some of the lagoons. A shelter at the eastern end allows comfortable views over the confluence of the Rivers Crouch and Roach.

Marsh Flat Trail – a circular 2.7-mile (4.4-km) trail passing the Grass Farm and Acresfleet lagoons, some grazing marsh and wet grassland.

The site is great at any time of the year and holds different arrays of birds depending on the season.

Summer sees healthy breeding populations of Avocet and Little Ringed Plover. Migration will bring waders aplenty, both on the reserve and the surrounding river estuaries. These include everything from Grey and Golden Plovers to Whimbrel, both godwits and a profusion of stints and sandpipers. Because of the mix of saline and freshwater, species such as Wood Sandpiper and Greenshank also appear in small numbers. Waders become more plentiful in autumn when hirundines, chats and warblers also begin piling through.

Winter provides great spectacles. While Brent Goose numbers are larger at some other sites, Wigeon, Teal, Pintail and other ducks are present in their hundreds or thousands. The notable flocks of Dunlin and other waders on the mud are often strafed by a marauding Peregrine or Merlin. Black-tailed Godwit numbers on site are Internationally Important. Spoonbill and Great Egret have become more regular.

The estuaries provide seaduck, including Red-breasted Merganser, along with Red-throated Diver and, less often, Slavonian Grebe. Mediterranean Gull gatherings can be well into three figures in summer. Onshore, Kingfisher hunt along the reedy channels and Bearded Tit thread the reeds. The site becomes raptor central in winter, with Marsh and Hen Harriers (up to three, some winters), Peregrine and Merlin all present, and Short-eared Owl likely. Rough-legged Buzzard has wintered twice in recent years, while autumn 2023 produced a long-staying juvenile Pallid Harrier.

The lagoon islands support nesting Avocets, Black-headed Gulls and Common Terns in summer, with numerous singing Skylarks, a few Yellow Wagtails and Reed and Corn Buntings. Marsh Harriers also breed, nesting deep in the reeds, and can be watched 'sky-dancing'.

59 NEARBY: LION CREEK EWT TO LOWER RAYPITS EWT

Creeksea Ferry Road, Rochford, Essex SS4 3PW
Website: www.essexwt.org.uk/nature-reserves/lion-creek-lower-raypits
TQ927947; desk.mavericks.goats
(16.19 hectares; 40 acres)

This seawall walk not far from the entrance to Wallasea Island can be relatively eventful and taken in as part of the same trip.

Park in the lay-by near the entrance of **Lion Creek**, which holds about three cars, and take the public footpath about 80 m to the south-west, which follows the River Crouch.

The mud, river and saltmarsh of the reserve hold hundreds of roosting ducks, geese and waders in winter, featuring many of the same species as at the RSPB reserve. You can also walk further to the permissive footpaths and enter the hides at **Lower Raypits** (46.54 hectares; 115 acres), where the habitat is specifically managed to help waders breed.

This short walk gives you a further chance of Marsh and Hen Harriers, and Short-eared Owl too. The surrounding fields can also hold Brent Geese, and small numbers of White-fronted and even Tundra Bean Geese have been seen.

60 NEARBY: PAGLESHAM LAGOON

TQ924915; humidity.puddings.laughs

This area of open water is officially named Stannets Creek Reservoir, and its situation close to the banks of the tidal River Roach means that it attracts regular scarce seaduck, grebes and divers, particularly in bad weather. In winter there are also plentiful goose flocks on the fields, which are quartered by the odd raptor.

However, it can be a bit of a slog to get there. To reach the closest parking place, leave Rochford on Stambridge Road to the T-junction, turn right onto Gore Road and take the next right east onto Paglesham Road at the Shepherd & Dog pub to Jubilee Cottages, where you can park. Follow the footpath to your left by the tiny Paglesham Congregational church building, then the often very muddy footpaths along the stream to the reservoir.

Another route is easier but is further away: park by Stambridge Meadows care home and walk two miles to the end of Hampton Barn Lane onto the uneven footpath opposite the north end of the lay-by in front of the care home; this goes east to the lagoon.

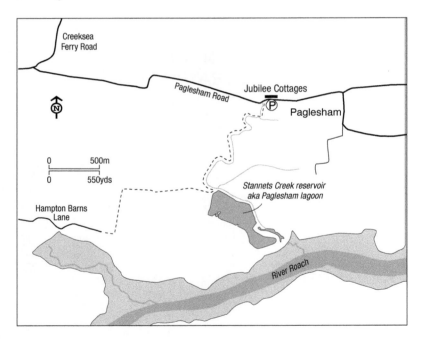

BENFLEET TO CANVEY ISLAND
61 RSPB VANGE MARSH

RSPB South Essex Visitor Centre, Wat Tyler CP, Pitsea Hall Lane, Pitsea, Basildon, Essex SS16 4UH
Website: www.rspb.org.uk/reserves-and-events/reserves-a-z/vange-marsh
TQ731871; yards.blank.gifted
Phone: 01268 498620
Email: southessex@rspb.org.uk
Open: all day, every day
Vange has very limited wheelchair access and unsurfaced, often muddy footpaths. Turn right at the level crossing and walk west to the entrance. Once you're through the kissing gate, you have a choice of footpaths leading you through scrub and along low bunds, from which you can scope the somewhat distant pools.
(4.5 hectares; 11.12 acres)

A reclaimed patchwork of wetland, fields and scrub that holds breeding Avocets and Little Ringed Plovers and has a burgeoning reputation for attracting scarce migrants.

SPECIES
All year: Shelduck, Gadwall, Shoveler, Marsh Harrier, Water Rail, Snipe, Avocet, Redshank, Oystercatcher, Ringed Plover, Barn Owl, Kingfisher, Peregrine, Cetti's Warbler, Bearded Tit.

Summer: Little Ringed Plover, Common Tern, Hobby, Swift, hirundines, warblers.

Winter: Wigeon, Teal, Pintail, Greenshank, Grey and Golden Plovers, Ruff, Dunlin, Curlew, Black-tailed Godwit, Jack Snipe.

Passage: Garganey, Little Stint, Common, Green, Wood and Curlew Sandpipers, Spotted Redshank, Bar-tailed Godwit, Whimbrel.

ACCESS
Bike: good bike trails connect Vange Marsh with Wat Tyler CP (page 134) and Bowers Marsh (page 135), crossing the entire reserve.

Bus: route 5 (Basildon–Pitsea) serves the stop at Tesco, Pitsea, less than a 10-minute walk from the reserve.

Train: The closest railway station is Pitsea on the c2c line out of London Fenchurch Street; the exit is 600m from the reserve entrance.

Car: leave the A13 at the junction for Pitsea and follow the brown tourist signs for Wat Tyler CP. Park for free at Wat Tyler CP, or in Pitsea station's pay-and-display car park to your left, just before the level crossing.

YOUR VISIT
This compact but productive reserve is sandwiched between the A13 and Pitsea Creek, where there is a small saline pool, plus a larger brackish pool covering most of the reserve's surface area. It's part of, and contiguous with, the much

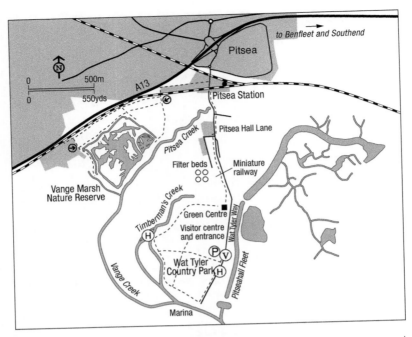

larger SSSI area that comprises the 164.6 hectares (407 acres) of Vange and Fobbing Marshes.

From the entrance kissing gate, the saline lagoon can be viewed by following the track to a viewing screen overlooking the open water. You'll pass a reedbed to your left that hosts the usual species, plus the odd Water Rail and Bearded Tit (both breed).

More of the brackish pool can be seen when walking directly on from the kissing gate for about 0.5 mile (0.9km) along the pool's northern shore, which will take you to a raised bank, from which the marshy areas and wildfowl and waders can be scanned. The whole site is open to the elements.

62 NEARBY: WAT TYLER CP

Website: www.rspb.org.uk/reserves-and-events/reserves-a-z/south-essex-wildlife-garden
SSSI
50.6 hectares (125 acres)

Wat Tyler CP is formed from former munitions works, now transformed into grassland and hawthorn scrub (with a little woodland). It's bordered by tidal creeks and saltings to its south and west, and Pitsea Hall Fleet to the east, where there is a large reedbed. Two hides (with disabled access) overlook the fleet. A key is available from either VC.

Several trails cross the park, one of which is surfaced and suitable for wheelchairs. You can also get to the trails via the Green Centre and marina car parks.

Perhaps the best route around takes in the perimeter of the CP and extends about 1.2 miles (2km) on a hard, level tarmac surface. This will enable you to visit both hides and explore the creeks, pools, woodland and marshland. It can easily be combined with a visit to Vange.

The VC next to the main car park has a shop, toilets and café.

63 NEARBY: RSPB BOWERS MARSH

Church Rd, Bowers Gifford, Basildon SS13 2HG
Website: www.rspb.org.uk/reserves-and-events/reserves-a-z/bowers-marsh
TQ755867; manual.dress.decreased
Phone: 01268 498620
Email: southessex@rspb.org.uk
Open: all day, every day (car park 9am–5pm, or dusk if earlier)
(270 hectares; 667.19 acres)

ACCESS

Bus: route 22 (Basildon–Canvey) stops on the B1464 nearby. Alight and use the subway underneath the A13 to reach Church Road for the entrance.

Train: the nearest stations are Benfleet (1.7 miles; 2.3km) or Pitsea (2.3 miles; 4km), on the busy c2c Fenchurch Street–Shoeburyness line. From Benfleet, turn right at the end of Station Approach, right down Brackendale Avenue, and follow the public footpath alongside the railway line to turn right onto Church Road.

Car: leave the A13 onto Broadway Link (signposted 'Pitsea centre') and turn right onto London Road (B1464) towards Basildon Crematorium. Turn right onto Church Road at the mini-roundabout following the brown tourist sign, turning left at the T-junction to the car park.

YOUR VISIT

Bowers Marsh is a relatively new RSPB reserve situated between Pitsea station and Benfleet station in South Essex and attracting similar birds to RSPB Vange Marshes and Wat Tyler CP. With saline and freshwater lagoons, plus a large area of restored grazing marsh, this reserve has already attracted a wide variety of species, including breeding Avocets. In April 2020, a pair of Black-winged Stilts was present – the seventh year in a row a pair had appeared in southern Essex, exciting hopes of breeding. Two pairs of Bearded Tits breed on site, while there were five pairs of Grasshopper Warbler in 2020.

There's no VC, but it does have a picnic area, along with 4 miles (6km) of trails of varying lengths and evenness, and three viewpoints. There are public footpaths on site, including the Manor Way, which the RSPB has extended to enable easy access for walkers, horseriders and cyclists.

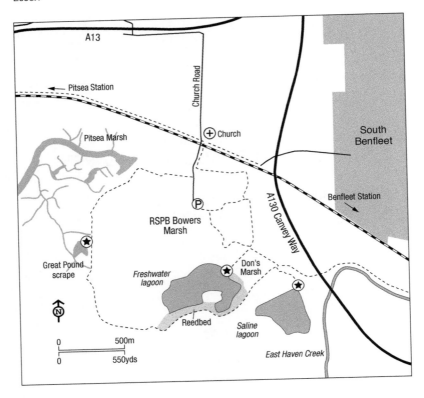

64 RSPB WEST CANVEY MARSH

Canvey Road, Canvey Island, Essex SS8 0QR.
Website: www.rspb.org.uk/reserves-and-events/reserves-a-z/west-canvey-marsh
TQ775842; player.trial.strike
(30 hectares; 74.13 acres)

SPECIES

All year: Shelduck, Gadwall, Shoveler, Little Egret, Marsh Harrier, Snipe, Redshank, Oystercatcher, Lapwing, Reed Bunting.

Summer: Hobby, Swift, warblers, hirundines.

Winter: Brent Goose, Wigeon, Teal, Greenshank, Grey and Golden Plovers, Dunlin, Curlew, Black-tailed Godwit, Peregrine, Merlin.

Migration: Common and Green Sandpipers, Whimbrel, Common, Green and Wood Sandpipers, Wheatear, Whinchat.

YOUR VISIT

West Canvey is a somewhat bleak but surprisingly bird-rich site surrounded by industrial sites and roads. Its 2-mile (3.2-km) network of wet grassland (often dry), reedbeds and scrapes has plenty of dragonflies (attracting Hobbies in summer), as well as Skylarks and Swallows.

Three viewpoints overlook the more productive areas. Winter often sees a Short-eared Owl quartering the grass for voles, along with Marsh Harrier, Peregrine and the occasional Merlin. Spring thrills with displaying Lapwings, Redshanks and Oystercatchers.

Migration brings Green and Common Sandpipers to the creek and Curlews to the fields, while winter hosts hordes of wildfowl, including large numbers of Wigeon.

Leaving the spacious gravel car park, you can take the 0.5-mile (0.8-km) or 2-mile (3.2-km) trails. The former is circular and follows the edges of the grassland and hedges, allowing access to the Roadside Hide, which overlooks a lagoon. The long route allows you to observe the grazing marsh, lagoons, grassland and seawall from two hides and a few viewpoints.

The whole site is accessible to wheelchair users (except the seawall); the kissing gates can be opened with a RADAR key.

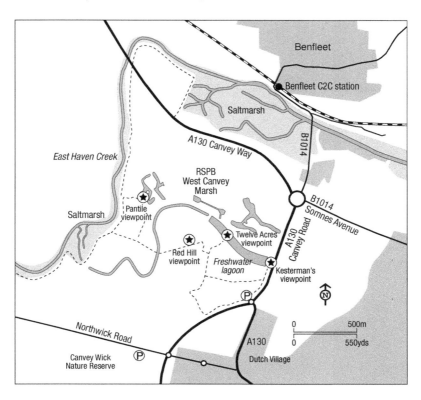

65 NEARBY: RSPB CANVEY WICK

276 Northwick Rd, Canvey Island, Essex SS8 0PT
Website: www.rspb.org.uk/reserves-and-events/reserves-a-z/canvey-wick
TQ766837; pans.tricks.speak
Phone: 01268 498620
Email: southessex@rspb.org.uk
Open: all day, every day
SSSI
(93.2 hectares; 230.3 acres)

Part-managed by the RSPB and Buglife, Canvey Wick is a former industrial site strewn with grassland, scrub and estuarine habitats owned by The Land Trust.

Spring sees commoner migrants arriving, with most warblers breeding. Several singing Nightingales are vociferous early in the season, and Skylark and Yellow Wagtail breed. Winter sees Stonechats on land, while the commoner waders and wildfowl assemble offshore.

The site is served by the 21 bus route (alight at Canvey Village Morrisons) and the nearest train station is Benfleet (London Fenchurch Street–Shoeburyness), 3.7 miles (6km) to the north. The reserve is signposted from the A130.

THE SOUTHEND-ON-SEA AREA
Despite its burgeoning commuter population and urban sprawl, Southend and its surrounding towns and countryside are surprisingly bird-rich due to its Continent- and estuary-facing aspect, coastal location, extensive mudflats, and good variety of habitats. There are several sites worth visiting.

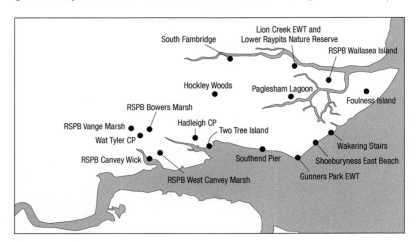

SPECIES
All year: Shelduck, Peregrine, Water Rail, Avocet, Redshank, Oystercatcher, Ringed Plover, Cetti's Warbler, Bullfinch.

Summer: Cuckoo, Swift, Swallow, Nightingale, commoner warblers.

Winter: Brent Goose, Wigeon, Teal, Shoveler, Pintail, Curlew, gulls, Merlin, Kingfisher, Short-eared Owl, Redwing, Fieldfare.

Migration: seabirds, commoner waders, Whimbrel, Little Stint, Curlew Sandpiper, Bar-tailed and Black-tailed Godwits, Greenshank, Grey and Golden Plovers, Knot, Dunlin, gulls, terns, skuas, auks, warblers including Yellow-browed, chats, finches.

66 SOUTHEND PIER

Marine Parade, Southend-on-Sea, Essex SS1 2EH
TQ884850; mild.really.gross

Essex's premier site for Mediterranean Gull. Several are usually present at the far end by the lifeboat bay all year, with the biggest numbers at the end of the breeding season. Turnstones also roost on the pier's iron supports (with occasional Purple Sandpipers).

When the tide is out, the pier offers an excellent place to scan the myriad geese and waders – Brent Goose, Oystercatcher, Redshank, Ringed Plover, Dunlin and Sanderling are the most likely species – and it's good for passage and winter seawatching when the tide is in. Sandwich Tern, Kittiwake and the odd Shag pass by, while a full array of seabirds has been logged, with divers, terns and auks all possible when winds are in the north-east sector. There have been day counts of more than 100 Red-throated Divers.

The 1.34-mile (2.16-km) pier can be walked easily, or you can catch the mini-train to the end for a £3 return ticket. There are plenty of pay-and-display car parks nearby, including roadside bays very close to the pier entrance, and it's a 10-minute walk from Southend Central station.

67 NEARBY: POUND, BELFAIRS AND WEST WOODS

POUND WOOD NR EWT
St Michael's Rd, Thundersley, Benfleet, Essex SS7 2UW
Website: www.essexwt.org.uk/nature-reserves/pound-wood
TQ815888; labels.method.soil
(22.26 hectares; 55 acres)

BELFAIRS WOOD EWT
Eastwood Road North, Leigh-on-Sea, Essex SS9 4LR
Website: www.essexwt.org.uk/nature-reserves/belfairs
TQ832874; export.agreed.relay
(469 hectares; 1,158.92 acres)

WEST WOOD NATURE RESERVE EWT

Hedge Lane, Hadleigh, Essex SS7 2SQ
Website: www.essexwt.org.uk/nature-reserves/west-wood
TQ806878; hooks.flown.vague
(23.47 hectares; 58 acres)

These three allied forest fragments are the most bird-rich of the county's biggest remaining area of ancient woodland. Hawfinch can be present in winter – historically up to ten have been seen, particularly around the Wombat Bridge area (TQ805881; desire.motel.upper), though one or two is more likely. Woodcock may have bred and is certainly present in winter, as is Firecrest sometimes.

Scarcities such as Golden Oriole and Nightjar are occasionally found in spring, but Marsh Tit has now gone. The coppicing encourages Nightingale in spring and summer, while all three woodpeckers, Nuthatch and Treecreeper breed. Hobby flies over the area in summer and coppicing encourages Nightingale. This is also one of the better spots to find Hazel Dormouse.

68 HADLEIGH CP

High Street, South Benfleet, Essex SS7 1ND
Website: hadleighcountrypark.co.uk
TQ778858; topped.nobody.acute
Open: all day, every day
SSSI
(152 hectares; 387 acres)

Deciduous woodland, grassland, scrub (Benfleet Downs), grazing marsh, saltmarsh and intertidal mudflats border Benfleet Creek, providing a rich jigsaw of habitat. There is a healthy profusion of songbirds and Bullfinch hangs on. There's always the chance of a surprise on the creek, where the commoner waders and wildfowl feed or stop off on migration.

Pay-and-display parking (£2) is just south of the A13 at Chapel Lane, while the CP is very close to Benfleet station (c2c from Fenchurch Street–Shoeburyness). A cycle route covers the northern half from St Mary's Road, while a partly cyclable bridleway enables views of the southern half.

69 TWO TREE ISLAND LNR EWT

Main car park: Belton Way, Essex SS9 2GB; TQ824853; coats.talent.push
Leigh Marshes NR car park: Castle Drive, Leigh-on-Sea, Essex SS9 2NL
Website: www.essexwt.org.uk/nature-reserves/two-tree-island
TQ830856; upset.gown.defeat
Open: all day, every day
LNR, NNR, Ramsar, SSSI, SPA
(257 hectares; 640 acres)

One of the more accessible sites to witness thousands of Dark-bellied Brent Geese on the Essex coast in winter.

ACCESS

Bus: several routes serve Leigh-on-Sea station from Southend and Shoeburyness.

Train: c2c services from Fenchurch Street–Shoeburyness stop at Leigh-on-Sea, a 15-minute walk from Two Tree Island.

Car: from Leigh-on-Sea station, follow the unnamed road past Leigh Marshes car park, over the humpback bridge across Benfleet Creek, and you'll see the car park just the other side, to your left.

YOUR VISIT

The Two Tree Island reserve is a site of two halves, divided by the access road. To the west, you'll find a 1.5-mile (2.4-km) circular cinder path through rough grassland to the western tip. There are two wheelchair-accessible hides, including the Lagoon Hide, which overlooks a brackish lagoon that Grey, Ringed and (less often) Little Ringed Plovers, Avocet, Dunlin, Snipe and other commoner waders favour, depending on the season. Numbers can be plentiful, and there's quite a vista to scan.

In winter, Kingfisher arrives, while Spotted Redshank and Greenshank can linger long after migration ceases. Keep an eye out for the winter Corn Bunting flock and resident Skylark and Stonechat (sometimes with Dartford Warbler in tow). Up to three Short-eared Owls can be present, hunting over the saltings and rough grassland.

The eastern half is not wheelchair accessible owing to its muddy, uneven paths, but can be explored along the grassy track through the scrub, via the kissing gate at the car park's southern end. Keep your eyes and ears open for Water Rail in the dykes on the 1-mile (1.6-km) circuit.

The path will take you to the point where you can scan a packed wader roost on the saltmarsh from a hide at high tide, including up to 90 Little Egrets, Oystercatchers, Golden and Grey Plovers, both godwits, Knot and Dunlin. Even more dramatic are the flocks of up to 6,000 Brent Geese feeding on the low-tide eelgrass, which annually conceal the Pale-bellied and Black Brant subspecies. Barn Owl hunts from a winter roost in the large trees. Scan the freshwater lagoon from the fourth hide for other wandering waders.

If there aren't too many people around, park in the Leigh Marshes (Leigh NNR EWT) car park and have a look around. The mudflats are a continuation of the habitats at Two Tree Island.

70 GUNNERS PARK EWT AND SHOEBURYNESS EAST BEACH

New Barge Pier Road, Shoeburyness, Essex SS3 9FD
Website: www.essexwt.org.uk/nature-reserves/gunners-park-shoebury-ranges
TQ933843; parts.scout.pass
Open: all day, every day
(Gunners Park: 25 hectares; 61.8 acres)

The accessible **Gunners Park** is a mile to the east of Southend, on a headland projecting out into the Thames Estuary. This means it's a decent migrant magnet, with annual Ring Ouzel, Spotted and Pied Flycatchers, Wheatear, Redstart and Whinchat, along with a chance of Yellow-browed Warbler. Check the old ranges inland for autumn and winter finch flocks and passing chats and other migrants, and explore the park after easterlies – rarities such as Olive-backed Pipit and Parrot Crossbill have lingered. It's good for seawatching with onshore winds, as well as waders on the foreshore and wintering Kingfisher – all dodging the local Peregrines.

Combine a visit with **Shoeburyness East Beach**, which is notable for its large high-tide wader roost. It's worth scanning the 0.6-mile- (1-km-) long Shoeburyness Anti-Submarine Boom, which projects over the mudflats, for gulls and terns at most times of the year; numbers of non-breeding Mediterranean Gulls in summer recently topped 100. Purple Sandpiper has roosted in winter along the stretch of beach further east, along with many Dunlin, Sanderling and Ringed Plover. Snow Bunting is possible at that time of year, and good numbers of Redpoll and Siskin sometimes use the park's trees.

There is a bike rack in the car park, and tarmac paths that can be cycled. Arriva bus route 9 (Rayleigh–Shoeburyness) stops at Church Road, near the park entrance, while c2c trains from Fenchurch Street terminate at Shoeburyness, about half a mile away. The free car park (50 vehicles) on New Barge Pier Road is open from dawn to dusk.

71 BLUE HOUSE FARM EWT

Blue House Farm Chase, North Fambridge, Essex CM3 6GU
Website: www.essexwt.org.uk/nature-reserves/blue-house-farm
TQ856970; outgoing.bungalows.panels
Phone: 01621 740687
Email: www.essexwt.org.uk/contact-us
Open: all day, every day
MCZ, Ramsar, SSSI, SAC, SPA
(267.1 hectares; 660 acres)

SPECIES

All year: Shoveler, Marsh Harrier, Avocet, Barn Owl, Skylark, Stonechat, Corn Bunting.

Summer: Little Ringed Plover, Common Tern, common wetland warblers, hirundines.

Winter: Brent Goose, Wigeon, Teal, Pintail, Shoveler, Peregrine, Merlin, Golden Plover, Snipe, Short-eared Owl, Fieldfare, Redwing.

Migration: terns, Ruff, Green, Common and Wood Sandpipers, Black-tailed Godwit, Yellow Wagtail, Water Pipit, Wheatear, Whinchat.

ACCESS

Bike: you can only cycle on the seawall on the border of the reserve.

Bus: there are no regular bus services nearby.

Train: Greater Anglia trains (London Stratford–Southend Victoria) stop at Wickford. Change onto the Southminster service, alight at South Woodham Ferrers and walk, cycle or get a cab the remaining few miles.

Car: from the A130, take Burnham Road (A132) north from Battlesbridge around South Woodham Ferrers onto the B1012 (Woodham Road/Lower Burnham Road). At the T-junction, turn right onto Fambridge Road and park (there's room for up to eight vehicles) just before Blue House Farm itself.

YOUR VISIT

This reserve comprises grazing marsh, open water, reedbeds and mud. There is a circular walk of 5 miles (8km) and three hides, with a grassy permissive footpath (not wheelchair advisable) connecting them to the seawall.

The site is great year-round, with hordes of wintering wildfowl including Brent

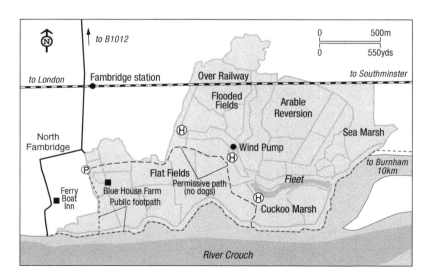

Geese (rarely with Black Brant and Red-breasted Goose), scarce summer breeders and some migration surprises.

Follow the path from the car park along the north side of Flat Fields, which host Brent Geese, Curlew and Lapwing in winter; the geese are easily flushed and are often more readily seen on the river and mudflats.

The first hide (TQ864973; diets.hammocks.paused) overlooks an expanse of flooded fields and a new scrape, which looks like it'll become very productive for migrating waders. In winter, Golden Plover can assemble in numbers there, and you'll have your first chance of Marsh Harrier.

The second (TQ867972; breathing.cracks.purely) and third (TQ870968; anno-tated.crusher.shelved) hides overlook Cuckoo Marsh, Upper Fleet and the arable conversion beyond, and provide great views of wildfowl, including Wigeon and Pintail. The reedbeds support breeding warblers in summer.

Your walk will take you right at the river, along the banks of the Crouch, and will include several muddy bays in which Curlew Sandpiper, Spotted Redshank and Little Stint may conceal themselves among the godwits, Dunlin and Knot – sometimes even in winter.

Summer holds many of the expected marshland and farmland species. Of note are the six or so pairs of Corn Buntings, which form much larger flocks in winter.

North Fambridge Hall Wood – equidistant north from the village as Blue House Farm is to the south – hosts a substantial Little Egret heronry with 36 nests in 2020. Yellowhammer still breeds in the area.

72 NEARBY: CLEMENTS GREEN MARSH, AKA STOW MARSH

Hogwell Chase, Stow Maries, Maldon, Essex CM3 6SE
TQ825978; sandpaper.generals.rhino

Just south-east of South Woodham Ferrers, south of Stow Maries and west of RSPB Blue House Farm is another flat, open expanse of grazing marsh and mudflats, replete with dykes and ditches: Stow or Clements Green Marsh.

It's particularly good in winter when more than 1,000 Brent Geese, 1,100 Wigeon and 800 Golden Plover can be present. They may be accompanied by dozens of Russian White-fronted Geese, the odd Pink-footed Goose and Snipe. Waders on the mud will include Black-tailed Godwit, Avocet and Grey Plover, while Ruff feeds in the short grass.

Raptors are obvious and can include Marsh and occasional Hen Harriers and Peregrine, with Merlin strafing the Redwings, Fieldfares and Rock Pipits. Water Rail numbers are well into double figures, and a few Grey Partridges are still resident. Shag is regular on the river, and there's always an outside chance of seaduck.

Healthy numbers of Corn Bunting stay on site all year, forming winter flocks of up to 75 recently, while migrants can include White Wagtail, Water Pipit and Nightingale. Raven pops in regularly, and passage periods bring Mediterranean Gulls loafing on the fields and sometimes an Osprey. Waders also pass through in good numbers, including Bar-tailed Godwit and Greenshank.

Occasional scarcities have included Black Brant, Tundra Bean Goose, Velvet Scoter, Montagu's Harrier, Water Pipit, Twite, and Lapland and Snow Buntings.

There is limited parking at the end of Hogwell Chase, a turning off Lower Burnham Road (B1012). Cross the railway line carefully and head south along the track to follow the paths along the shoreline.

Nearby **Hawe's Wood** (Hackmans Lane, Maldon, Essex CM3 6RN; TQ818996; walked.fattening.novelists) has an impressive rookery with more than 800 birds present in winter.

73 NEARBY: WOODHAM FEN NATURE RESERVE EWT

Ferrers Rd, South Woodham Ferrers, Essex CM3 5ZF
Parking: TQ798977; mysteries.vans.verdict
Website: www.essexwt.org.uk/nature-reserves/woodham-fen
Phone: 01621 862960
Email: enquiries@essexwt.org.uk
Open: all day, every day
LWS, Ramsar, SSSI, SAC, SPA
(8.09 hectares; 20 acres)

Divided by railway tracks, this ancient grazing marsh near the River Crouch is managed as a nature reserve within a larger area of common land.

The southern side of the tracks sustains a small area of saltmarsh and rough grassland. Species that can be seen all year include Buzzard, Barn Owl, Kingfisher, Bullfinch and Reed Bunting, while commoner migrants including chats and hirundines drop in. Summer produces Cuckoo, Yellow Wagtail (try the adjacent fields) and numerous warblers. Winter finds Wigeon, Teal, Snipe, Jack Snipe, Kingfisher, Rock and Water Pipits, and Siskin in residence. This is a fine potential local patch that is currently under-watched.

74 NEARBY: SOUTH FAMBRIDGE

Fambridge Road, South Fambridge, Rochford, Essex SS4 3LD
TQ854959; encrusted.spades.sound

This small village on the opposite side of the River Crouch to Blue House Farm can provide an off-piste opportunity to enjoy the Brent Goose spectacle in winter. Other seasonal possibilities then include Short-eared Owls and Hen Harrier. Wintering waders and ducks can be profuse on an outgoing or incoming tide, while finch flocks along the hedgerows can hold the odd surprise.

A saltmarsh to the west of the village has produced Water Pipit, and migrating Osprey occasionally passes through. Divers and scarce grebes are possible on the river. The seawall has produced Snow Bunting more than once. Midsummer congregations of Mediterranean Gull can top 100.

Park at the far end of Fambridge Road and walk straight ahead on the muddy footpath to the seawall. Don't ignore the field next to the road, which can have large finch flocks in autumn and winter, while summer sees several pairs of Corn Buntings breeding.

75 FOULNESS ISLAND

Bridge Road, Great Wakering, Rochford, Essex SS3 0DH
Landwick Police Lodge: TQ960876; plugs.essays.vocals
(2,430 hectares; 6,004.66 acres)

A remote island bordered by the Crouch and Roach rivers and the open North Sea, Foulness (Shoebury Ranges) is the largest island in Essex. It's managed by the MOD with very restricted public access but provides a true sanctuary for wildlife. It has a similar avifauna to other nearby areas such as Osea Island, but in very large numbers – for example, 7,045 Wigeon were counted in October 2020, just on the Thames side of the island, while 12,211 Dunlin used the site in January 2020, with 8,160 Golden Plovers and 2,640 Bar-tailed Godwits in February 2020. An October day count of 11,790 Brent Geese provided a great spectacle. Grey Partridge just about hangs on as a breeding bird. Habitats include arable

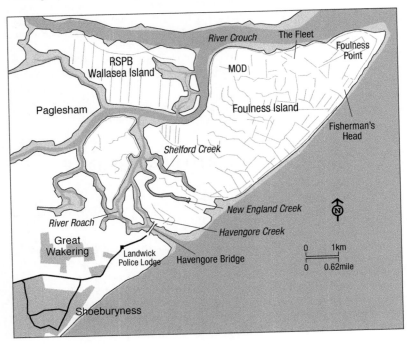

farmland, mudflats, saltmarsh, scrub and open sea. There are a few shops in the nearby villages.

Permission to walk is restricted to weekends (when bus route 14 runs there four times a day) and some evenings. Road access is via Landwick Police Lodge, from where you need to obtain a permit to cross the Havengore Bridge onto the island.

Despite this inconvenience, birders do visit for the plentiful migrants and estuarine birds, and there have been significant finds, including Lesser White-fronted Goose, Rough-legged Buzzard, Montagu's Harrier and Rosy Starling. Part of the western end of the island can be distantly scanned from Wallasea Island RSPB reserve.

76 WAKERING STAIRS

New Road/Stairs Road, Great Wakering, Essex SS3 0DH
Checkpoint: TQ959875; tiredness.unheated.kitchens

Another restricted access MOD area. The gateway to Foulness, and just to its south, Wakering Stairs has interesting birds of its own and can be accessed via a checkpoint at the end of New Road, Great Wakering. It's open to the public at weekends and bank holidays, along with some summer evenings.

Keep your eyes peeled on the drive down, as Barn and Short-eared Owls quarter the adjacent fields to the checkpoint. Drive along Stairs Road, stopping and scanning, or park for free at the coast by the start of The Broomway and walk the tracks, carefully observing all the signs.

Havengore Creek (TQ971884; sides.clapper.rumble) – actually part of the River Roach – can conceal interesting waders and marine species at times, while the saltmarshes support a substantial high-tide wader roost, notable for large numbers of Oystercatcher, Ringed and Grey Plovers, Turnstone, Knot, Dunlin, Redshank and Black-tailed and Bar-tailed Godwits. Brent Geese are a given in winter, and high water can also bring the likes of Common Scoter, Red-breasted Merganser, Red-throated Diver, Slavonian Grebe and Guillemot closer to shore.

You are likely to see Rock Pipit in winter, while Snow Bunting is annual and Dartford Warbler occasional. Scan the fields and Foulness to the north on a late winter's afternoon for the assembling roost of Marsh and Hen Harriers, as well as Merlin and Peregrine. Seawatching can be good in onshore winds, with all four skuas possible, although Arctic is by far the most likely.

77 HEYBRIDGE BASIN, NORTHEY ISLAND AND OSEA ISLAND

A complex area of tidal river mudflats and a gravel pit on the confluence of the estuarine Chelmer and Blackwater rivers, just to the west of Maldon. Heybridge Basin is probably the most productive area, with a historic list including Terek Sandpiper and Great Grey Shrike.

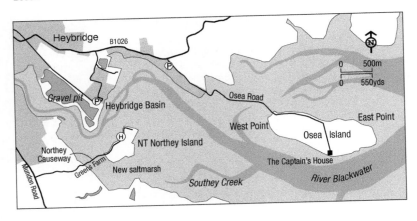

Your efforts are probably best concentrated on the gravel pit, which acts as a haven for waterbirds during migration and rough weather. Smew and Goosander are regular, and elusive Bearded Tits frequent the small reedbeds. Short-eared Owl is regular in winter over the riverside saltings, while Corn Bunting and Rock Pipit are also likely. Black Redstart breeds in Maldon town. Don't ignore the reed-beds at the northern end – a Northern Waterthrush wintered there into 2024, after transatlantic storms blew record numbers of American passerines into Britain the previous autumn.

SPECIES

All year: Shelduck, Water Rail, Cattle Egret, Avocet, Redshank, Oystercatcher, Ringed Plover, Peregrine, Cetti's Warbler, Bearded Tit, Bullfinch.

Summer: Cuckoo, commoner warblers.

Winter: Brent Goose, Wigeon, Teal, Shoveler, Pintail, Curlew, gulls, Merlin, Kingfisher, Short-eared Owl.

Migration: common seabirds, Whimbrel, Little Stint, Curlew Sandpiper, Bar-tailed and Black-tailed Godwits, Greenshank, Grey and Golden Plovers, Knot, Dunlin, gulls, terns.

ACCESS

For **Heybridge Basin** (6.07 hectares; 15 acres), there is pay-and-display parking on Daisy Meadow (TL870069; when.inflamed.pines) at the end of Basin Road (Heybridge Basin is signposted from Goldhanger Road), and then walk to the Blackwater on Lock Hill, turning right onto the footpath to scan the gravel pit and river. You can also park on Battle Rise (TL860072; fantastic.braced.comedians) and walk south on the path signposted 'seawall' to scan the northern end. A full circuit is sometimes possible depending on whether there are building works. Parts of the paths are wheelchair accessible.

Northey Island (120 hectares; 296.53 acres) is great for appreciating the full experience of huge Brent Goose flocks in winter, along with estuarine wildfowl and waders. The walk to the causeway starts from the Maldon Marine Parade Recreation Ground car park (TL860063; valuables.froze.treble) and along the promenade, where you turn south past the recycling centre (TL863062; fractions.keen.lousy).

The causeway there (TL868056; darts.diplomat.retaliate) isn't walkable for two hours on either side of high tide, but it takes you on a circular walk around the island. Keep an eye on the tide times or be prepared for a lengthy stay! Accommodation is available.

Osea Island (124.4 hectares; 307.4 acres) has very similar species, and dramatic in number. Take the road signposted 'Osea Leisure Park' (actually Osea Road) from Goldhanger Road (B1026) straight onto the island. It's more of a tourist attraction than Northey Island and has more accommodation.

78 CHIGBOROUGH LAKES

Chigborough Road, Heybridge, Essex CM9 4RD
Website: www.essexwt.org.uk/nature-reserves/chigborough-lakes
TL877086; lengthen.surprise.scrambles
Phone: 01621 862960
Email: enquiries@essexwt.org.uk
Open: all day, every day
LWS
(18.61 hectares; 46 acres)

Just to the north of the Blackwater Estuary and Heybridge Basin (page 147), this area of flooded gravel pits is in a good position to attract migrants. It provides enough willow carr, open water, reedbed, marsh, grazing and scrub habitat to

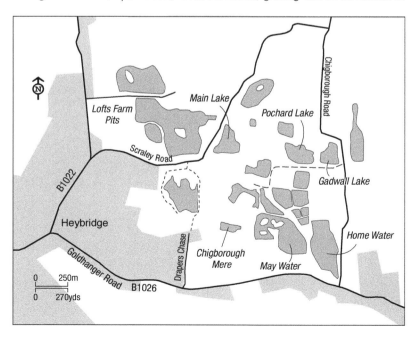

hold interesting breeding and wintering species year-round. More than 120 species of bird have been recorded, and at least 40 have bred.

The reserve comprises five main lakes surrounded by trees and scrub. Across the unnamed dirt track to the south, 10 fishing lakes also attract birds, though these are more managed and have less habitat. A Cormorant colony has about 20 nests.

A circular path around the reserve passes the most important areas, with smaller side paths. Little Owl, Kingfisher, Cetti's Warbler and Bullfinch are resident, and there is a sizeable Little Egret roost in summer. The Little Egret breeding colony has held a few Cattle Egrets after the species bred for the first time in 2019. Scarcer breeding species include Turtle Dove, Cuckoo and Nightingale, while Lesser Whitethroat and sometimes Garden Warbler are seen.

Garganey is anticipated in spring, while Black-necked Grebe is fairly regular. Autumn sees a few Green Sandpipers and Black-tailed Godwits, mostly on Main Lake. Winter attracts the expected wildfowl species, including Brent Goose, Wigeon and Pintail.

Vagrants have included Baikal Teal, Ring-necked Duck, White-tailed Eagle, Wryneck and Red-rumped Swallow, while Night Heron has lingered in the heronry more than once.

79 NEARBY: SHUT HEATH WOOD NR EWT

Tiptree Road, Great Totham, Essex CM8 3ED
Website: https://www.essexwt.org.uk/nature-reserves/shut-heath-wood
TL854135; merge.tripods.runner
(10.93 hectares; 27 acres)

This ancient woodland on the crest of the Great Totham Ridge is one of the better sites to see and hear Lesser Spotted Woodpecker, where 14 birds were counted in 2020. The EWT's coppicing of some trees also encourages a healthy Nightingale population. Raven has been noted in recent years, while woodland species include Coal Tit, Nuthatch and Treecreeper. Winter regularly produces Siskin and Redpoll. This site is also famous for its Glow-worms on summer's evenings.

80 TOLLESBURY WICK NR

Woodrolfe Road, Tollesbury, Maldon, Essex CM9 8RY
Website: www.essexwt.org.uk/nature-reserves/tollesbury-wick
TL963106; flap.squashes.final
Open: all day, every day
MCZ, NNR, Ramsar, SSSI, SAC, SPA
(242.41 hectares; 599 acres)

This little-known coastal Essex reserve provides good views of wintering wildfowl and waders on tidal mudflats.

SPECIES

All year: Shelduck, Cattle Egret, Peregrine, Avocet, Redshank, Oystercatcher, Ringed Plover, Cetti's Warbler, Bearded Tit.

Summer: Cuckoo, commoner warblers.

Winter: Brent Goose, Wigeon, Teal, Shoveler, Pintail, Curlew, gulls, Merlin, Kingfisher, Short-eared Owl.

Migration: common seabirds, Whimbrel, Little Stint, Curlew Sandpiper, Bar-tailed and Black-tailed Godwits, Greenshank, Grey and Golden Plovers, Knot, Dunlin, gulls, terns.

ACCESS

Bus: several bus routes go through Tollesbury from either Colchester (50, 50A, 92), Witham (91) or Maldon (95, 95A), all stopping at The Square.

Train: the nearest station is Witham, 14 miles (22km) away.

Car: park on Woodrolfe Road or in the small car park at Woodrolfe Amenity Area, which holds about 20 cars.

YOUR VISIT

This coastal reserve is just east of the small village of Tollesbury and can provide a good selection of maritime and marsh birds at any time of year. The one hide was 'closed for urgent repairs' at the time of writing. The footpath is exposed, so check weather conditions beforehand and dress appropriately.

From the car park, take the footpath from the village towards the saltmarsh and marina. This leads to the seawall, where the reserve will be on your right. A long, roughly circular walk brings you back through the village to your car.

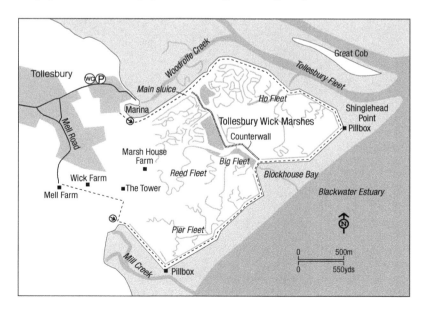

Marsh Harrier is often the most obvious bird over the channels; the marsh has a modest roost. The site comes into its own in winter, when it provides close views of Brent Geese (among which scarcer forms are sometimes found). The adjacent wet grasslands feature large flocks of grazing Wigeon, along with Lapwing and Golden Plover.

Migration brings more waders, including Spotted Redshank, Curlew and Wood Sandpipers, and Little Stint. The mud offshore is good for Grey Plover, while Avocet, Greenshank and Green Sandpiper visit the channels. Yellow Wagtail flocks pop in on passage, when hirundines whirl overhead. The reedbeds hold small numbers of Water Rail and Bearded Tit. Cattle and Great Egrets occur ever more frequently, with the former having a small breeding presence nearby, while Barn Owl hunts over the area, sometimes during the day.

Check offshore, as seaduck, Slavonian Grebe, and Great Northern and (more likely) Red-throated Divers come quite close. Bad weather can send the odd seabird inshore for shelter.

81 RSPB OLD HALL MARSHES

Old Hall Lane, Tolleshunt D'Arcy, Maldon, Essex CM9 8TP
Website: www.rspb.org.uk/reserves-and-events/reserves-a-z/old-hall-marshes/
TL960122; indicates.ushering.bags
Phone: 01621 869015
Email: oldhallmarshes@rspb.org.uk
Open: all day, every day. The free car park hours are officially 9am–5pm, though a few spaces can be used out of hours if you park carefully on the verge outside. Check the website for public holiday opening times. The reserve is reached from the villages of Salcott and Tollesbury by foot, although the paths are unsuitable for wheelchair users. Dog-walkers are allowed but must keep their charges on a leash. There are no facilities other than a picnic area.
NNR, SPA, Ramsar, NCA
(291 hectares; 719 acres)

SPECIES

All year: Shelduck, Shoveler, Gadwall, Little, Great and Cattle Egrets, Marsh Harrier, Oystercatcher, Avocet, Redshank, Lapwing, Barn Owl, Skylark, Cetti's Warbler, Bearded Tit, Reed Bunting.

Summer: Mediterranean Gull, Common and Little Terns, Hobby, Cuckoo, Turtle Dove, Yellow Wagtail, commoner warblers.

Winter: Brent and White-fronted Geese, Wigeon, Teal, Red-breasted Merganser, Goldeneye, Long-tailed Duck, divers, grebes, Hen Harrier, Golden and Grey Plovers, Short-eared Owl, Peregrine, Merlin, Stonechat, Fieldfare, Redwing, Twite, Snow Bunting.

Migration: Garganey, Little Ringed Plover, Whimbrel, Ruff, Spotted Redshank, Greenshank, Common, Wood and Green Sandpipers, terns, Wheatear, Whinchat.

ACCESS

Bus: Hedingham & Chambers routes 91 (Witham–Tollesbury), 92 (Colchester–Tollesbury), 95 and 95A (both Maldon–Tollesbury) stop opposite The Square in Tollesbury, 2 miles (3.3km) from the seawall and path.

Train: the Greater Anglia London Stratford–Ipswich service stops at Kelvedon, from where you get a cab or bus to Tollesbury and onwards.

Car: take the A12 east from London, turning onto Oak Road (signposted 'Rivenhall/Gt Braxted/Silver End'). Take the second right onto Henry Dixon Road, then follow this onto Braxted Road and Braxted Park Road. Turn left onto Maldon Road ('Tiptoe/Colchester'), right onto Station Road at Tiptoe, and follow the B1023 to Tolleshunt D'Arcy. Turn left onto North Street (B1026) at the village maypole, then right onto Chapel Road. At the right-hand bend, turn onto Old Hall Lane and follow this through the iron gates to the RSPB car park.

YOUR VISIT

One of the wilder areas of habitat on the Essex coast, Old Hall Marshes comprises open grazing marshes interspersed with brackish fleets, saltmarsh and reedbeds. Two small offshore islands act as roosting sites for waders, the most important of which is Great Cob Island.

Your visit will take in a circular route around the peninsula of the Blackwater Estuary NNR, bordered by the River Blackwater (north) and Tollesbury Fleet (south). That route takes in intertidal saltmarsh and mudflats, and enables scanning inland over extensive grazing marsh, brackish dykes and smaller fleets.

The reserve holds the largest area of traditionally managed grazing marsh in eastern England and the largest reedbed in Essex. It holds 2 per cent of the world population of Dark-bellied Brent Geese and migrant Ringed Plover, while the numbers of wintering Shelduck, Teal, Wigeon (2,500), Goldeneye, Grey Plover, Dunlin and Curlew are Nationally Important. In 2020, 36 pairs of Avocet bred.

Visitors have the choice of a 3-mile (4.8-km) or 6-mile (9.6-km) walk. I'll outline the more committed route, but it's possible to cut back about halfway. You can

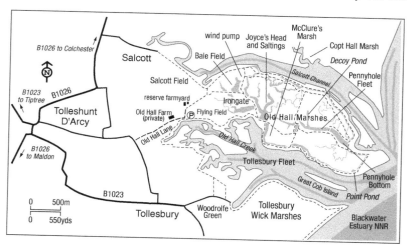

head north past the Bale Field first or east along Tollesbury Fleet – I usually take the latter, but read these instructions in reverse for the former.

Take the muddy and grassy footpath east from the north end of the car park (the bushes around there can hold migrants). Follow this through the Flying Field and Irongate bordering on Old Hall Fleet, which is the first bigger area of mud and saltings to scan. If the tide's out, there can be plenty of waders; a couple of hours on either side of high tide will produce the best views. This timing will then allow you to search for waders and then, in season, look for seaduck such as Red-breasted Merganser and Goldeneye, and grebes and divers as you reach the point and turn back along the Blackwater. The pool at Irongate allows viewing of breeding Avocets (30+ pairs) and Common Terns (40+ pairs) in summer. One or two pairs of Little Terns attempt to breed most years but are rarely successful.

Continue east to Joyce's Head and then south past McClure's Marsh – both good areas to scan for ducks in winter. The path then turns abruptly east and you can scan Great Cob Island. Morning views are distant and into the sun, but you might see Ruff, Spotted Redshank, Greenshank and other migrants among the hordes of Lapwing and Golden Plover in autumn, and a few sometimes linger into winter.

The path now turns abruptly north. Scan the sea for divers and examine the gulls that congregate on the shoreline – Mediterranean and Yellow-legged are possible. Now the path returns west but take the diversion to the screens that overlook Pennyhole Fleet to scan for geese; Cattle and Great Egrets are also likely among their Little cousins. The reedbeds at this end are the best bet for Bearded Tit. Marsh Harrier may well be quartering the area.

Your route back on the northern side allows further views of similar species, but the Blackwater may hold more maritime species as the tide rises. Check out Bale and Salcott Fields as you approach the car park for Hen Harrier, Merlin and other raptors.

The site has attracted many rarer species over the years, including Blue-winged Teal, Black Stork, American and Pacific Golden Plovers, Long-billed Dowitcher, Wilson's Phalarope and Lesser Grey and Woodchat Shrikes.

82 NEARBY: ABBOTTS HALL FARM EWT

Maldon Road, Great Wigborough, Colchester, CO5 7RZ
Website: www.essexwt.org.uk/nature-reserves/abbotts-hall-farm
TL963145; jokers.senders.bench
Email: www.essexwt.org.uk/contact-us
Open: closed at the time of writing so please contact the EWT for revised seasonal opening times. Please note the track to the reserve off Maldon Road is unmarked at the time of writing, so take it easy when approaching the last turn-off. There are lots of parking spaces.
Ramsar, SSSI, SAC, SPA
(283 hectares; 700 acres)

This huge coastal eco-farm surrounds the EWT's head office. Sited on the Blackwater Estuary, it enables visitors to see the results of an ambitious coastal realignment project. Its 'rewilded' reedbeds, trees and fields are visible from Old

Hall Marshes and the site could be considered an overspill from that even larger reserve.

The main focus is the hide during passage. The managed wetland has attracted 49 Spotted Redshanks at once, along with more than 100 White-fronted Geese, as well as Garganey, Great Egret, Black Stork, Spoonbill, Osprey, Curlew Sandpiper and Little Stint.

It's certainly worth scanning the area from the RSPB reserve, even if you don't visit, as Short-eared Owl and Hen Harrier quarter the site when they're not at Old Hall. Perhaps incorporate it with a visit to Old Hall or neighbouring Copt Hall, if you have time.

83 NEARBY: TIPTREE HEATH EWT

Maldon Road, Tiptree, Essex CO5 0PT
Website: www.essexwt.org.uk/nature-reserves/tiptree-heath
TL882148; bowls.endearing.smiling
(36.4 hectares; 90 acres)

Once part of a much larger area of heathland, the remnant Tiptree Heath still produces an interesting array of birds. Spring and summer are good for Cuckoo, Garden Warbler and Nightingale, while winter produces regular Woodcock, and Bullfinch and Yellowhammer are residents. Winter finches include Siskin and Redpoll, while Crossbill and Brambling have been seen.

84 COPT HALL MARSHES NT

Copt Hall Lane, Little Wigborough, Essex, CO5 7RD.
Website: www.nationaltrust.org.uk/visit/essex-bedfordshire-hertfordshire/copt-hall-marshes
TL980145; signature.trunk.track
Phone: 0344 8001895
Email: copthall@nationaltrust.org.uk
Open: all day, every day. Car park hours are 9am–5pm and there are limited spaces (bookable, if you're an NT member). There are no facilities on site.
(161.87 hectares; 400 acres)

This working farm on the edge of the Blackwater Estuary can hold more than 2,000 Brent Geese in winter.

Park in the roadside spaces (there's room for seven or eight cars) and walk south past St Nicholas' Church through the grazing marsh to the saltmarsh and estuary. Scan Abbotts Hall Saltings and Copt Hall Marsh towards Old Hall Marshes and the Blackwater Estuary NNR.

Autumn wader passage can be good and in winter the area holds large numbers of winter wildfowl, including White-fronted Goose, and waders such as Golden and Grey Plovers, Curlew and Avocet. Raptors should include Marsh and (sometimes) Hen Harriers, Peregrine and perhaps Merlin. Short-eared Owl is expected in winter, while Barn Owl breeds. The channel regularly holds Red-breasted Merganser.

The local farmland and marsh support breeding Yellow Wagtail, Corn Bunting and Yellowhammer, and the commoner species are parasitised by Cuckoo.

85 ABBERTON RESERVOIR

Church Rd, Layer-de-la-Haye, Colchester, Essex CO2 0EU
Website: www.essexwt.org.uk/nature-reserves/abberton
Layer Road/Layer-de-la-Haye causeway: TL963172; slurred.storyline.
informal
VC: TL963178; defectors.pavement.ready
Phone: 01206 738172
Email: abberton@essexwt.org.uk
Open: all day, every day, but the small, official EWT reserve opens from 10 am–4 pm. The VC has a café, shop, toilets, playground and baby-changing facilities. There is a large car park with bike racks. No dogs are allowed.
(36.42 hectares; 90 acres)

This huge body of water is the Rutland Water of the south. It's near the coast, has varied depths and plenty of shoreline, and attracts a profusion of waders, wildfowl and migrants all year.

SPECIES

All year: Great and Cattle Egrets, Marsh Harrier, Barn Owl, Water Rail, Cetti's Warbler, Yellowhammer, Corn Bunting.

Summer: heronry, Spoonbill, Common Tern, Cuckoo, commoner warblers, hirundines, Nightingale.

Winter: Bewick's Swan, Brent Goose, Wigeon, Pintail, Smew, Scaup, Goldeneye, Goosander, Bittern, Golden Plover, Ruff, gulls, Peregrine, Merlin, Stonechat, Rock Pipit, Redpoll.

Migration: Garganey, Red-crested Pochard, Little Ringed Plover, Green and Wood Sandpipers, Greenshank, Black-tailed Godwit and other waders, Little and Mediterranean Gulls, Black and Arctic Terns, Yellow Wagtail, Wheatear, scarcities and vagrants.

ACCESS

Bike: the perimeter roads can be easily cycled, but most of the viewing points are best accessed on foot. Most of the paths on the reserve are wheelchair accessible.

Bus: routes 50 and 50B (from Colchester) stop at Abberton Reservoir and Billetts Farm.

Train: the nearest stations are Colchester Town or Wivenhoe, both several miles away.

Car: each of the main viewpoints has free parking.

YOUR VISIT

Surrounded by farmland and small villages, this freshwater reservoir has many places from which to view the water and shore, particularly if you're prepared to do a little walking. Regulars tend to use the six main viewpoints described below.

With up to 40,000 ducks, geese and swans present in winter, including 2,500 Wigeon, more than 13,500 Teal and almost 500 Pintail, there will inevitably be notable species, and the 4.2 km^2 of open water has potential for scarce grebes, divers and seabirds. With more than 12 miles (19km) of shoreline fringing the water, waders can be numerous, while the surrounding farmland provides habitat for large numbers of passerines.

There are many places to stop and explore, and don't ignore the roadside lay-bys – sometimes thousands of Golden Plover and Lapwing can be present on the ploughed fields, and Cattle Egrets now forage among the livestock. The latter species has a small breeding presence in the heronry, which also holds about 20 Grey Heron nests.

Abberton easily warrants a full day's birding from autumn to spring. Perhaps start at the Layer Breton causeway to thoroughly scan the open water. Park on the causeway to scan from your car in bad weather or from the pavement on either side. Check the surrounding reeds, woodland and farmland as well. Numbers of Goosander (63 in January 2020) and Goldeneye (335, also in January 2020) in

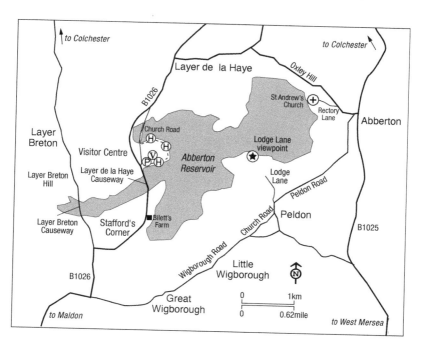

winter are Internationally Important and nowadays there is usually a Great Egret or two somewhere, with 65 present in October 2023.

The Layer Breton causeway is particularly good in the colder months for locating Smew (there were five in winter 2021–22) and provides a fair chance of Bittern. The water hosts huge rafts of diving ducks and often conceals several Scaup; a drake Canvasback was found in the flock during winter 2023 – astoundingly, the second to be seen at the site. Finches, buntings and pipits can feed on the bank in front of you as you watch the water. Spoonbill bred for the first time in Essex there in 2021.

It's also worth travelling the short distance to the east to the Layer De La Haye causeway, which runs along the top of a dam, and has a more exposed concrete bank and a panoramic view of the water. There are plenty of 'proper' parking bays here. There is a large Cormorant colony on the central section of the reservoir, while the hordes of Black-headed Gulls that feed on the millions of midges over the water are regularly joined by Little Gull and Black Tern in spring. This is the time to see Little Ringed Plover, while Redshank, Common Sandpiper and Rock Pipit are also possible outside the breeding season.

The short drive north to the EWT's Abberton Nature Discovery Park has three hides from which to escape the day-trippers and scan the shoreline, which is often crowded with ducks, waders and wagtails. The café has an elevated patio from which to scope in comfort with refreshments to hand – remember to check the feeders opposite the playground. The hides provide great views, though they are quite a long walk from the car park. Visit early or late on sunny days, as the hides are mostly south-facing and the glare will make viewing difficult around midday.

Heading back over the Layer De La Haye causeway, turn left and park in one of the lay-bys on the north side of the B1026, from where you can view the surrounding fields for gulls and Cattle Egrets, which have become regular; perhaps try your luck in the fields close to Garr House Farm (aka Great Wigborough Meats).

Other farmland species there include Yellowhammer and Corn Bunting, and flocks of up to 70 of the latter are still reported in winter. Check Billetts Farm for Yellow Wagtail in spring, as well as the commoner raptors in winter; park in the small area on its northern side. If the scrape on the western side of the road is wet, close views of migrant waders and wildfowl can be obtained.

Continue towards Peldon and turn down Lodge Lane. Continue to a small, dilapidated industrial estate to park, but don't block resident access. The footpath through the hedge there (signposted 'Viewpoint 500m') skirts a large field and leads to a viewing screen taking in a huge vista over Wigborough Bay. Scan the reed-fringed muddy shoreline, small bays and slacks, and view across to the other side of the reservoir. In winter, divers, grebes, waders and wildfowl are all possible; pay close attention to the shoreline if water levels are low. Don't ignore the field margins which attract flocks of finches and buntings in winter, while hedgerows are good for migrants in spring and autumn. Turning right onto the permissive footpath leads to a smaller viewpoint overlooking the same area, which can be closer to the birds. Several singing Nightingales are located every year, though they are widely spaced around the reservoir.

Your last port of call is St Andrew's Church (Abberton Church). Continue east and then turn north into Abberton village, turn left down Rectory Lane until you come to a small gravel car park with room for about eight vehicles. Take the permissive bridleway at the far end of the triangular area, heading down to the viewing screens; this path can get muddy at times. The spacious viewpoint has wooden plinths on which to stand, but only one is big enough for a tripod.

Scan the shoreline and the deep water beyond, which is good for grebes, divers and seaduck such as Common Scoter, Red-breasted Merganser and even Long-tailed Duck. Bewick's Swan has wintered and Red-necked Grebe and Velvet Scoter have been seen offshore. There is a desire line through the hedge taking you closer to the edge of the reservoir. Keep an eye out for warblers, finches, Yellowhammer and Reed and Corn Buntings in the hedgerows and scrub. The churchyard and trees are great for commoner farmland and woodland birds, including woodpeckers.

86 NEARBY: FRIDAY WOODS WT

Website: www.woodlandtrust.org.uk/visiting-woods/woods/friday-woods
TL986209; sprint.term.beam
Phone: 0330 333 3300
Email: enquiries@woodlandtrust.org.uk
Open: all day, every day
SSSI
(152 hectares; 378 acres)

Access to the main parking area for this MOD-owned forest is on Bounstead Road, the right turn at the T-junction at the western end of Oxley Road on the northern edge of Abberton reservoir. Please keep to the signposted paths and obey the signs.

This picturesque 'bluebell wood' is very popular with the public. It has resident Tawny Owl, Treecreeper and Nuthatch, as well as Cuckoo and warblers in summer (including about 12 pairs of Garden Warbler). The general area currently supports up to 38 pairs of Nightingales (in 2019) – one of the healthier populations in Essex. Firecrest has wintered and Raven is becoming more regular, while recent scarcities have included Golden Oriole.

THE DENGIE

Parking: Bradwell Power Station and St Andrew's Church, Bradwell-on-Sea, Maldon, Essex CM0 7HP
TM003085; snail.oxidation.coaching
Open: all day, every day
SSSI, SAC, SPA, NNR

Migration and wintering wildfowl and waders provide plenty of interest in this remote corner of Essex.

SPECIES

All year: Shelduck, Red-legged Partridge, Water Rail, Buzzard, Peregrine, Oystercatcher, Lapwing, Ringed Plover, Redshank, Cattle Egret (breeds), Marsh Harrier, Tawny, Little, Barn and Long-eared Owls, Skylark, Stonechat, Cetti's Warbler, Coal Tit, Raven, Bullfinch, Corn Bunting, Yellowhammer, Reed Bunting.

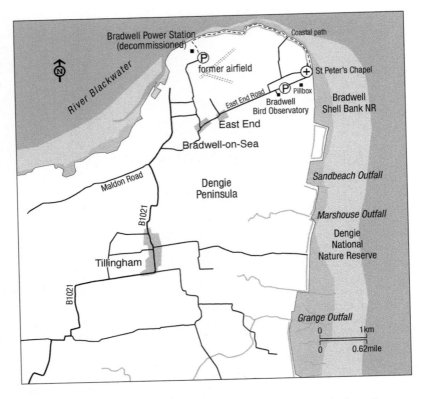

Summer: Hobby, Mediterranean Gull, Common Tern, Swift, Turtle Dove (increasingly scarce), House Martin, Swallow, Willow Warbler, Lesser Whitethroat, Yellow Wagtail.

Winter: Brent Goose, Wigeon, Teal, Pintail, Common Scoter, divers, grebes, Hen Harrier, Merlin, Jack Snipe, Snipe, Greenshank, Grey and Golden Plovers, Knot, Dunlin, Curlew, Bar-tailed and Black-tailed Godwits, Short-eared Owl, Rock Pipit, Redwing, Fieldfare, Snow Bunting.

Migration: Gannet, terns, skuas (autumn), Dotterel, waders, Wheatear, Whinchat.

ACCESS

Bus: bus routes 3 (Chelmsford–Tillingham), 104 (Tillingham–Burnham-on-Crouch), D1 (Bradwell-on-Sea–Maldon) and D4 (Bradwell-on-Sea–Burnham-on-Crouch) stop at the King's Head, Bradwell-on-Sea, about 0.6 miles (1km) from the seawall.

Train: the nearest station is at Southminster, a terminus on the Greater Anglia service from London Liverpool Street, 5.6 miles (9km) to the south.

Car: as well as the above addresses, parking for the bird observatory can be found at Eastlands Farm, East End Road, Bradwell-on-Sea, Essex CM0 7PW (though this is poorly signed); after parking, follow the track north-east for about 0.6 miles (0.9 km).

YOUR VISIT

This huge peninsula has extensive agriculture and small areas of woodland and neglected corners, along with a bird observatory. There's plenty to explore, especially if you like a long walk.

The River Blackwater forms its northern shore, the Crouch its southern, and it looks out on the vast expanse of the North Sea. Interest focuses on the coastal saltmarsh and the bushes and trees near the coast, which are attractive to migrants. The mudflats offshore form a large NNR.

The best place from which to explore the coastline is the large car park by the decommissioned power station at Bradwell. From there, walk east along the seawall once you reach the shoreline.

The two most important areas to visit are Bradwell Shell Bank NR and Bradwell Bird Observatory, but the coastal circular walk, which turns inland south of three outfalls and then north at the B1021 or any of the public footpaths, covers the area more thoroughly.

87 BRADWELL SHELL BANK NR AND DENGIE NNR

East End Road, Bradwell-on-Sea, Essex CM0 7PN
Website: www.essexwt.org.uk/nature-reserves/bradwell-shell-bank
TM030082; dubbing.surprises.baker
SSSI, SAC, SPA
(*Bradwell Shell Bank*: 80.9 hectares; 200 acres; *Dengie NNR*: 12 hectares; 30 acres)

This prime Essex viewpoint over the North Sea is co-managed by the EBS and EWT, and includes BBO (see page 162). **Bradwell Shell Bank** is notable for its dramatic high-tide wader roost of up to 20,000 Knot and Dunlin (including other species). Visit in autumn and winter for a couple of hours on either side of high water to thrill at the whirling flocks as they pulse over the water close to shore. Oystercatchers and Ringed Plovers stay to breed but are easily disturbed. About 5,000 Golden Plovers use the area in winter. Offshore, Red-throated Diver numbers can approach 300 at their peak in January, and scarcer species may be among them.

The grassland behind you – like most of the rest of the peninsula – has plenty of singing Corn Buntings and a few Yellow Wagtails in summer, both outnumbered by Skylarks. The inland fields are strafed by Marsh and (less frequently) Hen Harriers, Peregrine and Merlin, along with Short-eared Owl. The persistent may find all five British owl species on the peninsula.

For a wider range of wintering waders walk the shore south for a couple of miles to scan the **Dengie NNR**, where Grey Plover and Bar-tailed Godwit can be accompanied by scarcer species. An autumn trip of Dotterel occasionally drops in.

88 BRADWELL BIRD OBSERVATORY (BBO)

BBO: TM030085; unloading.averages.dazzling; East End Road, Bradwell-on-Sea, Maldon, Essex CM0 7PN
Parking: TM024078; unframed.ocean.plan; East End Road, Bradwell-on-Sea, Maldon, Essex CM0 7PN (use the public parking spaces on East End Road, then walk to the Othona Community by retracing your steps, turning right down the track to East Hall Farm then turning right again towards the coast). The Othona car park is for observatory staff only.
Phone: 01621 776564
Email: bradwell@othona.org
Open: While the area around the cottage can be partially observed all day, every day, there are no regular observatory opening days or times. When the hut is open, visitors are welcome and may even luck into a cup of tea.
SSSI, SPA, NNR

YOUR VISIT

The observatory cottage is placed in the centre of one of the largest publicly accessible clumps of bushes and trees on this part of the coast and acts as a migrant magnet.

The parking area is a short walk from the 'obs', which is now based at the religious Othona Community. Check the thickets and trees around the community as well, though this is sometimes not publicly accessible and must be viewed from the fringes instead.

Regular migrants are BBO's meat, but past rarities and scarcities have included Tawny Pipit, Pallas's Warbler, Short-toed Treecreeper, Rosy Starling and Isabelline Shrike. Yellow-browed Warbler is regular in autumn. Make sure you check the feeders.

Please note that the observatory has recently moved from its previous location at Linnets Cottage, which is now private. It's no longer possible to stay at the observatory, but overnight accommodation may be possible if you contact the Othona Community via the email address and phone number given above.

89 HOLLAND HAVEN CP

Pay-and-display car park: The Gap, Holland-on-Sea, Clacton-on-Sea, Essex CO15 5UB
Website: hollandhavenbirding.blogspot.com
TM214170; obey.squeaking.tinned
(40 hectares; 100 acres)

SPECIES

All year: Shelduck, Lapwing, Avocet, Redshank, Water Rail, Little and Barn Owls, Skylark, Meadow Pipit, Cetti's Warbler.

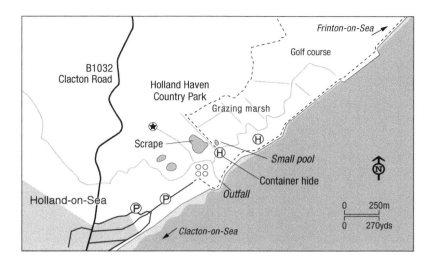

Summer: commoner warblers.

Winter: Red-throated Diver, Buzzard, Peregrine, Merlin, Snipe, Jack Snipe, Sanderling, Purple Sandpiper, Ruff, Short-eared Owl.

Migration: Garganey, waders, Yellow Wagtail, Wheatear, Whinchat, Redstart, flycatchers, warblers including Yellow-browed, Firecrest, scarcities.

A fine migrant trap on the coast rivalling The Naze to the north. It also produces good wildfowl and waders.

YOUR VISIT

Holland Haven comprises a large area of grazing marsh, grassland, scrub, wood-land, hedgerows, cliffs, pools, mudflats and open sea between Clacton-on-Sea and Frinton-on-Sea.

From the car park, walk the trees to the north and east, especially first thing before other people arrive – warblers are present in numbers at times, while Redstart and Spotted and Pied Flycatchers are annual in the scrubby area to the east.

Continue along Manor Way to the sewage farm, where regular ringing takes place, then cross the outflow sluice and turn left to the container hide (TM219175; spite.jetliner.prices). This overlooks a scrape and small pool that are good for scarcer waders such as Little and Temminck's Stints and even Pectoral Sandpiper. About 10 pairs of Avocet breed. Scan the grazing marsh for raptors, owls and ducks. To the south-east is a second hide overlooking a dyke (TM222176; screen-ing.output.deputy), which has produced Bearded Tit and commoner reed species.

Now proceed to the coast and scan the sea, where Red-throated Diver passage can be almost as impressive as at nearby Frinton-on-Sea (see page 164), or explore Frinton Golf Course for species that prefer shorter turf (Lapland Bunting and Shorelark have occurred).

The rarity and scarcity list includes Red-breasted Goose, Pacific Golden Plover, Lesser Yellowlegs, Marsh and Baird's Sandpipers, Citrine Wagtail, Barred, Yellow-browed, Pallas's and Icterine Warblers, and Woodchat.

90 NEARBY: FRINTON-ON-SEA

Esplanade, Frinton-on-Sea, Essex CO13 9EL
TM234190; listening.solids.opera

Sandwiched between Holland Haven and The Naze is the sleepy former holiday town of Frinton-on-Sea. Due to the efforts of one dedicated resident birder, the town has developed a formidable reputation as one of Essex's best seawatching sites, helped by its geographical location.

Hundreds of Red-throated Divers fly past during midwinter movements, and 656 were logged on passage on 1 April 2020. Spring visible migration can be impressive, as can the flocks of Brent Geese heading north. Other notable spring movements can be undertaken by the likes of Little Gull, Bar-tailed Godwit and Whimbrel – the latter has a substantial roost on the golf course at times.

Autumn wader migration generally begins in June, with wildfowl catching up from September. Thousands of hirundines and Swifts head through, along with scores of pipits and wagtails and hordes of finches. Terns, skuas and waders follow the coast south quite closely and the movements of Brent Geese have numbered more than 25,000 in one day at times, with single flocks of more than 2,000, as they fly into the Blackwater to winter on the estuary reserves and fields. Visible migration south is even better than in spring – with, for example, good numbers of Brambling among the hundreds of Chaffinches and day counts of more than 500 Siskins. Frinton can truly provide a real birding spectacle for the patient but judicious observer.

Park anywhere along Esplanade. The whole strip offers good views of the sea from the grass that separates the town from the beach, but one of the best positions to view is from Frinton Golf Club, the course that separates the town from Holland Haven (TM231183; soup.thatched.rent). The shoreline is very exposed, but some shelter is afforded by the chalets on High Wall Promenade (TM245203; diagram.showering.straw) during bad weather. There are several public toilets along the seafront and cafes and shops in the town.

91 THE NAZE AND HAMFORD WATER NNR

The Naze Nature Discovery Centre, Old Hall Lane, Walton-on-the-Naze CO14 8LE
Websites: www.essexwt.org.uk/nature-reserves/naze;
www.essexwt.org.uk/nature-reserves/john-weston
TM264234; entitles.irony.bless
Phone: 01255 679379
Email: naze@essexwt.org.uk
Open: all day, every day, but NDC hours are 10am–4pm (1 November–31 March) and 10am–5pm (1 April–31 October); for public holiday hours, visit the websites.
SSSI, NNR, Ramsar, SPA, ESA

(*The Naze*: 45 hectares; 111.2 acres; *Hamford Water*: 1,448 hectares; 3,578 acres)

A nationally important migrant trap, The Naze also allows views of huge numbers of wildfowl, seabirds and waders around its margins.

SPECIES

All year: Water Rail, Mediterranean Gull, Avocet, Redshank, Barn Owl, Cetti's Warbler.

Summer: Sandwich and Little Terns, Cuckoo, warblers.

Winter: Brent Goose, Wigeon, Teal, Shoveler, Grey, Ringed and Golden Plovers, Black-tailed and Bar-tailed Godwits, Curlew, Dunlin, Short-eared Owl, Redwing, Fieldfare, Snow Bunting.

Migration: gulls, Whimbrel, Greenshank, Wryneck, wagtails, warblers, Yellow-browed Warbler, Firecrest, Ring Ouzel, chats, flycatchers, visible migration, scarcities and rarities.

ACCESS

Bus: Hedingham & Chambers services 98 and 98A (Clacton–The Naze) terminate about 500m from the NDC.

Train: take the Greater Anglia service from London Liverpool Street to Colchester and then change to the Walton-on-the-Naze service.

Car: from the B1034, take Hall Lane, turn left onto Old Hall Lane and then take a quick right to the pay-and-display car park (£1.20–£5). This is open from 10.30am–9pm (summer) and 10.30am–6pm (winter), though spaces are available outside these hours and there are some disabled bays.

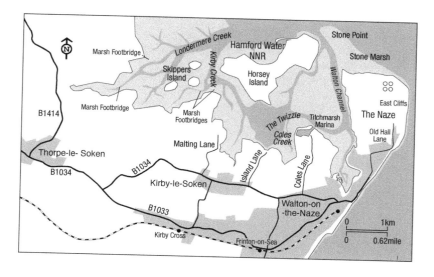

YOUR VISIT

Just a few miles south of the busy port of Harwich, this is the most easterly point in Essex. **The Naze** is in pole position in Essex to receive continental drift migrants and has a reputation for producing rarities and scarcities on an annual basis.

The site is best in autumn, but worth visiting any time of the year. It's just north of the village of Walton-on-the-Naze, and its trees and gardens also pull in migrants. If you include the John Weston NR at its northern end, the whole area supports a variety of habitats including woodland, scrub, cliff, marsh, grassland, freshwater pools, beach and the open sea.

The Naze is known as the gateway to **Hamford Water NNR**, and its Red Crag cliffs are a rich source of fossils as they erode at up to 2m per year. There is a good network of grassy paths through the trees and bushes that hold most of the migrants, and these can be combed thoroughly on a circular walk. The same paths lead to the blackthorn and bramble thickets of the compact 3.6-hectare (9 acres) **John Weston NR**, which has four small ponds with resident Water Rail and Cetti's Warbler; it is also an alluring migrant trap. There have been numerous rarities over the years including Red-breasted Goose, Red-throated Thrush, Blyth's Reed, Radde's and Arctic Warblers, and Blue Rock Thrush. Snow Buntings and Shorelarks can sometimes be found at Stone Point.

The Naze is the accessible part of the far larger Hamford Water. This huge area of mudflats, marshes, scrub, grassland and sand is a coastal embayment that's Internationally Important for its large numbers of wildfowl and waders. These include the ubiquitous Brent Geese in winter, when there are also large numbers of Shelduck, Ringed and Grey Plovers (1,092 in January 2020), Black-tailed Godwit and Redshank. There is a Nationally Significant colony of Avocet and numbers of that species in winter approach 1,000, while Little Tern nests, causing Stone Point at the northern tip to be closed to the public in summer. Up to 90 Sandwich Terns can be present in July, with more around Hamford Water, where the odd pair may nest. There's a roost of up to 18 Marsh Harriers in winter on Hamford Water, and they can be seen assembling earlier in the evening, while multiple Hen Harriers can winter on site.

Unfortunately, there is very limited access to these offshore areas. Hedge-end, Horsey and Skippers Islands are generally only viewable by boat, but you can scope the area from the seawall and footpath on the western side of The Naze, after parking by the NDC. Horsey Island also supports a small Little Tern colony. A good place to view the goose flocks is at the end of Island Lane/Island Road (TM234228; deflate.tripling.brush), from where Black Brant has been seen among the regular flocks of 3,000 or more Brent Geese. The small near-annual Colne Estuary Snow Bunting flock sometimes wanders into the Hamford Water area, adding to winter interest.

THE SOUTHERN STOUR ESTUARY

92 RSPB STOUR ESTUARY

Wrabness Rd (B1352), Harwich, Essex CO12 5NH
www.rspb.org.uk/reserves-and-events/reserves-a-z/stour-estuary
TM190310; resold.superbly.submit
Phone: 01206 391153
Email: stourestuary@rspb.org.uk
Open: all day, every day. There is very limited parking at the entrance of
Copperas Wood or at RSPB Stour Wood, from where you can walk along
the railway line to access Copperas Wood (page 168). Take the B1352 from
the A120 at Ramsey to find the reserve entrance.
SSSI/ASSI, Ramsar
(70 hectares; 173 acres)

Five miles (8km) of tracks are available to walk in this atmospheric estuarine
reserve, which also features a substantial tract of sweet chestnut woodland growing right down to the river's edge. It's possible to hear Nightingale song closely,
interspersed with the calls of waders – a true meeting of the habitats! Lesser
Spotted Woodpecker remains but is rapidly declining.

There are no hides on this reserve, so this is more of a fair-weather site than
Wrabness EWT (page 168), although there are picnic tables. It's open all day, every
day, but the car park closes at dusk. Dogs must be kept on leads on designated
rights of way.

The further 380 hectares (173 acres) of mudflats and saltmarsh in Deep Fleet and
Erwarton Bay often hold important numbers of wintering wildfowl and waders, with
total counts of 20,000 made in recent years. The intertidal roosts on the shoreline
and surrounding fields are almost as busy, but can extend away from the reserve,

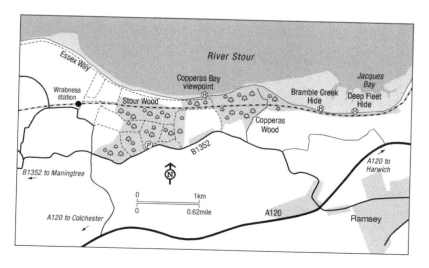

so exploring other sites in the area is recommended, depending on the state of the tide. Geese and Wigeon forage on the intertidal mud and grazing marsh in winter, when the saltmarsh is often hunted over by Short-eared Owls.

93 NEARBY: WRABNESS NR EWT

Wheatsheaf Close, Wrabness, Manningtree, Essex CO11 2TD
Website: www.essexwt.org.uk/nature-reserves/wrabness
TM166314; toenail.trickster.delved
Phone: 01621 862960
Email: enquiries@essexwt.org.uk
Open: all day, every day. The free car park at the end of Wheatsheaf Lane has a 2.1-m height barrier.
LNR, LWS, SSSI
(28 hectares; 69.3 acres)

This area of the River Stour shoreline faces Suffolk just downriver from RSPB Cattawade. It's immediately next door to RSPB Stour Estuary, with RSPB Copperas Bay and Copperas Wood EWT close to its east; all the sites can be combined in one day. Wrabness EWT is open all day, year-round.

The site is perhaps most interesting from late April when purring Turtle Doves return to the denser scrubby areas – this is one of the best sites in the county for this declining species. Come May, singing Nightingales will also be apparent, especially in the early morning. There is a substantial Sand Martin colony with 130 pairs, and a few Bullfinches still breed.

Winter is the time to scan the wildfowl and waders in Jacques Bay, with Grey Plover, Black-tailed Godwit, Avocet, Turnstone, Redshank, Dunlin and Knot expected. Brent Geese will be on the grazing marsh, with Short-eared Owl hunting low over the grassland. Barn Owl is present all year.

94 NEARBY: COPPERAS WOOD NR EWT

Wrabness Road (B1352), Wrabness, Essex CO12 5NE
Website: www.essexwt.org.uk/nature-reserves/copperas-wood
TM199312; occurs.position.overpaid
SSSI
(13.76 hectares; 34 acres)

Similar species as above frequent the grasslands, grazing marsh, woodland, mudflats and open water of Copperas Bay. One open shelter is available to watch geese on the fields in winter, and a hide overlooks the Stour. This provides opportunities from which to observe waders within a couple of hours of high tide, when Red-breasted Merganser comes closer. This is another great site for Nightingale and Turtle Dove in spring and summer.

A level, hard-surfaced path enables wheelchair users to make a complete circuit, but you'll need a RADAR key for one gate. Several other routes are available for the able-bodied, though they get muddy. Dogs must be on leads.

Winter will see resident Barn Owls hunting by day over the fields, perhaps with a Short-eared Owl or two. Brent Geese are as much a fixture here as anywhere else on the Essex coast, and they'll be joined by the odd scarcer species. The geese often assemble in the reserve's main inlet, known as Jacques Bay.

The presence of trees means autumn passage can be good, with Redstart, both flycatchers and many warblers possible.

There is limited parking for about three cars at the gate on the B1352 where the public footpath starts (at the coordinates mentioned above). Otherwise, access the reserve from RSPB Stour Estuary.

95 RSPB CATTAWADE MARSHES

1, Station Road, Manningtree, Essex CO11 2LE
Website: www.rspb.org.uk/reserves-and-events/reserves-a-z/cattawade-marshes
TM094321; preheated.dogs.cases
SSSI
(88.2 hectares; 218 acres)

SPECIES

All year: Shelduck, Lapwing, Redshank, Oystercatcher, Kingfisher, Skylark, Raven.

Summer: Common Tern, Little Ringed Plover, common warblers, hirundines.

Winter: Wigeon, Teal, Shoveler, Pintail, Curlew, Avocet, Peregrine, Fieldfare, Redwing, Water Pipit.

Migration: Black-tailed Godwit, Whimbrel, Green, Common and Wood Sandpipers, Snipe, Yellow Wagtail.

YOUR VISIT

Straddling the Essex/Suffolk border at Manningtree and between two branches of the River Stour, Cattawade is worth visiting for the spectacle as much as its number of species. Huge congregations of wildfowl assemble, with more than 1,500 Brent Geese, Wigeon and Teal present in winter, along with in excess of 500 Lapwing. Water Pipit is also possible in the colder months.

Cattawade can hold about 10 per cent of the wintering birds in the entire Stour Estuary. The riverside area between the white bridge (TM099327; inventors.miss.decorated) and red-brick barn (TM093329; nipped.fish.erupt) on the marsh to the north-west is particularly good.

Outside the official reserve, some of the best birding comes from what locals call 'The Splodge' (TM099325; dented.subtitle.button), a concise flooded area that dries up in summer but which attracts most species of migratory wader every year. The closest place from which to view The Splodge is looking south to the railway line from the footpath (TM099325; spirit.grain.agreeable) near that same white bridge. Cattawade is also important for breeding waders. Raven breeds a little further north in Dedham Vale and sometimes flies over.

Please note that there is no public access to the reserve, but much of it can be scanned from the south side of the Stour from the public footpath (TM091329; likely.subjects.polka).

Park at Manningtree station, or take a train via the Greater Anglia service from London Liverpool Street and walk to the river, choosing the paths north (for the reserve) and south (for The Splodge) that follow the river's edge.

96 FINGRINGHOE WICK NATURE DISCOVERY PARK EWT

South Green Road, Fingringhoe, Colchester, Essex CO5 7DN
Website: www.essexwt.org.uk/nature-reserves/fingringhoe
TM048192; triads.organist.swimsuits
Phone: 01206 729678
Email: fingringhoe@essexwt.org.uk
Open: all day, every day; the NDC is open from 10am–4pm (1 November–31 March) and 10am–5pm (1 April–32 October), seven days a week; for public holiday times see the website. Wheelchairs and a mobility scooter can be hired, as many of the paths are suitable. There are hides, toilets, a shop, café, picnic area and baby-changing area.
SSSI, SPA
(86.2 hectares; 213 acres)

SPECIES

All year: Gadwall, Marsh Harrier, Lapwing, Redshank, Tawny and Barn Owls, Kingfisher, Cetti's Warbler, Raven, Bullfinch.

Summer: Turtle Dove, Hobby, hirundines, Nightingale, Lesser Whitethroat, Garden Warbler.

Winter: Brent Goose, Red-breasted Merganser, Hen Harrier, Knot, Bar-tailed and Black-tailed Godwits, Avocet, Ringed, Golden and Grey Plovers, Merlin, Peregrine, Lesser Spotted Woodpecker, Dartford Warbler, Siskin, Redpoll.

Migration: Spotted Redshank, Greenshank, Whimbrel and other waders.

ACCESS

Bike: there is a bike rack at the NDC but cycling is not allowed on site.

Bus: the circular Hedingham & Chambers 50B service (Colchester–Great Wigborough) stops at the end of Weir Lane, a 2-mile (3.6km) walk from the NDC, while EssexBus services 174 and 175 (from Colchester) terminate in Fingringhoe, a short walk to the north.

Train: the Greater Anglia service from London Liverpool Street to Colchester Town is on the bus routes.

Car: follow Fingringhoe Road across the crossroads onto Furneaux Lane, where, after a couple of abrupt turns, you'll come to a grassy triangle. Turn left onto South Green Road to the car park.

YOUR VISIT

Fingringhoe Wick is about 5 miles (8km) south-east of Colchester, a few miles to the north of Mersea (see page 172) and west of Abberton Reservoir (see page 156). Its dense, expansive and complex habitat enables some seclusion, despite its popularity in good weather. There's a freshwater lake (formerly gravel workings), reedbeds, a scrape and the tidal River Colne with its mudflats and saltmarsh. There's also mature secondary woodland, conifer plantations, scrub and a small area of heathland. Geedon Marsh to the south has a productive area of saltings. The stars of its rich avifauna are breeding Turtle Doves and up to 40 pairs of Nightingales in spring and summer.

From the car park, go straight to Laurie's Hide (TM048191; livid.snaps.business) in autumn for migrating waders. Return to the car park to scan Warden's House Lake for strays and commoner waterbirds (including Kingfisher). The trees and scrub are your best chance for Turtle Dove in spring, when Cuckoo and Nightingale will also be announcing their presence (up to 25 of the latter have sung at the site recently). Lesser Whitethroat and Garden Warbler are likely. Dartford Warbler, Raven and Lesser Spotted Woodpecker are seen fairly regularly in winter.

Follow the southern lake shore, then turn right towards Crawshaw Hide (TM049191; perfumes.school.zeal), which overlooks some saltmarsh and a small scrape. Barn Owl is likely and Short-eared possible in winter. Continue towards the River Colne and use the Geedon Bay Hide (TM050191; thrones.engages.vessel) to scan the estuary for waders and wildfowl. Sightings of Spoonbill and Great and

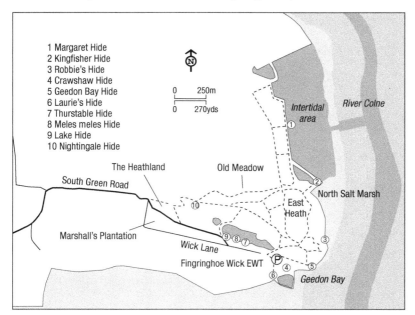

1 Margaret Hide
2 Kingfisher Hide
3 Robbie's Hide
4 Crawshaw Hide
5 Geedon Bay Hide
6 Laurie's Hide
7 Thurstable Hide
8 Meles meles Hide
9 Lake Hide
10 Nightingale Hide

0   250m
0   270yds

The Heathland
Old Meadow
South Green Road
North Salt Marsh
East Heath
Intertidal area
River Colne
Marshall's Plantation
Wick Lane
Fingringhoe Wick EWT
Geedon Bay

Cattle Egrets have increased recently, while spring and autumn may provide an Osprey.

Exit the hide and turn immediately right for an alternative view over the estuary, then continue north downhill. Turn right past the concrete bunkers through some scrub and turn right into Robbie's Hide (TM051193; excellent.novel.broad) for more estuary viewing. This can produce good views of Marsh and Hen Harriers, Peregrine and Hobby, and migrating terns will fly close.

Turn right out of this hide, heading past the picnic area. Just after Kit's Pond, you'll come to a viewpoint overlooking the huge new intertidal wetland area. First, scan the area from the new Kingfisher Hide (TM051197; leopard.companies.pinging), then head west, then right, then right again to walk along the banks of the water to the new Margaret Hide (TM049200; relaxing.repaying.vacancies), which extends out onto the mud, with viewing from three sides.

This extensive area is starting to produce scarcer waders among the impressive numbers of commoner migrants, with Spotted Redshank, Curlew and Wood Sandpipers and Little Stint regular. Time your arrival for a couple of hours on either side of high tide to get the best views. However, a dawn stint on the estuary is inadvisable as you'll be looking straight into the sun, so time your visit carefully.

Note also that more of the huge expanse of mud and saltmarsh of Geedon Bay (not part of the EWT reserve) can be scanned from tracks leading off Wick Lane and South Green Road.

97 THE COLNE ESTUARY NNR

Open: all day, every day
NNR, SPA, SSSI, SAC, Ramsar, MCZ, CPB, Nature Conservation Review site.
(576 hectares; 1,423.33 acres)

A rich and complex variety of coastal habitats produces good numbers of seabirds and land birds all year, but especially during migration.

YOUR VISIT

This very complex area of habitats, reserves and sites can be split into several discrete areas that are all worth checking on their own or as part of a prolonged visit.

This 2,915-hectare (7,203 acres) NNR comprises three major zones with varied habitats:

East Mersea – productive intertidal mudflats and open sea.

Colne Point – saltmarshes, shingle beaches and sand dunes.

Brightlingsea – grazing marshes, borrow dykes, ditches and pools.

The area is very attractive to many bird species. Much of it is accessible only to permit holders, so the publicly accessible areas are highlighted here.

Most of the sites listed are on **Mersea Island**, but a few are on the western bank of the estuary, which can be reached via a short drive through Wivenhoe to the north.

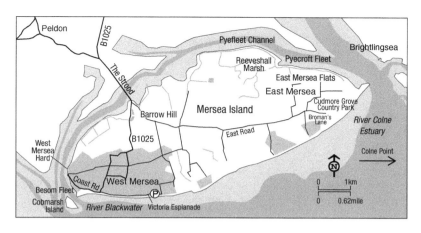

SPECIES

All year: Shoveler, Red-legged Partridge, Marsh Harrier, Mediterranean Gull, Lapwing, Redshank, Barn, Tawny and Little Owls, Skylark, Cetti's Warbler, Meadow Pipit, Reed and Corn Buntings.

Summer: Little and Common Terns, commoner warblers.

Winter: Brent Goose, Red-breasted Merganser, Slavonian Grebe, Great Northern and Red-throated Divers, Shag, Golden Plover, Avocet, Black-tailed and Bar-tailed Godwits, Curlew, Sanderling, Knot, Ruff, Merlin, Peregrine, Stonechat, Snow Bunting.

Migration: Osprey, Hobby, Green Sandpiper, Greenshank, Whimbrel, hirundines, Yellow Wagtail, Wheatear, Whinchat.

CUDMORE GROVE CP

Parking: Broman's Lane, East Mersea, Essex CO5 8UE
TM06414; rejoiced.combines.expecting
(41.28 hectares; 102 acres)

This popular country park has a spacious pay-and-display car park, a café and toilets. It's probably the best base for a prolonged exploration of the area.

There are few resident passerines of note other than Meadow Pipits and Skylarks, but songbird migrants drop in, and it's a good place to scan the low-tide mudflats for waders, along with the greater Colne Estuary for seaduck, grebes and divers at high tide, especially in winter. The adjacent grazing marsh attracts many Brent Geese (always with the chance of Pale-bellied or Black Brant), along with roosting waders at high tide.

Don't ignore the hide on the park's north side, as Kingfisher and Water Rail are often present on the pool.

REEVESHALL MARSH
Seawall mid-point at TM048163; weeknight.jokes.players
(198.7 hectares; 491 acres)

Just to the north-west of Cudmore Grove, about 1.5 miles (2.4km) upriver along the seawall beside Pyecroft Fleet, this expansive area of grassland, broken up with ditches and dykes, is a good area to scan for raptors.

Barn and Short-eared Owls, Marsh and (occasionally) Hen Harriers, Peregrine and Merlin are all possible in winter, with the additional chance of an Osprey in autumn over Pyefleet Channel or roosting on the many fenceposts dotting the marsh.

The mud by the fleets lures waders, which can include Wood and Curlew Sandpipers, Little Stint and Spotted Redshank, though Whimbrel and Greenshank are more frequent. Look out for Wheatear, Stonechat and Whinchat during migration.

EAST MERSEA FLATS
TM072152; ditching.proudest.signed

A small nature reserve just along the seawall at the north-east end of Cudmore Grove CP, this site provides more views over the mudflats of the Colne and the landward end of the estuary. In rough weather, seaduck, divers and grebes shelter and large numbers of Brent Geese and Wigeon (1,500 in January 2020) are reliable in winter, when there's always the chance of Grey Plover, Black-tailed Godwit and other waders on the mud or at their high-tide roosts.

WEST MERSEA
West Mersea Hard: TL999130; appoints.sandals.roofs
Victoria Esplanade: TM024124; stopwatch.soup.spells

Scan from West Mersea Hard for close views of Brent Geese. Check Besom Fleet on the River Blackwater from the publicly accessible causeway for seaduck, divers and grebes. Shag is regular in winter.

The beach huts on Victoria Esplanade at the end of Seaview Avenue provide awesome views of the Blackwater Estuary. Scan from the gap in the beach huts at the seaward end. There can be plenty of seaduck, divers and grebes in winter, along with perhaps Mediterranean Gull and Sanderling at the water's edge.

There are pay-and-display car parks by both West Mersea locations.

COLNE POINT EWT
Beach Road, off Lee Wick Farm, St Osyth, Essex CO16 8ET
Website: https://www.essexwt.org.uk/nature-reserves/colne-point
TM108124; wasps.business.helping
(276.4 hectares; 683 acres)

A complex, sizeable mix of saltmarsh, mudflats and open tidal water encloses the meandering Ray Creek. Myriad migratory waders use this area in spring and (especially) autumn, partially replaced by hordes of Brent Geese in winter.

Songbird migrants pass through in numbers. The shingle bank that edges the marsh holds a small, fragile colony of Little Terns that doesn't always manage to nest, along with breeding Ringed Plover and Oystercatcher.

Viewing from the remains of a Tudor blockhouse known as the Mersea Stone (TM072151; vivid.arranges.pigs), almost right on the point, often provides the best views of grebes and divers. Stonechat and Rock Pipit haunt the *Suaeda*, while Snow Bunting still occasionally shows up – there's usually a small flock wandering around the estuary. A few Grey Partridges still breed in the area too.

BRIGHTLINGSEA MARSH NNR
Promenade Way Car Park, Brightlingsea, Essex CO7 0HH
Website: www.wildessex.net/sites/Brightlingsea%20Marsh.htm
TM078162; shrug.stealing.orbited

On the opposite side of Brightlingsea Creek to Colne Point, and to its north, this is a productive area of grazing marsh with sluice-managed water levels. It holds waders, wintering wildfowl, and even more Brent Geese.

LANGENHOE MARSH
CO5 7DN (nearest)
TM045172; lingering.nurse.immunity

This, the western side of Brightlingsea Marsh can be scoped from the north side of Mersea Island. A winter Marsh Harrier roost, which can conceal a Hen Harrier, is notable on this private MOD land. Osprey also swings past on passage, sometimes lingering in autumn. Bearded Tit breeds but is usually only seen by official bird surveyors.

98 HOWLANDS MARSH NR EWT

Colchester Road (B1027), St Osyth, Essex CO16 8HW
Website: www.essexwt.org.uk/nature-reserves/howlands-marsh
TM118170; official.handover.games
Phone: 01621 862960
Email: enquiries@essexwt.org.uk
Open: all day, every day. Don't enter the private fields or walk on the seawall. Dogs must be kept on leads
LWS, MCZ, Ramsar, SSSI, SAC, SPA
(75.27 hectares; 186 acres)

Park in the small lay-by on the B1027 about 100m south of Oaklands Holiday Park (TM119169; detriment.forum.blues), which has space for about six cars. Don't go through the private gate but walk 600m downhill on the signposted public footpath to this coastal reserve. Alternatively, there is a free car park at Martin's Farm CP, about 300m to the north (indicated by the brown tourist sign).

Bordered by Brightlingsea Creek, St Osyth Creek and Flag Creek, this area of saltmarsh, grazing marsh, mudflats and tidal water has similar species to Mersea Island (page 173) and Copt Hall (page 155). Walk the rough public footpath on the western side to visit the hide on stilts (TM112169; flagpole.pictured.fence), providing unhindered views over the inland part of the estuary. There is another similar hide at the southern limit of the reserve.

Expect the usual large numbers of Brent Geese, with other winter wildfowl and good numbers of cold-season wanderers such as Golden Plover and Curlew. Common grassland birds such as Lapwing and Skylark breed in summer, while Marsh Harrier and Barn Owl can be seen year-round. To the east, **St Osyth Priory** (TM121156; fixated.montage.repelled) has a notable colony of Little Egrets with about 20 nests occupied. St Osyth Marsh to the south held Britain's second-ever Black-winged Kite during summer 2023, and can produce a good selection of farmland and estuarine birds from the seawall.

Unfortunately, there is no circular walk, so you'll have to retrace your steps back to your vehicle once you're done.

ESSEX WILD GOOSE CHASE

The extensive coastal fields, saltmarshes and sheltered shallow estuaries of this underrated county are some of the best sites in the UK to see impressive flocks of the Dark-bellied subspecies of Brent Goose – the population that breeds in the central Russian Arctic. Such a profusion of geese also carries small numbers of scarcer forms, usually an errant Pale-bellied from the eastern North American Arctic, but on rare but annual occasions a Black Brant from the western North American populations. The striking but rare Red-breasted Goose from Siberia's Taymyr Peninsula also tags along on occasion.

These huge flocks can wander widely but Essex's gatherings are some of the biggest on the East Coast of England. Here are the peaks from the last available WeBS counts to give you an idea of the numbers involved (sourced from *The Essex Bird Report 2020*, edited by Neil Sumner, 2022):

- Stour Estuary: 718 (January)
- Hamford Water: 3,334 (January)
- Colne Estuary: 2,887 (January)
- Blackwater Estuary: 7,005 (March)
- Dengie: 3,000 (November)
- Crouch/Roach/Wallasea: 7,995 (February)
- Foulness/Thames: 7,131 (February); 11,790 (October)

Specific sites to visit in these regions vary as the geese can be somewhat mobile, depending on foraging sites and tides, but there will always be some in the area in winter.

The best sites should provide particularly good numbers, and include Old Hall Marshes (page 152), Blue House Farm (page 142), The Dengie (page 159) and South Fambridge (page 145). Keep an eye on the bird news services for the whereabouts of which flocks include the rarer forms.

INLAND ESSEX

99 SEWARDSTONE MARSH AND GUNPOWDER PARK

Sewardstone Marsh: Godwin Close, Sewardstone Road, London E4 7RQ; TQ376982 (Cattlegate Bridge); member.roses.fuels; *Gunpowder Park:* Sewardstone Road, Waltham Abbey, Essex EN9 3GP
Website: www.visitleevalley.org.uk/gunpowder-park
TQ378982; deny.town.lazy
Phone: 03000 030 610
Email: info@leevalleypark.org.uk
Open: all day, every day. The two sites are connected by bridges and footpaths, and there are benches and picnic tables
(*Sewardstone Marsh:* 14.5 hectares; 36.5 acres; *Gunpowder Park:* 115 hectares; 284.17 acres)

A productive spring and winter site for waterbirds and songbirds, with regular Short-eared Owl in winter.

SPECIES

All year: Little Egret, Kingfisher, Cetti's Warbler.

Summer: Cuckoo, Nightingale, Garden Warbler and other migrant warblers.

Winter: Goosander, Water Rail, Snipe, Jack Snipe, Woodcock, Lapwing, Curlew, Short-eared Owl, Firecrest, Siskin, Redpoll.

Migration: chance of Garganey, Common and Green Sandpipers, Ring Ouzel, chats, Spotted Flycatcher, Yellow Wagtail.

ACCESS

Bike: Both sites are adjacent to Sustrans Route 1 and have paths suitable for cycling.

SEWARDSTONE MARSH

Bus: Red Arrow bus 505 stops near the end of Godwin Close.

Train: the nearest station is Enfield Lock on the Greater Anglia London Liverpool Street–Hertford East/Bishop's Stortford line, half an hour from the site on foot.

Car: park on Godwin Close, just off Sewardstone Road (A112).

GUNPOWDER PARK

Bus: routes 121 (alight at Enfield Island Village), 215 (Lea Valley Campsite) and 491 (Canal Side Walk) all stop nearby.

Train: see Sewardstone Marsh (above).

Car: there's a spacious, pay-and-display car park and VC at the north end of Sewardstone Road (A112) just before the roundabout

YOUR VISIT

While easily accessible from London, both sites are considered to be in Essex and can be visited in a single session.

Sewardstone Marsh provides enough varied habitats to attract interesting species. It holds two large fishing lakes – Knights Pits and Patty Pool Mead – and plenty of open grassland, scrub, marsh and wet meadow.

Now managed by the LVRPA, the interest centres around Knights Pits, former gravel pits surrounded by fencing, dense trees and scrub with muddy desire lines leading to favoured fishing spots. In spring, the profusion of warbler song includes Garden Warbler – often drowned out by Cetti's Warbler – and Nightingale in one of its few London strongholds, though numbers have declined.

Small reedbeds sustain common wetland warblers and Reed Bunting. In winter, the trees and dense thickets attract Treecreeper, Chiffchaff, Blackcap and Goldcrest to roving tit flocks, and the odd lone Firecrest appears. Impressive finch flocks lure in Siskin and Redpoll, and Spotted Flycatcher is regular in autumn. Most years produce a vocal spring Cuckoo.

To the south, the grazing meadow of Patty Pool Mead becomes waterlogged and attractive to Snipe, Lapwing and Curlew in winter and early spring. A peek at

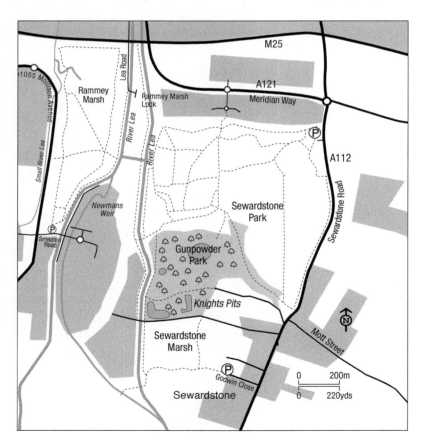

the River Lea can produce Goosander in winter and Little Egret and Kingfisher all year. Less often, Common Sandpiper, Water Rail or Pintail are present in autumn and winter, and Garganey pops in on passage. Sand Martins breed in drainage holes on the canalised river's walls.

The more open areas draw in migrating Yellow Wagtail, Wheatear and Whinchat, while Ring Ouzel and Redstart are near-annual and Stonechat sometimes stays for winter. Common grassland species such as Skylark, Meadow Pipit and Linnet are a fixture.

Wetter areas on Sewardstone Marsh are reliable for Redshank and Green Sandpiper on passage, and in winter Snipe – and occasionally Jack Snipe – secrete themselves away; the boggy sedges at the very south of the site, behind Northfield Nursery, can be productive for these and other passing waders. Your wellie-clad winter wanderings will sometimes flush a Woodcock from its leafy bed. Scarcer local species have included Grey and Little Ringed Plovers, Ruff, Black-tailed Godwit and Curlew.

The commoner raptors can be supplemented with Peregrine and Red Kite, while Hobby scythes overhead in summer. Scarce species have included Barn, Short-eared and Little Owls, Marsh Harrier, Osprey, Goshawk, Merlin, Raven, Yellow-browed and Grasshopper Warblers, Twite and Lapland Bunting.

Gunpowder Park has impressive finch flocks (73 Redpoll in November 2020) and a huge corvid roost. Enveloping Sewardstone Marsh, Gunpowder Park is ideal to incorporate during a visit. Almost all the grassland, scrub and woodland species found on Sewardstone Marsh are present in Gunpowder Park.

An important part of London/Essex birding lore is the presence of one or two Short-eared Owls every winter, which can allow close photography with patience and fieldcraft. Unfortunately, the popularity of these birds has resulted in some astonishingly poor behaviour on the part of the large numbers of people sometimes present – particularly photographers. Please try to keep your distance and be still and quiet – the birds may desert the site under these unusual pressures.

100 THORNDON CP

Thorndon Park North, The Avenue, Brentwood, Essex CM13 3RZ
Websites: www.essexwt.org.uk/nature-reserves/thorndon; www.explore-essex.com/places-to-go/find-whats-near-me/thorndon-country-park
Main car park: TQ607915; losses.windy.string
Second car park: TQ611913; echo.maps.silk
Phone: 01277 232944
Email: thorndon@essexwt.org.uk
Open: all day, every day. The NDC is open every day from 10am–4pm (1 November–10 February) and 10am–5pm, 11 February–31 October, with early closing on public holidays (check website). Any of the copious footpaths are accessible to wheelchairs and buggies, and dogs are allowed. There are hides, toilets, a shop and a café.
SSSI, Ancient Woodland
(226 hectares; 558.45 acres)

SPECIES

All year: Tawny Owl, all three woodpeckers, Nuthatch, Treecreeper and other common woodland species, Bullfinch, Yellowhammer.

Summer: Cuckoo.

Winter: Woodcock, Kingfisher, Fieldfare, Redwing, Brambling, Siskin, Redpoll, chance of Hawfinch.

Migration: Ring Ouzel, flycatchers, chats, hirundines.

ACCESS

Bike: bike racks are available by the VC.

Bus: routes 37, 251, 351 and 808 all stop on Eagle Way (Warley CM13 3BH), a walk of about 1 mile (1.6km) from the main entrance. Numbers 48, 49, 475, 481 and 565 stop at Thorndon Park Gates (Ingrave, Brentwood CM13 3RG), further from the main entrance but close to Public Footpath 42 that runs from the fork in the road at Thorndon Gate through the woods and past the golf course.

Train: the Elizabeth Line (London Liverpool Street–Shenfield) stops at Brentwood, about 1.5 miles (2.4km) from the entrance.

Car: an hourly parking charge is enforced by Essex County Council ticket machines. Season tickets are available from the NDC.

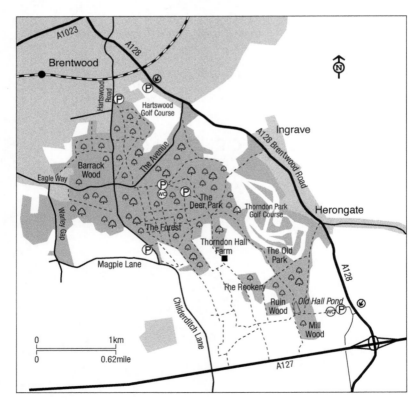

YOUR VISIT

Co-managed by the EWT and Essex County Council, this former deer park comprises ancient woodland, meadow grassland, some ponds and a small marsh.

It is perhaps best known for attracting large flocks of Siskin and especially Redpoll to its birches and alders in winter, and the larger flocks (which have topped 200, but have been no more than 40 recently) have held rarer forms such as Mealy and even Arctic Redpoll.

There are also healthy populations of regular woodland bird species and passage migrants. The beech mast attracts Bramblings among the hordes of Chaffinches, while a few Lesser Spotted Woodpeckers still breed, and there are Tawny Owls, Coal Tits, Nuthatches, Treecreepers and a few Bullfinches.

Perhaps also try the much smaller La Plata Wood (La Plata Grove, Brentwood, Essex CM14 4LA; TQ588932; votes.year.save) nearby, which also sometimes holds large finch flocks, including more than 50 Siskins in 2022.

101 CHAFFORD GORGES NATURE PARK EWT

Drake Road, Chafford Hundred, Grays, Thurrock, Essex RM16 6RW
Website: www.essexwt.org.uk/nature-reserves/chafford
TQ599793; united.arrow.life
(121.4 hectares; 200 acres)

A compact urban site holding a selection of common wildfowl and passerines, with Water Rail and the chance of Firecrest, good flocks of Redpoll sometimes in winter (42 in October 2020), and breeding common water, scrub and garden birds. Its proximity to Rainham Marshes and the Thames means that scarce species are occasionally found. Park in the small car park by the EWT visitor centre in the housing estate. A Little Egret colony of 18 nests (2020) is present during summer but disperses by September.

102 HOCKLEY WOODS

Main Road (B1013), Hockley, Essex SS5 4RQ
Website: new.rochford.gov.uk/hockley-woods
TQ834924; publisher.qualify.informs
(130 hectares; 321.24 acres)

Free car park: next to The Bull pub. There is a signposted footpath into this extensive but popular woodland.

This large wood is about 4 miles (6.4km) north-west of Southend. It was once the most reliable site for Hawfinch in Essex, and one or two can generally still be found in winter. The children's play area next to the car park can be viewed through the perimeter fence and is often where the species shows up. It's worth checking the tops of nearby tall trees and adjacent leaf litter.

Common woodland birds are present in winter and include Woodcock, Firecrest, Redpoll and Siskin. Winter finch flocks can be quite large and have concealed the odd Mealy Redpoll and Brambling. Tawny Owl, Lesser Spotted Woodpecker, Nuthatch, Treecreeper, Goldcrest, Coal Tit and Bullfinch are resident. A Goshawk displayed in 2011, while several Wood Warblers have been found singing in spring. Arrive as early as possible to avoid dog-walkers and prams, though Hawfinch can be found later in the day.

103 LANGDON NATURE DISCOVERY PARK EWT

Lower Dunton Road, Basildon, Essex SS16 6EJ
Website: www.essexwt.org.uk/nature-reserves/langdon
TQ659874; liked.stands.deflection
SSSI
(186.5 hectares; 461 acres)

Also known as Langdon Hills, this large reserve just south of the Basildon suburb of Laindon comprises woodland, meadows and lakes. It's the largest of the inland EWT reserves and comes into its own in summer when one or two Nightingales sing and roding Woodcock can be seen; there's still a slim chance of Turtle Dove.

In winter, Redwing, Fieldfare, Siskin and Redpoll are present, with a chance of Firecrest. Kingfisher can be found around the lake, and a few pairs of Bullfinch are resident.

104 BROOKES NR EWT

Tumblers Green, Braintree, Essex CM77 8BA
Website: www.essexwt.org.uk/nature-reserves/brookes
TL813265; regretted.chariots.snapper
Ancient Woodland, LWS, SSSI
(14.4 hectares; 36 acres)

Aka Belcher's and Bradfield's Woods, this reserve is an interesting oasis of ancient ash, oak and hornbeam woodland and meadows. Notable for wildflowers and butterflies, it supports a variety of scrub and woodland birds, including Nightingale (encouraged by regular coppicing), Willow Warbler, Goldcrest, Treecreeper, Nuthatch and Bullfinch. Marsh Tit still hangs on in small numbers.

105 HANNINGFIELD RESERVOIR

Hawkswood Road, Downham, Billericay, Essex CM11 1WT
Website: https://www.essexwt.org.uk/nature-reserves/hanningfield
TQ725971; cheater.teardrop.career
Phone: 01268 711001
Email: hanningfield@essexwt.org.uk
Open: 10am–4pm (November–January); 9am–5pm (February–October);
closed Christmas Day and Boxing Day. The large VC has a good café with
good views over the water, a shop and toilets. There is a 100-m disabled
access trail to Lyster Hide from the VC through Chestnut Wood; the paths
are otherwise not suitable for wheelchairs.
Access to areas of the reserve north-west of the reservoir is restricted to
permit holders; permits can be requested from the Hanningfield Warden
at the VC if you're serious about being a WeBS counter at the site and can
commit to the necessary time and dates.
LNR, SSSI
(352.1 hectares; 870 acres)

*A large reservoir holding the expected open-water species, with a good reputa-
tion for scarce migrants.*

SPECIES
All year: Gadwall, Shoveler, Shelduck, Mandarin Duck, Marsh Harrier, commoner
waders, Kingfisher, Tawny Owl, Bearded Tit, Nuthatch, Treecreeper.
Summer: Red-crested Pochard, Black-necked Grebe (scarce), Common Tern,
hirundines, Garden Warbler and other warblers, Nightingale.
Winter: Wigeon, Teal, Goldeneye, Goosander, Greenshank, Grey and Golden
Plovers, Dunlin, Curlew, Black-tailed Godwit, Ruff.
Migration: Red-crested Pochard, Osprey, waders, Black Tern, Little Gull,
passerines.

ACCESS
Bike: there are bike racks at the fishing lodge and VC, but cycling is prohibited on
the reserve footpaths.

Bus: the nearest stop is in Downham Village, half a mile (0.8km) to the south-west;
routes 2 (Billericay to Wickford), 10 (Shotgate to Wickford), 13, 13A or 14
(Chelmsford to Wickford) and 725 (Wickford to Brock Hill) all stop in Downham;
catch a bus from The Swans in Wickford for the shortest journey.

Train: the nearest station is Wickford, 3 miles (5km) away.

Car: in the early morning, free parking is available at the Fishing Lodge on
Giffords Lane. There is also ample but popular parking at the EWT's Nature
Discovery Park when it opens.

To get to the VC, take the B1007 (Billericay to Chelmsford) road to Downham
Road, and turn left onto Hawkswood Road along the reservoir's southern side.

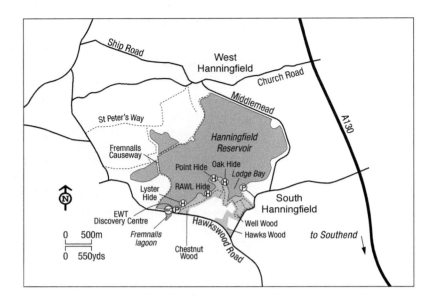

For the Fishing Lodge turn left onto South Hanningfield Road just after the reserve entrance, then left onto Giffords Lane.

YOUR VISIT

The relatively small 40.5-hectare (100 acres) terrestrial nature reserve is run by Essex & Suffolk Water and the EWT and abuts a huge area of open water surrounded by farmland and patches of woodland. It's popular for family days out but the site is large enough to avoid the crowds.

The water is deep and extensive enough to attract teeming wildfowl in autumn and winter, giving the site its SSSI status. It lures in thousands of hirundines and Swifts in late summer, when countless midges and flies hatch. The adjacent trees provide homes for classic woodland species such as Nuthatch and Treecreeper. The trails and hides can be visited via the Fishing Lodge when the reserve entrance is locked.

Scan the southern side of the reservoir from the causeway on Hawkswood Road (TQ721971; polices.boarding.gourmet). Don't ignore the parcel of woodland and small lake on the other side of the road, which can hold Water Rail and some wild-fowl overspill. Then move on to either the official reserve or the Fishing Lodge.

For the casual visitor, a good place to start is the EWT's Nature Discovery Park, within which all four bird hides are found. Park by the VC and follow the paths. To avoid the crowds, an early start is recommended, and you should park by the Fishing Lodge to the north on Giffords Lane for a more serious visit; follow the road sign to Hanningfield Waterside Park. Parking is possible pre-dawn at the lodge, where there are also toilets, a shop and a good café. This is where this itinerary starts, but it can be reversed if starting from the EWT centre.

Leave the Fishing Lodge car park through the gate to the east and follow the plentiful signs and paths to explore Well Wood and reach the hides. Before leaving, it's worth scanning the inlet adjacent to the café, which has good numbers of wintering wildfowl and extensive views of the open water at the northern end of the reservoir.

The mostly gravel paths can get muddy and slippery with leaves. You'll pass through secondary woodland with some young oaks, which are full of songbirds in spring and summer, including up to ten pairs of Garden Warbler, and mixed tit flocks in autumn and winter. Treecreeper, Nuthatch, Goldcrest and the two commoner woodpeckers should be apparent, and you may flush a Woodcock in winter. Tawny Owl is present, but very secretive. You'll skirt the Grazing Meadow on your way to the hides, and be sure to check this out. You can also follow paths further south to explore Hawks Wood before returning.

The route around the whole reserve runs to about 1.8 miles (2.9km) and you'll see signs to the Oak, Point, RAWL and Lyster Hides, all overlooking the water. Oak Hide overlooks Lodge Bay, directly across from the fishing Lodge. Point Hide is almost next door, and is the furthest out into the water, just about affording the best views of the western end. It also marks the border between the nature reserve, where boats are not allowed, and the more publicly accessible waters; birds don't seem to distinguish much but flush more from the public part.

Lyster Hide is closest to the VC. All the hides offer good views of the birds on the eastern side of the reservoir and on the water. There is a lot of weedy shoreline and shallow pools on the shoreline, which attract Wigeon and Teal in winter, and Little Egret any time. Goosander and Goldeneye are likely during the coldest months, while migration should bring wandering terns. One pair of Mandarin Duck and five pairs of Red-crested Pochard bred in 2020, as did Black-necked Grebe. Common Tern breeds on the tern rafts, which also provide roosting platforms for Lapwing and other waders outside the nesting season.

106 NEARBY: CROWSHEATH WOOD NR EWT

Crowsheath Lane, Downham, Billericay, Essex CM11 1QL
Website: www.essexwt.org.uk/nature-reserves/crowsheath-wood
TQ724966; expired.trespass.outsize
Open: all day, every day
Ancient woodland, LWS
(8.1 hectares; 20 acres)

A community forest consisting of open grassland and ancient coppiced woodland, including oak, Hornbeam and maple. In spring, its bluebells are popular. There is a good Nightingale population, while Barn and Tawny Owls, the two commoner woodpeckers, Treecreeper and Nuthatch are present. Winter finches can hold Redpoll and even Brambling. Turtle Dove (very scarce), Garden Warbler and Spotted Flycatcher have also been recorded.

107 HATFIELD FOREST NNR NT

Bush End Road, Takeley, Bishop's Stortford, Essex, CM22 6NE
Website: www.nationaltrust.org.uk/hatfield-forest
TL539197; trunk.booklets.snooty
Phone: 01279 870 678; 0344 249 1895 (car park bookings)
Email: hatfieldforest@nationaltrust.org.uk
Open: all day, every day; the car park is open between 9am–4pm (check with the NT for seasonal changes and fees – you may need to book a space). Parking is currently £8 for non-members (download the PayByPhone app or have a credit or debit card handy). You can also park for free at a few locations on the periphery of the park; the closest is a lay-by for six or seven vehicles outside St John the Evangelist church (TL547200; tonic. reeling.sprains); you can park for free there for two hours after 9am, but as long as you like before that.
SSSI, NNR
(424.52 hectares; 1,049 acres)

SPECIES

All year: Gadwall, Barn, Tawny and Little Owls, Marsh and Coal Tits, Nuthatch, Treecreeper, Raven, Bullfinch.

Summer: Garden Warbler, Lesser Whitethroat and common songbirds.

Winter: Fieldfare, Redwing, Firecrest, Brambling, Siskin, Redpoll, Hawfinch.

Migration: hirundines, Ring Ouzel, Wheatear, Whinchat, Stonechat.

ACCESS

Bike: National Cycle Route 16 runs along the Flitch Way CP (a disused railway track) between Braintree and Start Hill, just east of Bishop's Stortford. There are two entrances at the northern end of the forest at the eastern and western ends of Flitch Way, and there are bike racks by the café. Flitch Way is a public footpath. There are tarmac, gravel, grass and muddy paths throughout the forest, though cycling is not permitted on most. There are 24 official access points around the perimeter of the forest.

Bus: the nearest stop is on the Arriva 508 route (Harlow–Stansted Airport) at Green Man, Takeley Street, on the forest's northern edge, about 1.5 miles (2.1km) from the VC. Another 11 bus routes serving Stansted Airport also stop at the Four Ashes, Takeley, about 1 mile (1.6km) from the forest along the Flitch Way.

Train: the closest stations are Stansted Airport (3 miles; 4.8km) and Bishop's Stortford (5 miles; 8km), from where the 508 bus can be caught to the Green Man.

Car: from the M11, take the B1256 towards Takeley, if coming from the south or west; if coming from the east, use the A120. The forest is well signposted with brown tourist signs from both and about 1.5 miles (2.4km) from the motorway. The main car park is off Hatfield Forest Road.

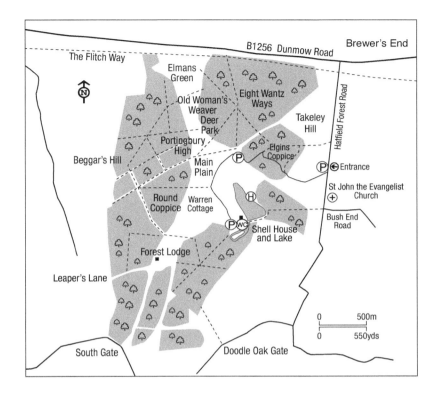

YOUR VISIT

This accessible, very large patch of remnant ancient forest has surprisingly rich habitats away from its more beaten tracks, including woodland, grassland, a lake and some marsh. It's significant for holding good numbers of Marsh Tit year-round and is one of the most reliable sites for Hawfinch in winter – numbers recently topped 28 birds, though fewer than 10 is more likely. They often conveniently feed on the ground or in bushes along the path to the west of the Entrance Car Park in Elgins Coppice (TL545202; adventure.agent.perused).

Most of the commoner woodland species are present, including Coal Tit, Nuthatch and Treecreeper, and Cuckoo and Garden Warbler arrive in summer. There are resident Bullfinch and Yellowhammer, while Woodcock winters, along with Redwing, Fieldfare, Siskin and Redpoll – mixed flocks are sometimes in the alders by the dam on the lake (TL541198; crops.playroom.surprises). Little Owl frequents the areas of grassland with scattered trees and hawthorns, while a few pairs of Tawny Owl make the wooded areas their home. Raven is frequently noted these days.

Dogs can be walked on most of the paths, and the central lake has a café, bookshop and toilets. It's worth checking early in the morning – there is a viewing shelter on the northern bank (TL540200; extremely.transmit.rentals) – as the occasional tern or wader can drop in before people arrive, but generally only common waterbirds are present.

108 DANBURY RIDGE EWT RESERVES

Scrubs Wood: Runsell Lane, Danbury, Chelmsford, Essex CM3 4NZ; TL787057; recruited.premiums.canal
Woodham Walter Common: Common Lane, Woodham Walter, Maldon, Essex CM9 6NF; TL795069; crumple.villa.glows
Website: www.essexwt.org.uk/nature-reserves/danbury-ridge
SSSI

A complex patchwork of ancient woodland, common, heathland, streams and bog, this managed green zone of 10 adjacent nature reserves has much of interest to the birder. The key species are Nightingale and Lesser Spotted Woodpecker. Scrubs Wood and Woodham Walter Common are the two main locations to visit to ensure you see the most species. Both have all three woodpeckers, Nuthatch, Treecreeper and Nightingale (spring) and are also great for butterflies and Hazel Dormice. Up to 17 Hawfinches have been logged in winter, though there have only been single figures recently.

Over the site as a whole, Tawny and Little Owls are resident, while a few Garden and Grasshopper Warblers are present in summer, and Long-eared Owl, Siskin and Redpoll have been noted in winter.

The nearby NT site at **Blake's Wood and Danbury Common** (Penny Royal Road, Danbury, Essex, CM3 4ED; TL784049; radar.cookie.tumblers) also has a comparable array of species, including all three woodpeckers.

KENT

Kent is one of the country's great birding counties. So much so that the 426 species recorded in the county ranks it eighth among Britain's recording areas in terms of records – as many as Orkney and only three behind Dorset.

While many of these are rare vagrants, the county hosts several scarce species in its varied habitats, even with the constant demands of farming, industry and new housing. With a large number of substantial nature reserves and coastline on three sides, there is plenty of habitat for breeding, wintering and migrant birds.

Autumn's down-Channel wader passage is light but spring's up-Channel passage is much stronger. Some flocks rest on the county's plentiful coastal wetland reserves, and numbers can be impressive on the North Kent Marshes.

The Continent is only 20 miles (33km) across the English Channel, which helps add a Gallic flavour to the migrants that occur on the Kent coast. The likelihood of notable visible migration and continental scarcities is very much improved by this proximity. Easterly winds will also blow birds onshore, but other directions can mean passage along the east coast is distant until it hits the Essex coast.

Many birding visitors to Kent concentrate on the North Kent Marshes and Dungeness, as both have a good number of specialised breeding species and a good chance of attracting scarce and rare migrants. However, there is much more to see inland, with enough freshwater marsh and woodland to encourage you to stray from the coast. The county still supported around 700 pairs of Turtle Doves in the most recent survey in 2021 – a whopping one third of the remaining UK population. Kent also holds a quarter of the UK's Nightingales.

Kent Breeding Bird Atlas 2008–13 by Rob Clements *et al* (2015) provides a recent, very detailed summary of the status and comprehensive description of Kent's birds.

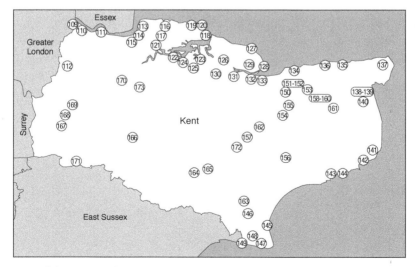

Map of the county of Kent. Numbers correspond to the sites in this section.

URBAN KENT

109 CRAYFORD MARSHES

Moat Lane, Slade Green, Bexley, London DA8 2ND
Website: https://londonbirders.fandom.com/wiki/Crayford_Marshes
Parking: Erith Yacht Club – TQ527777, fans.times.grand
Moat Lane – TQ526765, frost.fall.else
Open: all day, every day. Walk a few minutes from Slade Green station,
Forest Road, turning east onto Moat Lane. Some parts of the paths are not
suitable for wheelchair users, though many are flat and even.
SSSI

SPECIES

All year: Peregrine, Oystercatcher, Avocet, Redshank, Lapwing, chance of Turnstone, Mediterranean, Yellow-legged and Caspian Gulls, Little and Barn Owls, Kingfisher, Skylark, Meadow Pipit, Stonechat, Black Redstart, Reed and Corn Buntings.

Summer: Hobby, Little Ringed Plover, Common Tern, Yellow Wagtail, Nightingale, warblers, hirundines.

Winter: Wigeon, Pintail, Golden and Grey Plovers, Ruff, Woodcock, Jack Snipe, Snipe, Black-tailed Godwit, Short-eared Owl, Water and Rock Pipits.

Migration: waders, Black Tern, Tree Pipit, Ring Ouzel, Fieldfare, Redwing, Whinchat, Wheatear, Redstart, Spotted Flycatcher.

ACCESS

Bike: the public footpaths are part of the National Cycle Route and are sign-posted. Beware, though: bikes and equipment have been stolen in the past.

Bus: routes 89 (Maidstone–Coxheath) and 99 (Woolwich–Crayford) pass by Slade Green, while routes 492 (Sidcup–Bluewater), 96 (Dartford–Woolwich) and 428 (Erith–Bluewater) service Crayford and Dartford stations.

Train: the closest station is Slade Green. Both Crayford and Dartford stations are further but are equidistant from the marshes with more frequent trains. All are on the North Kent Line, reached via Southeastern and Thameslink trains from London Charing Cross and London Cannon Street. Dartford is also on the Bexleyheath and Dartford Loop Lines.

Car: Crayford Marshes are close to both the M25 and A2, and limited parking spaces in a muddy lay-by can be found on Moat Lane (there are other spaces in nearby residential areas around Slade Green station).

YOUR VISIT

This flat, open and large area of historical grazing marsh is situated on the western banks of the River Darent. The site is waterlogged in places for much of the year, with low hedgerows and a few trees in the northern part. The flooded areas support roosting waders in winter and on migration, particularly at high tide. Many waders, gulls and wildfowl use the tidal mud of the Thames for feeding too – particularly around the Darent Flood Barrier – so there is something to watch whatever the time or tide.

Your route will either start at the yacht club or Moat Lane. Starting at the former, the Thames Path runs east, parallel to the river. You'll pass a large recycling centre that attracts gulls, then turn right along the River Darent. The path runs south alongside this tributary and then turns right towards Moat Lane. You will either turn back and return to the yacht club the way you came or walk through the residential area back towards the river.

The first part of the footpath from Moat Lane has willows that often host a pair of Little Owls. The marsh can be somewhat quiet at times, but stay alert as Lapwing, Snipe and Redshank can be present during much of the year, and there may be a discrete Jack Snipe in winter.

Yellow-legged Gull is a speciality at Crayford and there are usually a few on the Thames, especially on low tides between late summer and spring. There's a chance of Caspian Gull and other good larids, while terns rest up on this side of the Thames more often than at Rainham, opposite. Species and numbers change seasonally, but Lapwing, Curlew, both godwits, Oystercatcher, Dunlin, Ringed Plover and Turnstone are all likely on the foreshore. Shelduck is often in the high double figures, while Teal, Wigeon and Gadwall may be apparent during the colder months.

Keep your ears attuned for the high whistles of Rock and Water Pipits outside

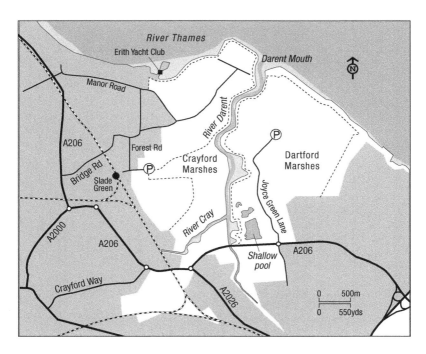

summer – there is quite a lot of interchange between Crayford, Dartford and Rainham.

Be sure to scan the boats by Erith Yacht Club in the warmer months, as terns favour this area. The river's also good for waders at low tide. To complete a full circle, you should follow the footpath south along the Darent and then turn right back towards Moat Lane or Manor Road. Short-eared and Barn Owls may be seen hunting over the open marsh.

The pools and industrial sites at the southern end of the marshes can be fantastic for the scarcer gull species – for more, see page 309.

110 DARTFORD MARSHES

Parking: Joyce Green Lane, Dartford, Kent, DA1 5RX
TQ542771; tube.indeed.landed
Open: all day, every day
SSSI
(Crayford and Dartford Marshes combined: about 500 hectares; 1235.53 acres)

SPECIES

The birds are very similar to those on the adjacent Crayford Marshes; both sites can be visited together on a longer visit.

YOUR VISIT

Park as far as you can go along Joyce Green Lane, just before Dartford Clay Shooting Club, and continue along the gated track towards the Thames. This will take you to the foreshore along the east bank of the Darent. You can then turn right along the Thames Path and observe the foreshore. Take your time to sift through the gulls, terns and waders on the mud, especially on a rising or falling tide. Yellow-legged Gull numbers have peaked at 48 in August 2021.

The path skirts Longreach Sewage Treatment Works and then the former Littlebrook Power Station. In summer, check the old wooden jetty, which hosts a small House Martin colony and roosting Oystercatchers.

Turn back and follow the dirt track onto the marshes, which runs almost straight along the eastern side, with the sewage works to your left (east). This is called Marsh Street North, but it's just a track. Before you get to Binnie Road, you can walk a few hundred metres to scan the lakes in the middle of the trading estate, or take the path right, across the marsh and through the open foundations of an abandoned building. This route will take you back to Joyce Green Lane, down which you can turn right and return to your vehicle.

It is worth crossing onto the marsh on the western side of the lane, where there are large pools that attract hundreds of loafing gulls. There is usually a scarcity or two among them, so sift through them carefully and try not to flush them. For more on watching gulls at Dartford Marshes, see page 309. There are also a couple of lakes in the industrial estate at the east end of Bob Dunn Way and Dartford Marshes.

With both Crayford and Dartford so productive bird-wise, it's hoped that something will be made of them as nature reserves one day, after the success of Rainham Marshes and Cliffe Pools.

111 SWANSCOMBE MARSHES

Manor Way, Swanscombe, Kent DA11 9BB
Websites: https://saveswanscombemarshes.wordpress.com;
https://londonbirders.fandom.com/wiki/Swanscombe_Marsh
TQ611756; system.dose.tiles
Open: all day, every day
SSSI
(205 Hectares; 506 acres)

This somewhat neglected area of marsh, scrub and wasteground regularly produces interesting birds.

SPECIES

All year: Marsh Harrier, Little Egret, waders, Skylark, Cetti's Warbler.

Summer: Little Ringed Plover, Common Tern, Cuckoo, Swift, Grasshopper Warbler, hirundines.

Winter: Teal, Shoveler, Wigeon, Snipe, Jack Snipe, gulls, Water and Rock Pipits, Dartford Warbler, finches.

Migration: seabirds, gulls, terns, waders, warblers, chats.

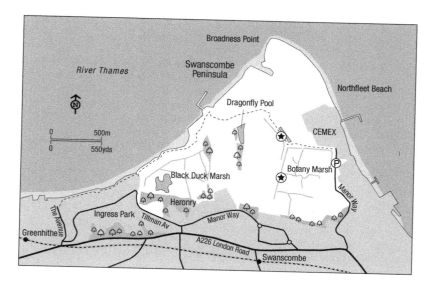

ACCESS

Bike: the paths aren't very suitable for cycling, being uneven, grassy and muddy.

Bus: routes 306 (Bluewater–Borough Green), 480 (Dartford–Gravesend), 490 (Gravesend–Bluewater–Dartford), Fastrack A2 (Dartford–Gravesend) and B/ Fastrack (Temple Hill–Gravesend) all stop at Taunton Road. Alight, and turn down Lower Road onto Manor Way where you'll see a metal kissing gate leading directly onto Botany Marsh. Explore the paths on Botany Marsh or continue north parallel to Manor Way until you come to Swanscombe Marshes proper.

Train: Greenhithe and Swanscombe stations (London Charing Cross–Dartford) are within walking distance.

Car: park in the lay-bys on Manor Way by the cement works, where there are paths directly onto the marsh.

YOUR VISIT

This extensive, abandoned industrial site originally gained its reputation among birders for the very productive sewage farm, which is now closed. However, there are still enough birds to make it worth a visit. Swanscombe Marshes covers most of the Swanscombe Peninsula and, despite being surrounded by industry, you can still lose yourself in solitude.

Three areas make up the marshes and they're fairly obvious when you're on the ground: Botany Marsh, Broadness Salt Marsh and Black Duck Marsh (aka Swanscombe Marshes proper). There's plenty of stony or muddy foreshore and river to watch, and a lot of scrub and grassland, as well as meadows, reedbeds and open water.

Black Duck Marsh (TQ598755; learn.tools.oldest) is the part you'll go through first, via grassy paths through hawthorn scrub, rich in finches and thrushes in winter. There's a large area of open water (TQ603759; loud.dizzy.fluid) which can produce something interesting almost any time of the year. It's surrounded by reeds which can conceal wetland warblers, Water Rail and any wildfowl that aren't out on the water. The small woodland adjacent hosts a small heronry. There were eight Grasshopper Warbler territories around the peninsula in 2021.

Reedy channels bordered by bushes also hold avian interest, with Cetti's Warbler a cert. There's also the possibility of a wintering Dartford Warbler. One of the reedy channels runs past a grassy slope onto a central mound that was once the landfill, and this is a shortcut to the shore via some very rough footpaths. Be careful there, but this can give you a good view over the whole site and is a good place to scan for Buzzard and Marsh Harrier. To the south, you can see Springhead Valley, an important wildlife corridor and minor flyway, in the distance.

Broadness Salt Marsh and Botany Marshes are sizeable areas of wet grassland and reedbed. The former has decent patches of saltmarsh, attracting waders to its mud and rivulets; Short-eared Owl visits occasionally. The foreshore is a good place to look for Scandinavian Rock and Water Pipits in winter, as well as the likes of Turnstone, Curlew, Oystercatcher, Lapwing and other common waders. Broadness (TQ605766; issued.drops.longer) is probably the best place for Turnstone in the LNHS Recording Area; the area around the small light tower at the tip of the point can be good for the species between November and March, though most of it is private. This is also a good place to check for gulls and terns, and even the odd errant seabird, some of which cut overland across the peninsula.

Botany Marsh (TQ610755; hatch.dress.herds) has more reedbeds and is less disturbed by dog-walkers. The 204-m (670-foot) central pylon (TQ606759; reds. sorters.spray) is visible for some distance and has provided a perch for locally nesting Ravens, a scarce species anywhere near London.

Swanscombe Marsh is prime brownfield real estate and has developers conniving over it constantly. A recent scheme to build a theme park on the peninsula was thwarted, but such plans will certainly arise again. The more visitors it gets, the more its value for wildlife will be apparent and it may yet be preserved for nature.

112 FOOTS CRAY MEADOWS

Rectory Lane, Sidcup, Kent DA14 5NG
Websites: footscraymeadows.wordpress.com; londonbirders.fandom.com/
wiki/Foots_Cray_Meadows
Parking: TQ478715; churn.puzzle.wash
TQ485720; claim.sums.rock
Phone: 07858 762530
Email: ffcm06@gmail.com
Open: all day, every day
LNR, SINC
(97 hectares; 250 acres)

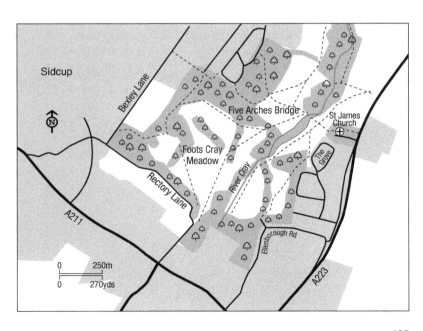

SPECIES

All year: Tawny Owl, Kingfisher, Grey Wagtail, Treecreeper, Nuthatch, Coal Tit.

Summer: Hobby, Swift, hirundines, Lesser Whitethroat.

Winter: Gadwall, Water Rail, Green Sandpiper, Snipe and Jack Snipe, gulls, Fieldfare, Redwing, Firecrest, Siskin, Redpoll.

Migration: Cuckoo, Yellow Wagtail, Tree Pipit, Garden Warbler, Spotted Flycatcher.

ACCESS

Bike: the London Loop (London Outer Orbital Footpath) passes along the River Cray through the whole site.

Bus: route 492 (Sidcup–Bluewater) stops at North Cray Road/Vicarage Road.

Train: Albany Park is the closest station; take the Southeastern service from London Charing Cross–Dartford or London Cannon Street–Gravesend.

Car: park on Leafield Lane, just off the A223 (Lower North Cray Road), or Rectory Lane (which connects Sidcup with Foots Cray).

YOUR VISIT

This LNR around the River Cray has associated wet meadows, plus a shallow, partially silted-up lake (with wooded islands). These water features support Kingfisher and Grey Wagtail year-round while, come winter, Green Sandpiper, Snipe, Water Rail and Gadwall appear, and Jack Snipe occasionally reveals itself.

In spring, the reedier fringes host Reed, Sedge and Cetti's Warblers, while Lesser Whitethroat breeds, though Garden Warbler only passes through. The areas of ancient woodland sustain Tawny Owl, Green and Great Spotted Woodpeckers, Treecreeper, Nuthatch, Coal Tit and Goldcrest, while Little Owl, Lesser Spotted Woodpecker, Tree Pipit and Firecrest have been noted occasionally.

Fieldfare and Redwing are reliable in winter, but small flocks of Siskin and Redpoll are less frequent. Migration sees the odd Cuckoo and Yellow Wagtail pass through, while in summer Hobby overflies the wetlands attracted by the Swifts, Swallows and prodigious dragonflies.

In its entirety, Foots Cray Meadows provides a spacious and pleasant suburban selection of habitats that can provide the odd avian surprise, despite human disturbance.

THE NORTH KENT MARSHES

Made up of the shorelines of the Thames, Medway and Swale estuaries, the North Kent Marshes make up some of the most attractive and bird-rich maritime habitats in Europe.

The whole area of the southern Greater Thames Estuary from Gravesend to the Isle of Grain is an SSSI and comprises the major habitats of estuarine river, mudflats, shingle, saltmarsh and inshore grazing marsh, with pockets of woodland and fresh-water, brackish and saline pools. The region is internationally important for more than 20,000 wintering wildfowl and waders, with often large numbers of threatened or decreasing species, some of which stay to breed.

The entire area contains eight RSPB reserves, with only short drives or train and bus journeys between most of the sites. It is one of 22 ESAs designated by DEFRA and includes numerous individual SSSIs, protected areas and other nature reserves. The marshes are governed by councils in Dartford, Gravesham, Medway, Swale and Canterbury, are fully protected under UK law and help protect the capital from flooding.

While no areas untouched by humans remain, this coast has been bordered by extensive marshland since the end of the Ice Age (about 10,000 years ago). More than 300,000 transient waterbirds also use the mudflats offshore during migration. Most of the species are the same as those on the Swale or Medway, highlighting that it is the entire, interconnected region that is important for birds rather than any one reserve or location.

The more expected species include breeding Avocet, Lapwing, Redshank and Oystercatcher, and migrating Spotted Redshank, Greenshank, Green, Common and Wood Sandpipers, Little Stint and usually a rarity or two each year. The area is important for seaduck and other wildfowl, including Goldeneye, Red-breasted Merganser and Common Scoter, while all three regular species of diver and five species of grebe are possible in winter. There is an expected seabird passage and some good seawatching points. Birds of prey winter in numbers, including the likes of Hen and Marsh Harriers, Peregrine and Merlin, and, in some winters, Rough-legged Buzzard, while all five species of owl can be found in winter and have bred at some point.

Numerous Birds of Conservation Concern are present, many of them songbirds. You can expect to find plenty of breeding Corn Buntings and Yellowhammers in spring, and migration provides room for scarcer European and Asian species to turn up. Snow Bunting is still regular in winter, though both Shorelark and Lapland Bunting have declined in numbers and regularity, while Twite has almost disappeared entirely.

THE HOO PENINSULA

The first major peninsula when heading east out of South London, this self-contained semi-island probably holds the greatest variety of habitats to be found among the North Kent Marshes and could easily absorb most birders all day during passage.

It's bordered by the Thames to the north, the Medway to the south and is full of nature reserves, including some significant RSPB properties. There are huge extents of tidal mudflats for waders, gulls and terns, large expanses of grazing marsh for wildfowl and considerable tracts of wetland and woodland for waterbirds and songbirds – and all include some of our scarcer species. Working from dawn to dusk in May, it's possible to see 120 species in the area. Some of these habitats hold Nationally and Internationally Important numbers of certain species.

113 RSPB CLIFFE POOLS

Salt Lane, Rochester ME3 7SX
Website: www.rspb.org.uk/reserves-and-events/reserves-a-z/cliffe-pools
TQ723760; target.clock.parade
Phone: 01634 222480
Email: northkentmarshes@rspb.org.uk
Open: all day, every day, but the car park is open from 10am–4pm. Check the website for holiday opening times. Pubs, shops, cafes and toilets can be found in nearby Cliffe. There are no facilities on site.
SSSI, SPA, ESA
(230 hectares; 568.34 acres)

SPECIES

All year: Shelduck, Gadwall, Shoveler, Red-legged Partridge, Spoonbill, Marsh Harrier, Red Kite, Buzzard, Peregrine, Water Rail, Oystercatcher, Avocet, Ringed Plover, Barn, Tawny, Little and Long-eared Owls, Stonechat, Cetti's Warbler, Reed and Corn Buntings.

Summer: Garganey, Hobby, Little Ringed Plover, Mediterranean Gull, Common Tern, Cuckoo, warblers, Nightingale, Yellow Wagtail.

Winter: Wigeon, Teal, Pintail, Goldeneye, grebes, divers, Hen Harrier, Merlin, Golden and Grey Plovers, Black-tailed Godwit, Ruff, Short-eared Owl, Rock Pipit.

Migration: seabirds, Green, Common and Wood Sandpipers, Greenshank, Whimbrel, Bar-tailed Godwit, Spotted Redshank, Curlew Sandpiper, Little and Temminck's Stints, skuas, gulls, terns, Yellow Wagtail, Whinchat, Wheatear.

ACCESS

Bike: no cycling is allowed on the reserve itself. Most of the tracks are unsuitable for wheelchairs.

Bus: ASD Coaches bus route 133 (Chatham–Rochester–Strood–Cliffe) stops in Cliffe, from where you can walk west to the Radar Pool down Pickle's Way at the very northern end of the village.

Train: the nearest stations are in Higham (3 miles/5km away) or Strood (5 miles/8km).

Car: leave the M2 at Junction 1 towards Cliffe onto the A289 for about 1.5 miles (2.4km), then take the left towards Cliffe Woods on the B2000. Enter Cliffe village and take the second left after the stone 'Cliffe' village sign on the ground onto Rectory Road, then turn right onto Buckland Road at the T-junction. Take the second left onto Salt Lane and continue to the end, where you will find steel gates. The set on your right enables you to drive into the reserve car park if open, but if you're early, you can discreetly park on the verge by the gate – don't block it please! A more traditional route onto the reserve involves parking on Pickle's Way and walking to the Radar Pool. If the barrier is open, you can carefully drive all the way to the Black Barn Mound and beyond – be aware that the dirt track is very pitted and troughed.

YOUR VISIT

The main areas of Cliffe Pools can be taken in via a 3.5-mile (5.6-km) circuit visiting all the main pools and other habitats.

Starting at the RSPB car park, head north-east along the track with the Crystal Pool to your left for an anticlockwise route. Turn left and walk along the southern side of that pool, a part of the Saxon Shore Way that can be very good for Nightingale (ten were singing in spring 2020).

Backtrack to continue a little further and scan the Conoco Pools. There is a very active Black-headed Gull colony there and you should be able to pick out some of the 130 or more pairs of Mediterranean Gulls that now nest among them. The edges of the bunds between the pools may conceal waders, particularly Greenshank in spring and autumn.

Continue further around the perimeter path to where it joins the Saxon Shore Way along one shore of the Radar Pool. Scan from there for ducks and other waterbirds, before turning left (north) along its western bank. The northern end of

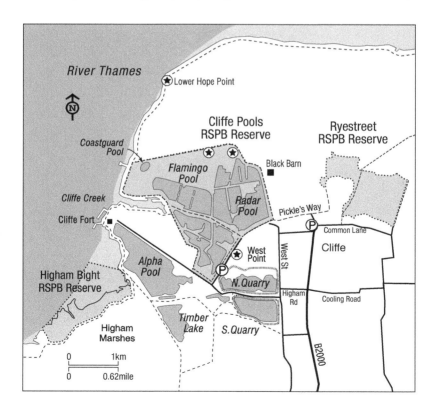

the Radar Pool has shallows and mud that serve as a roosting area for waders and is one of the hotspots for species such as Curlew Sandpiper and Spotted Redshank.

Just ahead, you'll see the building to your right known as the 'Black Barn', after which the Black Barn Pools emerging to your left are named. Around the bend in the road, you'll be able to walk up onto Hope Mound, which overlooks much of the reserve. You'll see the more distant Flamingo and Radar Pools, but much of your attention should be on the four nearer pools. These are particularly productive for scarcer species, having featured the likes of Glossy Ibis, Broad-billed, Marsh and Terek Sandpipers, White-winged Tern, Collared Pratincole, Lesser Sand-plover and many others over the years.

A scope will be handy here, as there is a lot of habitat to examine, and mornings are best as the light is behind you. You'll probably see a profusion of commoner species; up to 5,000 Black-tailed Godwits can roost on these pools during post-breeding dispersal, along with up to 3,000 Avocets (30–60 pairs nest on site), while more than 240 Little Grebes also winter. Wader and duck flocks build up in autumn until high-tide roosts of up to 7,000 Dunlin and 2,000 Lapwing amass. By the winter, up to 3,000 dabbling ducks are gathered on the more northern pools and more than 20 Goldeneye have featured in recent winters, making Cliffe the most important site in Kent for this species. Add up to 800 Shelduck and the reserve's importance is unarguable.

In summer, the mound is a good spot to see Cuckoo and the commoner reed-bed passerines. It also serves as a minor raptor watchpoint, with Buzzard, Red Kite and Marsh Harrier likely overhead, and resident Peregrine, joined by Merlin (winter) and Hobby (summer), all possible over the meadows to the north and east, towards Cooling Marshes.

You're likely to spend much of your time on this mound, which fortunately has a two-seater bench at the top. Once you've had your fill, continue further in the direction of the River Thames. The track bends left where you can scan the pools from another angle on the somewhat lower Pipe Pool Mound. Scan the farmland to the north-east, as Yellow Wagtail breeds in small numbers and Corn Bunting may be present.

Your arrival at the seawall is best timed for an hour before high tide for the chance of seeing seabirds heading upriver, as waders fly overhead to roost on the pools. The track takes an abrupt left at the seawall by the dry grassy depression formerly known as the Coastguard's Pool. Take a little time to scan the river, particularly if the winds are from the east. If seawatching looks promising, with winds in the north to east sector, turn right along the seawall up to where it turns north-east and scope the river from Lower Hope Point. The Thames becomes wider there, facing East Tilbury, but seabirds are usually closer to the Kent side.

Continue south (left, facing the river) along the seawall to Cliffe Creek, a large muddy inlet that can hold a lot of waders. This is a good place to view Curlew, Whimbrel, godwits and Oystercatchers, which can sometimes be very close.

Follow the seawall alongside the creek to the Flamingo Pool – another area at which to linger. The extensive shoreline mud on the far side is another hotspot; depending on the time of year, it can hold the likes of Bewick's Swan, Spoonbill, Glossy Ibis, Great Egret, Black-winged Stilt (the species has bred) and other waders, great or small.

Keep going along the path past the creek, and some of the high-tide waders may have pitched up on the very small reedy pool at the southern end, by the seawall. Approach with care for sometimes very good views. The path now leads back past the Conoco and Crystal Pools to a left turn back into the car park.

Cliffe Pools is such a large site that this long circular route doesn't cover all its options. At this point, instead of turning back to the car park you can take the footpath next to the cement works parallel to the route you've just taken in the direction of the coastal Cliffe Fort. This often-muddy path leads to the Alpha Pool. This is the largest pool, closest to the river, with deeper waters attracting scarcer species, including Slavonian and Red-necked Grebes and Great Northern Diver in winter. The fort, directly opposite Coalhouse Fort (page 125), is another good place to scan the river at high tide.

There is another option of walking back via Salt Lane (the road you drove in on). Find a gap in the hawthorns and scan the North and South Quarry Pits on either side of the road (note that there's nowhere to park). The deep waters are attractive to diving duck, and Peregrine nests on the quarry sides. Britain's first Canvasback was found there in December 1996.

At Cliffe Pools, the RSPB has recently begun to reduce the depth of the pools with material dredged from the Thames and waste from railway tunnelling. Different pools have different salinities, meaning that varying species may favour different locations onsite. The in-filled lagoons enable Lapwing and Redshank to breed, while carefully maintaining the scrub and grassland ensures that Long-eared Owl, Nightingale, Skylark and Corn Bunting sustain their fragile populations.

There's always something to see at Cliffe Pools, and exploring the site can easily take all day. It's also a short distance from Shorne Woods, Higham Bight and Cooling, Halstow and St Mary's Marshes.

114 NEARBY: SHORNE WOODS CP

Brewer's Road, Shorne, Kent DA12 3HX
Website: www.kent.gov.uk/leisure-and-community/kent-country-parks/
find-a-kent-country-park/shorne-woods-country-park
TQ684699; daring.data.onions
Open: all day, every day; the pay-and-display car park hours are 9am–8pm
SSSI, Kent Downs Area of Outstanding Natural Beauty
(118 hectares; 292 acres)

Shorne Woods comprises a mix of ancient woodland and commercial plantations, with broad paths and rides. Marsh Tit and all three woodpeckers can be found, while there is a chance of Hawfinch. Bullfinch is present all year, one or two Nightingales summer, and Spotted Flycatcher and Yellowhammer may just about hang on.

Shorne Woods CP is well signposted from the A2 London–Dover road, very close to the turn-off from either direction.

115 NEARBY: RSPB SHORNE MARSHES AND RSPB HIGHAM BIGHT

Shorne Marshes: Canal Road, Lower Higham, Rochester, Kent ME3 7JA; TQ703739; paints.sample.dull
Higham Bight: Church Street, Lower Higham, Rochester, Kent ME3 7LS; TQ716741; hike.fight.noisy
Website: northkent.birdwise.org.uk/events/ranger-walk-higham-shorne-marshes
(Total area: 159 hectares; 392.9 acres)

SPECIES

All year: Shelduck, Gadwall, Shoveler, Marsh Harrier, Peregrine, Water Rail, Oystercatcher, Avocet, Ringed Plover, Snipe, Stonechat, Cetti's Warbler, Bearded Tit, Corn Bunting, Yellowhammer.

Summer: Yellow Wagtail, warblers, Nightingale.

Winter: Wigeon, Teal, Hen Harrier, Merlin, Golden and Grey Plovers, Jack Snipe, Snipe, Redwing, Fieldfare.

Migration: Garganey, seabirds, Hobby, Yellow-legged Gull, skuas, terns, waders, Whinchat, Wheatear.

ACCESS

Bus: Arriva Kent & Surrey route 190 stops at Chalk Road at the west end of Gravesend, from where you can walk north along Castle Lane and Lower Higham Road to the marshes.

Train: the closest stations are via Southeastern services from London Stratford to Gravesend and Higham.

Car: Shorne Marshes: follow Canal Road north out of Higham to the limited parking at the end. Walk the track west, then north, to view the pools and marshes.

Higham Bight: take Church Street north out of Lower Higham and park at St Mary's Church. Follow the public footpaths north to the seawall to the Thames.

YOUR VISIT

Since **Shorne Marshes** is partly used by the Metropolitan Police's Milton Rifle Range, there is no public access to part of the site. However, the reserve can be viewed from public rights of way, and certain footpaths will take you all the way to the shore and back, if the red flags are not flying.

RSPB Higham Bight is more fully accessible and covers the shoreline to the south of Cliffe Fort, while Shorne Marshes is further south-west, inland of Shornemead Fort.

Winter is the best time to visit Higham Bight. Rapid tides push waders up the mudflats in front of you, before they fly to roost at Cliffe Pools. Shorne Marshes hosts breeding Water Rail, Lapwing, Redshank and Snipe, holds the highest

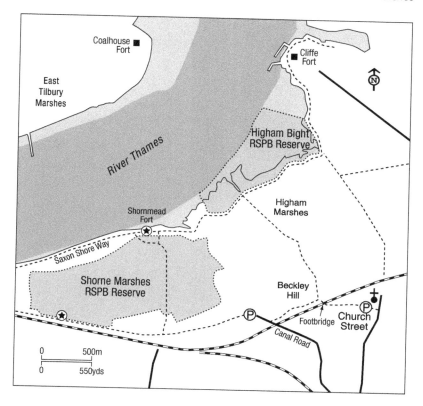

number of Jack Snipe in the county (14 in winter 2021), and provides stop-over habitat for Greenshank and Wood Sandpiper. The grazing marshes on Shorne and Higham sometimes support geese in winter, and scarce forms such as Tundra Bean and Russian White-fronted Geese sometimes drop in.

Higham Bight probably sees the largest numbers of Yellow-legged Gulls in Kent during their late-summer post-breeding dispersal. It's a decent vantage point for seabirds during autumn northerlies, though Cliffe Fort and Lower Hope Point are more productive. However, the narrowness of the Thames at this point means that smaller species such as auks and petrels pass by more closely when they occur.

Scrub and trees on either reserve support singing Nightingales in spring, particularly in the bushes around the Thames and Medway Canal forming the southern border of Shorne Marshes. Corn Buntings and the occasional Yellowhammer sing in summer, while good numbers of migrant chats turn up in autumn.

116 COOLING, HALSTOW AND ST MARY'S MARSHES

For approximate addresses, see Access.

SPECIES

All year: Marsh Harrier, Oystercatcher, Avocet, Redshank, Kingfisher, Bearded Tit, Corn and Reed Buntings.

Summer: Quail, Little Ringed Plover, warblers.

Winter: Bewick's Swan, Brent Goose, Wigeon, Teal, Shoveler, Pintail, Gadwall, Hen Harrier, Golden and Grey Plovers, Dunlin, Knot, Curlew, both godwits, Peregrine, Merlin, Short-eared Owl, Snow Bunting.

Migration: Garganey, Whimbrel, Greenshank, hirundines, chats, warblers.

ACCESS

Bike: the seawall only can be cycled with care.

Bus: Arriva Kent & Surrey service 191 (Chatham–Grain) stops at Harrison Drive, a short walk from High Halstow NNR (page 205), a short walk from Egypt Bay.

Train: the nearest station is Rochester, on the Southeastern London Kings Cross St Pancras–Ramsgate line, from where you will need to catch the 191 bus.

Car: parking places are at a premium for these sites; the best, in order of convenience, are:

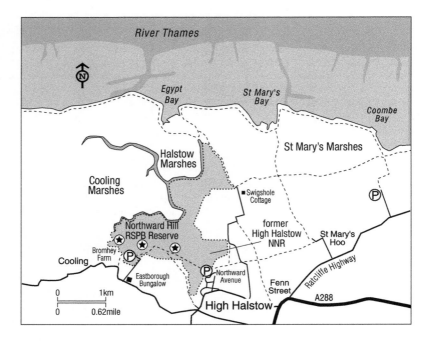

St Mary's Marsh – take Shakespeare Farm Road off the Ratcliffe Highway until you come to the Coombe Point Beach car park (TQ814776; digitally.congested. defends) and follow the footpath north to scope the river.

Halstow Marshes – from Britannia Road, turn onto Clinch Street, which becomes Decoy Hill Road after a couple of miles, and park on the verge (around TQ788762; vibrating.juror.currently) – not in front of any gates or access points – and continue north to the marshes and Egypt Bay (TQ777790; ambushes.track.starting). Spaces are very limited.

Cooling Marshes – turn down the unnamed dirt road at the bend between Common Lane and Rye Street (TQ747765; bluff.nozzles.dressings) and find a safe verge away from any farm access points, then walk north to the saltmarsh.

YOUR VISIT

These coastal marshes are lesser-known but productive parts of the peninsula, mostly comprising grazing marsh, scrub and reedbeds between Cliffe and Allhallows (the whole 12-mile/19-km section of coastal path can be walked by the more limber).

Wildfowl numbers can be substantial, with Bewick's Swan still a possibility, Brent Goose in their hundreds, and Wigeon and Teal in the low thousands. In the colder months, keep a lookout for Peregrine and Merlin, while Marsh Harrier is likely all year.

Time your arrival at the foreshore on a rising or falling tide to view the waders. A large proportion of the 10,000 or so Knot that use this part of the Swale foreshore can be seen, along with thousands of Dunlin and hundreds of Grey Plover, Redshank and Curlew – it's an impressive spectacle. Numbers of Golden Plover have declined, but some still use the grazing marshes. Salt Fleet Flats – the muddy foreshore at Cooling – has held up to 1,870 Avocets in autumn, depending on peak numbers at Cliffe Pools. The larids will conceal a few Mediterranean Gulls in late winter and plenty in the summer.

Songbirds include flocking Corn Buntings in winter, while a few Bearded Tits are resident but nomadic in the reedy ditches. Snow Bunting still shows up sometimes in winter.

117 RSPB NORTHWARD HILL AND HIGH HALSTOW NNR

Buck Hole Farm, Buckhole Farm Road, High Halstow, Rochester, Kent ME3 8SE
Website: www.rspb.org.uk/reserves-and-events/reserves-a-z/northward-hill
TQ768763; cleansed.glaze.product
Phone: 01634 222480
Email: northkentmarshes@rspb.org.uk
Open: all day, every day. Car park hours are 10am–4pm; there are a few spaces on the unnamed road from Lipwell Hill to the reserve entrance out

of hours. Check the website for national holiday opening times. Nearby High Halstow has basic amenities.

SSSI, Natura 2000, NNR

(*Northward Hill*: 52.5 hectares (130 acres); *High Halstow*: 270 hectares; 670 acres)

SPECIES

All year: large heronry, Marsh Harrier, Avocet, Lapwing, Redshank, Barn, Little and Long-eared Owls, Corn and Reed Buntings.

Summer: Garganey, Mediterranean Gull, Nightingale, Yellow Wagtail, warblers.

Winter: Hen Harrier, Merlin, Peregrine, Golden Plover, Woodcock, Short-eared Owl, Redwing, Fieldfare.

Migration: Ruff, Green, Common and Wood Sandpipers, Greenshank, Stonechat, Whinchat, Wheatear.

ACCESS

Bike: bikes are not permitted on the reserve's footpaths.

Bus: Arriva Kent & Surrey routes 10 (All Hallows–Hoo St Werburgh), 191 (Chatham–Grain), 193 (Chatham–Cliffe) and 692 (Rochester–Lower Stoke) all stop at Harrison Drive in High Halstow.

Train: Southeastern services from London Stratford–Ramsgate stop at Strood or Chatham, from where you can catch the 191 or 193 buses.

Car: there are two entrances. The closest to the car park is off Lipwell Hill. Turn into the RSPB-signposted track by Eastborough Bungalow and park but note that the gate at the bungalow closes at dusk. You can also take the entrance track to the old RSPB car park and walk through what used to be High Halstow NNR. Follow Lipwell Hill/Cooling Road into High Halstow, take a left onto The Street, then left onto Harrison Drive, then left onto Northwood Avenue. The RSPB is signposted immediately to your left.

YOUR VISIT

Perhaps the Hoo Peninsula's richest area of habitat, **Northward Hill** comprises a large area of reconstituted wet meadow and extensive woodland, with expansive views over grazing marsh and reedbeds. The bluebell woods are home to the UK's largest heronry, with around 150 Grey Heron and 50 Little Egret nests; Cattle Egret bred for the first time in 2019. The neighbouring rookery holds more than 500 pairs of Rook, and this is believed to be affecting Grey Heron numbers adversely.

Leave the car park at Bromhey Farm and follow the footpaths west or east to the reserve or the long path from the car park in **High Halstow**. Much of the reserve is inaccessible and a telescope is advised. There is now a wader scrape in the western half within a fenced-off area, distantly viewable from Gordon's Hide. The main part of the reserve is on a ridge enabling panoramic views north over the whole Swale SSSI, from Decoy Fleet to Halstow Marshes, Egypt Bay, St Mary's Bay and the

Thames, with Cooling Marshes to the north-west and Whalebone Marshes to the west.

Raptors such as Marsh Harrier and Buzzard are often obvious, while wildfowl movements at dawn or towards dusk can be fairly dramatic. The huge swathes of level marshes in the distance provide breeding sites for about 20 pairs of Avocet, plus Lapwing, Snipe and Redshank, and winter foraging for hordes of Wigeon and Teal. Up to 20 Woodcock roost in winter. It's possible to walk out as far as Egypt and St Mary's Bays, scanning the marshes and Thames foreshore on the way, though this will be time-consuming.

The edges of the woodland and scrub hold about 30 pairs of Nightingale, with numerous pairs of commoner warblers. The dense scrub encourages Long-eared Owls to breed and winter. There is a substantial rookery in the woods, which can be spectacular in winter. The reserve was once renowned for its Tree Sparrows, but these have now disappeared.

There have been many good birds over the years, including Red-breasted Goose, Montagu's Harrier, Black-winged Stilt, Marsh Sandpiper, Red-footed Falcon, Red-flanked Bluetail and Greenish Warbler.

118 THE ISLE OF GRAIN

The eastern part of the Hoo peninsula is less populous, particularly in winter, being somewhat isolated by Yantlet Creek, which partly divides the peninsula in half. The habitats and species are similar to those at Cliffe and Northward Hill. Most sites are accessible via the B2001, which runs from the A228 – the main route onto the Hoo.

SPECIES

All year: Shelduck, Gadwall, Shoveler, Red-legged Partridge, Marsh Harrier, Lapwing, Ringed Plover, Redshank, Mediterranean Gull, Peregrine, Barn and Little Owls, Cetti's Warbler, Bearded Tit, Corn Bunting.

Summer: Lapwing, Redshank, Oystercatcher, Yellow-legged Gull, Yellow Wagtail.

Winter: Bewick's Swan (scarce), Brent Goose, Wigeon, Teal, Pintail, Red-throated Diver, Hen Harrier, Golden and Grey Plovers, Purple Sandpiper, Knot, Dunlin, Black-tailed Godwit, Curlew, Snipe, Jack Snipe, Merlin, Short-eared Owl, Rock Pipit, Stonechat, Snow Bunting.

Migration: Garganey, seabirds, skuas, terns, waders, Kittiwake, Little Gull, auks, Hobby, Whinchat, Wheatear, Redstart, warblers including rarer species.

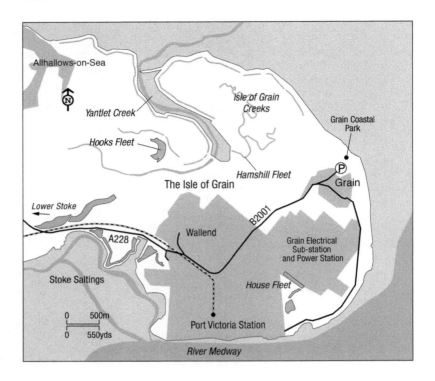

119 ALLHALLOWS AND STOKE LAGOON

Parking: Avery Way/Willow Close/Kingsmead Park, Allhallows, Kent ME3 9PZ
TQ844783; custard.glitter.repaying
Open: all day, every day. Allhallows has basic facilities

ACCESS

Bus: Arriva services 9 (Maidstone–Bearsted), 10 (Hoo ST Werburgh–Allhallows), 191 (Chatham–Grain) and 692 (Rochester–Lower Stoke) stop at Kingsmead Caravan Park, a short distance to the shore path.

Train: Southeastern services from London Stratford International–Ramsgate stop at Rochester, from where you should get the 191 bus.

Car: follow the A228 towards Grain, take the minor road north at Lower Stoke to Allhallows, then Avery Way and park at the British Pilot pub.

YOUR VISIT

This complex but discrete area of coastal marsh and farmland supports similar species and habitats to the nearby Northward Hill and Halstow shoreline.

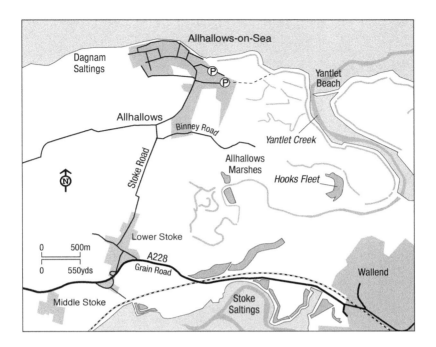

However, they're well worth exploring if you want to find your own birds. The mudflats host great numbers of waders, particularly during passage, and there's also grassland and scrub.

Lapland Bunting is much less frequent these days on the beaches and seawall between Allhallows and Yantlet Creek, but Snow Bunting still sometimes turns up in winter. Visible migration can be impressive on the coast, especially during light westerlies in spring or autumn, with particularly large numbers of hirundines and finches possible.

This is a good seawatching site in northerly or easterly winds; anything's possible – even petrels and shearwaters. Visit within a couple of hours of high tide to get the best views of the plentiful waders – otherwise, they can be very distant. There is often a large roost at Yantlet Beach, which can be scoped from the west side of Yantlet Creek (TQ855783; pouch.start.ears).

Inland, to the south-east of Allhallows, the footpath to Binney Farm overlooks **Allhallows Marshes** (TQ846775; scrum.prospers.teach), a small, isolated but productive area of flooded grassland. If you're following the meandering path east from that end of Binney Road, you'll get to **Stoke Lagoon** (TQ834751; nerve. reinstate.tribe) when it turns south then west, to the south of Allhallows. This private fishery is easily scannable and can host impressive numbers of Wigeon and other winter wildfowl, while it's also a good stopover point for migrating waders. It overlooks Stoke Saltings, providing refuge for waders that can be scoped from shore as the tide comes in or goes out. The area is often shot over but still produces good birds. It's best explored by walking the seawall from the village of Lower Stoke at the end of Burrows Lane towards Grain. Check the maze of creeks, pools and marsh on your way.

120 GRAIN COASTAL PARK

Parking: Grain Beach, High Street, Grain, Kent ME3 0BJ
TQ888769; duck.hurls.impose
Open: all day, every day. Grain village has basic amenities. Please use the
signposted public footpaths and avoid the fenced-off power station sites.

ACCESS

Bus: Arriva route 191 from Chatham terminates at Grain.

Train: Southeastern services from London Stratford International–Ramsgate stop
at Rochester, from where you should get the 191 bus.

Car: the B2001 takes an abrupt left to the village, where it becomes High Street.
Follow this to the beach car park next to Foreshore CP/Grain Coastal Park.

YOUR VISIT

This site, like much of the area, is most productive in autumn and winter, when the
seafront is worth exploring all the way around the coast to Kingsnorth Power
Station and Hoo. Most of the small coastal pools, some of which are former gravel
pits and filter beds, are very good for passage waders and can host Jack Snipe

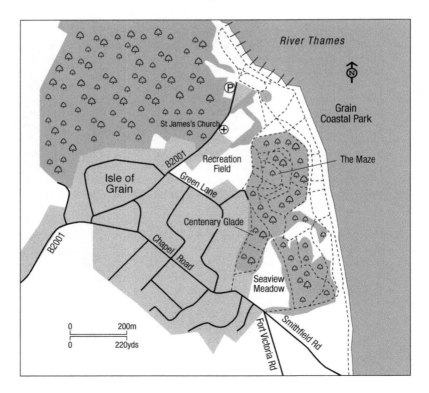

and Water Pipit in the colder months, and the fishing lakes hold breeding Kingfisher and have even attracted Red-rumped Swallow on passage.

Grain Foreshore CP (TQ890766; funds.last.disco) separates the village from the sea with a mix of grassland and scrub that is attractive to migrants, and there are many coastal and inland pools nearby – all worth checking. The shore allows good seawatching in autumn with winds in the north or east sector, particularly from the point at Grain (TQ890769; stand.slower.shells), just east of the car park (TQ888769; amused.fortunate.swear).

The huge areas of mud at low tide, contiguous with those at Allhallows to the west, hold numerous waders, but these are best viewed a couple of hours on either side of high tide. Visible migration is good in spring and autumn in lighter westerlies, with good numbers of finches and hirundines.

To the west of Kingsnorth Power Station and south of Abbots Court is **Coombe Bay** (TQ797717; driven.envy.clock), a further continuation of the same habitats; it has held more than 1,300 Brent Geese.

121 GREAT CHATTENDEN WOOD AND LODGE HILL CAMP

Chattenden, Medway, Kent ME3 8NZ
Website: www.kentwildlifetrust.org.uk/lodge-hill
TQ754737; grapes.raven.removed
Open: all day, every day
SSSI
(Total area: 163.5 hectares; 404.02 acres)

SPECIES

All year: Tawny, Little and Barn Owls, Nuthatch, Treecreeper, Firecrest, Hawfinch.

Summer: Cuckoo, Nightingale, commoner warblers.

Winter: Woodcock, Redwing, Fieldfare.

Migration: chats, flycatchers, warblers.

ACCESS

Bus: Arriva route 191 (Chatham–Grain) stops at Farm View Villas on Lodge Hill Lane, a short walk to the east from the woods.

Train: Southeastern services from London Stratford International–Ramsgate stop at Rochester, from where you can catch the 191 bus.

Car: parking spaces are limited on the verge at the sharp bend on Lodge Hill Road (TQ754737; steamed.newspaper.harnessed), by the private gate to Bridge Wood Field Archery Club.

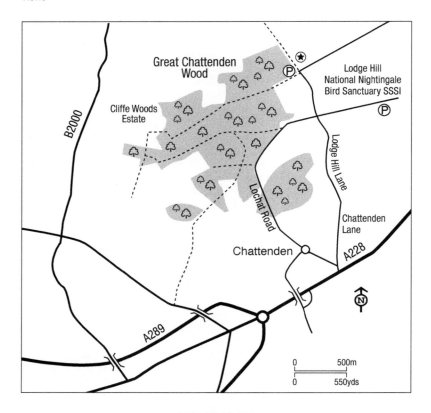

YOUR VISIT

Chattenden Woods in the south-west of the Hoo Peninsula is a sizeable area of ancient woodland, while Lodge Hill National Nightingale Bird Sanctuary, which connects to it in the south-east, holds the largest population of Nightingales in Britain, with more than 85 singing males recently.

Until December 2018, Lodge Hill was under threat from a 5,000-home development but this now seems to be cancelled owing to pressure from locals and conservationists. However, the prospect of houses being built nearby remains, which would still have a deleterious effect on wildlife.

This rich patchwork of grass, semi-heathland, scrub, coppice and mature trees supports healthy numbers of other birds, including Tawny, Little and Barn Owls, and Cuckoo. Nuthatch and Treecreeper are present, Firecrest has wintered and Hawfinch is still occasionally reported. Visit at dawn in late spring or early summer for bracing bursts of warbler song or take a chance in autumn for migrants.

THE MEDWAY ESTUARY

Website: ww2.rspb.org.uk/groups/medway; birdingsouthernmedway.blog-spot.com/p/a-site-guide-to-southern-medway.html
SSSI

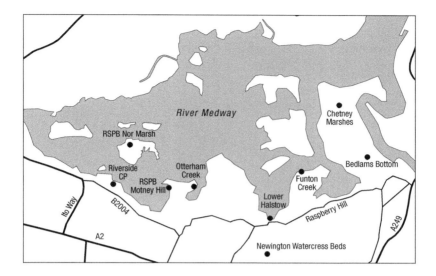

This is a huge area of tidal river estuary, with a huge tidal rise and fall too. The extensive areas of mud provide rich feeding grounds for wildfowl and waders over the whole shoreline, while the surrounding woods, hedges and fields provide refuge for migrants. The tide is your controlling factor for a good day's birding, but all the following sites are easily driveable or cyclable from each other and can be visited consecutively for a panoramic sweep of the whole riverside area.

The greatest numbers of Pintail in South-East England are concentrated in the Medway Estuary, with recent winter counts of more than 500, along with 3,500 Teal and similar numbers of Wigeon. Brent Goose counts peak in March, when more than 2,700 may be present, while the winter estuary can host more than 40 Red-breasted Mergansers. You may well find yourself in competition with shotguns for the wildfowl, as some of the private areas are shot over.

Winter waders are profuse too, particularly Grey Plover, Dunlin, Redshank, Avocet and Black-tailed Godwit, but many scarcer species pop up on passage. A full day on the Medway will provide a long day list, though you will need a scope handy to get the best from the location and try to arrive a couple of hours on either side of a high tide. Bad weather will increase the likelihood of seabirds offshore, particularly if winds are in the northern or eastern sectors. Visible songbird migration is best during the first couple of hours after dawn.

Make full use of the footpaths, seawall, Saxon Shore Way and roadside verges to scan the estuary. I've highlighted the best sites to view offshore waterbirds, but anywhere along the B2004 can produce good sightings.

SPECIES

All year: Avocet, Oystercatcher, Redshank, Mediterranean Gull (breeds).

Summer: Common, Sandwich and Little Terns, Turtle Dove (scarce), Hobby, Nightingale, Grasshopper Warbler, commoner warblers, Yellow Wagtail.

Winter: Brent Goose, Wigeon, Goldeneye, seaduck including Red-breasted Merganser, Black-necked and Slavonian Grebes, divers, Marsh and Hen Harriers, Grey and Golden Plover, Short-eared Owl, Merlin, Peregrine, Rock Pipit.

Migration: Garganey, Black-tailed and Bar-tailed Godwits, Spotted Redshank, Wood and Common Sandpipers, Greenshank, Little Stint and other migratory waders, Black Tern, Little Gull.

122 RIVERSIDE CP AND NOR MARSHES AND MOTNEY HILL RSPB

Parking: Motney Hill – Motney Hill Road, Gillingham, Medway, Kent ME8 7TZ ; TQ821675; sinkhole.competent.slippers
Riverside CP – VC, Lower Rainham Road, Gillingham, Medway, Kent ME8 7TL; TQ807683; quits.jumbled.doses
Website: www.medway.gov.uk/directory_record/523/riverside_country_park_greenspace
Open: all day, every day, but the Riverside CP VC hours are 10am–4.30pm; the car park is open from 8.30am–dusk (closed on Christmas and Boxing Days). You can book cruises on the Medway at the VC, which has basic amenities
Motney Hill and its car park are always open. Try nearby Rainham and Gillingham for more facilities
Ramsar, SSSI, Green Flag status

ACCESS

Bus: Nu-Venture route 131 (Chatham–West Malling) stops at West Motney Way, a short walk to the estuary shoreline, and at Lower Twydall Lane, an even shorter walk to the Riverside CP car park.

Train: Rainham station on the Southeastern service from London Stratford International–Faversham is the nearest, about a mile to the south of Motney Hill.

Car: both car parks can be accessed via the B2004 from Gillingham and Upchurch.

YOUR VISIT

Another expansive, complex mosaic of habitats on the Medway, giving views over the estuary and its multitude of waders and wildfowl, best seen in autumn and winter. There is plentiful scrub, grassland and reedbeds, with copious mudflats and open water offshore.

There are two promontories out into the Medway Estuary – Horrid Hill and Motney Hill (neither are really hills) – overlooking a deep channel (Bartlett Creek) about 1 mile (1.6km) offshore, a mile almost totally composed of exposed mud at low tide. No access is possible to **Nor Marsh**, an offshore saltmarsh island managed by the RSPB, though it can be viewed by boat when the tide is in. The island supported almost 150 pairs of nesting Mediterranean Gulls in 2021. Burntwick Island, further offshore, and **Riverside CP** also hold substantial breeding numbers of this relatively recent coloniser. Burntwick has also held more than 200 pairs of Sandwich Terns and a few Little Terns in recent years.

Motney Hill is also managed by the RSPB and is a better bet to view the wildfowl and waders, including overwintering Spotted Redshank. Walk the footpath along its western edge from the car park until you reach the northernmost tip – a grassy area that overlooks Bartlett Creek and a high-tide wader roost. The creek can hold seaduck outside the breeding season. On your way, be sure to check the scrub and reeds for migrants, but keep to the path as other areas are part of a private reserve managed by the Kent Wildfowlers' Association. Check the telegraph wires for purring Turtle Doves in summer.

Horrid Hill (TQ811689; alternate.afflicted.slurred) is part of Riverside CP and managed by Medway Council. It will also give you good views of the wildfowl and waders around the small islands of mud and saltmarsh, though the area is popular with local dog-walkers and joggers.

If you're looking for migrants, explore the scrub around the car park (TQ807683; flagpole.manage.booklet) and the sheltered pond (TQ806684; retailing.strike. visits) and scrub at Eastcourt Meadows to the west (central point: TQ801686; perky. recorders.crest). The tip of Horrid Hill is the best place to scan Nor Marsh RSPB, out in the estuary.

It's worth following the path to the east to Motney Hill (about 3 miles/4.8km) as a round trip. There are many more creeks and pieces of saltmarsh to scan during the walk for close views of large numbers of waders. In 2002 there was an 850-strong Avocet roost on Motney Saltings (TQ825686; signed.attending.certainly).

123 NEARBY: FUNTON CREEK, BEDLAMS BOTTOM AND CHETNEY MARSHES

Raspberry Hill Lane, Swale, Kent ME9 8SP
TQ882682; waggled.aged.juicy
Open: all day, every day

The Medway Estuary is viewable from several places along Raspberry Hill Lane (halfway point: TQ884683; masts.dusters.ridiculed). This minor road between Lower Halstow and the Kingsferry Bridge is further east than the previous site, though the road is sometimes rendered unusable by seasonal flooding.

Copious waders and wildfowl offer intimate views from the lay-bys, with rising or falling tides from autumn to spring being the best times to see these. The large Avocet flock present in winter is often distant, however, but numbered more than 800 in November 2020. Raptors and Short-eared Owls are often present at the same time along the shoreline. A few pairs of Yellow Wagtail nested in 2021.

Just to the north-east on the same road is **Chetney Marshes**, where 1,560 Brent Geese were present during a WeBs count in early February 2020, though the Bewick's Swans the site was known for are no longer reliable. The January Golden Plover peak can top 4,000 birds and there's a large wader roost on the saltmarsh at high tide, though birds are more easily seen on the mud. Park along the unnamed public byway (TQ898688; twinkling.trails.tripled) at the eastern end of Raspberry Hill Lane and explore using the public footpaths only.

Chetney is one of the most important areas for commoner waterfowl in Kent, with Shelduck, Gadwall, Teal, Shoveler, Pochard, Avocet, Lapwing, Redshank and Common Tern all nesting.

124 NEARBY: OTTERHAM CREEK

Essentially, this inlet on the eastern side of Motney Hill has little public access. However, it can be scanned from the beginning of the buildings halfway along the public footpath (TQ826681; tasteful.crabmeat.solar). Better views can be had from the seawall (TQ830681; preparing.outlooks.grapevine) by taking a right from the main path onto the tiny footpath that leads there (TQ828682; stardom. sunflower.printouts).

The lack of disturbance and sheltered aspect of the creek makes it one of the best spots to observe waders closely, particularly Spotted Redshank. Please keep as far away from the birds as possible and respect the area's solitude and privacy.

125 NEARBY: LOWER HALSTOW AND NEWINGTON WATERCRESS BEDS

Also known as **Newington Cress Beds**, this area of riverine watercress surrounded by woods, orchards and scrub a short drive west of Motney Hill is well worth visiting in winter. It's a fairly reliable site for Jack Snipe, as well as Water Rail and Green Sandpiper. Spotted Crake and Bittern have turned up on occasion.

To find the parking site, leave the A2 (High Street) in Newington north onto Church Lane. Take a right at the bend onto Wardwell Lane, and park anywhere you can sensibly near the bend by the start of Hawes Wood (Newington Enterprise Centre – TQ861655; soggy.steer.withdraw – can be a good spot). The public footpath onto the site begins just at the western end of the enterprise centre, and heads north.

The woods between there and Lower Halstow are also worth exploring for commoner species in winter and spring. There are buses from Sittingbourne and Gillingham, while the Southeastern service from London Victoria–Dover Priory stops at Newington.

There is extensive coastal marshland to explore nearby at **Lower Halstow**, which is best in winter for hordes of waders and wildfowl and the expected and less-expected winter raptors. Park at the end of Lapwing Drive (ME9 7DZ; TQ859674; bogus.masses.solve), walk the seawall north and view the mudflats and offshore islands, as well as the migrant-attracting fields and orchards around Ham Green (TQ846688; juniors.romance.trombone) further towards Rainham Creek.

Leave your vehicle, walk on the Saxon Shore Way to the wharf where the *Edith May* barge is moored to your right, and then head west, keeping the River Swale to your right. To return inland past the orchards, take a left at Callow's Cottages, then left again onto Poot Lane, then left onto Twinney Lane and walk back to the Saxon Shore Way coastal path.

THE ISLE OF SHEPPEY AND THE SWALE

The roughly rectangular, 36 square mile (93 km²) Isle of Sheppey is separated from the mainland by The Swale, a tidal channel supporting Internationally Important numbers of waders and wildfowl year-round, especially in winter.

Sheppey's northern coast is characterised by cliffs and a muddy foreshore, both of which are classed as SSSIs. The cliffs rise to about 55m (180 feet), providing a useful and alluring landmark for migrant songbirds crossing the North Sea.

The southern side has a complex array of arable and grazing grassland and marsh – very attractive to waders, raptors and passerines. The island is particularly notable for wintering Short-eared Owls, which regularly reach double figures. Sheppey's eastern side faces the sea and provides a good place to scan for seabirds as well as a further beacon for migrating birds. The western side is not as interesting for birds, being somewhat industrial and built-up, but still attracts interesting species – particularly Snow Bunting in winter.

The Swale (another SSSI) is a tidal channel rather than an estuary and holds more than 13,000 Wigeon in winter, along with up to 1,455 Grey Plovers and 3,700 Oystercatchers. Passing Brent Goose numbers on The Swale can top 3,400 during March, with White-front numbers in the high hundreds just before. Many of the waders concentrate on Oare Marshes, south of The Swale, at high tide.

Sheppey has several important nature reserves providing an opportunity to see scarcer species. Try to incorporate several Sheppey sites together.

Of peripheral interest, the isle's cliffs are well known as a site of great paleontological interest. They gave up the first-ever named fossil bird in 1825 – the kingfisher-like *Halcyornis toliapicus* – before yielding a further 16 bird families, of which this cliff site is the type locality for 20 fossil species. Clearly, Sheppey has been the home of a great diversity of birds for a very long time indeed.

SPECIES

All year: Grey and Red-legged Partridges, Little, Great and Cattle Egrets, Avocet, Redshank, Lapwing, Tawny, Barn and Little Owls, Skylark, Bearded Tit, Meadow Pipit, Stonechat.

Summer: Hobby, Mediterranean Gull, Common Tern, Yellow Wagtail.

Winter: Bewick's Swan, White-fronted Goose, Wigeon, Teal, Pintail, Shoveler, Red-breasted Merganser, Common Scoter, Eider, Red-throated Diver, Rough-legged Buzzard (not annual), Red Kite, Hen and Marsh Harriers, Merlin, Peregrine, Oystercatcher, Ringed, Grey and Golden Plovers, Sanderling, Turnstone, Snipe, Curlew, Long-eared and Short-eared Owls, Snow and Lapland Buntings.

Migration: Garganey, Osprey, shearwaters, petrels, Spoonbill, gulls, terns, skuas, auks, scarcer waders, Hobby, Yellow Wagtail, Wheatear, Whinchat, Ring Ouzel, Yellow-browed Warbler, Firecrest, Brambling.

126 ELMLEY NNR AND ELMLEY MARSHES

Kingshill Farm, Isle of Sheppey, Kent ME12 3RW
Website: www.elmleynaturereserve.co.uk
Car park: TQ938679; dare.digested.mooring
Phone: 01795 664896
Email: info@elmleynaturereserve.co.uk
Open: 9am–5pm, Wednesday–Sunday only (£6 entrance fee). Shops,
cafes, toilets and pubs are available in nearby Queenborough and
Sheerness. Expect a 6.5-mile (10.5-km) round trip on foot over the whole
reserve, most of which isn't suitable for wheelchairs.
SSSI, NNR
(*Elmley NNR*: 1300 hectares; 3212.37 acres)

ACCESS

Bike: cycling is not permitted.

Bus: Arriva route 334 (Maidstone–Sheerness) stops at Stray Marsh Farm,
Queenborough (the first stop after the Swale Crossing bridge). Walk south to the
reserve.

Train: the Southeastern Sittingbourne–Sheerness service stops at Queenborough
once an hour, about a mile from the reserve entrance on the A249.

Car: follow Sheppey Way over the old Kingsferry Bridge, roughly parallel to the
A249. After a mile, turn right onto Ferry Road at the brown tourist 'nature reserve'
sign. Take care – the turning can be easily missed. Take the immediate left, signposted 'Elmley'. If you're early, turn right down the minor road to scan the western
end of the fields and small pools.

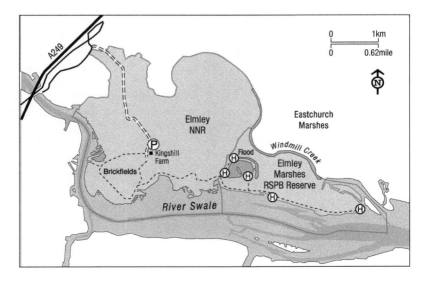

YOUR VISIT

Once one of the most popular reserves in the entire region, **Elmley Marshes** moved into private ownership in 2013 after many years of being successfully leased by the RSPB. Consequently, it's since become less easy to visit and is under-watched, though the owners say they are committed to conservation and access. The reserve now charges £6 for vehicular access and is closed on Mondays and Tuesdays – however, the main track and seawall are public footpaths, so some access is still possible. When open, a cafe, some toilets and picnic areas are available, and you can stay overnight in the barn, chalets and tents. That said, it's still a fantastic reserve and worth taking time to explore.

Elmley NNR is of National and International Importance for breeding and wintering birds and attracts a breathtaking number and variety of waders and wild-fowl. Overall, up to 64 pairs of Avocet now breed (if you include Spitend Marshes at the far end), along with around 100 pairs of Lapwing. During the winter all five regularly occurring owls can be found in the area, while raptors such as Merlin, Hen Harrier and Rough-legged Buzzard are sometimes present; there's always something interesting.

You should be alert the moment you turn into the entrance (taking care to drive slowly and safely, of course); the mile-long track to Kingshill Farm can enable intimate looks at commoner waders and duck, and the wintering flocks of larks and pipits can conceal the likes of Lapland Bunting. More than 1,000 Golden Plover can be present in winter. Use your car as a hide so as not to disturb the birds.

Once you've parked, check the oak trees behind the house for Little Owl, while the low, dense trees on the southern side of the car park often host a Long-eared Owl or two in winter – keep your distance to avoid disturbance. Once you're on the path heading downhill towards The Swale in winter, you're likely to see Barn and Short-eared Owls, as well as Marsh and (possibly) Hen Harriers quartering the fields. Peregrine and Merlin hunt the area in the cold months.

As you follow the 'nature trail' path along the Swale seawall, old hands at the site will be pleased to see that the screen overlooking the fecund mud is still there. This is one of the better places to scan for migrant waders, and can provide good views of Dunlin, Oystercatcher and other commoner species, along with the likes of Little Stint, Curlew Sandpiper and Spotted Redshank at low tide. Red-breasted Merganser can be seen in double figures in winter.

After about a mile on the rough path, turn left alongside a reedbed and scan the channels and pools to the east from the Well Marsh and Counterwall Hides. The waders and duck have historically included a substantial number of rarities, including American Wigeon, Black Stork, Pallid and Montagu's Harriers, and Marsh, Baird's and White-rumped Sandpipers.

Returning to The Swale, the South Fleet Hide allows views of the same area from a different angle, and the Spitend Hide remains at the far end, 1.5 miles (2.4km) away, enabling viewing of the central Swale. This enables you to observe a large Black-headed Gull colony in summer, which now includes Mediterranean Gulls. Among the passerines, a few pairs of Yellow Wagtail still breed.

If you're going to walk the whole site, be sure to allow about four hours for stopping and scanning, and dress for strong sunshine or cold weather depending on the season – the reserve is very exposed.

127 WARDEN POINT AND HENS BROOK

Thorn Hill Road/Warden Road, Eastchurch, Kent ME12 4HG
TTR016724; tubes.latest.supposing
Open: all day, every day
SSSI

ACCESS

Bus: Chalkwell Garage route 360 (Sheerness–Leysdown) runs to Eastchurch, an hour's walk to Warden Point.

Train: Southeastern trains (London Victoria/London St Pancras–Ramsgate) stop at Sittingbourne. Change for Queenborough, from where you'll need to cycle or get a cab.

Car: from Eastchurch, follow Warden Road north until it runs out just before the cliffs. Turn right onto Thorn Hill Road to park.

YOUR VISIT

This seaward north-east corner of Sheppey consists of clifftop fields with clumps of scrub and trees, set between farmland and caravan parks. Be careful on the crumbly cliff edges, especially when looking over the edge at the small patches of scrub below.

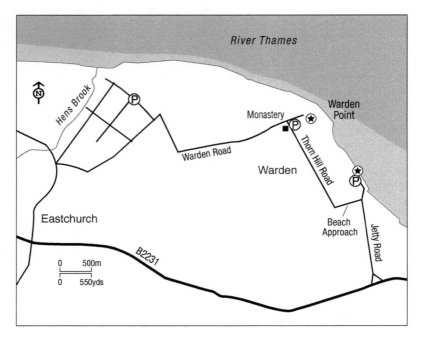

This is mostly a site for scarcities and drift migrants, particularly when winds are southerly in spring or easterly in autumn. The area hosts good numbers of passerines at these times, but especially in autumn, with Pallas's and Yellow-browed Warblers and Red-breasted Flycatcher possible among commoner migrants. Firecrest, Pied Flycatcher and Ring Ouzel are regular.

Don't ignore the trees on Thorn Hill Road as Firecrest and Yellow-browed Warbler have been seen there, and walk all the habitat, including around Warden Springs Caravan Park.

128 SHELLNESS, THE SWALE NNR AND LEYSDOWN COASTAL PARK

Shellness Road, Shellness, Leysdown-on-Sea, Kent ME12 4BS
TR051681; married.gymnasium.organs
SSSI, NNR

ACCESS

Bus: Chalkwell route 360 and 361 (Sheerness–Leysdown) and Travelmasters routes 370D, 370L and 371 (Leysdown–Sittingbourne) serve Leysdown, but it's another mile to Shellness.

Train: Southeastern trains (London Victoria/London St Pancras–Ramsgate) stop at Sittingbourne. Change for the Queenborough train, and then cycle or catch a cab.

Car: in Leysdown take Rowetts Lane/Leysdown Road (B2231) to the coast, then follow it round to the right as it becomes Shellness Road. This briefly dog-legs inland, then peters out into a dirt track. Follow this very rough and pitted route to the car park.

YOUR VISIT

Shellness borders the southern edge of The Swale NNR and shares its parking area, so visits to all three of these sites can easily be combined. Leysdown Coastal Park hosts a secondary wader roost and can be good for songbird migrants.

Drive down the last stretch of Shellness Road very carefully, as it's deeply pitted and rutted. It's worth stopping in places to scan the fields beyond from the top of the bund, as there can be large numbers of Golden Plover on the field. Various raptors sometimes quarter the area too.

Once parked at the end (TR051681; knowledge.tiptoes.release), check the scrub around the small pool adjacent, as migrants shelter there in autumn and other passerines use the pool for drinking. The small patch of wet long grass between the car park and the beach can hold Jack Snipe in winter (TR052682; courier.treatment. flops). You now have the choice of walking the landward side of the seawall through The Swale NNR or walking south behind the cottages to Shellness.

Taking the latter and heading towards **Shellness**, the path below the wall separating the saltmarsh from the cottages is often waterlogged. This is the better route to respect residents' privacy, so wear appropriate footwear. Sometimes it's impass-able, and then you have to walk the shingle beach in front of the cottages. This is best done away from high tide, to avoid trespassing.

The stretch of shingle beach allows close photos to be taken of Sanderling and other waders if you're careful, though you may have to lie on your stomach for the best shots. Sometimes the birds perch photogenically on the wooden groynes sloping down into the sea. South-westerlies in August can produce impressive movements of species such as Whimbrel, Bar-tailed Godwit, Little Stint and Curlew Sandpiper, so keep an eye on the weather charts. Snow Bunting is not as regular as it was, but still possible, and Lapland Bunting and Twite are even less likely now.

Once past the houses, the path skirts the shore, often close to roosting Ringed

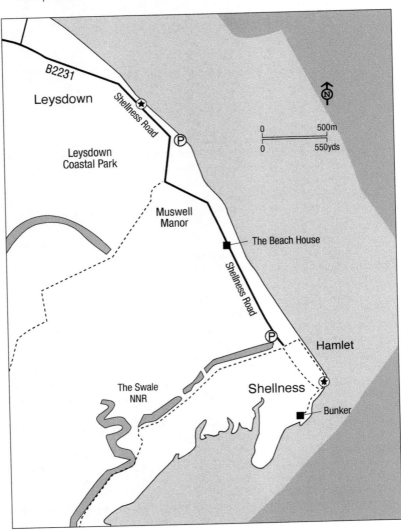

Plovers, down to a concrete building ahead. This blockhouse (TR052676; steadily. wired.scorching) has a large ATM mural (*atmstreetart.com*) of a male Hen Harrier on its estuary-facing side, and its size enables a few sea-watchers or wader counters to shelter from the wind.

Scanning the sea is a good idea, particularly if the winds are in the eastern half of the compass. Northerlies blow seabirds past Sheerness towards Oare, allowing close views as they pass Shellness. A good place to watch from is hunched under the seawall in front of the cottages. Easterlies will blow birds straight into The Swale where they are scopable mid-river, while southerlies will blow them close to the blockhouse, allowing even better views. When the birds realise they might have to fly overland, many of them turn back, enabling you to log them twice. Even during north-westerlies (counter-intuitively, often the best conditions for seawatching), birds will fly into the wind and get pushed into The Swale, closer to Oare Marshes but still visible from the northern shore. Depending on the time of year, almost anything can turn up and all four species of skua are occasionally seen in one session. Look high, too, as skuas can tower up and head inland.

Wader watching is also good on incoming tides, as Oystercatcher, Curlew, Whimbrel, Redshank and other species assemble on the point just to the south-west, often in huge numbers, before flying to the saltmarsh or Oare to roost. Please take care not to get too close and disturb them.

Scan the marsh, too – in winter, Short-eared Owls hunt low over the vegetation, especially in the hour or so before dusk, while Merlin can also be whizzing past. There is a winter raptor roost in the middle that can hold the odd Hen Harrier and Merlin among the more numerous Marsh Harriers.

Choosing **The Swale NNR** option, walk west along the raised bund overlooking

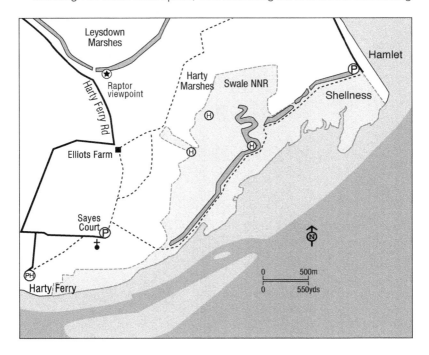

the saltmarsh to your left and the grazing marsh and farmland to your right. Pay attention, as scarce winter passerines such as Lapland Bunting and even Richard's Pipit have spent time around the path.

After a mile, the path bends fairly sharply left (TR041675; crisps.inflamed. nuzzling), and you will see a hide ahead (TR038671; found.tugging.degrading) overlooking wet grazing marsh and a small flooded dyke. Wildfowl assembles on its banks in winter, including wintering geese and ducks. The largest flocks of White-fronted Goose in Kent build up at this reserve, with a peak of 220 in March 2020, and 390 the year before.

You may see Great and Cattle Egrets there, though Little is the most likely. Marsh Harriers can fly close to the hide as they follow the reedbed. There is another hide further along (TR034665; limiting.profiled.slipping) overlooking less productive habitat. The path finally stops at privately owned grassland by the shoreline, where more waders may be seen away from high tide.

While summer is relatively unproductive, at least 16 pairs of Avocet breed on The Swale NNR. In winter, though, counts of Golden Plover between Eastchurch and Shellness have topped 5,000, sometimes concealing American Golden Plover or Dotterel.

Having made it this far, you'll need to double-back to return to the car park. It's worth checking the hides again, as there can be some changeover.

As you depart, check the areas of good habitat at **Leysdown Coastal Park**, while a stop on Shellness Road to search the trees by Muswell Manor Holiday Park (TR043694; salutes.gazes.feeds) during easterlies in autumn is also wise – the likes of Yellow-browed Warbler have shown up.

You can park just above the beach and seawatch from your car if conditions are wet; seabirds are often blown along the beach in strong winds. If the tide is out, the extensive mudflats attract scores of waders and gulls, even if there are people wandering around onshore. High tide pushes waders and gulls into secondary roosts on the short grass inland of the road – Mediterranean Gull is likely there. Thoroughly explore the bushes and trees in this area from August, particularly with onshore winds – Wryneck has been found on occasion.

Leysdown has plenty of amenities and the small car park by the seawall (TR046692; pegs.suitably.eaten) serves tea and snacks in summer.

129 RSPB CAPEL FLEET AND HARTY MARSHES

Harty Ferry Rd, Leysdown-on-Sea, Sheerness, Kent ME12 4BE
Website: www.rspb.org.uk/reserves-and-events/reserves-a-z/capel-fleet
TR022681; thinnest.debut.panther
Open: all day, every day

One of the county's best raptor viewpoints, with a chance of Rough-legged Buzzard, while the surrounding area has plenty to offer.

ACCESS

Bus: Chalkwell routes 360 and 362 (Sheerness–Leysdown) and Travelmasters routes 370D, 370L and 371 (Leysdown–Sittingbourne) stop just at the end of Harty Ferry Road, a mile's walk to the watchpoint.

Train: Southeastern trains (London Victoria/London St Pancras–Ramsgate) stop at Sittingbourne; change for the train to Queenborough, from where you'll need to cycle or get a cab.

Car: there is a car park next to the watchpoint.

YOUR VISIT

One of the very best places to observe birds of prey in England, **Capel Fleet** Raptor Watchpoint is at the south-eastern end of Sheppey on the Harty Ferry

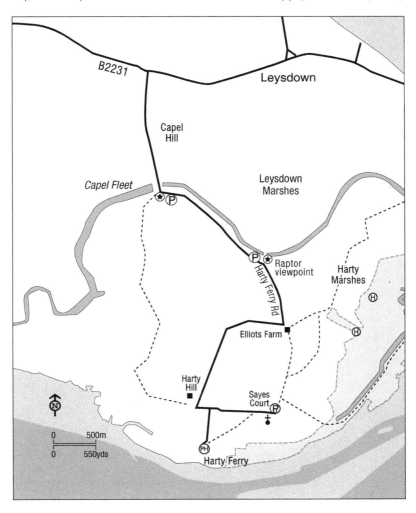

Road and overlooks **Harty Marshes** and much of Elmley. To get the best from this site, stop safely wherever you can to repeatedly scan, as birds are often close but also often mobile.

Marsh and Hen Harriers are almost guaranteed in autumn and winter, as are Peregrine and Merlin. Rough-legged Buzzard is not present every year, but there have sometimes been two birds in other years. Barn and Short-eared Owls fly by day in winter over the surrounding fields, and you can scan for Little Owl in the trees around Sayes Court Farm and St Thomas the Apostle Church, or on the fences to the north of The Fleet. White-fronted Geese are regular in winter flocks to the north and east of the watchpoint as well as in the fields around Sayes Court Farm, and the likes of Bewick's Swan, Pink-footed, Barnacle and Tundra Bean Geese are possible.

The wider part of The Fleet by the sharp bend in the Harty Ferry Road is a good place to scan for waders and wildfowl, which assemble there in larger numbers than you might expect; use the small parking space (TR010690; inherit.cages.proof-read). Mediterranean Gull is possible in summer, while passage Bearded Tits peaked at 52 in 2020.

For the closest amenities, follow the Harty Ferry Road all the way to The Swale and visit the Ferry House Inn (closed on Mondays), where the hot food is good and affordable (book ahead, though, if possible). There are good views over The Swale, and I've watched both Osprey and Glaucous Gull while having a pint there.

130 NEARBY: LITTLE MURSTON NR

Tonge Corner, Tonge, Sittingbourne, Kent ME9 9AX
TQ931654; baking.robe.belly

Bordered by gravel workings, farmland and Milton Creek draining into The Swale, this small reserve is on the Kent mainland, opposite Elmley and a couple of miles west of Oare Marshes (see page 228). It has extensive reedbeds, relatively deep lagoons and an oyster pond just inside the seawall. There's woodland and scrub, and the whole site is essentially a microcosm of its surrounding area. It's an undiscovered jewel and worth visiting during migration or winter, particularly if you tie it in with a trip to Oare Marshes.

With pools and reeds positioned so close to The Swale, explore the site as thoroughly as you can. Skuas, petrels, Ring-necked Duck, Red-necked Grebe and many other scarce species have been found in recent years, while Scaup, Spotted Redshank and Jack Snipe are regular. The reedbeds harbour a Bittern most winters. The footpaths border The Swale, ideal to scan for waders, seaduck and Osprey at appropriate times.

There is no official entrance, but you should be able to sat-nav your way to Swale Way or Church Road from the A249, using the exit for the B2005 and then taking the first exit off the roundabout. There is also no obvious parking spot. If you have no luck in the golf club car park (TQ932643; tasty.cooks.soak) down the long dirt track off Church Road, then park at the end of Church Road (TQ931654; dance.slows.park) and walk west along the seawall, or leave your vehicle on the short track off Swale Way (TQ926648; ending.begun.oasis). There's an angling club on the reserve's southern half, where three more pools are worth checking.

Little Murston is open all day, every day, and has muddy and grassy public footpaths. The fishing lakes are privately owned but can be viewed without trespassing in places. Some of the tracks are cyclable and Murston is on the Arriva Kent and Surrey 349 bus route (Sittingbourne–Murston), which runs every half an hour or so. There are amenities in the village and nearby Sittingbourne.

131 CONYER CREEK AND CONYER NR

North Quay, Conyer, Sittingbourne, Kent ME9 9HL
TQ961648; licks.weeknight.cools

The tiny village of Conyer is east of Oare Marshes, next to Conyer Creek. In the centre of the southern Swale, it's best between autumn and spring, and many of the birds possible at Oare also appear at Conyer. It has saltmarsh, farmland and trees, plus good views of The Swale.

Park carefully in the village on Conyer Road, just past the Ship & Smuggler pub (TQ961648; licks.weeknight.cools) and walk north, with the marina to your left, then through the metal gate to the seawall footpath (the Saxon Shore Way/National Cycle Route 1). If you head east, you'll eventually come to Oare, and walking a return route there and back is possible during a single birding day.

The triangular area of scrub at the mouth of the creek can support Nightingale (about ten pairs) and Turtle Dove, along with commoner spring breeders and migrants. The creek holds Kingfisher and has mud that feeds Oystercatcher, Avocet, Ringed Plover and Redshank. Almost anything can join them during passage periods, including Grey Plover, Turnstone, Little Stint, Curlew Sandpiper, Spotted Redshank, Greenshank and both godwits.

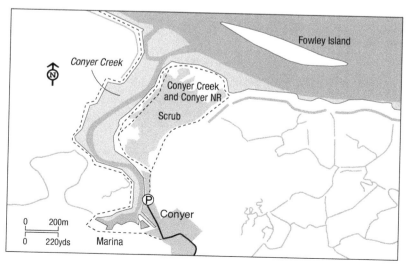

The surrounding land sometimes attracts White-fronted Goose and Bewick's Swan, while Rough-legged Buzzard and Hen Harrier have occurred. In spring, expect singing Corn Bunting, and there's a chance of Snow or even Lapland Bunting in the colder months. Water Rail and Bearded Tit frequent the reeds in the ditches.

Just offshore is a low sand and mud bank called Fowley Island, which Avocets and Red-breasted Mergansers favour in winter, and which hosts breeding waders, gulls and terns. These include Mediterranean Gull (more than 100 pairs in 2021) and Common Tern. Keep an eye out for Osprey in passage periods.

Conyer Marshes is open all day, every day, and there is food and drink in the Ship & Smuggler, and in nearby Teynham.

132 OARE MARSHES KWT

Church Road, Oare, Faversham, Kent ME13 0QD
Website: www.kentwildlifetrust.org.uk/nature-reserves/oare-marshes
Car park: TR013647; roughness.herring.watching; pay for parking on the RingGo app (currently £2.50 weekdays; £3.50 weekends). There is a small disabled car park to the south, on Church Road (TR012642; escalates.river-boat.cobbled).
Phone: Nadia Ward (01622 662012)
Email: Nadia.Ward@kentwildlife.org.uk
Open: all day, every day. The seawall, two hides, a section of the path and Church Road are wheelchair accessible (take care on the narrow road), but don't cover the full circuit. There are amenities in nearby Oare – including decent gastropubs – and Faversham. The part-time VC now seems to be closed but used to open at weekends.
Ramsar, ESA, LNR, SSSI, SPA
(71.4 hectares; 176 acres)

Probably the best wader-watching site in Kent, with birds only a few metres from the road.

SPECIES

All year: Shelduck, Gadwall, Teal, Shoveler, Little Egret, Marsh Harrier, Peregrine Falcon, Water Rail, Oystercatcher, Avocet, Ringed Plover, Barn and Little Owls, Kingfisher, Bearded Tit, Corn Bunting.

Summer: Garganey, Hobby, Little Ringed Plover, Common and Little Terns, Turtle Dove, Yellow Wagtail, Reed and Sedge Warblers.

Winter: Brent Goose, Wigeon, Pintail, Red-breasted Merganser, Bittern, Hen Harrier, Merlin, Golden and Grey Plovers, Knot, Dunlin, Black-tailed Godwit, Green Sandpiper, Short-eared Owl, Rock Pipit, Stonechat.

Migration: Osprey, Spotted Crake, Ruff, Spotted Redshank, Greenshank, Common and Wood Sandpipers, Little and Temminck's Stints, Curlew Sandpiper, Whimbrel, Bar-tailed Godwit, skuas, Kittiwake, Bonaparte's Gull (until at least autumn 2023), terns including Black Tern, Wheatear, Whinchat, warblers and other migrants, scarcities and rarities.

ACCESS

Bike: the narrow entrance track and seawall path are cyclable with care. There are no bike racks and cycling on the reserve is not permitted. The footpaths are level and mostly wheelchair accessible, except on the southern side of the reserve.

Bus: Stagecoach South East routes 638 (Whitstable–Faversham) and 666 (Faversham–Ashford) stop at the Three Mariners in Oare, a pleasant 1.7-mile (2.7-km) rural walk from the reserve, or even better, stay on for one stop more and walk the Saxon Shore Way north alongside Faversham Creek.

Train: Faversham is the nearest station, where the Southeastern service from London Victoria stops regularly.

Car: from the village of Oare, turn right onto Church Road and follow this to the seawall and KWT car park. Parking is pay-and-display (£2.50 on weekdays; £3.50 at weekends). A lay-by with space for about five cars overlooks the East Flood but cars should not be left unattended. Disabled users should be given priority.

YOUR VISIT

One of the best sites in the country for close views of waders. How many are present and how close they are depends on the sluice system; increasing water levels can markedly decrease the number of birds using the site, but levels have usually been productive recently.

On the south bank of The Swale (opposite Harty Ferry), the site is internationally important for migratory, wintering and breeding wetland birds. It comprises open

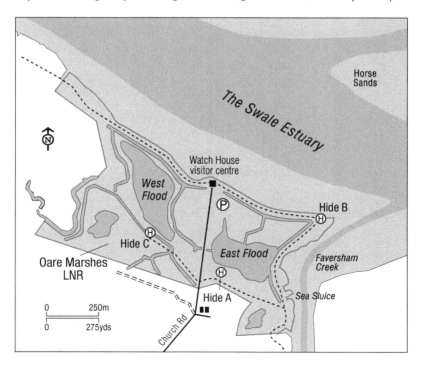

water, muddy scrapes, reedbeds, a little saltmarsh, ditches, scrub, muddy fore-shore, tidal river and grazing marsh.

The East Flood is one of the most reliable places in the country to see Curlew Sandpiper, particularly after south-west winds from late July to October. There are masses of waders on site for most of the year, including hundreds of Black-tailed Godwits, Avocets, Dunlins and Redshanks. These are joined annually by every regular passage wader species, including hundreds of Whimbrel and Bar-tailed Godwits, and the list of rarities is impressive.

Wader passage can also be spectacular in mid- to late spring, though birds linger less. Hide B on the point at Faversham Creek (TR018645; cookers.agency. grudges) can be very good for seawatching on incoming tides in onshore winds, with Long-tailed Skua annual and seabird rarities possible – including Britain's only Tufted Puffin in September 2009. Good views of the local seals can also be had from there.

Watching in winter at high tide will give you a chance of seeing seaduck, of which Red-breasted Merganser is most likely. Low tide will attract Brent Geese and waders to feed on and among the eelgrass. Snow Bunting is not so regular anymore, but Rock Pipit will be present. Also, check the foreshore for the returning adult Bonaparte's Gull in late summer and autumn – it's been returning to Oare since it was first seen in autumn 2013 and was still present in 2023.

The East Flood wader roost at high tide frequently holds thousands of birds if conditions are right. Not all can be seen, but when a Peregrine, Marsh Harrier or Short-eared Owl appears (or sometimes even an aeroplane), hundreds will take to the air at once, and unusual species are easier to pick out. The large flocks of Golden Plover that feed on fields on the Isle of Sheppey opposite will also roost on the flood, and American Golden Plover has been picked out more than once.

Don't just stay at Church Road, as waders can be hidden all over the flood. Take the circular route to scan from the seawall or Hide A (TR013642; tasteful.plantings. simulator), which is also good for wildfowl in winter and warblers, Whinchat and Corn Bunting in spring. The pools near Faversham Creek can hide Curlew Sandpiper and Little Stint, and occasionally even the likes of Red-necked Phalarope, and make sure you scan the mud on the creek. Common Tern breeds on rafts on the open water, while Little Tern may be on The Swale, though it no longer nests close to the site. Yellow Wagtail also breeds nearby.

The ditches, dykes and reeds hold Bearded Tit all year, especially on the western side. Explore these more vegetated and scrubby areas by crossing the road oppo-site the disabled parking area and taking the path to Hide C (TR009645; boils. headset.bride).

Pay attention on the road on the way in, too, as Little Owl is sometimes in the dead trees by the buildings at the last bend before the entrance track. Gatherings of hirundines feeding over the fields and on the telegraph wires can number in the hundreds. Turtle Doves cling on just about in double figures against all odds in the trees around the farms, but they can be very elusive. Try walking The Swale west as far as Uplees Copse, which can hold migrants.

133 SOUTH SWALE KWT, GRAVENEY MARSHES AND RSPB SEASALTER LEVELS LNR

Seasalter Road, Faversham, Kent CT5 4BP.
Website: www.kentwildlifetrust.org.uk/nature-reserves/south-swale
TR064648; occupy.tiny.chestnuts
Phone: Nadia Ward (01622 662 012)
Email: Nadia.Ward@kentwildlife.org.uk
Open: all day, every day. Enter through the kissing gate next to The Sportsman pub, climb up to the seawall and turn west for the circular walk.
ESA, LNR, Ramsar, SSSI, SPA, IBA
(*South Swale*: 420 hectares; 1037.84 acres;
Graveney Marshes: 360 hectares; 890 acres;
Seaslater Levels: 500 hectares; 1235.53 acres)

SPECIES

All year: Marsh Harrier, Peregrine Falcon, Ringed Plover, Oystercatcher, Redshank, Barn and Little Owls, Skylark, Meadow Pipit, Bearded Tit.

Summer: Hobby, Common and Little Terns, Yellow Wagtail, Grasshopper, Sedge and Reed Warblers.

Winter: Brent Goose, Wigeon, Teal, seaduck, divers, grebes, Rough-legged Buzzard (scarce), Hen Harrier, Golden and Grey Plovers, Avocet, Knot, Black-tailed and Bar-tailed Godwits, Short-eared Owl, Merlin, Rock Pipit, Stonechat, Snow Bunting.

Migration: seabirds, Osprey, waders, gulls, terns, auks, skuas, Wheatear, Whinchat.

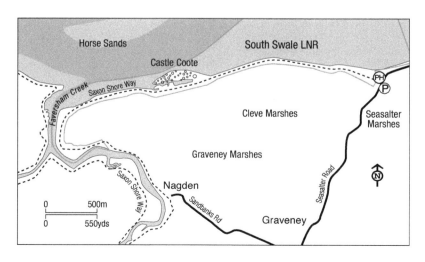

ACCESS

Bus: Regent Coaches bus route 660 (Stalisfield–Tankerton) runs infrequently from Monday–Saturday, stopping at The Sportsman pub.

Train: the nearest station is Faversham, 2.6 miles (4.2km) to the south-west.

Car: the reserve is just off Thanet Way/A299. As you approach the seawall on Seasalter Road there is limited parking at The Sportsman pub or by the gate to the chalets. There are also plenty more spaces about 500m in the direction of Whitstable, and the walk along the seawall enables excellent views of the marshes and sea.

YOUR VISIT

This lesser-known KWT reserve borders Faversham Creek and is directly opposite Oare Marshes KWT and adjoins Graveney Marshes and Seasalter Levels. It's an estuarine gem that can provide good birds, even for the casual visitor. It comprises saltmarsh, rough grazing, a shingle shoreline and some wet areas and ditches.

South Swale KWT comes into its own in winter, when outgoing or incoming tides enable great views of waders, geese and ducks as they feed on mud invertebrates and eelgrass. Particularly spectacular are the numbers of Wigeon and Brent Geese in winter – nationally important counts of 2,000 Brent have been logged from late September (including very occasional Black Brant or pale-bellied individuals or Red-breasted Goose); a few even linger into summer.

Passage periods see nationally important numbers of Black-tailed Godwits assembling on The Swale, along with Avocet, Curlew, Whimbrel and other waders. There's a good chance of Curlew Sandpiper, Spotted Redshank and Little Stint, while Wood Sandpiper can turn up on the reserve.

Keep an eye on the river well into November in northerlies: this is when skuas, Manx Shearwater, Gannet, Kittiwake and other seabirds can be seen. Arctic and Great Skuas are most likely in early autumn, but October regularly produces Pomarine Skua.

The site is also good for raptors in winter, with regular Barn and Short-eared Owls, Hen Harriers and Merlins joining the local Peregrine Falcons and Marsh Harriers, while Hobby appears in summer.

Access is via the Saxon Shore Way public footpath on the seawall, which provides a good vantage point. The footpath can get muddy so dress accordingly.

Over the years, the rich habitat has attracted respectable numbers of rarities, including White-tailed Eagle, Sociable Plover and Blyth's Pipit included.

Visitors should avoid disturbing the area around Castle Coote, to the north of Sandbanks Farm, at all costs, as the reeds and water there are very important for nesting and roosting birds, with breeding Yellow Wagtail.

The large area of saltmarsh inland from The Swale is also known as **Graveney Marshes** (the smaller northern part being known as Cleve Marshes, and the western, by Faversham Creek, Nagden Marshes). These extensive marshes are essential for wetland species but are currently under threat by the Cleve Hill Solar Power Station development (approved by the government in May 2020). For more information, visit *savegraveneymarshes.org*.

Graveney Marshes extends to **RSPB Seasalter Levels LNR** (off Faversham Road, Seasalter, Kent CT5 4BN; central point: TR 066 644; future.trombone.burns) on the South Swale reserve's eastern flank, just over the A299, north-west of RSPB Blean

Woods (see page 273). It has similar species to Graveney, and its major habitats are currently being restored. Seasalter is the stronghold for summering Grasshopper Warblers in the area.

The site was leased in 2007 and will eventually provide some 290 hectares (716.6 acres) of contiguous habitat for breeding waders and wintering wildfowl. It covers the Whitstable Bay, Monkshill, Alberta and Vikings Estate areas behind holiday cottages and caravan parks, and will eventually have the water, islands, scrapes and hides beloved of other RSPB wetland reserves. Work started in 2021 and is incomplete at the time of writing. Distant views across the area can be had from the seawall.

COASTAL KENT

THE THANET COAST

This area extends almost uninterrupted from Swalecliffe to Ramsgate, and comprises mainly unstable cliff and foreshore (including shingle, sand and mudflats), with smaller areas of saltmarsh, coastal lagoons, woodland and clifftop grassland.

The coast of Thanet has Internationally and Nationally Important numbers of wintering Turnstone, Sanderling and Ringed and Grey Plovers, with large numbers of waders and wildfowl during migration as well. Up to 12 Grey Partridges have been counted recently on the under-watched farmland inland in winter.

SPECIES

All year: Grey Partridge, Fulmar.

Summer: Ringed Plover, Little Tern, Yellow Wagtail, Sand Martin, common farmland and garden birds.

Winter: Brent Goose, Wigeon, Common Scoter, Red-throated Diver, Hen Harrier, Purple Sandpiper, Sanderling, Snipe, Jack Snipe, auks, Short-eared Owl, Dartford Warbler, Snow Bunting.

Migration: Eider, Marsh Harrier, seabirds including Manx and Sooty Shearwaters, terns, Little Gull, Kittiwake, skuas, Hobby, Ring Ouzel, flycatchers, chats, warblers, Lapland and Snow Buntings, scarcities and rarities.

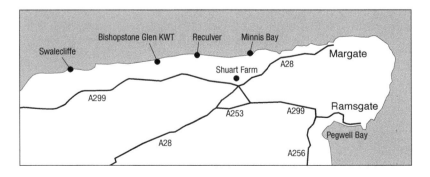

134 SWALECLIFFE

Swalecliffe Court Drive, Swalecliffe, Kent CT5 2NX
Parking: TR136674; hulk.moth.eaten
Open: all day, every day

An area of rough coastal grassland and scrub that has proved very alluring to migrants, especially in autumn.

ACCESS

Bus: Regent Coaches and Stagecoach 36, 903, 904, 906, 922 and Triangle services all stop at The Plough, just at the end of Plough Lane.

Train: the Southeastern London Stratford International–Margate and Chatham Mainline services stop at Chestfield & Swalecliffe Station, about 0.5 miles (0.8km) from the site.

Car: from the A299, turn left onto Herne Bay Road (following the brown tourist 'seafront' signs), then turn right onto Swalecliffe Court Drive. Park at the end by the small roundabout after the church, at the beginning of Plough Lane.

YOUR VISIT

Also known as Long Rock, Swalecliffe is best early in the morning, as the site is popular with joggers and dog-walkers. Its rough grassland and scrub are attractive to migrants, particularly in autumn. Scarcities are fairly frequent and there is good seabird passage in season.

Use the footpaths behind the church and up to the point (TR134673; pushy.peanut.field) in spring and autumn to explore the scrub and bushes, crossing the footbridge (TR135674; launch.spoil.formed) to the scrub around Swalecliffe Treatment Works (TR134673; plot.mock.drain) and along Swalecliffe Brook (TR135674; pops.signal.flood), which has recently held wintering Pallas's Warbler. The grass attracts birds early on, while the shingle beach encourages Snow Buntings to drop in. Most of the expected scarce autumn songbird migrants have occurred. Nearby **Hampton Pier** (Central Parade, Herne Bay, Kent CT6 8SS; TR172683; chins.visit.best), 1.5 miles (2.4km) to the east, is a regular spot for wintering Purple Sandpiper – very scarce in the region covered by this book.

While offshore Swalecliffe holds some of the county's largest numbers of Red-breasted Merganser in the region – up to 20 in mid-winter – seawatching overall is generally better at Reculver or Minnis Bay nearby (though 2019 produced Brown Booby!). However, scanning from the head (TR136677; same.vocal.wakes) or in front of Whitstable Skatepark (TR133674; many.rift.rival) can produce scarce divers, grebes and seaduck in winter.

Food, drink and toilets can be sought in Swalecliffe itself or in nearby Tankerton.

135 MINNIS BAY AND SHUART

Minnis Bay: The Parade, Minnis Bay, Birchington, Kent CT7 9QR; TR287696;
lamp.steeped.shameless
Shuart Farm: Shuart Lane, St Nicholas-at-Wade, Kent CT7 0NB; TR268677;
parading.distanced.maybe
Open: all day, every day. Birchington has plenty of amenities.
*This stretch of coastal farmland has a great reputation for attracting
migrants, especially in autumn – on land or at sea.*

ACCESS

Bus: Birchington station is just four stops on Stagecoach Southeast bus 34 from
Canute Road on The Parade. Route 8 (Canterbury–Westwood Cross) runs to St
Nicholas-at-Wade from where you can walk to Shuart, where there's a footbridge
over the A229.

Train: the Southeastern service from London Stratford International–Ramsgate
stops at Birchington, one mile to the east of Minnis Bay.

Car: take the A28 from the St Nicholas at Wade roundabout into Birchington, turn
left onto Kent Gardens, right onto Surrey Gardens and then left onto Minnis
Road. Turn left at the end onto The Parade and take the first available parking
space.

YOUR VISIT

There are three main areas at Minnis Bay, which can all be taken in on a long walk.

MINNIS BAY AND SHUART

Minnis Bay is one of Kent's best seawatching locations. There is a convenient
shelter at the clifftop to keep you out of the wind and rain – north-easterly or
northerly winds usually bring the best seabirds into Gresham Bay to the east and
Minnis Bay to the west of the headland (both are scannable from the shelter).
Auks, shearwaters and divers are expected, along with fairly regular Sabine's
Gulls, Long-tailed Skuas and Leach's Storm-petrels.

Scan the mudflats along the coastal path for waders and look for wandering
Snow Buntings in winter. Little Terns can still be seen offshore during summer, but
no longer seem to breed.

Though rather bare in most places, Minnis Bay can be great for vis-migging, too;
follow the coastal path out of Birchington on an early spring or autumn morning.
Continue west and explore the scrub around the Hawk Place Campsite and Plum
Pudding Riding School, which sometimes concentrate migrants as the only conspic-
uous shelter along this stretch. To explore the scrub, you'll need to turn down the
footpath running inland to the south-west.

SHUART LANE

Once on the scrubby footpath, continue south-west, carefully over the railway
tracks. After half an hour you'll come to more scrub and trees around the regular
ringing site at Shuart Farm, which has produced many notable birds during
passage including Masked Shrike and Western Bonelli's Warbler. Ring Ouzel and

other thrushes are regular, along with Yellow-browed Warbler and other scarce migrants.

Two small pools off the path are worth a quick check. Another dirt track heads towards the tiny village of Hale to the east; this is worth exploring. The lay-by (TR268677; parading.distanced.maybe) just before you get to the wooded area around Shuart Farm is an ideal place for scoping across the farmland and marshes for birds of prey.

A suggested route now is to follow the path back north-east to the railway line, then turn west (that is, left) and follow the railway embankment until you get to the River Wantsum. Grasshopper Warbler is occasionally found in the bushes in spring and summer, with Lesser Whitethroat and Yellowhammer regular. In a freeze-up, the narrow river can provide sanctuary for Smew, Goldeneye and even Slavonian Grebe. The railway embankment holds breeding Stonechat and commoner warblers, and is a vantage point to observe Hen Harrier, Merlin and Short-eared Owl over Reculver Marsh (see page 238).

From there, you have two choices: you can follow the path north along the river bank to the coast and scan **Coldharbour Lagoon** and **Plum Pudding Island**, a dune slack which can pull in a few waders, or continue south-west to Chambers Wall.

CHAMBERS WALL
The bushes alongside Wade Marsh Stream at Chambers Wall often provide shelter for songbird migrants, which have included Booted, Dusky, Yellow-browed, Pallas's, Greenish and Arctic Warblers – so brush up your ID skills! If you follow the concrete-paved Chambers Wall to the east you'll come to Shuart Lane again and can head back toward Minnis Bay in a nice circular walk (with diversions). Check the stream for waders and wildfowl.

If you decide to drive to Chambers Wall, take the unpaved Potten Street Road north from the A299, park in the very limited spaces at Chambers Wall (CT7 0QP; TR254676; sprouting.greyhound.copying), then take the minor track left just before the hamlet and follow it to the Wantsum.

136 RECULVER CP AND BISHOPSTONE GLEN KWT

Reculver/Towers and Roman Fort, Reculver Rd, Reculver, Herne Bay, Kent CT6 6SS.
Open: all day, every day. A pub, toilets, a few shops and cafes are nearby.
LNR, SSSI
(*Reculver CP:* 26 hectares; 62.25 acres)

SPECIES
See Minnis Bay (page 235).

ACCESS

Bus: Stagecoach route 7 (Whitstable–Canterbury) stops at Herne Bay and Reculver.

Train: the nearest station is Herne Bay, 1.5 hours on the Southeastern service from London Victoria/St Pancras–Canterbury/Margate.

Car:

Bishopstone: Reculver Country Park, Bishopstone Lane, Bishopstone, Kent CT6 6RL; TR210687; bleaching.snail.army. Leave the A299 left at the brow tourist sign saying, 'Reculver Towers & Roman Fort; Country park', then turn left, then right at the immediate T-junction, then right down Heart-in-Hand Road, following the white sign to 'Hillborough/Reculver' – this becomes Sweechbridge Road. Follow it for 2 miles (3.2km), then turn left at the thatched cottage onto Reculver Road. Finally, take a right onto Bishopstone Lane and follow it to the car park at the end. You'll need the RingGo app to pay for a space.

Reculver Towers: Reculver Roman Fort, Northern Sea Wall, Reculver, Kent CT6 6SU; TR226692; insolvent.heartburn.festivity. Follow the directions above onto Sweechbridge Road but follow this further onto Reculver Lane for a few miles until you reach the first car park.

Chambers Wall: Fisherman's Car Park, Potten Street Road, Chambers Wall, St Nicholas at Wade, Kent CT7 0QN; TR249681; stirs.ticked.keys – see directions under Minnis Bay (see page 235).

YOUR VISIT

Two miles (3.2km) further along the Thanet Coastal Path to the west from Birchington are Reculver and Bishopstone (a suburb of Herne Bay). The two areas are possible to cover in combination with Minnis Bay but are dealt with here as a single site. You can drive directly to each using the information above. This is a migration and seawatching hotspot with similar species to the Minnis Bay area (page 235) likely. It's most productive in spring and, especially, autumn with winds in the north or east.

You can walk the coast west for migrants, but pay some attention to **Bishopstone Glen KWT**, a small valley that leads inland from the low cliffs of the coastal path, and has plenty of trees and bushes beloved of wandering warblers. Explore the whole of this area in autumn during or after northerlies and easterlies, as the likes of Wryneck, Yellow-browed, Hume's, Pallas's, Greenish, Arctic, Dusky, Icterine and Barred Warblers and Red-breasted Flycatcher are always possible. At the time of writing, the area is fenced off and partly inaccessible, so much less productive, but it may open again – keep an eye on the news services.

To the east, **Reculver Towers** – the remains of a twelfth-century church overlying a Roman fort – is one of the county's great seawatching outposts. Northern winds in autumn bring regular shearwaters, Pomarine and Long-tailed Skuas, terns, auks and Sabine's Gull, while Leach's Storm-petrel is more regular than on the rest of the coast. The bushes on the edge of Waterways Caravan Park & Amusements have a proud reputation for wandering warblers, while Wryneck and Snow Bunting can show up anywhere along the seawall, along with errant wheatears. Check the whole area up to Coldharbour Lagoon – and try to cover the paths inland too.

Don't ignore the beach and muddy foreshore; this can produce good waders.

The grass around the church ruins can also offer up songbird migrants. It's also easy to walk east onto the seawall and scan the nearby oyster farm for migrant waders; Long-tailed Duck and Red-necked Grebe have also sheltered on the site. High tide will bring seabirds closer, while the shingle may produce occasional Snow Bunting. Dartford Warbler has recently become quite regular in the seawall brambles.

The seawall allows observation of vis-mig wagtails, pipits, wheatears and warblers, along with thousands of hirundines, while the parallel 'Green Wall', running just inland, is quartered by Hen Harrier and Short-eared Owl.

Reculver Marshes, inland of the seawall, though mostly farmed, can support more than 1,000 Brent Geese in late winter; Black Brant is almost annual among them. Look out for flocks of Corn Buntings in winter and spring; 160 have been counted recently.

Walking around the whole site can take more than three hours on a good day, and away from the glen it's pretty exposed, so dress accordingly. An early start is advised.

137 MARGATE: FORENESS POINT, NORTH FORELAND, MARGATE CEMETERY AND NORTHDOWN PARK

Foreness Point: Prince's Walk, Northdown, Margate, Kent CT9 3PP; TR383715; jolly.needed.trees;
North Foreland (Joss Bay car park): Joss Bay, Broadstairs, Kent CT10 3PG; TR399700; filed.slips.float;
St John's (Margate) Cemetery: Manston Road, Margate, Kent CT9 4LY; TR350692; rewarding.chew.spine;
Northdown Park: Queen Elizabeth Avenue, Northdown, Margate, Kent CT9 3LF; TR377702; live.scrap.stars.
Open: all day, every day, except Margate Cemetery, which usually opens from 9am–6pm.
Various clifftop and coastal habitats combine to provide great migrant traps in an up-and-coming coastal town.

SPECIES

All year: Grey Partridge, Fulmar, Rock Pipit, Black Redstart.

Summer: Mediterranean Gull, commoner seabirds and passerines.

Winter: Eider (scarce), Common Scoter, Red-throated Diver, Sanderling, Purple Sandpiper, auks.

Migration: seabirds, raptors, hirundines, Redstart, Wheatear, Whinchat, Stonechat, Ring Ouzel, Yellow-browed and Pallas's Warblers.

ACCESS

Bus: Stagecoach East 8A Breeze and 8X Breeze services (Cliftonville, Richmond Avenue–Northdown Park) stop at Springfield Road, close to Foreness Point. Both routes and the 937, 946, 960 and Loop services all stop at the Wheatsheaf, Cliftonville, close to Northdown Park. There are no bus services to the cemetery.

Train: high-speed trains to Margate from London St Pancras International, London Victoria or London Charing Cross take about 1.5 hours.

Car: Margate is on the main roads from London (A299) and Dover (A256). Leave Margate on the B2051 coast road for Foreness Point and park opposite the pumping station. Northdown Park is 0.5 mile (0.8km) south of there, with free parking on Queen Elizabeth Avenue. St John's Cemetery is 1.5 miles (2.4km) to the south-west of the park, with parking bays by the entrance and along Manston Road. North Foreland is 1 mile (1.6km) south-east of Foreness Point. Park in the Joss Bay Car Park and walk south-east along the cliff path to the lighthouse.

YOUR VISIT

This part of the coast is best in autumn. Get there early for a seawatch in onshore winds. Scoping from Foreness Point or **North Foreland** is best with winds from the north or east, and the likes of Little Auk can pass through from late October. There can be good birds on the sea at any time of year, and scarce divers and grebes sometimes linger offshore. Northerly winds can produce occasional raptor movements.

Expect skuas, auks, divers and shearwaters in autumn and winter. The area around **Foreness Point** sewage pumping station is a migrant trap, while the surrounding cabbage fields can also produce an array of migrants, including Ring Ouzel, Wryneck, flycatchers and warblers. Remember to check any area of grass,

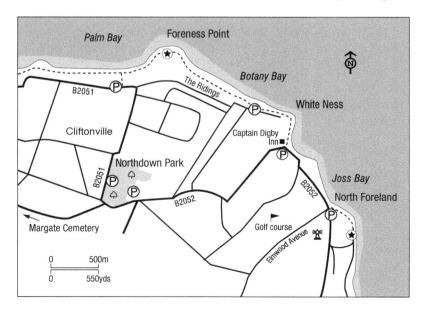

scrub or trees in the right conditions, including local gardens. Don't ignore the shoreline: there are Rock Pipits aplenty, and Purple Sandpiper and Black Redstart are regular.

Northdown Park is a popular urban green space that produces regular autumn Yellow-browed and Pallas's Warblers and Firecrest, as well as choice rarities. Early mornings are best, but birds can arrive all day in autumn. The local Ring-necked Parakeets roost there – this was one of the first places in the UK to have a viable population.

Margate Cemetery is as good as Northdown Park for migrants at times. This inland graveyard and crematorium is well-wooded, turns up regular scarcities – and even the occasional rarity, such as Dusky Thrush in May 2013. The farmland south of nearby **Dane Valley Woods** has held several pairs of Grey Partridge in recent years.

There are plenty of amenities in Margate and nearby Broadstairs.

THE SANDWICH BAY BIRD OBSERVATORY RECORDING AREA

SSSI, NNR

This highly productive, bird-rich web of habitats is best dealt with as a single entity. It includes the major reserves of Sandwich and Pegwell Bay NNR KWT, Sandwich Bay Bird Observatory and its associated habitats, and RSPB Worth Marshes. It has an international reputation for attracting migrants, and its important ornithological work includes a decades-long constant-effort ringing programme.

The SBBO recording area is one of Kent's major rarity hotspots, continuing to host a growing list of exciting species that includes Caspian Tern, Short-toed Lark, Isabelline and Lesser Grey Shrikes, Radde's and Greenish Warblers, Zitting Cisticola and Tawny Pipit, as well as regular scarcities such as Roseate Tern and Osprey.

With access to a car, you can cover much of the area in a long day's birding, or book lodgings at the 'obs' and take a bit more time to explore the region.

138 SANDWICH AND PEGWELL BAY NNR KWT

Pegwell Bay CP, Sandwich Road, Ramsgate, Kent CT12 5JB
Website: www.kentwildlifetrust.org.uk/nature-reserves/sandwich-and-pegwell-bay
TR341632; padlock.absorb.propose
Phone: John Wilson 0780 568821
Email: John.Wilson@kentwildlife.org.uk
Open: all day, every day, though the car park has variable opening and closing times

Country Park, County Geological Site, LNR, NNR, Natura 2000, Ramsar, SSSI, SAC, SPA
(615 hectares; 1,520 acres)

An open coastal bay with an admirable reputation for attracting noteworthy species, and worth a visit at any time of the year.

SPECIES

All year: Grey Partridge, Avocet, Lapwing, Redshank, Mediterranean Gull, Stonechat, Corn Bunting.

Summer: Ringed Plover, Common and Sandwich Terns, Cuckoo, Nightingale, Yellow Wagtail.

Winter: Brent and White-fronted Geese, Common Scoter, Eider (scarce), Red-breasted Merganser, Red-throated Diver, Golden Plover, Jack Snipe, Water Pipit, Snow Bunting.

Migration: Garganey, Marsh Harrier, Kentish Plover, Black-tailed and Bar-tailed Godwits, Greenshank, Curlew and Wood Sandpipers, Little Stint, Whimbrel, Yellow-legged Gull, Arctic, Sandwich, Little and Black Terns, Turtle Dove, Whinchat, Wheatear, Redstart, Black Redstart, flycatchers, warblers, White Wagtail, visible migration, scarcities, rarities.

ACCESS

Bus: the main bus routes between Ramsgate and Sandwich (45, 48, 48A, 9 and 9X) stop right outside the entrance to the park.

Train: Southeastern services from London Kings Cross St Pancras run to Ramsgate, the nearest station. You'll need to cycle or take a cab for the 2 miles (3.2km) to the park entrance.

Car: the large pay-and-display car park is off the A256; you may need loose change, as the phone reception for online payments can be patchy and the machines don't take cards. A wide range of amenities is available in Sandwich, Ramsgate and Deal. There is a café and plenty of benches.

YOUR VISIT

The coastal refuge of **Pegwell Bay** is a fairly complex but compact mix of habitats at the mouth of the River Stour and is of International Importance for its waterbird populations. The site is just to the north of Sandwich and co-managed by Kent County Council and the KWT.

The area's patchwork of habitats includes Kent's only ancient dune pasture, as well as farmland, dunes, beach, golf courses, mudflats, saltmarsh, wooded areas, scrub and gardens – plus, of course, the open sea. Numerous species are seen on passage, with the whole area alive with the songs of warblers, Nightingales and Cuckoos in spring and summer.

On arrival, explore the scrub and trees around the car park during passage for migrants. Choose one of the obvious footpaths and turn right or left along the waterfront; both directions enable you to scan the sand, mud and sea beyond, depending on the tide. Bring a telescope and check tide times before your visit. For roosting waders, gulls and terns it's best to arrive a couple of hours before or after high tide; the incoming tide often has the edge – the birds are distant but give decent scope views.

Pegwell Bay NNR is the broader zone between Cliffsend and Ebbsfleet, and the most accessible and productive part. Stonelees, at the south-western end of the NNR, is also part of the SBBO recording area but is largely taken up by a lorry park.

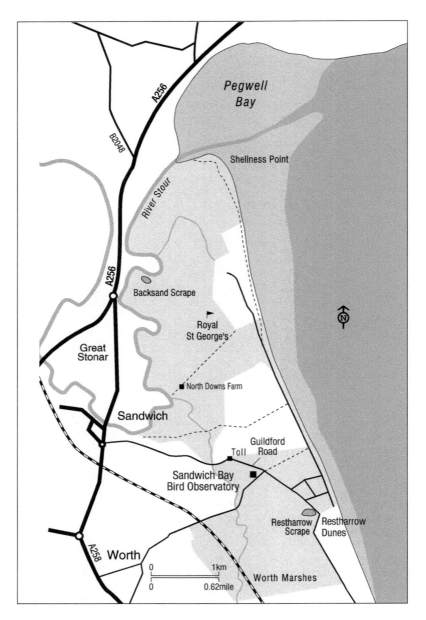

The site is particularly good for migrants during or after south-east winds in spring or autumn; Kentish Plover has occurred in such conditions. Garganey is regular on the saltmarsh in spring.

Follow the shoreline to the right (south-west). There, you'll find several benches and a hide, with the path winding through the scrub between the shore, road and power station. Passerine migrants often use the vegetation behind the path, particularly where it gets thicker past the hide at Stonelees, and at the point (also the best place to view seals in winter).

There's a substantial wader roost on the other side of the river mouth at Shellness Point, which is worth scrutinising from the Pegwell side; hundreds of waders come and go as the tide rises and falls. The path provides plenty of optimum observation points, though it can be exposed. If you turned left out of the car park, the northern part of the path (which continues around the coast past Ramsgate) provides good views of the shoreline in front of the village of Cliffs End.

In winter, look among the sizeable gull flocks for Little, Caspian, Yellow-legged and Glaucous Gulls. Wintering waders include Black-tailed Godwit, Dunlin, Knot and Grey Plover. Brent Goose is the most likely coastal goose, especially in front of the Western Undercliff. In winter, Pintail and other wintering ducks will haunt the saltmarsh fringe.

139 SANDWICH BAY BIRD OBSERVATORY

Sandwich Bay Bird Observatory Trust, Guilford Rd, Sandwich Bay, Sandwich, Kent CT13 9PF
Website: https://sbbot.org.uk
TR354575; websites.replying.tools
Phone: 01304 617341
Email: info@sbbot.org.uk
Open: the Field Centre (with its sightings board, shop and toilets) is open from 10am–4pm, but most of the SBBO recording area is open all day, every day. Most of the estate is managed by the Sandwich Bay Bird Observatory Trust (SBBOT) and the KWT. It's possible to stay at the observatory VC, which is self-catering and sleeps 16, including five twin rooms and a family room that sleeps six. The nearby town of Sandwich should have everything you need in the way of amenities. Please note that estate residents' privacy should always be respected.

A complex, nationally renowned migration hotspot that has hosted many of Kent's major scarcities and rarities; the county's best site for wild geese in winter.

SPECIES
See Pegwell Bay (see page 240).

ACCESS
Bus: Stagecoach South East route 43 from Canterbury terminates at Sandwich Guildhall, a decent walk from the 'obs' (see page 224).

Train: the Southeastern service from London Kings Cross St Pancras–Sandwich takes about an hour and 40 minutes, with two trains per hour. Get a cab, cycle or walk the 2.3 miles (3.7km) to the 'obs' by turning down Delfside, taking a right into St Georges Road and then turning right onto Sandown Road. At the fork, take Guilford Road over the bridge and enter the SBBO through the toll.

Car: leave Sandwich, following the signs to the golf courses, and enter the Sandwich Bay Estate, turning right at the SBBOT sign after a quarter of a mile. There's a £1 toll for non-members; members have a windscreen sticker to allow free access. The toll only allows access to the Field Centre; you're not allowed to drive through the private areas.

The 'obs' can also be reached from Deal by driving north on Beach Street (A258) and turning left at the marina on Godwyn Road. Turn right onto Golf Road and follow this past Restharrow Scrape to the tollbooth. It's also possible to leave your car at Restharrow Scrape to walk onto the estate to avoid the toll.

YOUR VISIT

The north-east coast of Kent is placed well to receive eastern migrants and, along with them, the chance of a scarcity or rarity. Possibly the best location in that region is SBBO, one of two bird observatories in Kent and voted Site of the Year in *BirdGuides.com*'s Birders Choice 2022 awards.

Autumn is best for migrants, but no spring passes without a surprise or two, and it's worth visiting at any time of the year. The whole region can take days to explore at the right time of year, so pick your route judiciously. The 'obs' buildings now have a new observation tower and scrape, as well as upgraded accommodation, all accessible to members. Members also benefit from reduced accommodation rates at the Field Study Centre.

RESTHARROW SCRAPE

This flooded field was originally created in 2001. The shallow water, short turf and mud acts as a magnet to wildfowl and waders. In 2019, the land was bought by the 'obs', the scrape was enlarged, a new hide was installed and the original hide was refurbished.

To use the hides, park on the verge at the southern end of the scrape, just after Gold Road bends north, and enter through the gate. A bund surrounds the scrape above head height to prevent disturbance, but please be quiet.

The breeding season sees nesting Avocets and Little Ringed Plover among the Black-headed Gulls, Oystercatchers and Lapwings, with Mediterranean Gull also likely. Gadwall is usually the most notable duck, though Garganey pops in annually. Regular summer visitors include Hobby, Turtle Dove and Cuckoo.

Autumn migration sees two dozen or more of wader species lingering on their journey south, always including Greenshank and Common, Green and Wood Sandpipers. Scour the Dunlin carefully for concealed Little Stints and Curlew Sandpipers. Pectoral Sandpiper is almost annual.

Migration continues until mid-November, with Curlew and Lapwing flocks regularly dropping in. Other birds to watch for during this time include Ruff, Little Ringed Plover and Ringed Plover, Snipe and Jack Snipe, Black-tailed and Bar-tailed Godwits, and Whimbrel and Spotted Redshank.

As autumn turns to winter, Black-tailed Godwits, Snipe and Jack Snipe remain and are joined by typical winter duck species. The many Greylags may lure in a

Russian White-fronted or Pink-footed Goose or two. Yellow-legged and Caspian Gulls have become a cold-season fixture, though they don't hang around. Scan the fields nearby for large flocks of Golden Plover too.

RESTHARROW DUNES AND THE GULLIES

Immediately on the opposite side of the road to Restharrow Scrape is an SSSI composed of a dune system and three gullies: Waldershare, Little and Big Gullies. These act as migrant traps in spring and autumn and are set back not very far from the coast, behind a row of private houses.

Redstart, Wheatear, warblers and finches are all likely in spring, and Corn Bunting breeds. Autumn will bring Whinchat, Black Redstart and various warblers, including Grasshopper, Garden and Wood Warblers. Carefully explore the small copses scattered around the area, which can also conceal migrants.

Stonechats linger into winter, sometimes followed by a Dartford Warbler, and Short-eared Owl may also be seen (it's possible over most of the SBBO area).

THE ELMS

At the northern end of Restharrow Dunes is The Elms, a small mixed broadleaf and conifer woodland, specifically planted to attract migrants. This fairly isolated patch of cover is good for Firecrest and Goldcrest in late autumn. Warblers favour the area, which has resident Sparrowhawks and Jays. This is the best place in the SBBO area to search for flycatchers and 'continental' Coal Tits and gives you the best chance of finding a Yellow-browed or Pallas's Warbler. Winter produces mixed flocks of Siskin and Redpoll.

MIDDLE FIELD

A mosaic of pond, reedbed, alder and willow copse and grassland habitats sandwiched between housing just to the north of Restharrow Dunes, the Middle Field is good for migrating warblers and is your best chance for Tree Pipit in spring and autumn. The trees can host Brambling, Siskin and even Crossbill in winter, and the leaf litter can hide a Woodcock or two from late October.

DRAGONFLY POND FIELD AND JUBILEE FIELDS

Back on the road's western side, and adjoining Restharrow Scrape to the north, are Jubilee Fields and the Dragonfly Pond. The pond supports more than 15 species of Odonata (and, thus, Hobby in spring), including Dainty Damselfly. The scrub here is another good place to search for migrants among the more common Linnets, warblers and thrushes. These often include Whinchats and sometimes Redstart.

The grassy meadow provides hunting grounds for Barn Owl. Despite its small size, the pond can host Green Sandpiper during autumn and winter and the odd duck, while Oystercatcher sometimes breeds in this area. Check the neighbouring fields for Golden Plover and Curlew.

WHITEHOUSE AND OASIS

A little further to the north of the houses bordering the Middle Field, and to the east of Guilford Road and the Haven Stream, the Whitehouse is a grass paddock used by the SBBO Ringing Team, which also traps at the Oasis, a smaller fenced-off area in the field next door (please respect the ringing activities and leave the area undisturbed). The grassy areas attract loafing Shelduck, while Little Owl is a surreptitious resident at the edges.

Spring sees warblers arriving from the south, and sometimes visible migration in the form of departing winter thrushes. As spring becomes summer, Cuckoo and Turtle Dove sustain an ever-flimsy breeding presence, and this small area is their core range on site.

Autumn sees migration (and ringing) beginning in earnest, as warblers, chats and finches flow through the site. Species found at this time of year have included Arctic and Blyth's Reed Warblers, Red-flanked Bluetail and Great Grey Shrike. Common migrants arrive, and you'll see winter thrushes, Bramblings, Siskins and Redpolls in the berry bushes, alders and birches that ring the Whitehouse area. As ever, the leaf litter may conceal a cryptic Woodcock.

THE GREEN WALL
The Green Wall is the large wedge of habitat between the 'obs' and River Stour, incorporating the tollgate and the small Royal St George's Reservoir. Its jigsaw of reedbeds, fields and mixed woodland makes it another magnet for migrants. The reeds also host Bearded Tit in winter, while Cetti's Warbler is resident.

NEW DOWNS
North of the golf course and stretching to Sampher and the River Stour is this extensive area of mixed agricultural and wetland habitat, connecting the Stour Valley Walk and the England Coast Path.

During spring migration, its wet fields are the best spot for White Wagtail (among other possible migrants). In a wet spring, Avocet favours its pools, while Red Kites may drift overhead. The fields host breeding Skylarks and are known to attract congregations of Mediterranean Gulls in late summer. Grey Partridge is still present in double figures – the best counts in modern Kent; they can still be difficult to see, though.

Autumn passage sees the numerous pools attracting waders, including that ever-tempting quartet of Little Stint, Wood and Curlew Sandpipers, and Spotted Redshank. Don't ignore the scrub and hedgerows near the New Pool and Prince's Reservoir, which often hold scarcities such as Wryneck, Yellow-browed Warbler, Nightingale and flycatchers. The pools continue to attract birds in winter; waders always headline, but with perhaps the chance of a Black-necked or Slavonian Grebe.

SHELLNESS POINT
This is the northernmost section of the SBBO area, incorporating the region north of Royal St George's Golf Club, and including another golf course (Prince's Golf Club), along with Hundred Acre Field and Sandwich Flats – a long, shingle beach that stretches from the northern border of the estate to the Stour Estuary and Pegwell Bay.

The core of Shellness Point is a restricted-access area overlooking the river-mouth and bay, where hundreds of waders roost at high tide. Peregrines often perch on the ground there, and the waders are not usually disturbed by this until the raptors take to the air.

The shingle provides nest sites for Ringed Plovers and Oystercatchers in spring, when freshly arrived Cuckoos and Ring Ouzels are sometimes seen. Long grass adjacent to the golf course fairways supports a strong population of Skylarks.

The beach hosts departing Wheatears in autumn, when huge flocks of hirundines may assemble. This is the best time to scan the wader roost on the point, with Grey Plover, Bar-tailed and Black-tailed Godwits, Knot and Dunlin all present in numbers. The roost is best scanned from the southern end of Pegwell Bay (see page 240).

Winter sees Red-throated Divers, seaduck and auks offshore, and groups of Sanderling run along the beach. This is the best location for Snow Bunting in Kent.

BACKSAND SCRAPE

This small area of shallow open water is accessible only to members of SBBOT. It's about 3 miles (4.8km) from the SBBO and was recently reclaimed by the EA after being destroyed by a tidal surge. A new seawall has been constructed and new scrapes excavated to mitigate against future flooding. It can be very exposed, so dress accordingly.

Park on the small lay-by at the bend on the unnamed road that runs left from just before Royal St George's Golf Club (TR342587; mural.risk.clan). Walk through the wooden kissing gate and follow the seawall path right (towards the sea) along the southern bank of the Stour. Walk below the seawall onto the gravel path to avoid disturbing the birds and scope from where the path bends right.

The scrape is very good for all migrant waders, along with wildfowl, Spoonbill, egrets, gulls and terns. The site is renowned for its gatherings of migrant Clouded Yellow butterflies too. Don't wander onto the surrounding private land.

STONAR LAKE

This fishing lake is owned by the Canterbury and District Angling Association and consists of deep waters surrounded by narrow reedbeds and trees. Unsurprisingly, it attracts winter wildfowl and waterbirds and is in the SBBO recording area, being just inside the River Stour. Most of the lake is for anglers only and is fenced and locked, but much of the water can be scoped or binned through the fence on Ramsgate Road, which runs alongside the western shore. Parking is possible in the concrete lay-by (TR333590; fallen.wriggle.owned).

Unusual species such as Scaup, Ferruginous Duck, Black-necked and Slavonian Grebes, and Red-throated Diver have all been noted in recent years.

MONKS WALL

This small wetland near the river quay in Sandwich was reopened in 2000 and has a reputation for attracting rarer wildfowl. However, in recent times, water levels have been somewhat low.

Access is by permit only, obtainable from the Sandwich Tourist Information Centre at the Guildhall (Cattle Market, Sandwich, Kent CT13 9AH, open 10am–4pm) or from the Pfizer VC (Ramsgate Road, Sandwich, Kent CT13 9NJ, open 7.30am–7pm, except Sundays). The entrance is signposted at the end of the Stoner Road exit to Sandwich Industrial Estate (TR333585; downsize.mining.again), but parking is tricky and you may have to leave your vehicle in Sandwich, a five-minute walk away.

140 WORTH MARSHES (RSPB LYDDEN VALLEY)

Jubilee Road, Worth, Kent CT14 0DT
Website: sbbot.org.uk/our-wildlife-reserves/worth-marshes
Parking: Jubilee Road – TR337557; sues.weeks.haunts
Goretop Lane/Pinnock Wall – TR344566; meals.trap.cured
The Street/Jubilee Road – TR337561; cleans.could.reduction
Email: info@sbbot.org.uk
Phone: 01403 617341
Open: all day, every day. The reserve is about a mile (1.6km) south of the SBBO along a pleasant footpath walk.

SPECIES

All year: Grey Partridge, Avocet, Lapwing, Redshank, Stonechat, Corn Bunting.

Summer: Garganey, Hobby, Little Ringed Plover, Common Tern, Cuckoo, Turtle Dove, Nightingale, warblers.

Winter: White-fronted and Tundra Bean Geese, Water Rail, Golden Plover, Snipe, Jack Snipe, Ruff, Black-tailed Godwit, Merlin, Water Pipit.

Migration: Marsh Harrier, Greenshank, Curlew, Common, Green and Wood Sandpipers, Whimbrel, Turtle Dove, hirundines, Whinchat, Wheatear, Redstart, flycatchers, warblers, White and Yellow Wagtails.

ACCESS

Bike: the main footpath parallel to the Pinnock Wall can be cycled.

Bus: Stagecoach South East route 80 (Dover–Sandwich) stops on Jubilee Road at Church View and King George Villas, both equidistant to Jubilee Road.

Train: Southeastern services run from London Kings Cross St Pancras and terminate at Sandwich, the nearest station, about 1.5 miles (2.4km) to the north.

Car: several footpaths lead onto the reserve, all with adjacent parking. Try the junction of Goretop Lane and Pinnock Wall, from where you can walk south onto the reserve, via agricultural land.

You can also park carefully on Jubilee Road, and walk down the gravel track opposite, following the path right towards Great Wood; this option ultimately leads to the Pinnock Wall over a small wooden bridge. Parking in the village, there are a few official spaces at the junction of The Street and Jubilee Road.

The RSPB has plans to open a parking area in a field to the north-west of the Great Wood, just off Jubilee Way.

YOUR VISIT

This very new site, generally referred to as Worth Marshes, will be part of a greater reserve called RSPB Lydden Valley, and will include the Lydden Downs

SSSI once completed. It's already racked up an impressive list of scarce and rare birds.

The reserve is in the Sandwich and Pegwell Bay corridor and can be visited in tandem, but it's a self-contained reserve with its own agrarian and marshy character. Its wildlife-rich combination of wetland, grassland and woodland was developed from reclaimed farmland and first opened to the public in 2019. It's covered by a grid of water-filled ditches and hedgerows, providing plenty of discrete places for invertebrates to live, including the dragonflies beloved by falcons.

The gravel and mud central path of the Pinnock Wall runs throughout the site and is slightly elevated above the grassland and marshes in places, providing an ideal vantage point from which to scan the site east across grassland to Willow Farm beyond and west towards the Great Wood. This is an excellent place to watch Hobbies in spring and summer, and there can be several in the air at once. They are sometimes joined by Red-footed Falcon and, twice in 2022, by Eleonora's Falcon. The commoner raptors also overfly the area, including occasional double-figure flocks of Red Kites.

The warmer months see the reedbeds, bushes and trees bursting with warbler song, as well as the ostentatious hooting of their arch enemy, the Cuckoo. Garganey, Little Ringed Plover and Hobby are seen in spring succession, while Avocet, Lapwing, Redshank and Snipe all nest around the scrapes close to the path between Great Wood and Pinnock Wall. There were at least 13 Turtle Doves in the taller trees in May 2020, the largest count in Kent that year.

Post-breeding, the scrapes attract Green and Wood Sandpipers (the largest numbers in Kent, with five of the latter together in August 2020) and Black-tailed Godwit. Bearded Tits rove the rushes in winter.

White-fronted, Tundra Bean and Pink-footed Geese are regularly seen, with up to 10 Tundra Beans on passage in early winter, though one or two is more usual, when White Stork has also stayed for long periods. Water Rail and Jack Snipe are also present, and Merlin and Peregrine hunt the area. Most of the few Grey Partridges left in the Sandwich Bay area have been counted on or near Worth Marshes.

This fine parcel of habitat has robust connections to the greater landscape. It provides an accessible and convenient opportunity to see wetland and grassland specialists, and the avifauna can only improve as the greater site develops.

DEAL TO DOVER

The coast between Deal and Dover has a deserved reputation both for 'vis-migging' and for grounded scarcities and rarities, mostly during migration. If the passerines aren't behaving, there is good raptor passage, and potentially some productive though distant seawatching during onshore winds.

141 BOCKHILL: KINGSDOWN TO ST MARGARET'S AT CLIFFE

Granville Road, St Margaret's at Cliffe, Dover, Kent CT15 6DT
Website: bockhillblog.blogspot.com
TR374452; pacemaker.fork.orange

> *Open:* all day, every day
> *SSSI*

This picturesque and productive area for migrants has a strong track record for vis mig and rarities.

SPECIES

All year: Grey Partridge, Fulmar, Gannet, Rock Pipit, Stonechat, Raven, Bullfinch, Corn Bunting, Yellowhammer.

Summer: Peregrine, Kittiwake, Rock Pipit.

Winter: seaduck, divers, grebes, auks, Woodlark.

Migration: Honey-buzzard, Wryneck, Ring Ouzel, Whinchat, Redstart, Black Redstart, Pied and Spotted Flycatchers, Yellow-browed and Pallas's Warblers, Firecrest, visible migration, vagrants.

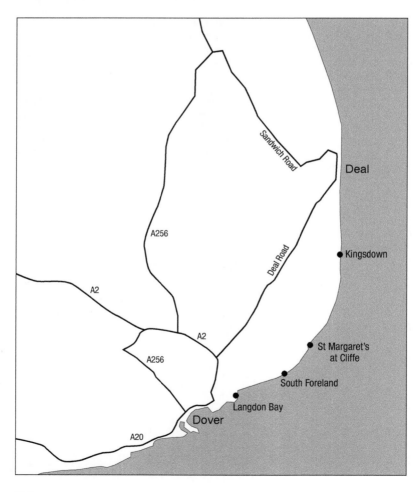

ACCESS

Bike: cycling is permitted but is hard going along the clifftop paths.

Bus: Stagecoach South East route 12 (Canterbury–Deal) stops at the Swingate Inn, Guston, and Oxney Bottom, Ringwould; both are a mile's walk to the north-west of St Margaret's.

Train: Southeastern services from London Kings Cross St Pancras terminate at Dover.

Car: Bockhill Farm is accessed via St Margaret's. Drive towards the sea, turn left onto Granville Road, and follow this to the car park by the monument.

YOUR VISIT

Owned by the NT and private farmers, the Bockhill patch stretches from the famous white cliffs to the A258 Dover–Deal road, about two miles (3.2km) inland. The footpaths are freely accessible, and you can wander almost anywhere except for the golf course and arable fields. Both attract migrants and should not be visually ignored, however.

It's always a tough decision whether to bird Bockhill or the South Foreland area during migration. They make up two sides of the same valley, which serves as a minor fly-way. Both are very attractive to migrants of all kinds, and locals are committed to their patches but frequently swap vital information on what's about and movements. There is a Bockhill Bird Group for regulars, which has discovered many rarities over the years, including Blue-cheeked Bee-eater, Nutcracker, Red-rumped Swallow, Red-flanked Bluetail, Radde's Warbler and Red-breasted Flycatcher.

Regular visits during migration will guarantee a scarcity, particularly during autumn, with Yellow-browed Warbler headlining. Kingsdown to the north-east provides the best seawatching, with regular, though distant, seaduck, divers, grebes, gulls, skuas, terns and auks seen from the shelter in the bay, and a constant-effort seawatching group keeps recent sightings updated.

Fulmar and Rock Pipit breed on the famous white cliffs, while migrant Black Redstarts can appear in numbers in spring and a few Honey-buzzards are expected between spring and autumn, even in midsummer. There's a regular passage of Red Kites and occasional influxes of Buzzards too. This is also an excellent vis-mig site, particularly at the monument, so bone up on your calls and flight identification.

Most of the birding is from the clifftop path, which can be followed inland across the fields toward the woods next to the A258. Pay particular attention to the bushes – the vegetation can heave with commoner migrants during easterlies, but vis mig is usually best with winds in the north-west. The ploughed fields also draw in migrants, while the NT land and golf course are attractive to waders and pipits (but private).

After prolonged easterlies, falls are possible with rain or fog just before dawn. The bushes and trees around Bockhill Farm can be as productive as the coastal gorse, so don't ignore those.

There are no facilities on site, and refreshments will need to be sought in St Margaret's or Dover.

142 DOVER TO ST MARGARET'S: LANGDON BAY AND SOUTH FORELAND

Parking: St Margaret's beach car park, Bay Hill, St Margaret's at Cliffe, Dover, Kent CT15 6DX (TR368445; inflict.rehearsed.spindles); White Cliffs of Dover National Trust car park (Level 4), Upper Road, Guston, Dover, Kent CT16 1HJ (TR335423; professes.famed.global) *SSSI*

A vagrant trap extraordinaire, this picturesque chalk grassland location produces scarce and rare migrants annually.

SPECIES

Very similar to Bockhill (see page 249), though Honey-buzzard is perhaps more likely.

ACCESS

Bike: most paths are generally unsuitable for bikes.

Bus: Dover station is serviced by several buses; walk east uphill to the paths.

Train: Southeastern services from London Kings Cross St Pancras terminate at Dover.

Car: for the White Cliffs of Dover car park, drive along Reach Road to or from Dover until you come to the sharp turn at the end of the loop. Take the sign-posted gravel track and continue upwards to the paid car park at Level 4.

If starting from St Margaret's, take Station Road then Bay Hill all the way to the beach, where there is pay-and-display parking on the seafront.

YOUR VISIT

With resident Fulmar, Peregrine, Raven, Stonechat, Black Redstart, Bullfinch, Corn Bunting and Yellowhammer, the famous White Cliffs and the chalk downs above them are worth birding at any time. However, the area truly comes into its own during passage, when almost anything can turn up.

Common and scarcer migrants can appear almost anywhere. With so much habitat available you can pretty much adapt the routes that follow to your fancy. If you have the time and the winds are good, you can spend all day here, so come prepared. Try after easterlies for grounded migrants, or north-westerlies for visible migration.

Begin at the top of the White Cliffs of Dover car park. Don't be in a hurry to leave, as the likes of Hoopoe and Yellow-browed Warbler have been found there and this is probably the best site for Ring Ouzel in Kent. There is plenty of cover and bushes bordering all four levels, with more scrub down to Langdon Hole below, to the north-east, though this habitat can be hard to work because there's so much of it. On early mornings during passerine movements, it's all worth checking. Birds continue to drop in during the day, and often 'wake up' a couple of hours after dawn – consequently, revisiting areas you've checked already can be worthwhile.

Foxhill Down is the gorse-covered chalk downland above the car park and its footpaths are accessed from the trees at the south-west end of the car park or the kissing gate to the north-east. Taking the south-west option enables you to scan the fields to the north of Reach Road; Golden Plover, and even Dotterel, are possible here in small numbers from August.

Take the north-east gate into an extensive area of scrub above the cliffs. Here, different species can turn up at different stages of the spring and autumn: the scrub in late summer and early autumn should produce Pied and Spotted Flycatchers and Redstart, along with Lesser Whitethroats and Willow Warblers aplenty, and scarcities and drift migrants become more frequent as the autumn develops. Bullfinches, Goldfinches and Linnet will often be apparent, and this is one of the best places in the country to find Serin.

Fulmars, Peregrines and Ravens will appear above the cliff edge. Red-throated Diver winters offshore in good numbers, and other divers, grebe and seabird species may be seen, though mostly at a distance.

Follow the footpath along the cliffs. Birds sometimes bottleneck overnight before launching themselves across the Channel or making landfall on their return. The path follows the edge of Langdon Bay, Fan Bay and then South Foreland before you reach St Margaret's. Search the vegetation surrounding both lighthouses and the trees and scrub surrounding Wanstone Farm Cottages (a Short-toed Eagle flew over in autumn 2022). The small wood inland of the lighthouses is attractive to flycatchers and warblers.

Beyond the Old Lighthouse you'll see the densely vegetated valley at South Foreland, where constant-effort ringing takes place. It acts as a funnel for raptors, including Marsh and Hen Harriers, Red Kite, Common Buzzard and Sparrowhawk. This is one of the best sites in the country to see Honey-buzzard, which is seen coming 'in-off' and soaring along the valley several times a year; the species can appear throughout the spring to autumn period. All wooded areas could hold Yellow-browed or Pallas's Warblers in late autumn.

Circle back around once you reach St Margaret's. The inland section of the path brings you close to Reach Road, where Hen Harrier and Merlin hunt in winter. The fallow areas of tall weeds, fences and grass are attractive to Wheatears, Whinchats and passing warblers.

Regular watching has produced choice scarcities and rarities such as Bee-eater, Sardinian, Greenish, Radde's and Dusky Warblers, and Little Bunting.

Three pairs of Black Redstart also nest in Dover docks, if you miss the species up on the clifftops. This site can also be worth checking for Caspian Gull.

There is a sizeable NT cafe with spacious toilets at the foot of the cliffs on the road up.

DOVER TO FOLKESTONE

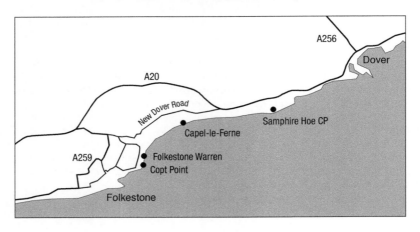

143 CAPEL-LE-FERNE, FOLKESTONE WARREN AND COPT POINT

This stretch of coastline – also featuring the famous White Cliffs of Dover – provides more well-known migrant traps.

The White Cliffs area as a whole has an enviable reputation for producing scarcities and rarities, as well as dramatic visible migration. Resident Fulmar, Kittiwake, Mediterranean Gull, Peregrine, Black Redstart, Firecrest, Raven, Rock Pipit and Bullfinch make the birding attractive year-round.

ACCESS

Stagecoach South East bus service 15 runs between New Romney and Dover, stopping within walking distance of most sites, but otherwise, driving is recommended. See each entry for parking information.

COPT POINT
Car parks:

Wear Bay Road, East Cliff, Folkestone, Kent CT19 6AT (TR238363; refills.claims. faster);

Wear Bay Road, East Cliff, Folkestone, Kent CT19 6PU (TR239365; easy.bake. unguarded);

East Cliff, Folkestone, Kent CT19 6PR (TR240372; horses.spent.remainder).

This clifftop viewpoint just to the north of Folkestone holds one of the largest congregations of Mediterranean Gulls in the country, with some 4,000 estimated in September 2020. Winter is best, but some are found throughout the year (though there are few in mid-summer). Check the short grass between the road and the shore for gull congregations, particularly between July and March.

The site also provides reasonable seawatching, with the bay offshore providing shelter for grebes, divers, seaduck such as Red-breasted Merganser, and seabirds such as Kittiwake or even Shag during bad weather. Viewing from the bay or harbour wall can provide views of commoner seabirds.

FOLKESTONE WARREN LNR

Car park: East Cliff, Folkestone, Kent CT19 6PJ
TR243375; volunteered.taxed.leathers
LNR, SSSI
(299.4 hectares; 739.8 acres)

This sizeable CP is found just to the north of Copt Point and is managed by the White Cliffs Countryside Project. It's a compact pocket of habitat, with scrub, woodland, grassland, cliffs and sea all holding good birds at any time of the year.

Migrants are often logged overhead, including passerines and birds of prey, while seawatching over the bay can be good, particularly with onshore winds; there's the chance of divers, grebes, seaduck and seabirds at these times.

Migrants will settle in the bushes – but get there early before they're disturbed. Unusual past sightings have included a flock of nine Bee-eaters 'in-off' and Greenish Warbler, while the Copt Point Mediterranean Gull flock sometimes wanders a little north to the Warren area and has numbered close to 1,000 recently.

The site can be explored via the Four Seasons Nature Trail, which covers the whole reserve, through the scrub to the cliff edge and foreshore. This is an almost circular route that entertains all the site's possibilities. Chiffchaff and (sometimes) Firecrest overwinter, while Peregrine hunts overhead all year. Black Redstart and Rock Pipit are resident at the cliff base, often perched on the rocks and concrete wall.

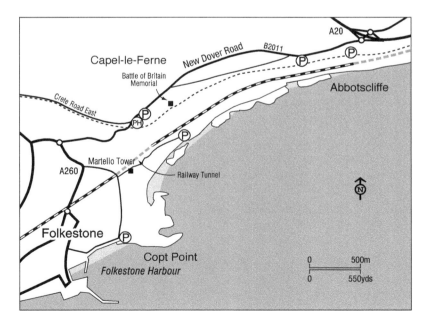

The area of chalk ridge between The Warren and the town of **Capel-le-Ferne** (North Downs Way, off Old Dover Road, Capel-le-Ferne, Kent CT18 7HW; TR250382; configure.steered.music) is also great for visible migration, sometimes luring passing migrants to its scrub.

The site has logged many exciting species during migration, including Black Kite, Alpine Swift and Kent's first-ever Isabelline Wheatear. Remember to check everywhere nearby during passage, including the imposing Battle of Britain Memorial (Beazley Way, Capel-le-Ferne, Kent CT18 7ND; TR245381; stub.berated. answers), which provides a handy viewpoint from which to take in a glorious vista of coast and sea, and thoroughly check the skies.

A little further up the coast from The Warren is **Abbotscliffe** (park at Old Folkestone Road, Hougham Without, Dover, Kent CT15 7AE; TR275387; expecting.promoted.icons) – another good place to find scarce migrants. Whinchat, Ring Ouzel and Wryneck turn up most years, while raptors – once including a juvenile Pallid Harrier – are expected overhead. It's also another productive spot for seawatching.

144 SAMPHIRE HOE CP

Fishermens Litter, Samphire Road, Aycliffe, Dover, Kent CT17 9FL
Website: www.samphirehoe.com/
TR294390; vitals.thrashing.rips
Phone: 01304 225 649
Email: paul.holt@whitecliffscountryside.org.uk
Open: The reserve is open daily from 7am–dusk and is wheelchair friendly. There is a small tea kiosk that's open 'most days' from 11am–5pm, between Easter and September. Samphire Hoe is managed by the White Cliffs Countryside Partnership and publishes an annual bird report available online at *www.samphirehoe.com/biodiversity-wildlife/birds.* (30 hectares; 74.13 acres)

A unique, compact reserve that acts as a decent migrant trap, replete with Black Redstarts and Peregrines.

SPECIES

All year: Fulmar, Peregrine, Rock Pipit, Stonechat, Raven.

Summer: cliff-nesting House Martin, Black Redstart.

Winter: seawatching.

Migration: seabird movements including skuas and terns, Ring Ouzel, Wheatear, Whinchat, migrants, scarcities.

ACCESS

Bike: the North Downs Way footpath and Sustrans NCN Route 2 cyclepath pass close to the entrance.

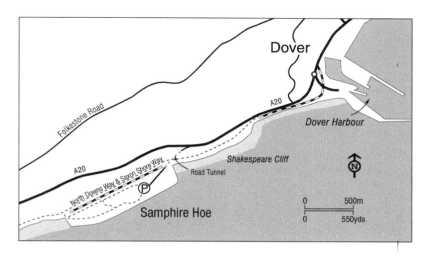

Bus: Stagecoach route 64 (Aycliffe–Dover) stops at Aycliffe Community Primary School, from where you use the footbridge to cross the A20 and walk to the reserve.

Train: the Southeastern service from London Kings Cross St Pancras terminates at Dover; continue south-west by bike, bus or taxi.

Car: Samphire Hoe is signposted on the A20 Dover–Folkestone road. It's accessed via a tunnel cut into the cliff, which is controlled by a traffic light system. There is a spacious fee-paying car park (£2.00 for two hours or more, free for disabled people).

YOUR VISIT

Created from the spoil produced by the Channel Tunnel excavations and owned by Eurotunnel, this small reserve is a hidden gem and acts as one of the better migrant traps during passage.

Peregrine, Rock Pipit, Black Redstart and Raven all breed. Fulmar is resident, but other seabirds are best scoped for during passage and winter and can include grebes, divers, terns and skuas.

Samphire Hoe comes into its own for migrants, but the site is popular with day-trippers, so the earlier you visit, the better. Keep an eye overhead, as visible migration can be good and raptors such as Honey-buzzard pass overhead on occasion. Dartford Warbler has wintered.

Despite being relatively new, Samphire Hoe has already notched up a few rarities, including Crag Martin, Asian Desert Warbler and Short-toed Treecreeper. A couple of shallow pools at the cliff base sometimes pull in a wader.

THE DUNGENESS PENINSULA

SSSI

This shingle headland on the south coast of Kent has a deserved reputation as one of the best birding destinations in Britain. The combination of farmland, coastal and marshland habitats means that there is a unique combination of birds, including scarce breeders, while its position close to France and at a decisive bend on the coast, as the English Channel meets the North Sea, provides ample opportunity for seeing active migration, seawatching, and scarcities and rarities. The region's list is enviable, including several firsts for Britain.

An aerial view of the peninsula gives you a grasp of its geography: the ancient shingle stretches from Camber and Rye in East Sussex to the cliffs at Hythe in the east, taking in all the areas to the north-west in a curve through Appledore, Hamstreet and West Hythe. There are good birds in the countryside inland too, but most birders concentrate in the hotspots (below) during spring and autumn.

Even so, there are enough birds at any time of the year to keep anyone busy. Spectacles include the 6,000 Golden Plover the area holds each winter, up to 7,660 Brent Geese passing offshore during March and huge numbers of Mediterranean Gulls – 1,350 in October 2020. Add to this the possibility of rarities such as Penduline Tit or Kentish Plover (Dungeness is probably the best site in the country for these continental vagrants), and the reserve, the 'obs' and the peninsula as a whole can be a truly world-class birding experience.

While there are few facilities on site, the fairly central towns of Lydd, Lydd-on-Sea, Greatstone and New Romney all have pubs, shops, cafes and toilets. Dungeness has fish'n'chips, a few pubs and a café.

The birds you will see on your visit can be somewhat dependent on the weather, especially during migration. Winds from the eastern quarter during spring or autumn can bring the more interesting migrants to the peninsula, and this situation can be boosted further by southerly airflows during May. Winds from the northern quarter are good in autumn, while seawatching can be improved by onshore airflows or westerlies in spring and easterlies in autumn.

SPECIES

All year: Shelduck, Gadwall, Common Scoter, Bittern, Cattle and Great Egrets, chance of Glossy Ibis, Water Rail, Red Kite, Marsh Harrier, Oystercatcher, Curlew, Common Gull, Kingfisher, Barn Owl, Peregrine, Bearded Tit, Cetti's Warbler, Black Redstart, Stonechat, Tree Sparrow (scarce), Corn Bunting.

Summer: Garganey, Hobby, chance of Black-winged Stilt, Little Ringed Plover, Common Tern, Turtle Dove, Cuckoo, hirundines, Wheatear (breeds), Reed and Sedge Warblers, Lesser Whitethroat, Nightingale, Yellow Wagtail.

Winter: Bewick's and Whooper Swans, White-fronted Goose, seaduck, Smew (scarce), Goosander (scarce), Black-necked and Slavonian Grebes, Snipe, Jack Snipe, Caspian, Glaucous and Iceland Gulls, Guillemot, Razorbill, Merlin, Water Pipit.

Migration: Brent Goose, Pintail, divers, Gannet, Spoonbill, Sooty, Manx and Balearic Shearwaters, Avocet, Turnstone, Bar-tailed and Black-tailed Godwits, Whimbrel, Common, Green and Wood Sandpipers, Spotted Redshank, Greenshank, Sanderling, Dunlin, Knot, Ruff, Kittiwake, Mediterranean, Little and Yellow-legged Gulls, Arctic, Sandwich, Little and Black Terns, Pomarine, Arctic and Great Skuas, Swift, Ring Ouzel, Spotted Flycatcher, White Wagtail.

145 GREATSTONE BEACH, LADE SANDS AND LADE PITS

SPA, SAC, SSSI, Ramsar

Long, sandy **Greatstone Beach** (The Parade, Lade, Kent TN28 8RE; TR082229; poorly.lifts.teaches) between New Romney and Dungeness is of a very different nature to the shingle of the southern end of the peninsula. Here, Oystercatcher, Grey Plover, Sanderling, Turnstone, Knot and Bar-tailed Godwit occur, and it's also good for loafing gulls in winter.

RSPB Lade Pits (TR078217; romance.differ.tilt) is just inland of the beach behind Romney Sands Holiday Park, formed from former gravel diggings. A similar range of species can be seen there, including Smew, Marsh Harrier, Bittern and Bearded Tit, though it's much smaller in area. The site is good for Scaup in winter, while divers and scarce grebes turn up regularly.

A sizeable wader roost at the pits mostly involves Oystercatchers, along with Curlew, Bar-tailed and Black-tailed Godwits, and Grey Plover (Dunlin and Ringed Plover tend to roost on the tideline shingle at Dungeness). They can be seen flying over the holiday park between the beach and lake as the tide comes in. Perhaps the best place to observe these movements is from the bare paved area opposite the Romney Tavern (TR082219; guarding.earlobes.insurers) on the seafront.

There are several free car parks along the coastal road, from where the coastline and sea can be scanned from the opposite side of the road. There are a couple of public toilets along this stretch, sometimes closed outside the tourist season. You can enter Lade Pits via Taylor Road (TR081207; coaster.inefficient.scoping), Leonard Road (TR 082 211; lengthen.chain.begins) or Seaview Road (TR078221; encodes. develops.farmer), but you still need to use the nearby public car parks if you're driving.

Of special interest at Lade are the huge wartime sound mirrors (aka acoustic mirrors, or 'listening ears'), built between 1928 and 1935 as part of the British National Defence Strategy). They were intended to monitor the sounds of approaching enemy aircraft but were made redundant by the invention of radar.

146 WALLAND AND ROMNEY MARSHES

Romney Marsh KWT: Dymchurch Road, New Romney, Kent TN28 8AY.
Website: www.kentwildlifetrust.org.uk/nature-reserves/romney-marsh-visitor-centre-and-nature-reserve
TR077260; mirror.protester.circus
Email: romneymarsh.vc@kentwildlife.org.uk
Phone: 01797 369487
LNR, SSSI

ACCESS

Bus: Stagecoach route 102 (Folkestone–Rye–Lydd) stops at several points along Dymchurch Road.

Train: change off the Southeastern London Stratford International–Margate service at Ebbsfleet onto the Ashford International–Dover Priory service and alight at Folkestone, from where you can catch the 102 bus.

Car: park carefully on the verges of the A259 and minor roads to scan the fields.

YOUR VISIT

Walland and Romney Marshes comprise large areas of farmland north of the region's more famous birding areas, with irrigation ditches and small patches of woodland throughout. It can be hard work exploring the minor roads and tracks that lace through the area's habitats, but it often pays off. A car or bike is advisable. National Cycle Route 2 crosses part of the region, all the way to Scotney (page 269).

In winter, the sizeable Mute Swan flock that haunts fields on Walland Marsh to the south of the A259 can attract Whooper and Bewick's Swans in small numbers, but both have become less numerous in recent years – although more than 50 Bewick's turned up during winter 2022–23; Whooper Swan numbers are usually in low single figures. The distant white blobs can be scoped by parking carefully in lay-bys or on verges, but beware: there are countless Mute Swans in the same fields too.

A few pairs of Nightingales can be heard in spring in the coppices dotted around the area. Tree Sparrow is still present in small numbers around farm buildings (a waning ten pairs in 2020), while Turtle Dove just about hangs on in a couple of places; try the areas close to the railway line at Kenardington on the north-western fringes of the marsh (TQ971326; crunching.lightens.melt).

The farmland has patchy populations of Corn Bunting and Yellowhammer, forming mixed flocks in winter that sometimes attract other seed-eaters. Yellow Wagtail is common during passage and in summer – check out any wet areas on the fields for this species (and rarely its scarcer subspecies). The likes of Dotterel, White Stork and Common Crane have been found on the ploughed fields in spring and autumn, though a few Golden Plover are more likely. Barn and Little Owls hunt over the fields, best seen early or late in the day.

In winter, there's a small winter roost of Marsh and, sometimes, Hen Harriers in reeds south of the Woolpack Inn on the A259, Guldeford Lane (TQ978244; fires.grudge.cushy). This can be reached by the footpath that runs opposite the pub; get there an hour before dusk. Another site that is good for harriers is the small area of wetland to the north of St Thomas à Becket Church in Fairfield (TQ966264; humidity.conductor.presumes), where ducks and waders can also be seen in season.

Many of the more interesting species are possible on extended walks out of New Romney. **Belgar Farm** (on an unmarked road off Romney Road/B2075 TN28 8AF; TR065226; fall.usages.movements) to the south of the village of Belgar supports Yellowhammer, Corn Bunting and Yellow Wagtail. Try **Faggs Wood** (aka **Orlestone Forest** – Malthouse Lane, Warehorne, Ashford, Kent TN26 2EL; TQ986347; junior.trees.refusals) for Nightingales in season (68 singing in 2021), along with Garden and Willow Warblers, Siskin and Redpoll, and woodland birds such as Woodcock and Tawny Owl. **Park Wood/Great Heron Wood** (Woodchurch Road, Appledore, Ashford, Kent TN26 2BJ; TQ954317; beans.term.clapper), near Appledore, and

Warehorne (Warehorne, Ashford, Kent TN26 2LL; TQ989325; removable.milky. impaled) also continue to support a few Turtle Doves and Nightingales.

Romney Marsh NR KWT (TR077261; hindered.ending.dinner) at the northern end of the region has scant birding interest but the 24-hour parking is free and it's close to the coast and eateries. There is also a small, 11-ha (27 acres) nature reserve called **Romney Warren KWT** (TR078261; perch.even.dwell) at the eastern end of the A259, where refreshments can be had. Again, there is little avian interest, but Cuckoo occurs in summer and seawatching over the bay from the beach can be productive in bad weather.

Note also that the village of Lydd has a heronry with bonus nesting Little Egrets, as well as a rookery, views of which are sometimes allowed by visiting the top of All Saints Church (TR042209; merge.blip.idea). About 10 wintering Tree Sparrows were counted in nearby **Brenzett** in January 2020.

147 DUNGENESS BIRD OBSERVATORY (DBO)

11 RNSSS Cottages, Dungeness, Romney Marsh, Kent TN29 9NA
Website: www.dungenessbirdobs.org.uk
TR084172; craftsman.rapport.today
Phone: 01797 321309
Email: dungenessobs@vfast.co.uk
Open: all day, every day
NNR, SSSI

One of mainland Britain's greatest migration observation sites, with breeding Wheatear and Black Redstart, and always the chance of excitement.

ACCESS

Bike: all the main tracks and roads are cyclable, but the shingle is best explored on foot.

Bus: routes 11 (Ashford–Lydd–New Romney), 102 (Rye–Dover), 105 (Dover–Lydd) and 553 (Brookland–Rye) all stop outside Dungeness Power Station.

Train: the Romney, Hythe and Dymchurch Light Railway runs somewhat unpredictably from near the 'obs' and provides a pleasant way to travel across the scenic width of the peninsula. The nearest mainline station is Ashford International, from where you can catch the number 11 bus.

Car: head east out of Lydd on Dungeness Road, pass the RSPB pits and the turning for the power station and turn right at Lydd-on-Sea along the concrete-topped Dungeness Estate Road. Follow this to the power station perimeter wall and turn down the narrower tarmac road to your right to the end. The 'obs' is the first door by the limited parking spaces. There is also a small parking area on the right side of the road near the fishing boats – the official nature reserve car park – and a much larger car park by the café and lighthouse. The smaller one at the beach end of the power station wall is often used by seawatchers as it's close to hides.

STAYING AT DBO

The obs offers cheap and basic accommodation for visitors. A stay at DBO has become a rite of passage for many a birder over the years – particularly those interested in ringing or rarity finding. The obs has resident wardens and there are two small dormitories with five and four beds respectively, costing £15 a head, or £10 if you're a 'Friend' (see below). It's more of an old-school hostel, and you'll need a sleeping bag, pillow case and your own food, drink, toiletries and towels. There is a café, fish'n'chip shop and pub close by, and more are available in Lydd-on-Sea or Lydd.

YOUR VISIT

Combined with the RSPB reserve – and even without taking in Lade GPs – this is a huge area to cover and your strategy will depend on the weather conditions, the time of year and what has been seen recently. The obs is a constant-effort ringing site in the heart of the shingle peninsula. It is in pole position to receive the lion's share of the migrants that hit land in the area. Consequently, the scrubby area around the obs has an enviable reputation of attracting outrageous rarities, while scarcities are a site staple.

You can become a Friend of DBO for a small annual fee, which entitles you to a key to the seawatching hides and a cup of tea at the obs, as well as discounted accommodation – see *www.dungenessbirdobs.org.uk/p/friends-of-dbo*.

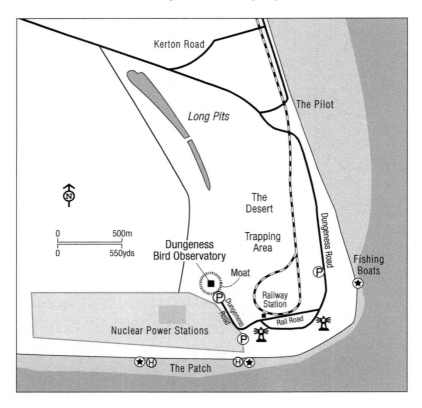

The main areas are:

- the low scrub that surrounds The Moat, which circles the 'obs' entirely, and often conceals 'crests' and warblers, the most likely of which are Chiffchaff, with the odd Firecrest and occasional Dartford Warbler (all may overwinter at times). There is a large Heligoland trap close to the entrance path, while the circular shingle ridge gives good height to observe visible migration.
- the Trapping Area to the north of the 'obs' is a large area of shingle and scrub where most mist-netting is performed. Ringing takes place in spring and between July and November; any rarities that are trapped tend to be held for release for a short time, enabling nearby birders to see them. You can walk these areas freely but please be considerate.

The Desert is an area of extensive shingle dotted with thick bramble, gorse and willow clumps to the east of the 'obs', backing onto the houses. It's very attractive for passerine migrants, especially wheatears, redstarts, chats, pipits and larks, while up to 20 pairs of Wheatear breed in the area.

The only area of open water is the Long Pits, which can produce the occasional scarce waterbird. However, the dense willows and scrub surrounding the pits can conceal plenty of songbirds, often later in the day.

The lighthouse and gardens provide shelter for avian waifs and strays too, but try not to be intrusive while searching and consider the privacy of residents.

The fishing boats are attractive to small groups of larids, which can include Yellow-legged and Caspian (26 in December 2020) Gulls from late summer to spring. This location is a sheltered place for a seawatch, with migrating seabirds passing close to shore as they turn 'England's corner'. This eastern part of the shoreline is more productive in autumn as the birds migrate north to south.

The hides and The Patch are the main seawatching locations. The two lockable hides are intended for use by the Friends of Dungeness Bird Observatory (see page 262). Members are entitled to a key to these shelters and can invite a friend. Non-members should check the weather to ensure they don't get caught in the rain or a freezing blast, but there's a little room at either end of the huts, out of the wind. The westernmost hide – after a heavy trudge over the shingle – overlooks The Patch, an area of upwelling warm seawater created by the power station outflow that pulls in passing gulls and terns. South-westerly winds are the best for pushing wader, wildfowl and seabird movements towards your scope in spring, while south-easterlies perform the same task in autumn.

The breeding birds in this unique environment include Wheatear and Black Redstart, the latter usually present all year around the power station (six pairs in 2021).

Continental birds pass through in small numbers every year, including Hoopoe and Bee-eater. Black Kite and Honey-buzzard have become more regular in spring. Every spring and autumn, various warblers and chats, including Whinchat, Redstart, and Pied and Spotted Flycatchers, file through, and can be seen in varying numbers throughout the two periods – though they often linger longer in autumn. Serin is more possible in spring.

Autumn can also host large, mobile hirundine flocks. Visible migration peaks in October when finches and thrushes are on the move, especially when winds are in the north-western quarter under cloudless skies.

Dungeness is the closest part of Kent to the Continent, and the narrowness of the English Channel at the peninsula creates a bottleneck. This geographical fortune means that the best seawatching in the south-east can be had there, with classic seabirds such as auks and skuas, plus flocks of wildfowl and waders. The hides are useful but not essential to experience this spectacle – some of the best sightings come from observers staked out at the fishing boats at the point of the peninsula.

Park by the power station wall for the hides and walk up the high shingle bank ahead, turning right (west) at the top. While good seabirds can be seen all day, the earlier the start, the better. Check the weather forecast, as the shingle banks are very exposed. The species and numbers are best with onshore winds, as birds otherwise pass on the French side, but good sightings have been logged in all conditions at all times of year.

Winter can provide interesting movements, with good numbers of Red-throated Diver and Guillemots seen in calmer conditions from the point. There can be thousands of gulls at The Patch then, with 'white-wingers' and Caspian Gull very possible. You'll often see the trailing, back-heavy black blobs of Common Scoter in the middle distance for much of the year; day-counts have recently peaked at 1,365 in April 2020.

As spring develops or summer begins, expect flocks of Whimbrel and Bar-tailed Godwit, along with terns of all kinds. The main event is usually the passage of Pomarine Skuas in early May, when small groups (sometimes in double figures) of this chunky jaeger can be seen passing east close to shore. Observers further along the south coast often radio or phone in sightings, so birders at Dungeness can have a heads-up when they are likely to appear.

Despite the summer lull at most sites, the sea remains productive at Dungeness, and small numbers of Manx Shearwater can assemble, although the largest numbers pass in May (with 421 logged in May 2021), attracting the Critically Endangered Balearic Shearwater, which is now seen reliably often, with 161 being logged in September 2021. Don't ignore the beach at the water's edge, where gulls and terns often loaf near The Patch, with scarcer species among their number. Pay attention to the weather – bad conditions are difficult for humans, but good for interesting seabirds, and shearwaters and petrels can be seen through the rain-drops on your scope lens.

Some Dungeness rules of thumb: onshore winds are best for autumn and spring migration, but calm conditions don't mean you won't see anything. Stillness means The Patch may be your best option, especially towards the end of summer or in winter. That said, the best conditions can be birdless and the worst produce a stonking rarity – nothing ventured, nothing gained!

148 RSPB DUNGENESS

Dungeness Rd, Romney Marsh, Kent TN29 9PN
Website: www.rspb.org.uk/reserves-and-events/reserves-a-z/dungeness
Entrance: TR063197; bulletins.resolved.arose
Phone: 01797 320588
Email: dungeness@rspb.org.uk
Open: every day (9am–5pm; VC 10am–4pm). The reserve has a basic shop and refreshments, spacious toilets, picnic and play areas, and binoculars for hire. Check the website for public holiday opening times.
NNR, SSSI
(approximately 1,000 hectares; 2,471 acres)

One of the RSPB's jewels, this reserve attracts copious waders, wildfowl and passerines, hosts breeding Bittern and Bearded Tit, and attracts many scarce migrants.

ACCESS

Bike: National Cycle Route 2 runs from Rye railway station all the way to Camber, passing the reserve, where there are bike racks.

Bus: Stagecoach routes 11 (Ashford–Lydd–New Romney), 102 (Rye–Dover), 105 (Dover–Lydd) and 553 (Brookland–Rye) all stop outside Boulderwall Farm at the entrance.

Train: Rye is the nearest station at 10 miles (16km) away; Ashford (16 miles, 25km) and Folkestone (20 miles, 32 km) are further (see also the access entry for the 'obs' on page 261). Whichever you choose, you'll need a bus, taxi or bike.

Car: follow signposts from Lydd until you see the reserve entrances (see map). The car park opposite the main entrance is always open, allowing for an early start at the ARC Pit.

YOUR VISIT

RSPB Dungeness takes up most of the peninsula and is close enough to the English Channel for migrants to drop in almost constantly in spring and autumn, and for wintering species to arrive from the Continent at the first sign of hard weather.

It has a cross-section of the peninsula's unique habitat, including swathes of open shingle and scrub, former gravel pits with reedbeds and open freshwater, wet grassland with sedges, grazing marsh and wet meadows. There is a profusion of wildflowers, and it's one of the most biodiverse sites for insects in England.

Dungeness RSPB is a large site and a lengthy visit will pay off. However, the frustratingly late (for birding) opening time of 9am means that the keenest visitors will start at the ARC pit car park, conveniently opposite the main entrance.

Once parked, take a short walk down the Willow Trail to the nearest hide, the Hansen ARC Hide, which is placed off a path running east, parallel to Dungeness Road. This will allow you to make a grand visual sweep across the open water, which often hosts good numbers of wildfowl, with wading birds on the fringes.

Walk back to the car park through fairly dense willow scrub that can host good numbers of warblers and flycatchers during migration.

Head north, then north-east, from the car park past the smaller Water Tower Pits and more trees and scrub. Oystercatcher breeds on the shingle near the path, while the trees hold Cuckoo and Garden Warbler in spring, and the occasional Turtle Dove may be purring away. The pits can host migrants in the fringing willows and scrub.

Soon, you'll come to a viewing shelter on your right overlooking some small muddy islands, shallow water inlets and reedbeds. These can be good for scarcer 'drop-ins' such as waders, and the likes of Glossy Ibis and Black-winged Stilt. Walk north past the viewing shelter, keeping an eye on the pines to your left, to a minor railway crossing. Cross carefully to scan the typical shingle scrub of the peninsula, where migrants sometimes perch or even root around among the pebbles.

Just before 9 am, you'll want to turn back to your car and venture into the reserve proper. Through the main gate, you'll immediately see Boulderwall Farm on your right from the gravel access track (Reedbed Road). Pull onto the small lay-by on your right just past the farm building and roadside pool. From there, scan the grazing marsh, the small area of open water (Cook's Pool), the larger Tanner's Pool beyond and the reedbeds. Take care not to block the track.

Year-round, this is a good place to see Cattle and Great Egrets and perhaps Glossy Ibis (although none are guaranteed), as Marsh Harriers quarter the reeds beyond and Hobbies wheel high in the warmer months – there may be several in the air at one time. Barn Owl is possible, either around the farm or across the road

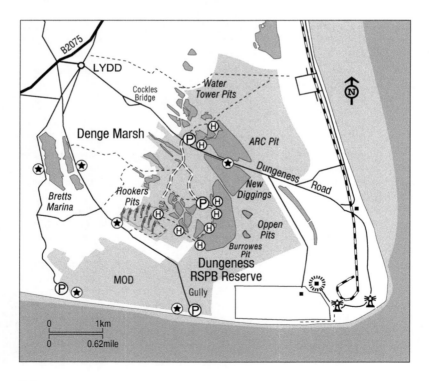

around the Water Tower Pits. Yellow Wagtail and Water Pipit visit during passage and winter respectively.

Drive slowly along the road, keeping an eye on the scrub and fields. You'll come to a bend in the track where there is a shortcut on foot to Hooker's Pit and Denge Marsh, but drivers must go the full mile to the VC and park there. You'll find there are plenty more parking spaces, friendly staff and decent amenities, along with free colour maps of the site and a regularly updated list of recent sightings. You can get snacks and coffee, but the RSPB is rather missing a trick without a café at such a popular reserve.

As you near the VC, pause and scope the gulls that roost on the shingle crests to your left. There are usually a few Common Gulls and Oystercatchers (both breed) but, although Mediterranean, Yellow-legged and Caspian Gull numbers fluctuate seasonally, they are possible at almost any time of year. Up to 50 pairs of Common Terns nest on the rafts provided, though the chicks were entirely predated in 2021.

Your circuit starts at the VC, taking you past most of the reserve's main attractions. Burrowes Pit – visible from the VC, Dennis's, Firth and Scott Hides, and a new watchpoint built where the Makepeace Hide used to be – often lures in unusual waders, gulls and ducks, so time spent scoping the water and islands is advised.

The winding gravel path leads past smaller pools to your right, all of which are worth scanning; the Christmas Dell Hide often provides a good excuse to do this. Any of the pools on the reserve can hold Smew in winter, and Penduline Tit is possible in the reeds, especially in October or November.

To your left, the gorse gives way to hawthorn, beyond which lie wet grassland and meadows interspersed with streams and pools. This is the edge of Denge Marsh and can be very good for migrating waders. Late summer brings good numbers of post-breeding Lapwing and Redshank, boosted by Green and Wood Sandpipers, and Black-tailed Godwits – always with the chance of something juicier. Garganey lingers into summer here, sometimes breeding, with up to 18 through during passage. The grass and mud can be observed from many points, with the birds often close.

This path – the Nature Discovery Trail – reaches a crossroads where you have the option to turn left and scan more of the same productive habitat; some of the best birds can be tucked away deeper into the sedges and grasses on Hayfields 1, 2 and 3. The path stretches as far as Dengemarsh Sewer, which sometimes conceals herons and other waterbirds, and Yellow Wagtail (summer), while Yellowhammer and Corn Bunting (all year) may be present in the greater area.

Amble back to the crossroads, turn left down the narrower path and pop into Denge Marsh Hide. Depending on water levels, species such as Yellow Wagtail can give confiding views, while Spoonbill and various egrets are regular on the far side. With higher levels, interesting wildfowl may appear. The scrub around the path to this hide is good for Sedge Warbler and Lesser Whitethroat, and Dartford Warbler is sometimes found in winter.

Continue north, following the path round to the left. You'll come to a grassy raised viewpoint overlooking Hooker's Pits with a circular wooden bench. This modest mound with its panoramic view over the pits, reeds and farmland beyond can provide one of southern England's greatest birding experiences on a warm spring or summer evening. Bittern is resident in the reeds, and its resonant booming is often heard among the squealing Water Rails, and patience will almost certainly reward you with close and photogenic flight views. Bearded Tits will be uttering their laser-gun *choo*s and can provide intimate views. Herons and egrets of many hues can fly past, but the numbers of Marsh Harriers and Hobbies in the air can be distracting. Purple Heron and Cattle Egret have bred in the reeds and Great Egret will surely follow soon. It's one of South-East England's ultimate wetland experiences and the equal of almost anywhere in the UK.

Continue along the Nature Discovery Trail, following it to the right back to the VC. Anything after a good session at Hooker's Pits might seem like a comedown, but there can yet be good birds to see in the scrub or flying over on your way back – Dartford Warbler and Red-backed Shrike have occurred in this area.

After your session on the main reserve, an option is to turn right out of the reserve entrance and head towards the village of Dungeness until you get to the eastern end of the ARC Pit. There, it's possible, with care, to park on the edge of the road (though the police are likely to move you on, so it's better to park further on and walk back). Scan over the marshy areas at this end, as the likes of Great Egret and Black-winged Stilt can haunt this quieter area. With more care, cross the road to scan the New Diggings, which is probably the best area of open water for sawbills in winter, as well as scarce grebes and divers. Terns favour waters on either side of the road, but stay aware of the traffic.

DENGE MARSH

While hardier walkers can scan over Denge Marsh to the south-west from the reserve paths, it is sometimes easier to drive along Dengemarsh Road from the south end of Lydd and scan the area outside the reserve from the road on the southern and northern sides. This long, curved road leads all the way to the sea, but it's best to pull off at Springfield Bridge (TR054181; shackles.studs.thickened), a short distance after Dengemarsh Farm; from there, you can gain wider views of the area and it's a short walk to the nearest hide on the reserve.

The open fields host marauding Marsh Harriers and Hobbies in summer and the occasional Hen Harrier and Merlin in winter. Ravens are likely as they're resident in the area. Whooper and Bewick's Swans are much less frequent than they were, but the odd wild swan and Arctic goose still turns up. Afterwards, it can be worth driving to the end of the road to seawatch from the beach, but it's usually easier to do this from the seawatching hides to the east.

It's also possible to view the area from the north, off Dungeness Road. Halfway between Lydd and the reserve entrance is a small track called Marshfield Lane. Turn off there and park carefully at the far end (TR054202), where the lane curves back and joins Dungeness Road again. This can enable better views of the waterbirds and raptors seen from Boulderwall Farm. The bridge over Dengemarsh Sewer there is known as Cockles Bridge and is sometimes referred to in sightings reports.

149 NEARBY: SCOTNEY PIT

Jury's Gap Road/Lydd Road, Lydd, Kent TN29 9JN
TR009187; frog.stood.century
Open: all day, every day
SSSI

ACCESS

Bus: Stagecoach services 11, 102, 293 and 553 stop at the 'Camp' bus stop at the north end of Jury's Gap Road in Lydd, 1–2 miles (1.6–3.2km) from the pits.

Train: see other Dungeness sites above.

Car: from Lydd, head south-west on Jury's Gap Road and park in the lay-bys. Park at the grid reference given and on no account stop in front of any of the MOD access points.

YOUR VISIT

The westernmost part of the greater Dungeness peninsula, and on the East Sussex border, the former gravel workings at Scotney Pit (some are still being worked) are just along the coast from Denge Marsh. They are very productive for errant wildfowl and seabirds, especially after hard weather. They are easily, if sometimes distantly, scoped from the roadside at the grid reference above, though the site is very exposed to wind, cold and precipitation; you can also watch from anywhere on the bike path that runs alongside the pit.

The main attraction is the open water, an area of rest and refuge during storms. Duck flocks can be sizeable and have hidden American species including Lesser Scaup. Flooded areas around the pit, even close to the road, can hold waders, and flocks of Golden Plover should be scoured carefully for the likes of Dotterel. Occasional Little Stints and Ruff can also occur on migration. Waders are also attracted to the grassland next to the pit in spring when roosts of Whimbrel can be quite large. There is an entertainingly active Herring Gull colony in the summer.

In winter, Brent, White-fronted and Bean Geese irregularly turn up on the fields behind the pit at its western end, but swans are less likely. At nearby Scone Court GP, there is a naturalised flock of about 200 Barnacle Geese.

The surrounding countryside can be productive, with Yellowhammer, Corn Bunting and Barn and Little Owls resident; it's quite a good site for occasional singing Quail at the height of summer. A few Tree Sparrows (ten were counted in February 2020, down to one pair in 2021) and Corn Buntings continue to breed on Scotney Farm, at the north-eastern end of the main pit, but Yellow Wagtail and Skylark are much more numerous.

There are no amenities at the site, but refreshments can be found in nearby Lydd or Camber.

OFFSHORE KENT

The Kent coast can provide some of the best seabird passage in England with onshore winds and a bit of turmoil in the weather. While it can be quiet, there's almost no time of year when something of interest isn't possible. Winds in the southern half blow birds towards the South Coast, while easterlies and northerlies blow birds up-Channel or onto the East Coast, and even westerlies push migrants overland and upriver on the Thames.

Seawatching is an acquired taste, however; views are rarely great and you spend a lot of time being alternately pounded and abraded by sun, rain and strong winds – especially if conditions are good for seabird passage. Light is often your enemy, changing plumage tones with glare or shadow, making dark birds look pale and vice versa. You'll need plenty of practice to hone your seabird identification skills, and while there are some excellent books and videos available, nothing beats field experience for nailing a distant seabird on jizz at two miles out (and, oddly, sometimes distant birds are easier to put a name to than closer ones). You'll have to let more birds go past unidentified than you might on land, and you don't often get long to view them, either!

Here are a few of the best sites to visit after you've checked the weather and wind charts.

Lower Hope Point, Cliffe Pools (page 198). If winds are in the north-eastern quarter, this is a good Thameside option. Turn right along the seawall where it turns north-east (TQ710775; pools.sprint.jump) and scope the river from the Point, where the River Thames widens. Winds usually push seabirds closer to the Kent side there, though this site can be rather exposed.

Grain Fort (TQ890769; farmer.mute.whips). Good during easterlies, when seabirds are blown onshore from the wider Thames Estuary.

Warden Point (TR017724; bombshell.drain.harmonica). Looks out onto the North Sea and is great with onshore winds. Get some height and shelter at the top of the cliffs instead of trying to watch from the beach.

Oare Marshes (page 228). The Sea Wall Hide overlooking the Swale (TR018645; flagpole.frosted.betrayed) can be almost devoid of seabirds at low tide (though the waders can be good), but this changes at high tide during north-easterlies when migrating skuas and other seabirds can fly very close to the shore. And you get to stay warm and out of the wind.

Seasalter Sailing Club (TR068649; shrugging.crusher.workbook)/ **Whitstable Harbour** (TR107671; identify.dynamics.highlight). Both these sites look out onto the North Sea and are good in northerlies, though easterlies can blow seabirds on shore and westerlies direct those trying to head south along the seafront. Whitstable has more options at the head of either side of the quay or from the beach in front of the Lobster Shack.

Tankerton. Try watching during winds in the northern quarter from the foot of Fraser Hill on Marine Crescent at the Swalecliffe end of Tankerton (TR130673; skill.frozen.rushed), in front of the huts.

Long Rock, Swalecliffe (TR139677; drill.reef.moss). Onshore winds during the prolonged autumn are your best bet, though this concrete promontory can be exposed. Other useful points at Swalecliffe are in front of **Seaview Holiday Park** (TR141677; fades.full.alert and TR146677; deaf.tower.alarm).

Reculver Towers (page 236). Another site that's best with winds in the northerly quarter, particularly in autumn north-westerlies (light rain helps). At high tide in these conditions, birds can fly very close to shore, providing memorable sightings. Reculver has the advantage of some shelter from the wind and rain – a few seats if you arrive early – and plenty of pay-and-display parking spaces.

Minnis Bay (page 235). Often as good as Reculver in similar conditions. The Promenade around Grenham Bay has plenty of cliff nooks to shelter in, but best are the blue and white shelters on top of the cliffs (TR296700; dinner.alarming.petulant and TR297699; thanks.relegate.loser).

Foreness Point, Palm Bay, Cliftonville, Thanet (TR383716; visits.holly. woke) has some slightly insalubrious shelters on the west side of Palm Bay and is right on the shoulder of the coast looking west, north and east onto the North sea, ensuring that birds can be seen in most winds and weather, though onshore is always best. Margate Pumping Station affords some more shelter at the furthest point on the eastern side, and there's a small wader roost below that features Sanderling, Turnstone and occasionally Purple Sandpiper.

North Foreland (page 238). The Coastguard Station offers some shelter from the onshore winds and weather conditions needed for seabirds to be viewed from the cliffs, overlooking either side of Joss Bay, just north of Broadstairs.

Dungeness (page 265). Access to the seawatching hides is for keyholders only but they provide tolerable shelter outside – depending on which way the wind is blowing (though this option is inadvisable in anything other than very light rain).

INLAND KENT

It's not just Kent's coasts that hold interesting birds – there are large tranches of productive habitat inland, particularly many rich areas of woodland in what has been called 'the Garden of England'.

With the trees, come their specialists – though many have declined over the last few decades. Nightjar and Woodcock are sporadically distributed in summer, but there are some healthy populations in pockets, though Turtle Dove has been extirpated from most. Lesser Spotted Woodpecker is still present at a few sites, while more still hold Marsh Tit and Bullfinch, though they're also in decline. Nightingale is doing fairly well, but Woodlark, Redstart, Pied Flycatcher and Wood Warbler are long gone as breeding birds, though still trickle through as migrants. Spotted Flycatcher is still found in a few woodland glades in summer, but only a few pairs of Tree Pipit now turn up each summer. Plenty of Redpolls and Siskins arrive in winter, though few breed, while numbers of the more irruptive Crossbill fluctuate from year to year. Hawfinch is hanging on in small numbers and still worth searching for in suitable woodland at any time of year.

There are also some fine inland wetlands with a different character to the coastal marshes, the crown jewel of which is the Stodmarsh–Grove Ferry complex, which can host some very rare species such as breeding Savi's Warbler or migrating Spotted Crake. Others present a robust ecosystem that supports the more expected wetland species in good numbers. The following are sites that can give you a memorable day's birding without setting eyes on the sea.

THE CANTERBURY AREA

The Canterbury area is rich in varied habitats, chief of which is its extensive wooded surrounding ring. The historic, picturesque but very accessible city is worth visiting of its own accord and is a good base from which to bird the region.

Its birding sites can be divided into two main zones: the Canterbury Ring Woods to the north and west – particularly those known collectively as The Blean – and the wetlands to the north-east, most notably in the Stour Valley.

The presence of these woodland and wetland habitats makes the city one of the best places in the country for a prolonged birding trip, especially in spring and autumn.

CANTERBURY RING WOODS

Most of this substantial halo of forest is part of The Blean, one of the largest areas of reclaimed woodland in the country. Formerly an extensive area of commercial Sweet Chestnut and conifer plantations, each of the area's tracts has gradually developed a mature mixed deciduous and coniferous character, allowing a more complex fauna and flora to develop. Much of this forested area is now managed and protected under the NNR designation, and almost all of it is also an SSSI.

With such a large tranche of timber, several scarce and hard-to-see bird species maintain a presence, including Nightjar, Turtle Dove, Lesser Spotted Woodpecker (13 pairs overall in 2020), Marsh Tit, Tree Pipit and Hawfinch, though all are still in decline and the last two are teetering on the precipice of extirpation.

SPECIES

All year: Woodcock, Tawny and Long-eared Owls, Lesser Spotted Woodpecker, Firecrest, Coal and Marsh Tits, Nuthatch, Treecreeper, Yellowhammer.

Summer: Turtle Dove, Nightjar, hirundines, Nightingale, Spotted Flycatcher, Lesser Whitethroat, Willow and Garden Warblers, Tree Pipit.

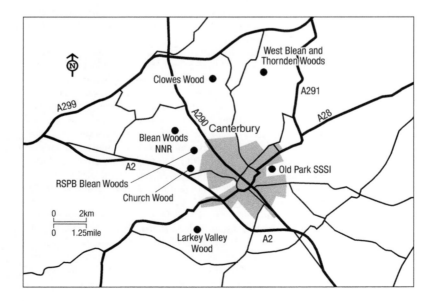

Winter: Kingfisher, Redwing, Fieldfare, Brambling, Siskin, Redpoll, Crossbill.
Migration: Hobby, Redstart, warblers, Hawfinch.

150 RSPB BLEAN WOODS AND CHURCH WOOD

Rough Common Rd, Rough Common, Canterbury CT2 9DD
Website: www.rspb.org.uk/reserves-and-events/reserves-a-z/blean-woods
Nightjar walks: events.rspb.org.uk/bleanwoods
TR121594; ended.eagles.saturate
Phone: 01227 464898
Email: blean.woods@rspb.org.uk
Open: all day, every day, but car park hours are 8am–8pm. There are no amenities, so stock up in nearby towns
SSSI, NNR
(509 hectares; 1,257 acres)

ACCESS

Bike: a major circular cycle route through the forest starts from the car park. A map of the route is available at: tinyurl.com/bleancycle. The Green Trail is suitable for wheelchair users.

Bus: Stagecoach Triangle (Whitstable–Canterbury–Herne Bay), 6 and 6A (Greenhill–Canterbury), and 4 and 4A (Herne Bay–Canterbury) routes all stop on Rough Common Road.

Train: Southeastern services from London Victoria/Kings Cross St Pancras/Charing Cross all terminate at Canterbury East and West – about two miles (3.2km) from the reserve.

Car: turn onto Rough Common (signposted) from the A2050 (Rheims Way) or A290. Go through the village until you see the brown RSPB sign.

YOUR VISIT

With such a large area of woodland, it's difficult to pick a route. However, on-site, you'll see signs showing five colour-coded trails. The longest is the Black Trail at 8 miles (13km), but the Red Trail should enable you to see all the important species and is more manageable at 2.6 miles (4km). There are shorter Green, White and Brown Trails too, and maps are usually available in the car park.

RSPB Blean Woods (formerly known as Church Woods) is part of a much larger forested area to the north of Canterbury, but with the reserve covering such a large area, there is plenty to explore, with all the scarcer species likely to be found at the right time of year. Unless you happen upon a roosting bird, Nightjar will have to be listened for just after dusk; the RSPB runs guided tours for this species, so use the events link for details. One Tree Pipit still sang in 2020.

The woods are a smorgasbord of coppiced Sweet Chestnuts to encourage Nightingales and Hazel Dormice, ancient oak and beech forest (ideal for Lesser

Spotted Woodpecker – which is relatively easy to find, with 10 pairs located during a 2021 survey), secondary birch woods, a bracken understorey and sunlit glades and heath (where you can find the rare Heath Fritillary butterfly). There are several streams and a pond which attract wandering Kingfishers.

A winter visit will have lengthy birdless periods enlivened by wandering parties of tits, which can include Marsh Tit and Nuthatch. Treecreeper, Goldcrest and the odd Chiffchaff may also tag along, and if you're lucky, a Firecrest.

From mid-April, look for Garden Warbler and Nightingale (at least 47 singing in 2020) in the coppices – they'll be most audible at dawn or dusk. As spring warms up, a few Turtle Doves and up to seven pairs of Spotted Flycatcher may join them, though both are becoming scarcer. Nightjar uses both coppiced areas and heathland, but your best bet is to join an RSPB group on a warm late May or June evening, as the ranger will know exactly where to find the one or two pairs present. You may also be rewarded by a roding Woodcock (though numbers had declined to an all-time low of seven in 2020).

Late summer is the best time to see Crossbill in the pines, but otherwise the best period to visit is spring: early on (even late winter) for vocal Lesser Spotted Woodpeckers, and later (May into June) for Nightingale.

151 WEST BLEAN AND THORNDEN WOODS KWT

Parking: Thornden Wood Road, Canterbury, Kent CT6 7NZ
Website: www.kentwildlifetrust.org.uk/nature-reserves/west-blean-and-thornden-woods
South – TR144632; passenger.news.employer;
North – TR147642; fully.fork.funded
Phone: (Will Douglas) 01622 662012
Email: william.douglas@kentwildlife.org.uk
Open: all day, every day. The paths are often muddy in winter. Dogs must be kept on leads. Bring a torch and insect repellent if visiting for Nightjar. No amenities.
Ancient Woodland, SSSI
(Total area: 490 hectares; 1,211 acres)

ACCESS

Bus: the nearest bus stop is Broomfield Gate at the north end of Radfall Road on the west side of Thornden Wood.

Train: the closest station is Canterbury West, about 5.6 miles (9km) to the south (see above).

Car: leave the A299 at the exit marked 'Canterbury/Whitstable' and take the Thanet Way. Take the second exit at the third roundabout after this, onto Millstrood Road, and then turn onto South Street at the T-junction. At the next T-junction turn right onto Radfall Hill, drive all the way past the Clowes Wood car park until you get to a sharp left turn. This is Thornden Wood Road, on which you'll pass both pay-and-display car parks, with the southern first (£2.00 week-days, £2.50 weekends). Download the RingGo app to your phone to pay.

YOUR VISIT

This huge area of mature mixed deciduous and coniferous woodland is daunting to explore but has many paths – plus most of the birds can be seen near the car parks. Sweet Chestnut coppicing encourages Nightingales and makes up 40 per cent of the trees, while about 40 per cent of the rest is coniferous.

From the southern car park, cross the road onto the track opposite to hear and, if you're lucky, see churring Nightjar and roding Woodcock on a late spring or early summer evening. Three singing Tree Pipits hung on in the summer of 2020. You may see the commoner woodland raptors displaying across the skyline above the trees, with the chance of a scarcer species, while Turtle Dove may also be purring. Skirt the cleared areas to stand your best chance of all these species.

Similar birds can be seen from the northern car park. Take the central track of the three available into the woods, leading to some cleared areas. Explore any open areas and forest edge to connect if the main options don't produce the birds. There are five trails in all.

With such a huge wooded area, most of the woodland passerines, including Nuthatch, Treecreeper and Marsh Tit, should be picked up on your walk – they're almost always more apparent on the woodland edges. The site's speciality is Lesser Spotted Woodpecker, and there were up to 16 territories located during a 2021 survey.

NB: the car parks are sometimes used for nefarious purposes, so don't leave any valuables in your car and bring a torch for an evening visit.

THE WILDER BLEAN PROJECT

Website: www.kentwildlifetrust.org.uk/wilderblean/faqs
Apart from the birds, West Blean Woods has an interesting selection of mammals, including Hazel Dormouse – and now European Bison. In 2022, three bison from wildlife parks in Scotland and Ireland joined the Konik ponies already grazing the woods and are now living in Britain for the first time in 6,000 years.

Within large fenced-off enclosures in West Blean Woods (now rechris-tened 'the Wilder Blean'), the bison will roam freely in their roles as 'ecosystem engineers'. The animals have already carved out trails and dust baths, and opened up the forest floor to sunlight. Bison like eating tree bark and consequently increase the amount of rotten wood for woodpeck-ers and Nuthatches to feed on and nest in. The female and two juvenile bison have now been joined by a bull, and it is hoped they will soon breed.

You're unlikely to see any bison unless you're very lucky, as footpaths don't go through the fenced-off area, but on the Continent European Bison now roam unfettered in several places where people walk and there has never been a dangerous incident. It's expected that the bison's natural behaviour will help increase the ecological viability of West Blean, much of which was formerly composed of monocultural pine plantations, and increase the numbers and variety of animals and plants that depend on the woods – including birds.

152 NEARBY: CLOWES WOOD

Radfall Road, Canterbury, Kent CT5 3ER
TR136629; warmers.develop.waltzes
Open: all day, every day. No amenities
(236 hectares; 583.17 acres)

Clowes Wood is north-east of RSPB Blean Woods and west of Thornden Wood. It's a WT-managed conifer forest, with broad-leaved trees interspersed. Similar species to the other forested areas are present.

This used to be one of the easiest sites in Kent for Nightjar, as they could be heard from the car park on stiller evenings, but only one churring bird has been present in recent years. This is still a good place to hear Firecrest in spring.

153 NEARBY: EAST BLEAN WOOD NNR KWT

Hicks Forstal Road, Canterbury, Kent CT3 4JS
Website: www.kentwildlifetrust.org.uk/nature-reserves/east-blean-wood-nnr
TR193643; that.speech.page
Phone: (Will Douglas) 01622 662012
Email: william.douglas@kentwildlife.org.uk
Open: all day, every day. Maximum headroom for vehicles is 2.13m. No VC or amenities
Ancient Woodland, NNR, SSSI
(151.4 hectares; 374 acres)

One of the smaller woods in the Ring, East Blean still supports some good species. Its coppiced Sweet Chestnuts support Nightingale, while the mature oaks encourage Lesser Spotted Woodpecker (perhaps most easily seen accompanying tit flocks in winter), along with more expected species, such as Nuthatch and Treecreeper. It's noted for a healthy population of Tawny Owl, and Woodcock breeds. Hawfinch used to be possible but has not been seen recently.

Leave the A291 Canterbury Road onto Hicks Forstal Road towards Hoath to find the car park after about a mile, just past a fairly sharp right bend.

154 NEARBY: DENGE AND PENNYPOT WOODS

Penny Pot Lane, Petham, Canterbury, Kent CT4 7HA
Website: www.woodlandtrust.org.uk/visiting-woods/woods/denge-penny pot-wood
TR098524; pencil.answer.raven
(25.77 hectares; 63.68 acres)

Situated between Chilham and Petham, a few miles south-west of Canterbury, these extensive woods are good for the full suite of woodland species.

Lesser Spotted Woodpecker, Tawny Owl, Coal and Marsh Tits, Treecreeper, Nuthatch and Bullfinch are all resident. Winter should provide Fieldfare, Redwing, Brambling, Siskin and Redpoll, while summer provides a chance of Nightjar. A Crossbill irruption may bring birds in late summer. A single Tree Pipit sang in the spring of 2020, so it's worth keeping vigilant for this fast-declining species.

155 NEARBY: LARKEY VALLEY WOOD LNR

Cockering Road, Canterbury, Kent CT1 3UR
Website: group.rspb.org.uk/thanet/local-wild-places/larkey-valley-wood-lnr
TR123556; cubs.curry.boots
Open: all day, every day
SSSI, LNR
(44.21 hectares; 109.24 acres)

Formerly one of the best sites in Kent for Hawfinch, but the species is only rarely seen now. However, Marsh Tit is still present, Firecrest is often seen and Lesser Spotted Woodpecker may hang on.

These beech woods are just a short hop from the North Downs on the slopes of a chalk downland valley and provide a picturesque stroll, though progress can be difficult in places after rain.

Exit Canterbury on the A28, taking Milton Manor Road at the first major roundabout outside the city. Take a sharp left onto Cokering Road at the end and the car park is about 500m on your right.

Nearby: **Old Park SSSI** is an acid grassland and woodland area on the eastern outskirts of Canterbury. Firecrest breeds, as do about ten pairs of Nightingale. Turtle Dove is still present in summer in relatively good numbers. There is a new viewing mound to scan for raptors.

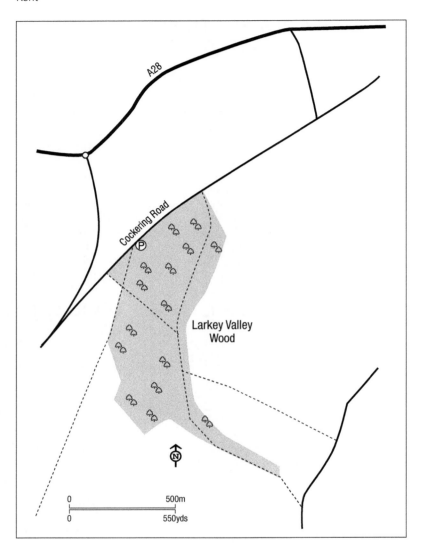

156 LYMINGE FOREST

West Wood Car Park, Mockbeggar, Lyminge, Kent CT4 6DN
Website: www.visitfolkestoneandhythe.co.uk/attractions/lyminge-forest-2259
TR143439; grasp.rotations.floating
(178 hectares; 440 acres)

Situated about 6.8 miles (11km) inland to the north-west of Folkestone, Lyminge Forest is composed largely of mature fir and spruce, with an area of young conifers. Neatly divided into two separate areas – Park and West Woods – this isolated forest is best visited in spring and early summer, as the most interesting species are its breeding birds.

Commoner woodland birds are found year-round and include Marsh Tit (Willow Tit is now extirpated in Kent). Their songs are joined in spring and summer by Nightjar, Nightingale, Firecrest and Garden Warbler. Turtle Dove may just about hang on.

Grassy paths and rides enable exploration throughout but try the more open areas for Nightjar, and you should pick up most of the other species around the edges of the trees too.

Leave the B2068 (Hythe–Canterbury) road at the Murco garage (following the sign to Rhodes Minnis and Elham) onto the unsigned road (actually called Mockbeggar) that connects it to Longage Hill, and the West Wood Car Park is two-thirds of the way along on your left. Cross the road to visit Park Wood, where the same species are also possible. There is an entrance height limit of about 2m.

157 KING'S WOOD, CHALLOCK

Main car park: White Hill Road, Challock, Kent, TN25 4AP
Websites: www.forestryengland.uk/kings-wood; www.friendsofkingswood. org
TR023499; jousting.slimy.lump; TR030496; bagpipes.loss.wide (smaller car park)
(558 hectares; 1,379 acres)

About 5 miles (8km) north of Ashford, this extensive FC-managed area of mixed coppiced Sweet Chestnut, beech and oak, and coniferous woodland is situated in the very heart of the county.

Typical woodland species have healthy populations, with Tawny Owl and Woodcock breeding, while in spring and summer you are likely to hear and see Nightjar, Nightingale and Garden Warbler among the commoner migrants. There are plenty of paths through the wood but try the more open areas for churring Nightjars and roding Woodcock from late May. Marsh Tit, Nuthatch and Treecreeper are present year-round. Summering Turtle Dove and Tree Pipit are still possible, as might be Firecrest. Late summer will bring the occasional Crossbill irruption to the conifers, while winter provides a chance to see Brambling, Redpoll and Siskin among the sizeable finch flocks.

As with some of the other forests, an evening visit is best to explore the more open areas for Nightjar (four pairs in 2021) and Woodcock. Follow the main path from the car park north-east through the middle of the forest, where you'll find the trees opening out after about 150m or so. There is a chance of good raptor sightings in these areas – perhaps even one of the scarcer species. There are a couple of other cleared areas to explore nearby.

The car park is on the south-western edge of this patch of forest. From the A251 Faversham Road (Faversham–Ashford), turn onto White Hill (signposted 'Rye/Stour

Valley Arts'), and the car park is about 500m on your left. It has a height restriction of about 2m.

A little to the east, Longbeech Wood (park at Monkery Lane; TQ980509; rolled. resonates.perfected) has similar species including Nightjar, Firecrest and perhaps Tree Pipit.

THE STOUR/STOW VALLEY

Historically, the Stour Valley was at the heart of Kent's coal-mining industry. The closure of the valley's mines in 1969 (the whole Kent industry closed for good in 1989) led to considerable subsidence and flooding, and much of the gravel extraction industry also wound down not long after, adding to the valley's open water.

The results have been an extensive, connected mosaic of wetland environments, including reedbeds, lakes, wet meadows, wet woodland and gravel pits. These extensive areas of open water sustain mixed wetland habitats for a wealth of common and scarcer breeding and wintering bird species and rich pickings from passing migrants.

Website: *stourvalleysightings.blogspot.com*

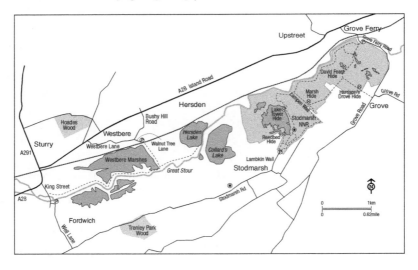

158 STODMARSH NNR AND GROVE FERRY

Parking: Stodmarsh NNR – Lambkin Wall, Stour Valley Way, Stodmarsh, Canterbury, Kent CT3 4BE; TR221609; carpentry.messing.denote.
Grove Ferry – Grove Ferry Road, Canterbury, Kent CT3 4BP; TR235631; freezers.unscathed.speaks.
Websites: https://birdingforall.com/england/kent/stodmarsh-reserve; http://www.kentos.org.uk/blogs-sightings/stour-valley

Open: all day, every day. The walk from Stodmarsh to Grove Ferry and back can be completed in a rough circle, with diversions. Basic amenities are to be found in several villages within a few miles of the reserve, while Canterbury has plenty of choice. The Grove Ferry Inn right next to the western entrance is recommended as an eatery but booking ahead is recommended at weekends – and you can even stay overnight.
SSSI, NNR, SPA, Nature Conservation Review site, SAC
(623.2 hectares; 1,540 acres)

The best of the Stour Valley's rich wetlands, with good populations of the commoner waterbirds and the chance of scarce breeders and migrants.

SPECIES

All year: Gadwall, Bittern, Marsh Harrier, Water Rail, Cetti's Warbler, Bearded Tit.

Summer: Garganey, Spoonbill, Little Ringed Plover, Hobby, chance of Red-footed Falcon, Yellow Wagtail, chance of Savi's Warbler, Spotted Flycatcher, Nightingale.

Winter: Wigeon, Teal, Shoveler, Hen Harrier, Green Sandpiper, Snipe, Jack Snipe, Water Pipit.

Migration: chance of Spotted Crake, waders.

ACCESS

Bus: Stagecoach route 8A Breeze (Canterbury–Margate) stops at Grove Ferry Hill in Upstreet; cross the road and walk down to the reserve.

Train: Southeastern trains from Ashford (change there from Stratford International, London, trains) stop at Sturry, which is the nearest station, 8 miles (8km) from the Grove Ferry entrance.

Car: from the A28, turn onto Grove Ferry Hill at Upstream for the Ferry Boat Inn car park, which is on your left just after you cross the Great Stour river bridge. For Stodmarsh NNR, continue on this road to Grove Road (right at the triangular roundabout), then take another right onto Stodmarsh Road, follow the sign to Stodmarsh, then turn onto Lambkin Wall in the village to reach the car park.

YOUR VISIT

Truly a reserve to get your teeth into, the extensive reedbeds, open water, grazing marsh, scrub, wet woodland and riverine trees of Stodmarsh and Grove Ferry always provide surprise sightings or memorable experiences. Just a few miles from Canterbury, the reserve provides plenty of opportunities for isolation despite its proximity. It's ideal for a lunchtime stop at a pub with good food, before heading back or leaving.

Grove Ferry to the east is now the more productive end, where former turf fields have been converted into excellent wetland habitats. Garganey is annual in spring in decent numbers, while substantial flocks of Hobby appear overhead in spring (with a group of 42 one day in 2021) and Spotted Crake is regular in late summer, though never reliable.

The older part of the reserve at **Stodmarsh** has a dramatic winter harrier roost that usually includes one or two Hen Harriers, while Bittern is resident (occasionally in double figures) and Bearded Tit almost inevitable. Early spring evenings are often the best time for Bittern, as they might be 'booming' and will almost certainly be leaving their reedbed roosts to feed, or performing their impressive pre-migration displays. The site is the best in the county for Water Rail and Green Sandpiper, with 16 of the former present in autumn 2020 and 25 of the latter passing through. Some 12 Water Pipits were counted in February 2021.

Woodcock is present in the wet woodland close to the car park and can be flushed from the grassy footpaths at dawn. The same woodland holds Treecreeper year-round, one or two pairs of Spotted Flycatcher in summer, and Redpoll and Siskin flocks, Firecrest and occasionally Yellow-browed Warbler in winter.

There are five hides over the whole site from which you can scan the reeds and open water, while the raised Lampen Wall provides an essential watchpoint, particularly if you're hoping to see Water Rail or Bittern. From here, a winter vigil for harriers can be thrilling and may be spiced up by a Merlin or Barn Owl. The two hides at the Grove Ferry end were the best for Spotted Crake, but much of the habitat is now overgrown, and Water Pipit is also most likely there (there were 25 on site in January 2020).

The extensive reedbeds have supported breeding Savi's Warbler more than once, though the species is not annual. At the Grove Ferry end, the raised slope that overlooks the first scrape to your left is the most productive for waders and raptors. It's a wise idea to keep your eyes on the skies there, as good birds of prey have passed over, including migrating Osprey and soaring Red-footed Falcon among the Hobbies, which may form impressive hunting parties.

If parked at **Grove Ferry**, it's just a short walk over the road from the car park through a kissing gate to the viewing mound. With lower water levels, waders can be plentiful and will include Golden Plover and Ruff in winter, and Little Ringed Plovers in spring. It's easy to spend all day on site in spring, early summer and autumn, and the beginning and end of the day can be as thrilling as any of the best wetland reserves in Britain. Oh – and keep an eye out for Beavers which can now be found at several sites along the Stour Valley.

Rarity records are plentiful and have included: Blue-winged Teal, Ferruginous Duck, American Coot, Baillon's Crake, Collared Pratincole, Long-billed Dowitcher, Marsh and Buff-breasted Sandpipers, Slender-billed Gull, Whiskered Tern and Red-footed Falcon (which is almost annual).

The grass paths that cover most of the reserve can be waterlogged and muddy outside summer, so please dress accordingly.

159 NEARBY: WESTBERE LAKE AND MARSHES AND FORDWICH

Walnut Tree Lane, Westbere, Canterbury, Kent CT2 0HG
Website: group.rspb.org.uk/thanet/local-wild-places/westbere-lake
TR196610; chiefs.competing.abolish

Westbere Lake is essentially a continuation of the wet habitats of Stodmarsh to its east (and north-east of Canterbury) and incorporates a greater area of land. However, Stodmarsh is the go-to destination for most birders, despite the fact that Westbere holds similar species. It isn't a reserve, however, and consequently has fewer birds overall.

To visit, park carefully on Walnut Tree Lane where the paved road runs out, and cross the railway via the obvious dirt and grass footpath (muddy at times). It's also possible to walk east from the village of Fordwich following the footpath just north of the Great Stour (for this option, park on King Street near the bridge and follow the sign for 'canoe and kayak hire', and continue along the grassy path).

The proximity of good public transport makes this a decent alternative to Stodmarsh for the carless. Trains run to Sturry (see above), about 600m to the north of the site: walk south out of the station and then turn onto the path by the small stone footbridge. Buses also run between Sturry and Westbere along the A28 – alight at the Pennington Lane stop, a 10-minute walk south from Walnut Tree Lane. To see the most birds, the route is best done by doubling back along the river, rather than pursuing a circular option, by following the railway track. Bear in mind that you are unlikely to be able to walk all the way to Stodmarsh from here, as the paths are often flooded.

As you head south from the railway track, there is a fishing platform to your right that used to allow you to scan much of the open water, but its use is now prohibited. That's a shame because this produces good numbers of wildfowl in autumn and winter; there is always the chance of a scarce grebe, diver or seaduck during passage. The best place to view now is from the grassy area alongside the railway track, though this is somewhat disturbed by boaters.

Similar species to Stodmarsh may be seen, though there is little wader habitat. The reeds conceal commoner wetland warblers in summer along with Bearded Tit and Water Rail, and there's a chance of Bittern and Kingfisher in winter. Little and Great Egrets are likely. Keep looking up during migration, as the site is part of the same mini-flyway as its neighbour, with Osprey, Marsh and Hen Harriers, and Hobby distinct possibilities. Check the alder clumps for Siskin and Redpoll in winter, and scan carefully through the hordes of hirundines in spring and autumn.

Plenty of woodland, hawthorn and willow fringes the area on your walk as you turn right to follow the Great Stour, and Lesser Whitethroat and Garden Warbler will be present in the warmer months.

The adjacent villages of Sturry, Westbere and Fordwich have decent pubs with menus, as well as shops, cafes and toilets.

160 NEARBY: COLLARD'S LAKE

Stodmarsh Road, Stodmarsh, Canterbury, Kent CT3 4AZ
Parking: TR212601; switched.master.chitchat

While there is no access to this site, much of the open water can be scanned from the verge on Stodmarsh Road (the main route out of Canterbury for the NNR). Park carefully on the roadside about 800m from the Red Lion and scan the water from the gate. In winter, there could be Goldeneye and a sawbill or two, with plenty of other diving ducks. It's a good raptor viewpoint, with the regular spring Hobby flock passing through, relatively frequent (though less than annual) Red-footed Falcon, and the chance of Marsh or Hen Harrier or Merlin flying past in winter. The Greylag and Canada Goose horde may conceal a properly wild goose or two.

The woods 200m or so to your left at this point are called Trenley Woods, where Lesser Spotted Woodpecker has been reported. The junction with Elbridge Hill (known colloquially as 'Cow Corner') also has Little Owl – scan the fences and trees to the north from the farm gateway there, parking sensibly.

161 NEARBY: SEATON GRAVEL PITS AND DEERSON AND PRESTON MARSHES

Parking: Seaton Road, Seaton, Canterbury, Kent CT3 1RR
TR224588; grumble.vision.clouding
SSSI

The three abandoned **Seaton Gravel Pits** are surrounded by reedbeds and willow scrub, providing the best habitat for diving duck in the Stour Valley. Smew, Goosander and Goldeneye are all regular in winter, while the reeds can hold Bittern. There are rows of alder for Siskin and Redpoll. Make sure you examine the grazing areas (which have breeding Lapwing and Redshank, and wintering Wigeon and Teal) and dykes around the site for Snipe and the occasional Jack Snipe. The reedbeds support Reed Buntings and Cetti's, Reed and Sedge Warblers, while there should be a few Bearded Tits.

Use the public footpath via the gate by the very limited parking space at the bend in Seaton Road. The biggest lake is properly viewable, but there is no public access to the other lakes, and you aren't allowed into the woods. Follow the path along the river to view the accessible part of the site, and double back to return.

To extend your visit, cross the Little Stour at Deadman's Bridge (TR234597; gazed.powers.permit), and follow the permissive footpaths east between the river and Wenderton Wood. These lead you through **Deerson and Preston Marshes** (named after the two nearest hamlets), which provide open grazing marsh attractive to wintering geese, ducks and raptors such as Merlin and Hen Harrier. Please observe the signage en route and stick to the routes indicated.

Tundra Bean and White-fronted Geese have turned up on the pasture, while recent oddities have included Ferruginous and Ring-necked Ducks, Black-throated Diver, Slavonian Grebe and Iberian Chiffchaff.

162 CHILHAM LAKE AND DENGE WOOD

Station Approach, Chilham, Kent CT4 8EG
TR078537; begin.type.crank
SSSI

SPECIES

All year: Gadwall, Mandarin Duck, Water Rail, Kingfisher, Lesser Spotted Woodpecker, Cetti's Warbler, Firecrest, Marsh Tit, Treecreeper, Bullfinch, Yellowhammer, Corn Bunting.

Summer: Nightingale, warblers, perhaps Tree Pipit.

Winter: Wigeon, Teal, Shoveler, Goldeneye, Goosander, Smew, Bittern (scarce), Lapwing, Snipe, Redpoll, Siskin.

Migration: Osprey, Hobby, hirundines, Yellow Wagtail.

ACCESS

Bus: Stagecoach services 1, 1A and 1X (Canterbury–Ashford) stop at the Old Alma pub on the A252 Canterbury Road, by the station entrance.

Train: the Southeastern Ashford International–Minster service stops at Chilham.

Car: from the A28, turn right into Chilham on the A252 and drive into the free car park right next to the station. Backtrack on foot briefly south-west on the A252 Canterbury Road, turn left onto the A28 Ashford Road and turn left onto the footpaths.

YOUR VISIT

Chilham Lake is the centrepiece of a string of former gravel diggings to the south-west of Larkey Valley Woods (page 277) and Canterbury and is the furthest inland of the major Stour Valley sites. Running through the site are the Great Stour River and Denge Woods, the combination of which makes for a rich patchwork of habitat attracting and supporting a good number and variety of birds.

Your visit could take in a circular walk around the lake via the two bridges over the River Stour at either end of the site, or a more wide-ranging exploration of the surrounding farmland, river and woods for a longer day list and the greater chance of a surprise or two. The shorter route takes in the north end of the lake (between the railway track and the fenced-off area), the river and the edges of **Denge Woods**. Viewing of the lake is limited due to private fishing rights, but the open water and edges can be scanned adequately in places. However, a public footpath takes you through the woods and skirts the lake on the southern side.

The lake's small islands should conceal a few Mandarin Duck, one of the few places in Kent where this exotic naturalised duck can be seen. Kingfisher is often obvious, while the alders and willows host the most interesting songbirds. Nightingale and Firecrest (23 singing in recent times, in the eastern part of the wood) breed in Denge Wood, there was one singing Tree Pipit in summer 2021, and Spotted Flycatcher may still hang on. There were three churring Nightjars in 2021, along with two roding Woodcock.

While there probably won't be too many unexpected sightings, unusual species have turned up, including Hooded Merganser (in 2005 and 2012), Spotted Crake and Dipper. Scan the farmland to add more to your day list.

Picturesque, historic Chilham village has amenities and is worth exploring after your visit. King's Wood (page 279) is a few miles to the south-west and worth combining in a visit.

THE WEALD

The rolling hills, woods and fields of the Weald have their own attractions, and while its sites are generally less speciose, there are a number of productive forested areas, reservoirs and lakes for you to explore.

SPECIES

All year: Goshawk (scarce), Woodcock, Lesser Spotted Woodpecker, Tawny, Barn and Little Owls, Cetti's Warbler, Marsh Tit, Hawfinch (scarce).

Summer: Honey-buzzard (scarce), Little Ringed Plover, Nightjar, Hobby, Tree Pipit, Nightingale.

Winter: Goosander, Smew, Goldeneye, Bittern, Brambling, Siskin, Redpoll.

Migration: Osprey, Green and Common Sandpipers, gulls, terns, Wheatear, Whinchat, Redstart, Crossbill.

163 HAM STREET WOODS NNR

Bourne Lane, Hamstreet, Ashford, Kent TN26 2HH
Website: www.woodlandtrust.org.uk/visiting-woods/woods/ham-street-woods
TR003337; truffles.cascaded.sobbed
Phone: 0330 333 3300
Email: enquiries@woodlandtrust.org.uk
Open: all day, every day
NNR
(175 hectares; 432.43 acres)

A discrete patch of designated ancient woodland south of Ashford on the border of Romney Marsh, with most specialist woodland birds present, including Nightingale and Garden and Willow Warblers in spring, and Brambling, Siskin, Redpoll and possibly Crossbill – with a chance of Hawfinch – among the commoner finches in winter.

The 10-space car park isn't obvious, but it's in the northern part of the village of Hamstreet at the end of Bourne Lane. Hamstreet has a railway station, serving Southern trains from Ashford International. Stagecoach buses 11, 11A and 11B and Traveline bus HS2 stop on Ashford Road, Hamstreet, a five-minute walk north-east of the entrance.

164 BEDGEBURY PINETUM AND FOREST

Bedgebury Road, Tunbridge Wells, Kent TN5 7QJ
Website: www.forestryengland.uk/bedgebury
TQ715336; dumpling.rivers.fermented
Phone: 01580 879820

Email: bedgebury@forestryengland.uk
Open: all day, every day. The car park and pinetum are open 8am–4pm
(winter) and 10am–5pm (summer); check the website for public holiday
times
(800 hectares; 2,000 acres)

SPECIES

All year: Mandarin Duck, Teal, Woodcock, Tawny, Long-eared and Little Owls,
Lesser Spotted Woodpecker, Raven, Firecrest, Goldcrest, Coal Tit, Nuthatch,
Treecreeper, Firecrest, Bullfinch, Crossbill, Yellowhammer.

Summer: Hobby, Nightjar, Turtle Dove, Cuckoo, Tree Pipit, Spotted Flycatcher,
Nightingale, Garden Warbler.

Winter: Fieldfare, Redwing, Hawfinch, Brambling, Siskin, Redpoll.

Migration: hirundines, Yellow Wagtail, common warblers, Wood Warbler, Pied
Flycatcher, Wheatear, Whinchat, Stonechat, Redstart.

ACCESS

Bike: there are cycling and mountain biking trails on site. Visit the link for more
details and trail maps: tinyurl.com/bedgeburybike.

Bus: Stagecoach route 254 (Tunbridge Wells–Hawkhurst) and Hamstravel routes
U1 (Wadhurst–John Cross), U2 (Hawkhurst–Wadhurst) and U3 (Uxbridge High
Street–Heathrow Airport) all stop at Aspect Wood, Flimwell, about 2.5 miles
(4km) south-west of the entrance.

Train: Southeastern services (London Charing Cross/London Bridge–Hastings)
stop at Tunbridge Wells, the nearest station.

Car: from the A21 between Hastings and Tunbridge Wells, leave at the turn-off
for the B2079 and follow this north-east to the entrance.

YOUR VISIT

The best-known site for Hawfinch in Kent, Bedgebury Forest is a huge area of
conifer plantations incorporating Bedgebury National Pinetum, with its 200
species of conifer (the most complete anywhere on Earth), managed by Forestry
England. The conifers don't hold a great variety of birds, but there is plenty of
coppiced Sweet Chestnut and quasi-heathland to enrich the avifauna.

Crossbills stayed on site to breed after a major irruption in the early 1990s, and
influxes still occur every few years in July or October. Other finches such as Siskin,
Redpoll and Brambling are best looked for in winter, particularly when coming in to
roost or when feeding in the larches, birches and alders.

Hawfinch is best sought on winter evenings, when birds fly in to roost and perch
at the top of the tallest conifers. The traditional spot to wait for them is at the
'Fallen Tree', which is on the edge of the large area of conifers, about 200m straight
ahead towards the Pinetum from the car park, just after Dallimore Valley – it's near
the second stop on Forestry England's handy 'Presenting the Pinetum' trail map.

Pick this up at the new VC, which has a cafe, shop and toilets. Bear in mind that Hawfinch has declined over the last couple of decades.

The pines also conceal a few resident Woodcock, and views of roding birds are possible in spring and summer. Those conifer specialists, Coal Tit and Goldcrest, are remarkably common, and there are still small numbers of Marsh Tit, along with Nuthatch and Treecreeper. Check the feeders near the VC for close views of these. Lesser Spotted Woodpecker is still present and is most vocal in late winter.

Up to four Nightjars have churred in the open areas and rides in recent summers along with up to six roding Woodcock, and Stonechat and perhaps Tree Pipit can also be found. Try the taller cypresses for Firecrest, which sings in spring, and can be joined by purring Turtle Dove.

Bedgebury has perhaps the greatest numbers of Mandarin Duck in Kent, with counts usually topping 40 individuals at the end of the breeding season. Other wetland birds are in short supply, however, but Little Grebe nests and Grey Wagtail and Kingfisher visit; Marshall's Lake to the north of the Pinetum is the best location for these.

165 HEMSTED FOREST

Cranbrook Road, Benenden, Cranbrook, Kent TN17 4AN
Website: www.forestryengland.uk/hemsted-forest

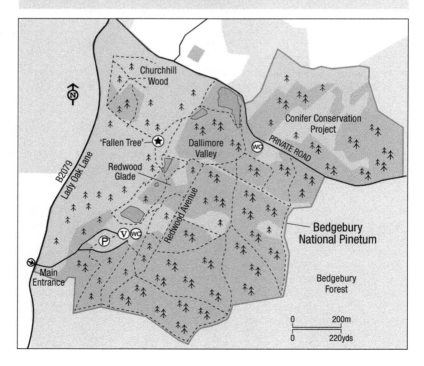

Parking: the four northern access points are off Cranbrook Road between Mockbeggar Lane to the east and the rows of houses that start with 'Brattlid' to the west: TQ831364; reacting.crackles.handsets; TQ825367; searching.carting.defender; TQ821370; admiringly.racing.surnames; TQ817370; chariots.puppy.washable
(398 hectares; 983.48 acres)

SPECIES

All year: Mandarin Duck, Woodcock, Tawny, Little, Long-eared and Barn Owls, Spotted Flycatcher, Marsh Tit, Nuthatch, Treecreeper, Crossbill, Yellowhammer.

Summer: Nightjar, Turtle Dove, Tree Pipit (scarce), hirundines, Spotted Flycatcher, Nightingale, Grasshopper Warbler (scarce).

Winter: Redwing, Fieldfare, Siskin, Redpoll, Brambling, Hawfinch, Crossbill.

Migration: warblers, chats.

ACCESS

Bus: Hamstravel route 297 (Cranbrook–Benenden) runs to the Golford Corner stop; alight and walk 1.25 miles (2km) along Cranbrook Road to the first access point.

Train: Southeastern services run every half hour from London Bridge to Headcorn, about 5 miles (8km) away.

Car: take the A229 from the M20 for 12.7 miles (20km), following signs to Cranbrook. Turn onto either Chapel Lane and take Cranbrook Road at the cross-roads, or Fosten Lane and take Cranbrook Road at the T-junction. Parking is free.

YOUR VISIT

This FE property between Tenterden and Cranbrook is particularly good for Nightjar and Woodcock on a spring or early summer evening. The copious paths and rides allow good views, especially from the four northern access points. Please keep to a reasonable distance, as bird numbers have declined due to the forest's popularity.

Hemsted Forest contains mature trees, secondary woodland and conifer planta-tions, providing a good range of habitats. Small streams and ponds, particularly in the western half, support Mandarin Duck; there were 23, post-breeding, in 2020. Turtle Dove also nests near the forest edge in enough numbers for the RSPB to consider it one of the county's most important sites for the species. In 2020, there were birds about 1 mile (1.6km) from the forest's southern edge around the village of Iden Green, between Standen Street and Moor Wood. Don't forget to explore the patch of forest to the north of the road.

There is a small population of Nightingale around the forest edges, while a few Marsh Tits and Spotted Flycatchers just about linger on as breeding species. Tree Pipit hasn't bred recently, but there's the chance of a bird on migration. Grasshopper Warbler has occasionally nested and Firecrest was present recently. Winter should supply Siskin and Redpoll, and Barn Owl can be seen hunting over the surrounding fields year-round. This is also one of the best sites in Kent for wintering Crossbills, with up to 58 present in winter 2021–22 while 120 Brambling roamed the area in early 2021.

166 RSPB TUDELEY WOODS AND PEMBURY HEATH

Half Moon Lane, Pembury, Tunbridge Wells TN11 0FW
Website: www.rspb.org.uk/reserves-and-events/reserves-a-z/tudeley-woods
TQ617433; fool.handed.bike
Phone: 01892 752430
Email: tudely.woods@rspb.org.uk
Open: all day, every day. Amenities can be found in Tunbridge Wells, four miles (6.4km) away. Dogs must be leashed and kept on public footpaths.
SSSI
(Tudeley Woods: 281.55 hectares; 695.71 acres)

SPECIES
All year: Tawny Owl, Lesser Spotted Woodpecker, Skylark, Marsh and Coal Tits, Nuthatch, Treecreeper, Crossbill.

Summer: Hobby, Nightjar, Turtle Dove, Tree Pipit, Stonechat, Nightingale, Spotted Flycatcher, Garden and Willow Warblers.

Winter: Woodcock, Dartford Warbler, Stonechat, Siskin, Redpoll, Brambling.

Migration: warblers, Wheatear, Whinchat.

ACCESS
Bike: the reserve is on a Sustrans Cycle Route.

Bus: Autocar Bus & Coach Services route 205 (Paddock Wood–Tonbridge) stops north-east of the reserve in Tudeley at the Turmeric Gold stop, from where it's a winding two-mile (3.2km) walk to the VC.

Train: Southeastern services (London Bridge/LondonCharing Cross–Hastings) stop at High Brooms, Tunbridge Wells, about 4.3 miles (7km) from the reserve.

Car: leave the A21 Pembury Bypass between Tonbridge and Tunbridge Wells, taking the slip roads signposted 'Capel/Kent college' from either direction. Take the first left turn (signposted Capel) onto Half Moon Lane (aka Dislingbury Road) and turn into the reserve car park after 500m.

YOUR VISIT
The rich, semi-natural, mixed broadleaved woodland reserve of Tudeley Woods holds some good birds and acts as the northern gateway to the remnant heathland of RSPB Pembury Heath (aka Pembury Walks).

It's managed by the RSPB, although owned by the Hadlow Estate, and there are plenty of permissive and public footpaths available to explore both sites. The sites are at their best in the breeding season, and the mature trees support waning numbers of Lesser Spotted Woodpeckers, along with the commoner species.

Tudeley Woods proper is on the northern side of Half Moon Lane, but you'll have to cross over and walk south for about half a mile to get to the heath. The woods can be explored via the Brakeybank Trail. The Heathland Link Trail takes in the southern areas, covering a comprehensive 3-mile (4.8km) route through the main habitats.

The heathland is currently being restored, with the heather spreading as the alder and birch secondary woodland are removed, and is surrounded by extensive pine and larch plantations, along with large areas of coppiced Sweet Chestnut.

The path onto the heath can be found when crossing **Pembury Walks** and there are plenty of open areas frequented by Nightjar in late May and June (although just one pair was present in 2020). Hobby hunts overhead, while migrant warblers breed in summer. Species such as Woodlark and Dartford Warbler have been found, especially in winter, and might be staging a slow comeback. There's still a chance of Tree Pipit on passage, while irrupting Crossbills use the conifer plantations and sometimes stick around. Keep an eye open for Hazel Dormouse too.

167 BOUGH BEECH RESERVOIR

Winkhurst Green Road, Chiddingstone, Sevenoaks, Kent TN8 7AN
TQ496491; lease.ramp.actual
Open: all day, every day, though the reserve and VC are now officially closed; see *www.kentwildlifetrust.org.uk/bough-beech*
(115 hectares; 284 acres)

SPECIES

All year: Mandarin Duck, Gadwall, Goshawk, Kingfisher, Lesser Spotted Woodpecker, Grey Wagtail, Marsh Tit, Nuthatch, Treecreeper.

Summer: Common Tern, Little Ringed Plover, Turtle Dove, Cuckoo, Nightingale, warblers.

Winter: Wigeon, Teal, Shoveler, Goosander, Goldeneye, Snipe, gull roost, Peregrine, Brambling, Siskin, Redpoll (scarce).

Migration: Brent Goose, Garganey, Osprey, Ringed Plover, Greenshank, Wood, Common and Green Sandpipers, Dunlin, terns, Hobby, Yellow Wagtail, Wheatear, Whinchat.

ACCESS

Bus: Metrobus routes 231 and 233 (Tunbridge Wells–Lingfield) serve Bough Beech village, 2 miles (3.2km) from the viewpoint.

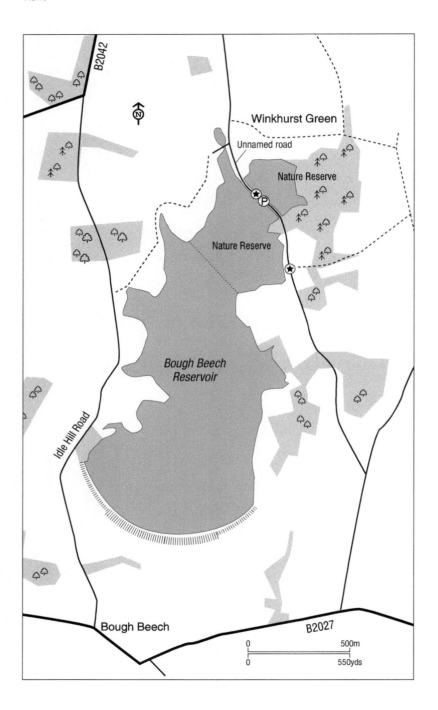

Train: take the Southeastern service from London Bridge–Tonbridge and change to Southern's Tonbridge–Penshurst service. Penshurst is 2 miles (3.2km) from the viewpoint.

Car: leave the A21 and join the B2021 west until you see the sign for Bore Place and turn right. Continue for about 600m and then take the left fork onto Winkhurst Green Road (unsigned). Park considerately on the southern side of the road at the reservoir's northern end.

YOUR VISIT

Just to the west of Tonbridge, this large working reservoir is no longer managed by the KWT as of July 2020 and has reverted into the care of its owners, SES Water. The VC is closed but there is limited public access to the former reserve. The reservoir is the biggest area of freshwater in the county.

The open water is very attractive to wildfowl, while the surrounding woodland and fields also support interesting bird species. There's a generous extent of wader- and gull-friendly shoreline which can be scanned along with the open water by the parking area. Also, cross carefully to check the much smaller North Lake on the other side of the road.

It's still possible to park near the old VC at the very northern end and explore the public footpaths through the habitats along the top half of the reservoir, which include an orchard, meadow, scrub and woodland. There is also a scrape and a Sand Martin bank just to the west of the old VC, though these are unlikely to be maintained in the foreseeable future. The former nature reserve area extends into the woods beyond the North Lake on the northern side. Go through the gate between the viewpoint and the old VC to explore.

Notable wildfowl include good numbers of resident Mandarin Duck; up to 45 have been counted in recent winters. This is one of the few reliable sites for the species in Kent, but they're not always obvious as they tend to perch out of site, low in the waterside trees. Gadwall is resident and up to 20 or so Goosander arrive for winter. Smew is possible and there are lots of wintering Wigeon, Teal and Shoveler. A cold snap or severe weather will substantially increase your chances of seeing wild swans and geese, seabirds and the scarcer grebes and divers.

The winter gull roost can approach an impressive 10,000 birds, and evening scanning has pulled out Caspian and Yellow-legged Gulls. Check the exposed shoreline for Little Ringed Plover in spring and summer, and wagtails and waders on passage.

The woods still support a healthy population of Marsh Tit among the commoner forest specialists such as Treecreeper and Nuthatch. Several pairs of Turtle Dove can be found between Bough Beech and Edenbridge a few miles to the west, though they're never reliable and are absent from Bough Beech itself. Speculative exploration of smaller woods close by might pay off.

The plentiful scrub, hedgerows and trees hold good numbers of warblers in spring and summer, thrushes and finches in winter, and perhaps the odd interesting migrant. Siskin and Redpoll are likely, while there have been counts of up to 100 Brambling in winter.

Osprey is possible on migration, and Buzzard and Red Kite nest in the area.

168 NEARBY: GOATHURST COMMON

The Pheasant Plucker, Wheatsheaf Hill, Chevening, Kent TN14 6BU
TQ499528; knots.reply.tides

A few miles north of Bough Beech, Goathurst Common supports Nightjar from late May, with Woodcock, Tawny Owl and Marsh Tit also present. Much of the woodland is private, but a public footpath runs from almost opposite the new Pheasant Plucker pub, which also has a car park and good food (it's a good idea to buy a drink and ask if you can use a parking space). Once on the edge of the woods, look for clearings and listen.

169 NEARBY: SEVENOAKS WILDLIFE RESERVE KWT

Bradbourne Vale Road, Sevenoaks, Kent TN13 3DH
Website: www.kentwildlifetrust.org.uk/nature-reserves/sevenoaks-wildlife-reserve-and-jeffery-harrison-visitor-centre
TQ521563; fits.taps.entry
Phone: 01732 741673
Email: sevenoaks.vc@kentwildlife.org.uk
Open: all day, every day (dawn–dusk); VC hours are 11am–3pm (Thursday–Sunday). Check the website for public holiday opening times. All three hides are wheelchair accessible, as is the VC with its cafe and toilets, and most of the nature trail. It's free to enter, with an optional donation.
SSSI
(73 hectares; 180.3 acres)

SPECIES

All year: Mandarin Duck, Lesser Spotted Woodpecker, Kingfisher, Grey Wagtail, Treecreeper, Bullfinch.

Summer: Lapwing, Little Ringed Plover, warblers, Reed Bunting.

Winter: Teal, Shoveler, Gadwall, Water Rail, Green Sandpiper, Snipe, Brambling, Siskin, Redpoll.

Migration: waders, songbirds.

ACCESS

Bike: there is a bike rack by the VC.

Bus: Arriva routes 8 (Maidstone–Barming Heath), 431 (Orpington–Sevenoaks) and 402 (Tunbridge Wells–Bromley) stop on request by the entrance.

Train: Southeastern and Thameslink trains from London Bridge serve three stations within 1 mile (1.6km) of the reserve: Bat and Ball, Sevenoaks and Dunton Green.

Car: adjacent to the M26, the entrance track and car park are on the north side of the A25 Bradbourne Vale Road (£2.50 weekdays, £3.50 weekends).

YOUR VISIT

Sevenoaks Wildlife Reserve is situated north of its titular town and was probably the first gravel pit to be developed for wildlife and conservation in the country. It has five lakes fringed by woods, grassland and reedbeds, and the River Darent emerges into the northern part before flowing to Dartford.

The reserve is a haven for wetland and woodland species, including resident Lesser Spotted Woodpecker (try the trees nearest to the car park), Treecreeper and Bullfinch, while in winter, the alders attract Siskin and Redpoll.

Nearby **Knole Park** (Knole House, Duchess Walk, Sevenoaks, Kent TN15 0RP; TQ538543; reward.belong.windy) may also still hold Lesser Spotted Woodpecker in its wooded areas, but Tree Pipit seems to be gone. Several pairs of Spotted Flycatcher still nested on site in recent years, and a Nightjar sang in 2021.

170 TROSLEY CP

Waterlow Road, Vigo, Kent, DA13 0SG
Website: www.visitkent.co.uk/attractions/trosley-country-park-2803
TQ632610; quarrel.flats.ideas
Phone: 01732 823570
Email: country.parks@kent.gov.uk
Open: all day, every day; the official car park hours are 8.30am–5pm
(68.79 hectares; 170 acres)

Six miles (9.6km) south-west of Rochester, this is one of the best sites for wood-land birds on the North Downs. Marsh Tit remains in good numbers among the Goldcrests, Nuthatches and Treecreepers, and there still seems to be a remnant population of Hawfinch – the trees near the car park provide your best chance of seeing this robust finch, especially in late winter and spring. Lesser Spotted Woodpecker may still be resident, but there have been no public reports over the last few years. Start early, as the paths are popular with dog-walkers and joggers.

171 MEREWORTH AND HURST WOODS

Parking: North – Long Mill Lane/Beechin Wood Lane, Platt, Tonbridge, Kent TN15 8QG; TQ624559; called.topped.chew;
South (NT Gover Hill viewing area) – The Hurst, Plaxtol, Tonbridge, Kent TN11 9SP; TQ631529; pages.dark.played
(Mereworth Wood: 120 hectares; 300 acres; Hurst Wood: 17.12 hectares; 42.30 acres)

This is another good site for roding Woodcock and churring Nightjar in late spring and early summer. Partly Woodland Trust-managed and partly private, it also holds a range of the commoner woodland species, plus Lesser Spotted Woodpecker.

Tree Pipit seems to have disappeared but may return to the more open areas. Crossbill is possible in late summer, while Siskin, Redpoll and perhaps Brambling are found in the colder months. Firecrest haunts the conifers and Goshawk has been reported.

The northern parking area is usually the best for Nightjar. Follow the path into the wood for about 300m to the open areas. Woodcock has declined but is still possible. The southern car park may be useful for finding some of the other species.

172 HOTHFIELD HEATHLANDS KWT

Cades Road, Hothfield, Ashford, Kent TN26 1HD
Website: www.kentwildlifetrust.org.uk/nature-reserves/hothfield-heathlands
TQ971458; thud.assemble.binder
Phone: Ian Rickards: *01622 662012*
Email: ian.rickards@kentwildlife.org.uk
Open: all day, every day
LNR, LWS, SSSI
(86 hectares; 210 acres)

SPECIES

All year: Lesser Spotted Woodpecker, Marsh and Coal Tits, Nuthatch, Treecreeper, Bullfinch, Yellowhammer.

Summer: Hobby, Nightjar, Cuckoo, Turtle Dove, Tree Pipit, Nightingale, warblers.

Winter: Woodcock, Fieldfare, Redwing, Dartford Warbler, Brambling, Siskin, Redpoll.

Migration: flycatchers, chats, warblers.

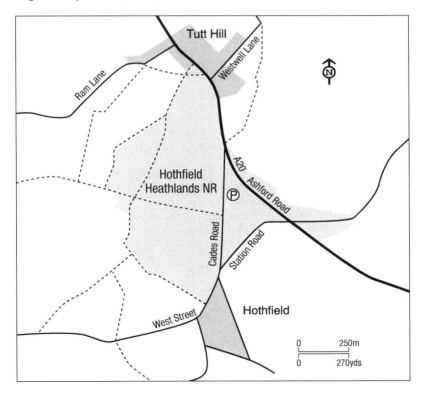

YOUR VISIT

Aka Hothfield Common, this small KWT-managed reserve comprises most of the remaining original open heathland and valley bog in Kent. Cross Cades Road to walk the reserve's footpaths, passing through a small patch of broadleaved woodland. After about 100m, you'll emerge on the open heather and gorse heath.

Well-signposted paths and boardwalks penetrate most of the site, but much of your birding will concentrate on the central area and woodland. All three wood-peckers could be present – though Lesser Spotted is rarely reported these days – along with Marsh and Coal Tits, Nuthatch and Treecreeper. The resident Yellowhammers and visiting Willow Warblers, Lesser Whitethroats and commoner songbirds will be singing and nesting in spring and summer. Winter will see Fieldfare, Redwing, Siskin and Redpoll appearing.

The habitat's extent and variety mean regular watching has produced good sightings, including recent Great Grey Shrike and Rough-legged Buzzard.

173 THE MEDWAY VALLEY AND SNODLAND

The River Medway's meandering course and the mining of its gravel deposits have resulted in a series of marshes and lakes in the vicinity of Snodland that can make for a productive birding trip. Despite being quite built-up, the habitat mosaic provides conditions suitable for several of the scarcer wetland species and migrants – just a short drive from the M20 motorway.

Much of the area is classed as an SSSI and there is open water, reedbed, hawthorn scrub, grassland and dry and wet woodlands. There is precious little exposed mud in the area, but the occasional wader is seen on the river.

In spring, up to 30 singing Nightingales have been logged recently around Snodland, along with good numbers of Garden Warblers. Hobby hunts over the sites. The open water sometimes holds Smew in winter, when an elusive Bittern or Long-eared Owl can also be present.

It is possible to spend the greater part of the day in the area, but there are some key sites with accessible car parks to concentrate on. Most are open all day, every day, and there are many permissive and public footpaths.

Visiting details for each of the major parts of this complex area follow, but please note that most of the area is worth exploring and can be accessed from any of the car parks.

SPECIES

All year: heronry, Water Rail, Kingfisher, Lesser Spotted Woodpecker, Grey Wagtail, Cetti's Warbler, Coal Tit, Bullfinch.

Summer: Little Ringed Plover, Common Tern, Cuckoo, Sand Martin, Nightingale, common warblers, Reed Bunting.

Winter: Shelduck, Wigeon, Teal, Shoveler, Gadwall, Smew (scarce), Goosander, Goldeneye, Bittern, Green and Common Sandpipers, Snipe, Long-eared Owl, Stonechat, winter thrushes, Brambling, Siskin, Redpoll.

Migration: Brent Goose, Osprey, hirundine flocks, Wheatear, Whinchat, Redstart, Grasshopper Warbler.

NEW HYTHE GP

Parking: New Hythe Lane, New Hythe, Kent, England, ME20 6US.
TQ708598; detergent.officers.soothing

Visit during spring migration to stand a good chance of seeing Cuckoo, Willow, Garden and Grasshopper Warblers, Lesser Whitethroat and Nightingale (the combined total with the next site was 27 singing birds in 2020).

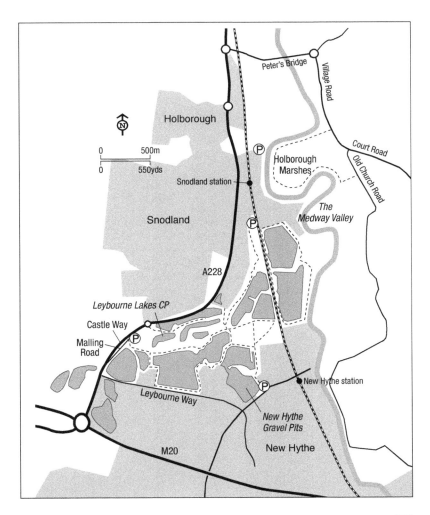

LEYBOURNE LAKES CP AND CASTLE LAKES

Parking: Lunsford Lane, New Hythe, Kent ME20 6JA
Website: tmactive.co.uk/locations/leybourne-lakes
TQ696602; january.delusions.scored

Lesser Spotted Woodpecker still hangs on in the trees around the lakes on either side of the M20, while Nightingale and sometimes Grasshopper Warbler sing close to the car park. Mature alders are attractive to Siskin and Redpoll, and Coal Tit is present.

ABBEY MEAD AND BROOKLAND LAKE

Parking: Brook Street, Snodland, Kent ME6 5UD
TQ707614; student.swarm.redeeming

Abbey Mead holds the greatest number of wildfowl in winter, as well as supporting a heronry in the surrounding willows. Its reedbeds are probably your best bet for a wintering Bittern, along with Water Rail and Bearded Tit. The scrub between the lake and the Medway has good numbers of Nightingales and warblers in spring.

HOLBOROUGH MARSHES KWT (AKA HOLBOROUGH LAKES) AND BURHAM MARSH

Church Field, Snodland, Kent ME6 5FB
Website: www.kentwildlifetrust.org.uk/nature-reserves/holborough-marshes
TQ707621; bits.prompts.warp
(*Holborough Marshes*: 35 hectares; 86 acres;
Burham Marsh: 11 hectares; 27.18 acres)

To the east of the River Medway and providing a panoramic vista of the North Downs, this is another area favoured by Nightingales, warblers and even the odd Turtle Dove in spring, along with a smattering of waders and wildfowl in winter.

Burham Marsh, just to the south-east of Snodland, is most notable for hosting Kent's first-ever Common Nighthawk for one day in November 2020, while the area held 22 pairs of Nightingale in 2021.

ADDITIONAL SITES WITHIN THE LNHS RECORDING AREA

Some excellent birding sites are just outside the remit of this book but are accessible from London by rail or car. Those listed and described below are included in the LNHS recording area, so birds seen at these sites count for your 'official' London list.

AMWELL NATURE RESERVE

Amwell Lane, Great Amwell, Ware, Hertfordshire SG12 9SS
Website: www.hertswildlifetrust.org.uk/nature-reserves/amwell
TL376127; shared.straw.noses
Phone: 01727 858 901
Email: info@hmwt.org
Open: all day, every day
Ramsar, SPA, SSSI

Former gravel pits that are very productive for locally and nationally scarce birds, especially on passage and in winter.

RSPB RYE MEADS AND STANSTEAD INNINGS LVRP

RSPB Rye Meads, Rye Rd, Hoddesdon, Hertfordshire SG12 8JS
Websites: www.rspb.org.uk/reserves-and-events/reserves-a-z/rye-meads/;
leevalleyfisheries.co.uk/venues/stanstead-innings
TL389103; they.foil.stands
Phone: 01992 708 383
Email: rye.meads@rspb.org.uk
Open: 9am–5pm (or dusk, if earlier) every day, except public holidays – check the RSPB website for updates. The surrounding habitat can be explored when closed
Ramsar, SSSI, SPA

An excellent wetland reserve with good numbers of summer and winter visitors and migrants. A long walk through excellent scrapes and reedbeds, with breeding Bearded Tits and Hobbies in good numbers in spring.

HILFIELD PARK RESERVOIR

Parking: non-members – viewing platform, Hogg Lane, Oldham, Hertfordshire WD6 3AL.
Website: www.hertswildlifetrust.org.uk/nature-reserves/hilfield-park-reservoir
TQ159962; local.double.vouch
Phone: 01727 858901
Email: reserves@hmwt.org
Open: access for HMWT members only. A key is available from the head office (Grebe House, St Michael's Street, St Albans, Hertfordshire AL3 4SN). For the somewhat exposed viewing platform, park by the aerodrome entrance and walk down the sometimes boggy signposted boardwalk and footpath.

The only site in the region covered where Black-necked Grebe breeds, and good for other commoner waterfowl.

THE SURREY COMMONS

Website: www.nationaltrust.org.uk/bookham-commons
Bookham Common: Commonside, Church Road, Great Bookham, Surrey, Nearest postcode KT23 3LT; TQ130557; judge.strict.violin
Abinger Roughs and Netley Park: NT Car park on White Downs Lane, Abinger Hammer, Surrey, RH5 6QS; TQ110479; pretty.defeat.pepper
Denbies Hillside: Ranmore Common Road, near Dorking, Surrey, RH5 6SR; TQ141503; files.fetch.hotels
Headley Heath: Headley Common Road, Headley Heath, Surrey, KT18 6NN; TQ205538; unwanted.prompting.remain
Limpsfield Common: Limpsfield, Oxted, Surrey, RH8 0TW; TQ426521; target.pigs.report
Reigate Hill and Gatton Park: Reigate Hill, Wray Lane, Reigate, Surrey, RH2 0HX; TQ262523; follow.unity.flank
Box Hill: The Old Fort, Box Hill Road, Tadworth, Surrey KT20 7LB; TQ187512; bridge.fact.finds
Hindhead Common: London Road, Thursley, Surrey GU26 6AB; SU891357; jokers.footpath.condense

An excellent range of common woodland and scrub birds is to be found in this huge area of Green Belt land, with a chance of Goshawk, Woodcock, Lesser Spotted Woodpecker, Nightingale and Hawfinch.

THE WEST LONDON RESERVOIRS AND AREA

STAINES RESERVOIR

Parking: Stanwell Moor Road, Surrey TW18 4HZ
Website: www.birdingplaces.eu/en/birdingplaces/united-kingdom/staines-reservoirs
TQ045728; divide.excuse.return
Or for the east side (on the verge, but less secure): Town Lane, Stanwell, Surrey TW19 7UL
TQ056733; force.dawn.normal
SSSI

A great site for waterbirds in general, and diving duck in particular, Staines Reservoir is probably the most accessible of the West London reservoirs and has an impressive list of scarcities and rarities attracted to its bleak surroundings. King George VI Reservoir is opposite Staines Reservoir on Stanwell Moor Lane and produces a similar range of scarce and rare waterbirds, but access is for permit holders only.

STAINES MOOR

Parking: Hithermoor Road, Spelthorne, Stanwell, Surrey TW19 6AZ (follow the path south past the fields and scrub to the moor)
TQ039743; hotels.notice.line
SSSI

Some 190 bird species have been recorded on this area of open ground and scrub adjacent to Beechin Wood Lane, Platt, Tonbridge. Migrants and vagrants are a speciality, and it has held as many as six Short-eared Owls in winter, as well as London's only Brown Shrike from October 2009–January 2010.

QUEEN ELIZABETH II STORAGE RESERVOIR

Park in Approach Road, Molesey, Surrey KT8 2LL
TQ133675; bought.raft.passes

At the time of writing, this large, productive reservoir was empty and closed for essential maintenance. Access is restricted at the best of times, but this and Island Barn Reservoir just to its east can both be scoped from higher points on Molesey Heath, to which a path runs from Approach Road.

QUEEN MARY RESERVOIR

Staines Road West, Ashford, Surrey TW15 2AB
TQ075704; froth.slower.survey

A large Surrey reservoir (plus two scopable former gravel pits) that's excellent for migrating and wintering waterbirds. Accessible by Thames Water permit only.

THORPE PARK

Coldharbour Lane, Thorpe, Egham, Surrey TW20 8TE
TQ030689; funds.acute.pulled

Despite the disturbance at this popular family leisure site, the huge amount of open water contained by Manor, Fleet, Abbey and St Anne's Lakes has gained a reputation for producing scarce wildfowl, particularly on Manor Lake. Park on Coldharbour Lane or Church Approach and walk down Monks Walk to the tree-lined causeway between the lakes.

QUEEN MOTHER RESERVOIR

Horton Road, Horton, Berkshire SL3 9NU
TQ018770; advice.skins.coach

On the very edge of the LNHS Recording Area, this huge waterbody is only accessible to members of the Berkshire Ornithological Club who hold Thames Water permits.

WRAYSBURY GRAVEL PITS

Douglas Lane, Wraysbury, Berkshire TW19 5NG
TQ007745; fees.book.quite

Some 12 waterbodies surrounded by scrub and willows by Junction 13 of the M25. One of the most reliable sites in South-East England for Smew in winter, it has regular Garganey during passage, when the occasional Turtle Dove is also seen. There is some wildfowl interchange with Queen Mother Reservoir.

For readers who wish to know more about many of these sites, please refer to *Where To Watch Birds in Surrey and Sussex* by Matt Phelps and Ed Stubbs (Bloomsbury 2024).

GULL-WATCHING
IN THE REGION

Essex, London and Kent are rich in gull-watching opportunities, particularly in the more urban and industrialised areas. Not only do the scarcer species occur reliably, but it's probably the best region in the country to learn the different ages and variations of every regularly occurring species and form, and perhaps find your own more interesting birds. Several firsts for Britain have revealed themselves among the gulls on the region's landfills and coasts.

Of special note is the fact that the Thames Estuary and Kent coasts hold the majority of the country's wintering Caspian and Yellow-legged Gulls. Hundreds of juvenile Yellow-legged Gulls arrive in July and August, with a scattering of Caspians joining them in the latter month, and small numbers remain through winter into spring, after being joined by older immatures and adults later in the autumn. A few non-breeding individuals of both species are present year-round. Caspian Gull peaks in August (juveniles), November and February, as birds arrive and relocate.

There are usually good numbers of juvenile Mediterranean Gulls in the outer estuary in late summer and some of these linger, while adults begin to disperse in small groups in early autumn – again, a few can be around at any time of the year. Several hundred now breed in the coastal areas of the region covered by this book.

One or two Iceland or Glaucous Gulls usually show up, and London has also produced records of such outlandish species as Glaucous-winged and Slaty-backed Gulls, while Dungeness produced the first British record of Audouin's Gull; almost all the gulls on the British list have occurred in the region. Learning the different calls can help pick out something unusual, and here, Xeno-Canto is your friend.

While gull-watching can be interesting at any time of the year, it's generally considered best between late July and March. That's when you stand your best chance of seeing birds dispersing after breeding and foraging en masse over the winter period. Check sheltered coastal pools, fields and surrounding buildings at high tide and the foreshore at low tide, while the birds are a constant presence at any working landfills, sometimes commuting between different loafing and feeding areas. The larger gatherings are obvious and can contain surprises. Many sites will enable you to take close photos to examine those all-important, educational plumage details.

The five commonest species are present on the Thames estuary all year, although Common Gull is by far the scarcest. Herring and Lesser Black-backed Gulls breed on or near the river, while Great Black-backed nests in small numbers and Black-headed Gulls form large colonies. All ages and conditions of plumage can be seen, providing a useful state of constant learning. Larger numbers of any of these species will always attract their less common congeners. Mind you, only the brave will try to sort out large white-headed gulls in mid-summer.

In London, the 'Mud Reaches' of the Inner Thames between Tower Bridge and Gravesend attract countless gulls year-round. They usually concentrate in several hotspots, and recycling plants, landfill sites and significant outflows on the coast also hold allure for them. Bear in mind that flocks can be mobile and are reliant on food sources; if these change, the birds move on. There are slim pickings at some of the traditional gatherings these days, but you can create your own temporary gull hub by bringing some cheap loaves of wholemeal bread with you as bait. It's surprising how quickly a bit of ground bait thrown out onto the water will lure them in.

Something to consider is that the state of the tide is important on the Thames – and to a lesser extent around the coast. Sites that hold good foreshore assemblies should be visited for 2–3 hours on either side of high tide, while feeding and roosting sites are more productive when the tide is fully in, both for sifting through the flocks and taking photos.

With all that in mind, the following are the best sites in the region for observing gulls at close quarters at the time of writing; many are some of the very best in the country.

THE NORTHERN INNER THAMES

BILLINGSGATE MARKET, LONDON

During the daytime, this busy fish market lures similar numbers of gulls to Rotherhithe (below). Easily accessible via Poplar DLR station, many gulls can be seen on the surrounding roofs but they are best seen resting behind the market on the North Dock, which is visible from the paved public footway (TQ378803; shorts.dock.stews) in front of the Barclays building opposite.

SILVERTOWN, LONDON

Thames Barrier Park by Pontoon Dock DLR station (see page 31) is a fantastic place to observe thousands of gulls on the exposed mud on either side of low tide (TQ412798; spicy.empty.flight), which usually include Yellow-legged and the odd Caspian Gull. Lyle Park nearby offers more limited views of the same birds. Numbers have decreased recently owing to the closure of a factory food source on the opposite side of the Thames.

CREEKMOUTH, LONDON

This is where the River Roding empties into the Thames opposite Thamesmead, next to a massive flood barrier (Barking Creek Barrier at TQ454816; nuns.drew. knee), a sewage outfall, a recycling centre, warehouse roofs, low-tide mud and Beckton Sewage Treatment Works – all ideal foraging habitat for gulls. Bonaparte's and several Iceland and Caspian Gulls have occurred among the many Blackheads. The site is isolated, almost a mile from the nearest car park at the Showcase Cinema in Newham, and further from a bus stop or DLR station. That said, this can be a pleasant, though very urban, riverside walk past the sewage works and through the tiny Beckton Creekside NR (open all day, every day, at TQ450826; deeper.thing.form), which has plenty of wintering Chiffchaffs (including regular 'Siberian'). You'll need to concentrate your gull-watching on the western side of the Roding (the eastern side is largely inaccessible). This site is best visited on overcast days, as you can be looking into the sun. Be prepared to peer through fences and onto roofs at times. NB: buses with 'Creekmouth' as their destination stop on the wrong side of the river.

RAINHAM MARSHES AND LANDFILL, ESSEX/GREATER LONDON

This huge site is dealt with in detail on page 56, but it's justly famous for the thousands of gulls attracted year-round by the massive landfill adjacent to the reserve. Yellow-legged and Caspian Gulls are always present, even in midsummer, and hundreds of the former and double figures of the latter have been counted in late summer and November respectively.

On weekdays and Saturday mornings, food waste being dumped on the working landfill will lure them in, but Sundays will see many, though not all, of the birds seeking food elsewhere. Bring a scope as gulls can be distant on the river or dump, particularly at high tide. There are several key locations at which to observe gulls, all bar one of which is accessible on foot or by car:

Coldharbour Point (TQ519788; hurt.costs.cove) A roosting point in front of the industrial estate by the landfill along the riverside footpath, this promontory has piles of rocks exposed at low tide that allow resting gulls to be scanned with ease at low tide, while some birds rest on the river at high tide. There is constant commuting between the dump and the river, meaning that birds change all the time and patience can be rewarded.

Aveley Bay (TQ534792; thank.dishes.golf) The small car park by the landfill site is the best place to leave your car and explore the riverside footpath on foot. At low tide, thousands of gulls can be present, loafing on the foreshore and bathing on the river between Aveley Bay and Coldharbour Point.

Veolia Rainham Landfill (TQ528789; hedge.taken.thigh) This site attracts many thousands of gulls that spill over onto the surrounding hotspots. Unfortunately, it's strictly not accessible to the public, though it can be viewed from the surrounding footpaths. The best vantage points constantly change according to where tasty waste is being dumped, but gulls are usually obvious from the perimeter. Observation can be through chainlink fencing, but birds will be coming and going to the other locations, providing better views.

Wennington Marshes NR (TQ533794; linen.pasta.eagles) This part of the RSPB reserve is not accessible on foot but can be viewed from the 'Serin Mound' at the eastern end of the footpath, and from the western end just before the common watercourse next to the 'Silts'. Gulls often roost on the wet grass and the shallow pools at the far, north-eastern, end.

RSPB Rainham Marshes Both the Target Pools (TQ540797; than.trend.leaps), and, to a lesser extent Aveley Pools (TQ545795; radar.bike.stews), provide loafing opportunities for resting gulls, and have held Caspian, Iceland and even Slaty-backed Gulls in the past.

Rainham is still productive at the time of writing but is projected to close over the next 10 years, bringing the most exciting phase of London gull-watching to an end. The amount of food waste dumped has decreased radically and the number of gulls present is already noticeably smaller.

THE SOUTHERN INNER THAMES

ROTHERHITHE, LONDON

Despite generally attracting no more than about 50 larger gulls, this site can hold a few Yellow-legged and occasional Caspian Gulls on its exposed mud beach, 2–3 hours before and after low tide. Try the beach (TQ365803; charmingly.bands. dull) just north of the Double Tree by the Hilton hotel for the biggest numbers. The nearby Russia Dock Woodland usually holds a wintering Firecrest.

SURREY QUAYS/GREENLAND PIER/ GREENLAND DOCK

Another good adjacent site (TQ360790; potato.ships.crash) for small numbers of close Yellow-legged Gulls, which happily come to bread, along with the occasional Caspian and Mediterranean Gull. Common Tern breeds locally.

GREENWICH PENINSULA/O2 ARENA/ANCHOR & HOPE

On the riverside frontage of the O2 Arena is a small beach (TQ391803; librarian. songs.sadly) that becomes exposed productively for 2–3 hours on either side of high tide and can also be distantly, but less satisfactorily, scoped from East India Dock Basin NR (TQ391806; brands.helps.mining). Hundreds of large gulls can be present, with Yellow-legged and Mediterranean likely among them, particularly between July and September. It's about a mile from North Greenwich underground station. Walking south-east, downriver, along Olympian Way will allow you to check out more of the foreshore and will bring you to the Anchor & Hope pub – a civilised place opposite Thames Barrier Park to scan from, with decent food and drink to hand.

WOOLWICH/KING HENRY'S WHARF

Continue walking to the other side of the Thames Barrier, or park for free on Harlinger Street and walk down to the riverfront to the pier (TQ418793; sling. rocks.term) in front of the Port of London Authority building, between the Thames Barrier and Woolwich Pier. Despite sometimes holding only dozens of gulls, point-blank Yellow-legged and Caspian Gulls are possible, even in mid-winter.

THAMESMEAD/PRINCESS ALICE WAY/GREENHAVEN DRIVE
(GREENHAVEN DRIVE, THAMESMEAD, GREENWICH, LONDON SE28 8FY; TQ 466 809; SULK.BEFORE.ORGANS)

A little further east along the same stretch of Thames, as it curves north again, Thamesmead can be productive for the scarcer large gulls at high tide – and this is an optimal site for Yellow-legged and Caspian Gulls from late summer through to early spring. Parking is available right next to the river on Princess Alice Way, just west of the waste ground, or on the western side of Greenhaven Drive. Gulls come very close at either place and you have the whole of the foreshore to examine, as well as the East Lake, viewable from Linton Mead, the tarmac path that runs parallel to Greenhaven Drive. That location is particularly good for photography, with the light behind you and the birds not too high or low.

SOUTHMERE LAKE AND CROSSNESS OUTFLOW

These two sites adjacent to Crossness NR (page 84) can pull in scarcer species as well as good numbers of commoner gulls. Southmere Lake (TQ476800; bids.

purple.heat) lies to the south-west of the reserve and is an urban lake with plenty of open water. Large numbers of smaller gulls use it for loafing. The Crossness sewage outflow (TQ490808; deaf.bells.spends) is close to the northern entrance of Crossness NR (park at the golf centre) and attracts many Black-headed Gulls. These have concealed five spring Bonaparte's Gulls since 2012, as well as Franklin's at the turn of the century, while the muddy foreshore has a high hit rate for Yellow-legged and Caspian Gulls.

ERITH PIER, KENT (WHARFSIDE CLOSE, ERITH, KENT DA8 1QW; TQ 517 779; FANS.CHIPS.IDEA)

One of the most convenient sites to visit by car, with lots of spaces in the adjacent Morrisons supermarket car park (handy for buying a few loaves). It's directly opposite Rainham Landfill, and gulls rest on the jetty upriver all day in the week and on Saturday, but they are more apparent on a rising tide. Regulars say that Saturday lunchtime, just after the tip closes, is the best time to visit and also rate it as the best site to study and photograph juvenile Yellow-legged and Caspian Gulls in the UK.

CRAYFORD AND DARTFORD MARSHES (PAGES 190–192)

Two of the best sites for Glaucous and Iceland Gulls in the estuary, their distance from the Thames results in fewer Yellow-legged and Caspian Gulls than at the other sites mentioned. The south-western edge of Crayford Marshes hosts Viridor and Serco recycling centre buildings along a short stretch on the northern side of the A206 between the Jolly Farmers (TQ527756; shift.plot.tracks) and the A206/Bob Dunn Way/A2026 roundabouts; these act as useful and very productive gull roosts, as does the obvious waste ground in the same area. There are plenty of places to park in the area (try Crayford Creek Road at TQ530756; empty.title.living), and the footpath on the north side of the river Cray probably provides the best place to observe. Viewing can be frustrating elsewhere, with chainlink fences, guard dogs and Harris's Hawks all present. This is another area best visited once Rainham Landfill has closed at the weekend.

This section of the book wouldn't be as informative and detailed without the pioneering fieldwork of Josh Jones, Dante Shepherd, Richard Bonser and Jamie Partridge, who have added so much to our knowledge of London's gulls and their movements. For more detailed information visit: *www.birdguides.com/articles/patch-birding/watching-gulls-in-east-london.*

OTHER LARID HOTSPOTS

DUNGENESS, KENT (PAGE 258)

While there are many birding reasons to visit Dungeness, among the best are The Patch (TR082166; depravity.catch.void) in front of the power station and the fishing boats pulled ashore at the very tip of the peninsula (TR097170; images.declining.vesting). The **Dungeness NR car park** is right by the boats where large white-headed species often loaf, and scoping the assembled small flocks from this area can provide close views of varying ages of Caspian Gull. The hide overlooking The Patch, which is the underwater outfall, provides good cover for scanning the hordes of Black-headed Gulls swooping over the churning water for more interesting species, of which many have occurred over the years. Also check the loafing birds on the shingle beach below to your right.

BEDDINGTON FARMLANDS, LONDON (PAGE 88)

The formerly productive landfill at Beddington has now closed but used to feature hundreds of gulls and regularly produce scarcities and rarities. Smaller numbers still use the shallower areas and mud for loafing and can include Yellow-legged and Caspian Gulls.

WILLIAM GIRLING AND KING GEORGE V RESERVOIRS, LONDON (PAGE 44)

Girling, and to a lesser extent King George V, are home to one of the largest gull roosts in London. There is no public access to Girling and access to permit-holders only at KGV, but the roost turns up regular Yellow-legged and Mediterranean Gulls, plus the odd Caspian. The birds assemble in the two hours before dusk so there is limited time to scour them thoroughly.

HACKNEY MARSHES, LONDON (PAGE 32)

This site suffers from disturbance and is only productive for a couple of hours. Hundreds of large gulls assemble on the playing fields just after dawn from autumn through to spring and are available for close scrutiny by scope or binoc-ulars until the dog-walkers and joggers arrive. Good for a few Yellow-legged Gulls, with other scarce species on occasion.

SOUTHEND PIER, ESSEX (PAGE 139)

The far end of this mile-long pier protrudes out into the North Sea and provides a resting place for dozens of Mediterranean Gulls of all three ages in late summer.

There are a number of great gull sites in the region covered by this book that are not open to the public but which host large numbers and regularly produce rare and scarce forms. These include: Kingston-upon-Thames Recycling Centre; Valencia Waste Management, South Ockendon; Pitsea Landfill, Essex (the second-largest tip in the country); and Barling Marsh Tip, Essex (on the south side of the River Roach, near the small Barling Magna Nature Reserve).

Sites come and go. For example, the formerly productive Mucking Tip where the late Martin Garner did so much of his pioneering fieldwork on Caspian Gull, is now closed. However, all landfills are likely to shut down in the next 10 years or so, as recycling, for the most part justifiably, becomes the primary method of waste disposal.

It is possible that the number of individuals of all species of gull that have devel-oped a commensal use of landfills will decline rapidly when this easy food source dries up. If you're keen on finding scarcer and rarer forms, the golden age of landfill gulling has already passed, but the next few years could still be productive. However, if you yearn to find the first American Herring Gull for the region, you'll need to get your skates on – sifting through those huge mixed flocks may soon be a thing of the past.

TOP SITES FOR DISABLED ACCESS AND PUBLIC TRANSPORT

BEST SITES FOR WHEELCHAIR ACCESS

Wherever possible in the text, I have highlighted the sites where part or all of the sites are accessible for those in wheelchairs. For ease of visiting, here is a list of those sites that are most suitable for disabled visitors:

RSPB Rainham Marshes, Greater London (see page 56)
The Chase LNR, Greater London (see page 72)
London Wetland Centre WWT, Greater London (see page 95)
Brent Reservoir, Greater London (see page 108)
Two Tree Island LNR EWT, Essex (see page 140)
Heybridge Basin, Northey Island and Osea Island, Essex (see page 147)
Abberton Reservoir, Essex (see page 156)
Oare Marshes KWT, Kent (see page 228)
Sevenoaks Wildlife Reserve KWT, Kent (see page 294)

BEST SITES ACCESSIBLE BY PUBLIC TRANSPORT

All Lea Valley sites (see pages 29–47)
All Greater London sites (see pages 27–121)
RSPB Rainham Marshes, Greater London (see page 56)
East Tilbury and Coalhouse Fort, Essex (see page 125)
Southend Pier, Essex (see page 139)
Gunners Park and Shoeburyness East Beach, Essex (see page 142)
RSPB Vange Marsh, Essex (see page 133)
Wat Tyler CP, Essex (see page 134)
RSPB Cattawade Marshes, Essex (see page 169)
Crayford and Dartford Marshes, Kent (see pages 190–192)
Foots Cray Meadows, Kent (see page 195)
RSPB Cliffe Pools, Kent (see page 198)
Margate area sites, Kent (see page 238)
Sevenoaks Wildlife Reserve KWT, Kent (see page 294)
Dover area sites, Kent (see pages 249–253)

THIRTY SPECIES TO SEE IN SOUTHEAST ENGLAND

GARGANEY

This attractive migratory dabbling duck can turn up at almost any of the wetlands mentioned in this book, but is most likely at the larger sites with richer habitat. The London Wetland Centre and Walthamstow Wetlands are the two best urban sites, with several birds sometimes passing through during spring or autumn. It's never reliable as a breeding species, but is likely to be seen in summer at RSPB Northward Hill, RSPB Dungeness, RSPB Worth Marshes, Stodmarsh NNR and Grove Ferry, and Oare Marshes KWT in Kent. Birds are often logged on migration at Pegwell Bay NNR, Bough Beech Reservoir and RSPB Cliffe Pools, Kent; Walthamstow Wetlands LWT, Cornmill Meadows, Fishers Green, RSPB Rainham Marshes, the London Wetland Centre (more regular in autumn) and Wraysbury Gravel Pits, London; and RSPB Vange Marsh, Chigborough Lakes, RSPB Old Hall Marshes and Abberton Reservoir, London; in fact, most larger marshes either side of the Thames.

MANDARIN DUCK

This naturalised resident Asian species is a habitué of wooded areas near freshwater with much of its core national range in the region covered by this book, particularly in London, and even more particularly in West London and beyond. Key Capital locations are at Connaught Water in Epping Forest, centrally in Kensington Gardens, and along the Thames past the London Wetland Centre west, including Richmond, Bushy and Osterley Parks, as well as up to Hampstead Heath and Trent Country CP. Kent has notable populations at Chilham Lake and Denge Wood, Bedgebury Pinetum, Hested Forest, Bough Beech Reservoir and Sevenoaks Wildfowl Reserve. Mandarins are much scarcer in Essex, but can be seen at Dagnam Park on the edge of London.

BLACK-NECKED GREBE

This scarce grebe actually breeds in very limited numbers in the region, most notably at Hilfield Park Reservoir (see page 302), but occasionally at Hanningfield Reservoir, Essex. Otherwise, it's a very scarce passage migrant and winter visitor, with the greatest numbers at the largely inaccessible William Girling Reservoir, where there can be more than 20. Passage birds randomly turn up at most of the reservoirs around the perimeter of London, sometimes lingering.

SPOONBILL

Now a scarce breeder in the region, Spoonbill's core range is the Greater Thames Estuary, with a few pairs breeding at Abberton Reservoir, Essex, and very small numbers annually pitching up at RSPB Rainham Marshes, London/Essex, RSPB Wallasea Island, Essex and RSPB Cliffe Pools and KWT Oare Marshes, Kent, arriving from the Continent or the larger British breeding colony at Holkham, Norfolk.

CATTLE EGRET

In line with much of the rest of England, occurrences of this cosmopolitan species have increased greatly this century. Small numbers now tentatively breed in the region, mostly in heronries, including at RSPB Northward Hill and RSPB Dungeness, Kent, and on The Dengie, Essex. Wandering individuals and small flocks are more widespread post-breeding, and will pitch up at larger sites such as Abberton Reservoir and RSPB Rainham Marshes, the North Kent Marshes, and even along the Lea Valley between Walthamstow Wetlands and Fishers Green.

GREAT EGRET

While not as plentiful as the garrulous Cattle Egret, Great Egret is now expected at several sites in the region, as well as popping up at most wetlands from time to time. Among the most likely sites are RSPB Rainham Marshes, Abberton Reservoir, RSPB Wallasea Island, RSPB Dungeness. It can't be long until the species nests in the region, and increasing numbers are seen overflying regional wetlands in general every year.

BITTERN

Though scarce, Bittern has several regular haunts in the region, including a few key breeding sites. The best place to see birds in summer is from the bench on the grassy knoll overlooking Hookers Pits at RSPB Dungeness, where an often short vigil will produce the odd bird in flight and plenty of 'booming'. Stodmarsh NNR also has a few booming males, generally taken to indicate breeding at this extensive site. Wintering birds are more widespread, with annual appearances at the London Wetland Centre and the Fishers Green Bittern Watchpoint. In Kent, the main breeding sites remain the best for seeing the species, while in Essex, where the species is much scarcer, Abberton Reservoir in winter is your best bet.

FULMAR

While Fulmar is common at many sites in northern England, its cliff breeding sites are limited to the east Kent coast in the region. The species is easily seen in the south-east 'white cliffs' corner of Kent, on the stretch of coast from Capel-le-Ferne north-east to Kingsdown, particularly around Dover and at South Foreland, mostly between February and August. Smaller numbers can also be seen from Pegwell round the 'corner' to just west of Margate. The species becomes pelagic after breeding and is rarely seen from land.

HEN HARRIER

A very scarce wintering species, as its breeding fortunes take a turn for the better in Britain, it can now be expected at a few sites in winter. Regular Kent birds occur on the Isle of Sheppey, where they can sometimes be observed at RSPB Capel Fleet and the other reserves there, as well as potentially at RSPB Dungeness, RSPB Cliffe Pools or almost anywhere on the North Kent Marshes. The roost between Shellness and the Swale NNR can be particularly productive. The most regular Essex birds are at RSPB Wallasea Island, RSPB Old Hall Marshes and on The Dengie.

HONEY-BUZZARD

Always patchily distributed in Britain, Honey-buzzard regularly breeds in small numbers in a few woods in Kent which are kept secret to avoid disturbance. The species be seen overhead on migration at other sites, with the stretch of coast from Dungeness to St Margaret's in Kent being particularly productive through late spring and early autumn, when sometimes several birds are logged coming 'in off', though they are never predictable.

GOSHAWK

Similarly to Honey-buzzard, Goshawk is a very scarce woodland breeder in Britain found in a few forested areas in the region. Its precise breeding sites are kept quiet to avoid disturbance, and it can be very secretive in any case, but watching clear-felled areas of coniferous woodland from February to April can be productive, and the species has been noted in the past from Copped Hall and Hockley Woods, Essex, Denge Wood and Mere Worth and Hurst Woods, Kent, as well as at woods on the Surrey Commons.

SHORT-EARED OWL

Though it occasionally breeds, this charismatic owl tends to winter in more coastal areas with extensive saltmarsh and grassland, though it can occasionally be seen migrating overhead almost anywhere. The few birds that winter at Gunpowder Park, Essex, have proved popular among photographers, and have proved fairly resilient to disturbance, but other sites are just as reliable and are more recommended: RSPB Wallasea Island, RSPB West Canvey Marsh, Two Tree Island LNR EWT, Blue House Farm EWT, South Fambridge sea wall, Wakering Stairs, Heybridge Basin, Tollesbury Wick, RSPB Old Hall Marshes, The Dengie, Holland Haven, Staines Moor, Crayford/Dartford Marshes, Shellness/The Swale NNR, the whole of the North Kent Marshes and Sheppey, and Pegwell/Sandwich Bay can all allow good views without interference. Rainham Marshes, RSPB Cliffe Pools, East Tilbury and other Thameside sites also sometimes produce birds.

LONG-EARED OWL

Never the most common nocturnal bird of prey in the region, LEO's communal roosts have largely disappeared and the species, although scarce, can turn up at almost any sizeable area of woods and fields in winter. One or two birds still occur regularly in the copse near the car park at Elmley NNR, where you should keep your distance and try not to disturb any owls present. Elsewhere, birds are best listened for (and observed if you're lucky) at dusk on The Dengie (where several pairs breed), RSPB Cliffe Pools, RSPB Northward Hill (where it also breeds), the Canterbury Ring Woods and Bedgebury Pinetum.

LITTLE RINGED PLOVER

LRP's specialised nesting requirements of bare gravel close to freshwater make it a scarce breeder in the region, with just a few pairs at each site, as well as an expected passage migrant in small numbers. The best sites include RSPB Rainham Marshes, the London Wetland Centre, RSPB Cattawade Marshes, RSPB Dungeness, Crayford, Dartford and Swanscombe Marshes, RSPB Cliffe Pools, Oare Marshes KWT, the Sandwich Bay area, RSPB Worth Marshes, RSPB Dungeness, Snodland and Bough Beech Reservoir. The species can turn up on passage at almost any wetland with bare mud or gravel. Walthamstow Wetlands and East India Dock are fairly reliable in spring for London sightings.

AVOCET

Having thoroughly replenished its British population since the Second World War, the Thames Estuary is now one of this elegant wader species' European hubs. Large numbers can be seen on passage and in winter at East Tilbury/Thurrock Thameside and West Thurrock Marshes, and along the Essex coastline (RSPB Wallasea Island and RSPB Vange Marsh are also notable breeding sites), while RSPB Rainham Marshes has good numbers away from winter, and several pairs now breed. Kent has lots, especially at RSPB Cliffe Pools, the North Kent Marshes coastline, Elmley NNR, Oare Marshes KWT, Pegwell and Sandwich Bays, Worth Marshes and RSPB Dungeness. Wandering individuals are possible at almost any regional wetland during passage.

JACK SNIPE

Probably far less scarce than it seems, this highly secretive reedbed wader can be seen (or, more accurately, probably flushed) at a number of key sites in the region. In London, Rainham Marshes and the London Wetland Centre will hold one or two, and Walthamstow Marsh and Wetlands also have potential. Rammey Marsh is a hotspot, as is the Ingrebourne Valley. In Kent, try Stodmarsh/Grove Ferry, Newington Watercress Beds, Pegwell Bay and Worth Marshes. In Essex, try any of the marsh reserves in the Southend area or further out into the Thames Estuary. You can be sure that you're near a Jack Snipe at any of these sites, but beware – you're still unlikely to see one!

CASPIAN GULL

Distinctive once you've got your eye in, this south-eastern European larid turns up in small numbers from every August to overwinter, and is a regional speciality of the Thames Estuary in particular. There are one or two birds present all year, but the best sites are the foreshore and landfill at Rainham Marshes, and the southern stretch of the Thames between Rotherhithe and Dartford Marsh. Birds are also regular at the fishing boats near Dungeness NR and around Dover harbour, while autumn and winter at Walthamstow Wetlands have begun to be reliable too. Read the section on gull-watching (pages 305–310) and check any gathering of larger gulls.

LITTLE TERN

A summer visitor and breeding specialist of pebble beaches, Little Tern has disappeared from most of its sites in the region, turning up on passage more frequently. Kent does best, with small numbers still apparent in summer on The Swale and less frequently along the Thanet coast. The only (tiny) Essex colony is on Horsey Island next to Walton-on-the-Naze.

POMARINE SKUA

While all four skuas pass the North Sea coast in varying numbers every autumn, you're most likely to see this species on its spring migration along the south coast. By far the best place to observe this species is from the seawatching hides or fishing boats at Dungeness during May. The species is irregular elsewhere.

NIGHTJAR

The secretive Nightjar favours heathland in Britain, but breeds sparsely in Kent, although it's absent from London and Essex except as a vagrant. Sites with always low numbers include the Canterbury Ring Woods, Lyminge Forest, King's Wood, Bedgebury Pinetum, Hemsted Forest, Pembury Heath, Goathurst Common, Mereworth and Hurst Woods, Hothfield Heathlands KWT. To experience more guaranteed sightings, contact the RSPB or Wildlife Trust offices to find out when special walks to see the species are taking place.

LESSER SPOTTED WOODPECKER

Despite a severe ongoing national decline, this shy woodpecker can still be seen in the more ancient woodlands of the region, especially when it is displaying and calling in February and March. In Kent, the Snodland area, Canterbury Ring Woods, Denge Wood, Bedgebury Pinetum, RSPB Tudeley Woods, Bough Beech Reservoir, Sevenoaks Wildfowl Reserve and Hothfield Heathlands hold breeding birds. In London, try Cely Woods or Belhus Woods CP, where the species can be fairly obvious, or roll the dice in Richmond Park or Trent CP. Heading out into Essex, Hainault Forest, Dagnam Park, Shut Heath Wood NR EWT, Fingringhoe Wick EWT (winter) and the Danbury ridge reserves are all worth a try.

TURTLE DOVE

With a fast-decreasing British population, Turtle Dove is now rather scarce in the region, though some sites remain reliable. It's now a vagrant in London, but a few Essex sites can come up trumps for passage birds, though few regular sites remain. Canterbury Ring Woods, Bedgebury Pinetum, Hemsted Forest, the Bough Beech Reservoir area, Hothfield Heathlands, Stodmarsh/Grove Ferry are the most likely sites in Kent.

HOBBY

While breeding locations are sparser, this medium-sized migratory falcon continues to increase in numbers and can be seen overhead almost anywhere on passage, especially near wetlands. Substantial numbers pass through Stodmarsh/Grove Ferry and the rest of the Stour Valley in May, while RSPB Rainham Marshes and RSPB Dungeness are other excellent sites for the species.

NIGHTINGALE

A Mediterranean species with a stronghold in Southeast England, the best sites in the country for this stentorian species are found within the region – and there are quite a lot! In Greater London, Fishers Green is by far the best location and it's best to visit in late April when birds can still be seen among relatively bare branches. Essex sites such as Stanford Warren, Chigborough Lakes, Shut Heath Wood NR EWT, Tiptree Heath, Abberton Reservoir, RSPB Stour Estuary/Copperas Wood NR EWT, Fingringhoe Wick and Hanningfield Reservoir produce singing birds each spring. Kent is the species' true stronghold, with many pairs at Great Chattenden Wood/Lodge Hill, Faggs Wood/Orlestone Forest, in the Canterbury Ring Woods, RSPB Northward Hill and Snodland.

BLACK REDSTART

Partly replacing Robin on the Continent where it is far more common, this sleek chat tends to prefer urban environments with sparse vegetation and gravel in England. Traditional sites include Dover and South Foreland, Dungeness Power Station and random sites in the centre of London: Soho rooftops, Westfield, Stratford, Liverpool Street station and on the Isle of Dogs have all held singing males very recently. Territories can move, though, and former sites such as East India Dock no longer sustain the species.

FIRECREST

There has been a boon in the population of this tiny kinglet this century, and it is now expected to be profusely singing in spring in many broadleaved woodlands as well as wintering widely, especially where there is a dense holly and ivy under-storey. Try the Snaresbrook area of Epping Forest, Wanstead Park, Warley Place NR EWT, Wimbledon Common, Great Chattenden Wood, the moat around Dungeness Bird Observatory, Canterbury Ring Woods, among many other sites.

MARSH TIT

Though its decline hasn't been as precipitous as that of Willow Tit (now entirely extirpated in the region), Marsh Tit is becoming harder to see and has virtually deserted the Greater London area. Extensive areas of secondary and primary woodland are best, so head to sites such as Hatfield Forest and Brooks NR EWT, Essex, and Shorne Woods CP, the Canterbury Ring Woods, Lyminge Forest, Bedgebury Pinetum, Hemsted Forest and Bough Beech Reservoir. Make sure you check more obscure woods in either county, as the species lingers on at some sites where there are otherwise only common species.

BEARDED TIT

Sparsely distributed across the larger wetlands of the region, Bearded Tit favours more coastal and estuarine sites in the region despite preferring freshwater habi-tats. Its stronghold is in East Anglia, but Essex, Kent and even London have pairs. More acclimatised birds can be seen at RSPB Rainham Marshes, which is as close as the species gets into London, but plenty of sites in Essex hold birds, including RSPB Rye Meads, Hornchurch CP, RSPB Wallasea Island, RSPB Vange Marsh, RSPB Bowers Marsh and RSPB Old Hall Marshes. There are a number of Kentish hotspots: the Isle of Grain, the Isle of Sheppey, RSPB Dungeness, Oare Marshes KWT and Stodmarsh NNR are all worth trying.

WATER PIPIT

A very scarce winter visitor, this montane species haunts a few favoured sites in the region, exceptionally showing up on passage at other wetland sites too. In Kent, Stodmarsh/Grove Ferry and RSPB Worth Marshes are regular sites. In Essex, try RSPB Wallasea Island and Blue House Farm EWT. The Thames fore-shore at RSPB Rainham Marshes and the grazing marsh at the London Wetland Centre are both reliable metropolitan locations.

HAWFINCH

Another broadleaved woodland species in sheer decline, Hawfinch still breeds in a few of the larger ancient woodlands of the region, turning up in winter more widely as local birds move and Continental birds arrive in unpredictable numbers, although it's always scarce and always difficult to see. A few mobile breeding pairs linger in the Canterbury Ring Woods and Trosley CP, while a small wintering roost clings on in Bedgebury Pinetum/Forest. The odd bird is still reported around Epping Forest every autumn and winter, while a small flock sometimes forages at Hatfield Forest near the entrance.

ONLINE RESOURCES AND CONTACTS

GENERAL BIRDING WEBSITES

Birdforum: *www.birdforum.net* Popular online forum for the discussion of everything related to birding.

BirdTrack: *www.bto.org/our-science/projects/birdtrack* The BTO's website for recording your bird sightings in Britain. Make your birding contribute to our deepening knowledge of our birds.

British Birds Rarities Committee (BBRC): *www.bbrc.org.uk* The official adjudicator of records of rare birds in Britain, and publisher of the journal of record *British Birds*.

British Trust for Ornithology (BTO): *www.bto.org* The UK charity devoted to the study of changes in bird populations and associated research.

eBird: *ebird.org/home* Cornell Lab of Ornithology's global bird recording website, app and software, which has become the main resource for recording your own sightings and discovering which species are likely at a site you are visiting, anywhere in the world.

European Colour-ring Birding: *cr-birding.org* Have you seen a darvic ring on a bird? If it comes from a European ringing scheme, it will be registered here and can be traced by their helpful contacts. Please try to pass on any such rings seen or photographed in the field to help contribute to our knowledge of the movements of birds.

Fat Birder: *fatbirder.com* A fairly comprehensive go-to hub for all manner of birding information, including the regions covered by this book.

RSPB: *www.rspb.org.uk* All birders should be a member of Britain's biggest and most constructive conservation organisation – not least because membership allows free entry to every one of its substantial reserves (though a few aren't open to the public).

Xeno-Canto: *xeno-canto.org* A huge bird sound resource, with countless and ever-increasing recordings of almost every species and subspecies in the world.

News services – paid subscription services for finding out 'what's about' in terms of scarce and rare birds, immediately and in detail.

BirdGuides: *www.birdguides.com*

Rare Bird Alert: *www.rarebirdalert.com*

REGIONAL BLOGS AND WEBSITES

GENERAL

Hertfordshire Bird Club: *www.hnhs.org/herts-bird-club/home*

Hertfordshire and Middlesex Wildlife Trust: *www.hertswildlifetrust.org.uk*; *info@hmwt.org*; 01727 858 901

Surrey Bird Club: *surreybirdclub.org.uk*

LONDON
London Bird Recorder: Roger Payne *rogerwpayne@gmail.com*
London Bird Records: *www.lnhs.org.uk/index.php/recording/birds*
Dave Morrison (with the accent on Peregrines): *davemobirding.blogspot.com*
Jim Anderson (Lea Valley and beyond): *jj-anderson.blogspot.com*
Josh Jones (plenty of regional entries): *www.joshrjones.com/blog*
Lee Valley Park: *https://www.visitleevalley.org.uk/nature-reserves-open-spaces*
London Bird Club: *www.lnhs.org.uk/index.php/sections/london-bird-club*
London Bird Club wiki (for daily sightings): *londonbirders.fandom.com/wiki/ London_Bird_Club_Wiki*
London Wildlife Trust: *www.wildlondon.org.uk*; *enquiries@wildlondon.org.uk*; 020 7261 0447
London Natural History Society: *www.lnhs.org.uk*
Peter Alfrey (Beddington and beyond): *peteralfreybirdingnotebook.blogspot. com*
Richard Smith (London and Kent): *mybirdwatchingdaysout.blogspot.com*
Walthamstow Wetlands monthly sightings round-up: *walthamstowbirders.blogspot.com*
Wanstead Birding (Wanstead Birders): *wansteadbirding.blogspot.com*

KENT
Kent Bird Recorder: Barry Wright *umbrellabirds66@gmail.com*
Kent Bird Records: *kentos.org.uk/index.php/recording/how-to-submit-records*
Alan Woodcock (Snodland): *snodlandblogspotcom.blogspot.com*
Birding Paradigms: *birding-paradigms.blogspot.com*
Canterbury RSPB Group: *group.rspb.org.uk/canterbury*
Dungeness Bird Observatory (blog): *www.dungenessbirdobs.org.uk*
Gary Howard: *garyhowards.blogspot.com*
Graham Barker (mostly Kent): *grahambarker.blogspot.com*
Gravesend RSPB Group: *group.rspb.org.uk/gravesend*
Jamie Partridge (Kent and further afield): *perdixbirding.com*
Kearsney Birding (Dover area): *mrphil-kearsneybirder.blogspot.com*
Kent Birding Adventures: *robs-birding.blogspot.com*
Kent Ornithological Society: *kentos.org.uk*
Kent Wildlife Trust; *www.kentwildlifetrust.org.uk*; *info@kentwildlife.org.uk*; 01622 662012
Kevin Thornton: *birdingsouthernmedway.blogspot.com*
Maidstone RSPB Group: *group.rspb.org.uk/maidstone*
Martin Casemore (Dungeness sightings blog): *ploddingbirder.blogspot.com*
Martyn Wilson (Stour Valley): *stourvalleysightings.blogspot.com*
Medway RSPB Group: *group.rspb.org.uk/medway*
Mike Gould (Kent wildlife photography): *mikegouldwildlifephotography.blogspot.com*
Nick Upton (Kent, national and international): *dartfordwaffler.co.uk*
North Kent Marshes: *group.rspb.org.uk/gravesend*
Phil Sharp (New Hythe and more): *sharpbynature.blogspot.com*
Reculver Marshes blog (Chris Hindle): *reculverbirding.blogspot.com*
Rob's Birding Blog (mainly Kent): *robs-birding.blogspot.com*
Romney Marsh blog: *ploversblog.blogspot.com*
Ross Newham: *baldbirder.blogspot.com*

Sevenoaks RSPB Group: *group.rspb.org.uk/sevenoaks*
Swalecliffe Birds: *www.kentlisters.club*
Swale Wader Group *http://swalewaders.co.uk*
Thanet RSPB Group: *group.rspb.org.uk/thanet*
Tonbridge RSPB Group: *group.rspb.org.uk/tonbridge*

ESSEX
Essex Bird Recorder: Mick Tracey *micktrac@aol.com*
Essex Birdwatching Society Identification Panel (EBSIP): *ebws.org.uk/index.php/society/ebsip*
Brian's Birding Blog: *briansbirding.blogspot.com*
Brightlingsea: *essex.bna-naturalists.org/brightlingsea-a-special-place*
Chelmsford and Central Essex RSPB group: *group.rspb.org.uk/chelmsford*
Colchester RSPB Group: *ww2.rspb.org.uk/groups/Colchester*
Essex Wildlife Trust: *www.essexwt.org.uk*; *enquiries@essexwt.org.uk*; 01621 862960
Mick Rodwell: *hollandhavenbirding.blogspot.com*
North Thames Gull Group: *www.ntgg.org.uk*
South-east Essex RSPB (Graham Mee): *group.rspb.org.uk/southeastessex*; *grahamm@southendrspb.co.uk*
Southend Ornithological Group (Paul Baker): *www.sognet.org.uk*; *baker22@btinternet.com*
Southern Colour Ringing Group: *www.southern-colour-ringing-group.org.uk*
Wakering: *wakeringnaturalhistory.weebly.com*

BIBLIOGRAPHY

Clements, R, Orchard, M, McCanch, N and Wood, S. 2015. *Kent Breeding Bird Atlas 2008–13*. Kent Ornithological Society, Canterbury.

Fitter, R S R. 1945. *London's Natural History*. Collins, London.

Gartshore, N. 2022. *The Birdwatcher's Yearbook 2023*. Calluna Books, Wareham.

Harrison, J and Grant, P. 1976. *The Thames Transformed: London's River and its Waterfowl*. Andre Deutsch, London.

Mitchell, D. 1997. *Where to Watch Birds in the London Area*. Christopher Helm, London.

Phelps, M & Stubbs, E. 2024. *Where to Watch Birds in Surrey and Sussex*. Christopher Helm, London.

Privett, K. 2022. *Kent Bird Report 2020*. Kent Ornithological Society, Maidstone.

Self, A. 2014. *The Birds of London*. Bloomsbury, London.

Self A. 2017. *Birds of Brent Reservoir: Facts & Figures* (3rd edition). London: Welsh Harp Conservation Group.

Sumner, N. (ed.). 2022. *The Essex Bird Report 2020*. The Essex Birdwatching Society, Chelmsford.

Taylor, D, Wheatley, J and James P. 2009. *Where to Watch Birds in Kent, Surrey and Sussex* (5th edition). Christopher Helm, London.

Wood, S. 2007. *The Birds of Essex*. Christopher Helm, London.

Woodward, I, Arnold, R and Smith, N. 2017. *The London Bird Atlas*. The London Natural History Society and John Beaufoy Publishing, Oxford.

Yalden, D W and Albarella, U. 2009. *The History of British Birds*. Oxford University Press, Oxford.

SOUTHEAST ENGLAND BIRD LIST

This following list contains every species of wild bird officially recorded by the local recorders as having been seen by the time this book was published. Note that many species on this list are either scarce or rare and are unlikely to be seen on a casual visit. Please use the list to keep a tally of what you see on your visits to the region, and refer to the lists on the following links if you would like to keep score using more county-based context.

Essex: https://www.ebws.org.uk/essex-bird-list
London: https://lnhs.org.uk/index.php/recording/birds
Kent: https://kentos.org.uk/index.php/recording/the-kent-list

COMBINED ESSEX, LONDON AND KENT LIST

1	Red-legged Partridge	32	Pintail
2	Grey Partridge	33	Teal
3	Quail	34	Green-winged Teal
4	Pheasant	35	Red-crested Pochard
5	Brent Goose	36	Canvasback
6	Red-breasted Goose	37	Pochard
7	Canada Goose	38	Ferruginous Duck
8	Barnacle Goose	39	Ring-necked Duck
9	Snow Goose	40	Tufted Duck
10	Greylag Goose	41	Scaup
11	Taiga Bean Goose	42	Lesser Scaup
12	Tundra Bean Goose	43	King Eider
13	Pink-footed Goose	44	Eider
14	White-fronted Goose	45	Surf Scoter
15	Lesser White-fronted Goose	46	Velvet Scoter
16	Mute Swan	47	Common Scoter
17	Bewick's Swan	48	Long-tailed Duck
18	Whooper Swan	49	Goldeneye
19	Egyptian Goose	50	Smew
20	Shelduck	51	Hooded Merganser
21	Mandarin Duck	52	Goosander
22	Baikal Teal	53	Red-breasted Merganser
23	Garganey	54	Ruddy Duck
24	Blue-winged Teal	55	Nightjar
25	Shoveler	56	Common Nighthawk
26	Gadwall	57	White-throated Needletail
27	Falcated Duck	58	Alpine Swift
28	Wigeon	59	Swift
29	American Wigeon	60	Pallid Swift
30	Mallard	61	Great Bustard
31	American Black Duck	62	Little Bustard

63 Great Spotted Cuckoo
64 Cuckoo
65 Yellow-billed Cuckoo
66 Pallas's Sandgrouse
67 Rock Dove / Feral Pigeon
68 Stock Dove
69 Woodpigeon
70 Turtle Dove
71 Oriental Turtle Dove
72 Collared Dove
73 Water Rail
74 Corncrake
75 Spotted Crake
76 Moorhen
77 Coot
78 American Coot
79 Baillon's Crake
80 Little Crake
81 Crane
82 Pied-billed Grebe
83 Little Grebe
84 Red-necked Grebe
85 Great Crested Grebe
86 Slavonian Grebe
87 Black-necked Grebe
88 Stone-curlew
89 Oystercatcher
90 Black-winged Stilt
91 Avocet
92 Lapwing
93 Sociable Lapwing
94 White-tailed Lapwing
95 Golden Plover
96 Pacific Golden Plover
97 American Golden Plover
98 Grey Plover
99 Ringed Plover
100 Little Ringed Plover
101 Kentish Plover
102 Killdeer
103 Greater Sand Plover
104 Tibetan Sand Plover
105 Dotterel
106 Whimbrel
107 Curlew
108 Bar-tailed Godwit
109 Black-tailed Godwit
110 Turnstone
111 Knot
112 Ruff

113 Broad-billed Sandpiper
114 Stilt Sandpiper
115 Curlew Sandpiper
116 Temminck's Stint
117 Sanderling
118 Dunlin
119 Purple Sandpiper
120 Baird's Sandpiper
121 Little Stint
122 White-rumped Sandpiper
123 Buff-breasted Sandpiper
124 Pectoral Sandpiper
125 Sharp-tailed Sandpiper
126 Semipalmated Sandpiper
127 Western Sandpiper
128 Long-billed Dowitcher
129 Woodcock
130 Jack Snipe
131 Great Snipe
132 Snipe
133 Terek Sandpiper
134 Wilson's Phalarope
135 Red-necked Phalarope
136 Grey Phalarope
137 Common Sandpiper
138 Spotted Sandpiper
139 Green Sandpiper
140 Solitary Sandpiper
141 Lesser Yellowlegs
142 Redshank
143 Marsh Sandpiper
144 Wood Sandpiper
145 Spotted Redshank
146 Greenshank
147 Greater Yellowlegs
148 Cream-coloured Courser
149 Collared Pratincole
150 Oriental Pratincole
151 Black-winged Pratincole
152 Kittiwake
153 Ivory Gull
154 Sabine's Gull
155 Slender-billed Gull
156 Bonaparte's Gull
157 Black-headed Gull
158 Little Gull
159 Ross's Gull
160 Laughing Gul
161 Audouin's Gull
162 Franklin's Gull

163 Mediterranean Gull
164 Common Gull
165 Ring-billed Gull
166 Great Black-backed Gull
167 Glaucous-winged Gull
168 Glaucous Gull
169 Iceland Gull
170 Herring Gull
171 Caspian Gull
172 Yellow-legged Gull
173 Slaty-backed Gull
174 Lesser Black-backed Gull
175 Gull-billed Tern
176 Caspian Tern
177 Lesser Crested Tern
178 Sandwich Tern
179 Little Tern
180 Least Tern
181 Bridled Tern
182 Sooty Tern
183 Roseate Tern
184 Common Tern
185 Arctic Tern
186 Forster's Tern
187 Whiskered Tern
188 White-winged Black Tern
189 Black Tern
190 Great Skua
191 Pomarine Skua
192 Arctic Skua
193 Long-tailed Skua
194 Little Auk
195 Guillemot
196 Razorbill
197 Black Guillemot
198 Puffin
199 Tufted Puffin
200 Red-throated Diver
201 Black-throated Diver
202 Great Northern Diver
203 White-billed Diver
204 Black-browed Albatross
205 Storm Petrel
206 Leach's Petrel
207 Fulmar
208 Cory's Shearwater
209 Sooty Shearwater
210 Great Shearwater
211 Manx Shearwater
212 Balearic Shearwater

213 Barolo Shearwater
214 Black Stork
215 White Stork
216 Gannet
217 Brown Booby
218 Cormorant
219 Shag
220 Glossy Ibis
221 Spoonbill
222 Bittern
223 American Bittern
224 Little Bittern
225 Night Hero
226 Green Heron
227 Squacco Heron
228 Chinese Pond Heron
229 Cattle Egret
230 Grey Heron
231 Purple Heron
232 Great Egret
233 Little Egret
234 Osprey
235 Egyptian Vulture
236 Honey Buzzard
237 Short-toed Eagle
238 Greater Spotted Eagle
239 Golden Eagle
240 Sparrowhawk
241 Goshawk
242 Marsh Harrier
243 Hen Harrier
244 Pallid Harrier
245 Montagu's Harrier
246 Black-winged Kite
247 Red Kite
248 Black Kite
249 White-tailed Eagle
250 Rough-legged Buzzard
251 Buzzard
252 Barn Owl
253 Scops Owl
254 Snowy Owl
255 Tawny Owl
256 Little Owl
257 Tengmalm's Owl
258 Long-eared Owl
259 Short-eared Owl
260 Hoopoe
261 Roller
262 Bee-eater

263 Blue-cheeked Bee-eater
264 Kingfisher
265 Wryneck
266 Great Spotted Woodpecker
267 Lesser Spotted Woodpecker
268 Green Woodpecker
269 Lesser Kestrel
270 Kestrel
271 Red-footed Falcon
272 Eleonora's Falcon
273 Merlin
274 Hobby
275 Gyrfalcon
276 Peregrine Falcon
277 Ring-necked Parakeet
278 Acadian Flycatcher
279 Red-backed Shrike
280 Daurian Shrike
281 Turkestan Shrike
282 Brown Shrike
283 Lesser Grey Shrike
284 Great Grey Shrike
285 Woodchat Shrike
286 Masked Shrike
287 Red-eyed Vireo
288 Golden Oriole
289 Jay
290 Magpie
291 Nutcracker
292 Chough
293 Jackdaw
294 Rook
295 Carrion Crow
296 Hooded Crow
297 Pied Crow
298 Raven
299 Waxwing
300 Coal Tit
301 Crested Tit
302 Marsh Tit
303 Willow Tit
304 Blue Tit
305 Great Tit
306 Penduline Tit
307 Bearded Tit
308 Woodlark
309 Skylark
310 Shore Lark
311 Short-toed Lark
312 Crested Lark

313 Calandra Lark
314 Sand Martin
315 Swallow
316 House Martin
317 Red-rumped Swallow
318 American Cliff Swallow
319 Cetti's Warbler
320 Long-tailed Tit
321 Wood Warbler
322 Western Bonelli's Warbler
323 Hume's Warbler
324 Yellow-browed
     Warbler
325 Pallas's Warbler
326 Radde's Warbler
327 Dusky Warbler
328 Willow Warbler
329 European Willow Warbler
330 Iberian Chiffchaff
331 Chiffchaff
332 Greenish Warbler
333 Arctic Warbler
334 Great Reed Warbler
335 Aquatic Warbler
336 Sedge Warbler
337 Paddyfield Warbler
338 Blyth's Reed Warbler
339 Reed Warbler
340 Marsh Warbler
341 Booted Warbler
342 Eastern Olivaceous Warbler
343 Melodious Warbler
344 Icterine Warbler
345 Savi's Warbler
346 Grasshopper Warbler
347 Zitting Cisticola
348 Blackcap
349 Garden Warbler
350 Barred Warbler
351 Lesser Whitethroat
352 Asian Desert Warbler
353 Eastern Subalpine Warbler
354 Western Subalpine Warbler
355 Whitethroat
356 Sardinian Warbler
357 Dartford Warbler
358 Firecrest
359 Goldcrest
360 Wren
361 Nuthatch

362 Treecreeper
363 Short-toed Treecreeper
364 Northern Mockingbird
365 Rose-coloured Starling
366 Starling
367 White's Thrush
368 Ring Ouzel
369 Blackbird
370 Red-throated Thrush
371 Black-throated Thrush
372 Dusky Thrush
373 Naumann's Thrush
374 Eyebrowed Thrush
375 Fieldfare
376 Redwing
377 Song Thrush
378 Mistle Thrush
379 American Robin
380 Swainson's Thrush
381 Grey-cheeked Thrush
382 Rufous-tailed Scrub Robin
383 Spotted Flycatcher
384 Robin
385 Bluethroat
386 Thrush Nightingale
387 Nightingale
388 Red-flanked Bluetail
389 Red-breasted Flycatcher
390 Pied Flycatcher
391 Collared Flycatcher
392 Black Redstart
393 Redstart
394 Rock Thrush
395 Whinchat
396 Stonechat
397 Siberian Stonechat
398 Wheatear
399 Isabelline Wheatear
400 Desert Wheatear
401 Black-eared Wheatear
402 Pied Wheatear
403 Dipper
404 House Sparrow
405 Tree Sparrow
406 Alpine Accentor
407 Dunnock
408 Yellow Wagtail
409 Eastern Yellow Wagtail
410 Citrine Wagtail
411 Grey Wagtail

412 White/Pied Wagtail
413 Richard's Pipit
414 Tawny Pipit
415 Meadow Pipit
416 Tree Pipit
417 Olive-backed Pipit
418 Red-throated Pipit
419 Water Pipit
420 Rock Pipit
421 Chaffinch
422 Brambling
423 Hawfinch
424 Bullfinch
425 Pine Grosbeak
426 Trumpeter Finch
427 Common Rosefinch
428 Greenfinch
429 Twite
430 Linnet
431 Mealy (Common) Redpoll
432 Lesser Redpoll
433 Arctic Redpoll
434 Parrot Crossbill
435 Crossbill
436 Two-barred Crossbill
437 Goldfinch
438 Serin
439 Siskin
440 Lapland Bunting
441 Snow Bunting
442 Corn Bunting
443 Yellowhammer
444 Pine Bunting
445 Rock Bunting
446 Ortolan Bunting
447 Cirl Bunting
448 Little Bunting
449 Yellow-browed Bunting
450 Rustic Bunting
451 Yellow-breasted Bunting
452 Black-headed Bunting
453 Reed Bunting
454 Dark-eyed Junco
455 White-throated Sparrow
456 Golden-winged Warbler
457 Common Yellowthroat
458 Blackpoll Warbler
459 Baltimore Oriole
460 Rose-breasted Grosbeak

INDEX TO SPECIES